Proof of Work

Rhea Myers

Proof of Work

Blockchain Provocations 2011–2021

URB
ANO
MIC

Rhea Myers
Proof of Work
Blockchain Provocations
2011–2021

Simple Blockchain Art Diagram

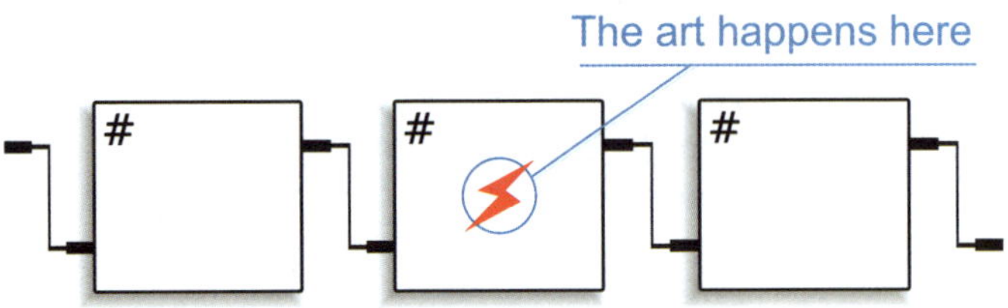

R Myers ca. #422422 after MTAA ca. 1997

'Hurt Me! No, Not Like That!' A Conversation with Rhea Myers

Maya B. Kronic
Your work is obviously about more than technology. It's full of formulations like 'Blockchain Aesthetics' and 'Blockchain Poetics', and I was struck by your description of Bitcoin as a 'development in cyberculture' rather than just a technology. Many of your works exhibit a sensitivity to the charm and energy of the cultural scenes that assemble around technological platforms and indeed play a part in their growth. Dogecoin, Ethereum, Rare Pepes, these are all instances of the collective charisma that can burgeon around an online project, even something as apparently nakedly financial as a cryptocurrency. In an article that you cite in 'Blockchain Poetics', Brett Scott argues that a rational account of the emergence of money is always inadequate because, in order for exchangeable objects to accrue social value, they have to already be imbued with some kind of cultural energy, something akin to artistic value.[1]

Rhea Myers
Prior to Bitcoin I was looking at bronies, and before that at more general internet culture, I just immerse myself in these things. I describe culture as Dogecoin's secret sauce, because it didn't have a particularly better algorithm than Bitcoin, although it is slightly faster. The thing that was different was its community's *Bill-and-Ted*-esque spirit of excellence and charity and support and welcoming and inclusion. Something which I assume was calculated to begin with, but as far as you could tell, was pure and in earnest. Even today, if you dropped the Bitcoin and Ethereum and Doge communities in a barren wasteland somewhere and came back in two years time, I know which one I would put my money on still having any kind of functioning social fabric. That in part is what 'Bad Shibe' is about. Unfortunately the social is all but invisible to the crypto bros who believe that conventions just appear and communities just spring up. That wilful ignorance of the social labour of reproducing crypto culture is just fascinating, not to mention that it's transparently and ridiculously gendered too. So looking at those more social aspects does give you a critical way into the culture. And gaps in the culture give you clawholds on the sloping glass roof of the nice happy libertarian-to-VC pipeline of crypto technology.

MBK The word 'currency' understood not just in terms of money but also as involving a cultural current, a nowness which has a social and emotional dimension.

RM Yes, which allows the bootstrapping of a socially valued currency—and makes FOMO, the fear of missing out (e.g. on a token drop), the original source of value! If we take Marx's view of the evolution of money—treated very trollishly in 'Why Bitcoin is Money According to Marx'—there's no mysterious meteor that hits the earth and imbues everything with value, there's a base layer of things, people

1 B. Scott, 'Much Soul, Very Emotion: Why I Buy into the Cult of Dogecoin', *MCD*, 27 December 2014, <https://www.digitalmcd.com/dogecoin-2/>.

want one thing more than any other for some irrational reason, and it becomes a medium of exchange precisely because of this charm. This then spins up into financial hyperspace and turns into money.

MBK As Scott points out, Bitcoin, for example, is imbued with the mystique of Satoshi Nakamoto.

RM And he's absolutely right there. Technology is of course socially embedded and produced, and technology has a cultural history and is a part of the history of ideas. The mythology of Satoshi is incredible, they're the absent founder who has, not ascended to heaven, but returned to perfect cypherpunk secrecy, and that's so generative for Bitcoin. Just as the figure of the doge for Dogecoin means that you have this sort of non-human benevolent avatar, and for Ethereum Vitalik Buterin is this monklike figure who does his best not to get drawn into squabbles whether they come from outside or within the Ethereum project. So those sort of founding myths or prophet figures are there.

But the choice of technology also shapes the kind of culture you're engaged with. Like the representation schemes used for different cryptocurrency addresses—Bitcoin addresses are easy to recognise and contain a checksum to ensure you type them correctly, Ethereum uses a format that is very easy to get wrong. That generates different social conversations. There is a culture to coding, to the choice of technology, to the mixing and prioritising and valuing of different technological elements. I may be overdoing it, this may be only one percent and the culture around it is the other ninety-nine, but the dream of the cypherpunks is that you can somehow match technologies to your political objectives. And in the case of Bitcoin, that succeeded beyond anyone's wildest dreams.

MBK That suggests that there may be a politics embedded in the technology, and yet you seem to appeal to your readers to pare Bitcoin, and blockchain technology more generally, away from the various political ideologies that have appropriated it, or with which it's associated by its denigrators. Is ideology baked into Bitcoin as a project, or not?

RM Bitcoin is a practical solution to an open problem in the cypherpunk political project. The cypherpunks wanted private communication, and they got it, and that's amazing—that's what the Crypto Wars were fought for, and we're all very grateful to them for that, it was a positive outcome for society. But beyond that, what they wanted was state-free everything, because they have a strong anarcho-capitalist bent. They wanted state-free money, and there were various sketches for that which almost worked, but if they involved the technical necessity for a central authority, then that can be compromised and the state or some other party can interfere in the social exchange of value at the moment of transaction. The thing that Bitcoin does is to make it impossible to interfere at the moment of transaction. This is a very modest achievement. There are many other things that you need to do in order to have a free society, however conceived. But within the cypherpunk political project, Bitcoin is a genuine solution to a problem in how they wish to justly organise social relations.

So to the people who get so mad about Bitcoin as a product of ideology: you're absolutely right, it's the product of cypherpunk ideology, it is antistatist, and it does not take a stance against the commodity form of either property or money. That's something I talk about in great detail in 'Blockchain Poetics' because, as far as I can tell, the difference between anarcho-capitalists and anarcho-socialists comes down to whether they believe it is possible or desirable to abolish the commodity form. But when it comes to Bitcoin, the Left in general has been very upset that, with this exclusion of a potential moment for injustice at the moment of the transaction, there's also an exclusion of a potential moment for redistributive justice. No redistribution of wealth can happen here. But whether you're a left- or right-wing anarchist, you want the state out of people's social relations. And after the abolition of the bourgeois/neoliberal/etc. state there won't be a state to redistribute anything anymore anyway, so why are you getting so upset about this? In 'Blockchain Poetics' I go into a lot of detail mapping from anarcho-capitalism and the cypherpunk program to the specific design choices that Bitcoin makes, to try and inform imagined socialist interventions in the technology. There is a history of projects that take cryptocurrency and say, *Okay, we're gonna change this and make it work in a more benevolent way*, and in doing so change the very finely tuned engineering constraints on Bitcoin and end up with something that is exploitative, unstable, or gameable in ways they simply wouldn't want. Unfortunately there's a belief that your good heart will get you there and you won't need to get your hands dirty with the engineering. But however problematic the figure of the engineer is for socialist theory, and however little you may like these ideological underpinnings, you have to make an attempt to understand them.

I'm not exactly shocked when people who think all technology is fascism decide that Bitcoin is fascism. But it's not, it is a genuinely anarchist technology, it is an anti-statist technology. I can fully understand how uncomfortable it is for the reformist 'the best we can hope for is trivial modifications to the state until we all die baking in the anthropocene sun' tendency to encounter something that actually operationalises a political programme, but this technology precisely excludes the possibility of an actual fascist state intruding into your ability to carry out exchanges. Take a look at the United States today, where Bitcoin might come in extremely useful if you want to pay for an abortion, pay for hormones, pay to flee the country. These are all things we've been told no one would ever need to use money to do, or need to do without the state watching. Lo and behold, it's 2022 and people are almost beginning to put together the idea that a state panopticon of money and a government that is not your friend may not be the best combination.

None of this means that you can or have to ignore the large pools of capital involved, which are very easy to examine—precisely because current public blockchains are transparent. Actually taking the time to find out how to perform that kind of examination is another part of the demand that I make for competence in critical engagement with this technology. With Bitcoin you are beholden to those who came before you because they mined Bitcoin back when it was possible to do so with a modest amount of computing power. Or, in the case of Ethereum and other later currencies, they were smart enough and/or privileged and/or well-informed enough to get in on the pre-sale. So there is a tendency for there to be a hierarchy of early versus late adopters, something which is obviously not friendly to left anarchism. It's very friendly to right anarchism because right anarchism, anarcho-capitalism, views the state as an impediment to your personal power and particularly to the power of your money. In contrast to this, left anarchists view the state as an impediment to a more equal society. These are very different views on what removing the state will achieve for society.

So Bitcoin has that first-mover advantage, not quite by accident but certainly with less of a programme than the later cryptocurrencies—those that followed it do really bake in first-mover advantage in a way that I'm tempted to say wouldn't be such a problem for the Left if they had been mining from day one.

MBK That brings us to your relation to left-wing politics, which is obviously not without its complexities. In many of these texts you seem to be espousing an extreme accelerationism—removing all the brakes, whether social, technological, or psychological, on the tendencies unleashed by blockchain technology. Your writing deliberately makes it difficult to evaluate the level of irony at play, something that has been a constant source of amusingly heated Twitter exchanges.

RM I've had a lifelong feeling of being an outsider. I've certainly been socio-economically privileged: I'm from the end of the post-war settlement, the state paid for my education, I'm white-passing, I know people who had to work far harder than me to be part of the technology industry in England, and some of those people gave me a chance in that industry as a newly graduated art student. But that didn't give me any secure or lasting sense of belonging or security. And so, to a degree, since I was chronically unsuccessful at 'finding my people', my work tended to be addressed to whatever group of people I was annoyed with at the time. Usually a group that I was or am a part of. For example, I describe 'Bad Shibe' as my exasperated love letter to the Vancouver crypto scene.

One of the techniques I often use came originally from a conversation on an old mailing list with one of the writers of the *Twilight 2000* role-playing game. One thing I liked about the imagined future historical scenario of that game was that it disappoints everyone's expectations for a Third World War equally. If you're a hawk, the military effort just grinds down to a degrading and shameful standstill; if you're a political wonk, the American government breaks down to the point where there are running gun battles in Congress; if you're someone who's anti-nuclear, well, there's a nuclear conflict with horrific effects but civilisation is crawling on and things are really only about as bad as they were in the mid-twentieth century, and so on. Nobody gets to say *Aha, I told you so!* This is bathos, the deflation of grand claims.

Rhea Myers, *Shared Secret*, 2020. TOTP QR Code.

This movement of bathos—which is something I also find in the work of the artist collective Art & Language—is present in everything I do in these projects, where however grand the claim made at the start, there's a moment where you have to say, *Okay, but is that it? There's got to be more to this*...and there is always more to it, but you have to be able to make the jump to those coordinates, to be able to say, for *Shared Secret* (2020) for instance, *Possibly the world's most ridiculously secure unknowable secret isn't just there for me to go wow, they put*

Rhea Myers, *Tokens Equal Text*, 2019. Ethereum ERC-998 and ERC-721 tokens.

MICHELANGELO'S DAVID
NEON GREEN GRID
REFLECTIONS ON THE GROUND
HYPERSPACE STARFIELD

a hash on the blockchain. Or for *Tokens Equals Text* (2019), *Maybe there's more going on in this little vaporwave typography display than meets the eye....*

However ironic the work, I am reflexively left-wing. I trust the Left to at least kill me more slowly than the Right. I feel no joy (and didn't from a very early age) in anything restrictively traditional or in any kind of reproductive ideal that you have to live up to. And I'm certainly a very boring atheist. But I really felt the critique of Nick Srnicek and Alex Williams's 'Manifesto for Accelerationist Politics'.[2] I know that you can make a very good career from beating up on identity politics, and as someone who 'has an identity', I would like to be very clear that I do not wish to do that. But at the same time, the genteel libidinal security of merely symbolic resistance is essentially a ritual blessing for whatever it is supposedly against. The insufficiency of the institutionalised Left and of always-already-defeated mediatised leftist politics, which the Manifesto really nails, is something that's always deeply irritated me.

So what you see here is my exasperation and heartbreak and my aching wish for a better world—which I don't have the economic or psychological or rhetorical or discursive security to put into mere dreamwork. I am unable to say *I'm starting this artist's cooperative, we're gonna pay artists a living wage and everything will be great* without also thinking *Okay, where does the money come from for this?*

MBK Asking questions about money is particularly unwelcome in the contemporary art community, which is simultaneously deeply complicit with capital, and requires everyone present to affirm it as a singular site of criticality and resistance against capitalism. What does it mean to introduce into that world artworks made in a medium that is transparently (in every sense) a monetary instrument?

RM Remember that old Ad Reinhardt cartoon of a gentleman in a trilby pointing at an abstract painting and saying *What does this represent?*, and the painting pointing back at him very angrily and saying *What do you represent?* In the context of the contemporary art world I would modify it to say *Who pays for this?* And then the painting (or the NFT) points back and says *Who pays for you?* It's a milieu where you're always working for some blob of capital that has come from taxing miners or selling slaves or taking the tops off of mountains and digging rubies out of them or whatever, but there is generally a comfortable ignorance of how

2 N. Srnicek and A. Williams, 'Manifesto for an Accelerationist Politics', in R. Mackay and A. Avanessian (eds), *#accelerate: The Accelerationist Reader* (Falmouth: Urbanomic, 2014), 347–62.

the sausage is made, and you get to sit there and say to people that money is this horrible dirty thing. This has happened to me on a number of occasions: *I can see that you are getting your money from a venture-capital-funded corporation, that's terrible. I have this unproblematic position from which I can say that you should do this other thing that I have in mind*. And that other thing turns out to be some sort of pantomime of value which only works if you have secure income and healthcare, which of course you have if you work for a big nonprofit or state institution. The fact that the money paying for it is the heat noise of historical capitalist exploitation seems to be far less problematic in that context because you can't see it clearly, whereas Bitcoin is pure messenger, in the sense that it gets shot every time because you can see the money. My response to that isn't to point out how terrible what we are seeing is, it's to point out that being aware of it in this way is a useful thing. Here we have a transparent and plastic medium for looking at the exchange of value, where it comes from and where it goes to.

This lack of plausible deniability, the fact that not only do you know how the sausage is made, but you've got a sausage machine here whirring away on your own desktop—it changes things. Of course I know that there is no ethical production under capitalism. But why is this the production we're objecting to so vocally? I appreciate that part of it is because people feel that crypto genuinely has no value, that it genuinely has no social utility that could not be achieved by more just and less socially and economically and ecologically harmful means. But as I often say to people, and as they often get very annoyed at me for saying, if it could be achieved in another way it would already have been, and if had been, then the same people who you don't like buying up blockchain projects would be buying up projects on that because, you know, we're like little financial amoeba around these financial gravity wells.

Blockchain technology is a tiny crack, a tiny shifting of the ass cheeks of capital, it's a moment of potential for a temporary autonomous zone. And I've been amazed by how long that moment has lasted. I'm not here preventing revolution, I'm here trying to get a minor redistribution of wealth within this moment where capital has not yet slammed shut the door on any alternative or any support for anything other than adopting a hyperextractivist attitude in every single social relation. And frankly, I regard that as more useful than most of what the people who get terribly upset with me for doing that are trying to do.

MBK So should we also add some salt to the tacit antihumanist suggestion in some of these works that, if we left the market to it, it could probably do a better job than humans at most things?

RM I don't actually believe in markets. I'm a 'real markets have never been tried' person, because the 'markets' we have are structured by the state: you need fiat money, you need the state legal system, you need the violence of the state to protect the commodity form and break strikes. You need all of that for markets of the kind that people game-theorise and insist upon naturalising. There may be a possible post-revolutionary anarcho-marketist 'markets-but-not-capitalism' wonderland, but I don't have the heart to see it. 'Bad Shibe' is as close as I can get to seeing it, but it's a scary world: it has child labour and there are black helicopters doing who knows what, and there's a bug in the code that's gonna cause the blockchain to jam in about two days time (if I ever get around to writing the sequel)....

So I'm not a market anarchist, I just play one on the internet. And in those moments you mention, what I'm doing is not entirely a bit, but it is a critical move.

The reason I make it in the form of an apparently first-order statement is that no-one is going to listen or give me the benefit of the doubt if I distance myself from it by saying *Here are my complex emotional and history-of-ideas feelings about markets, now let's talk about them.*

And when it comes to blockchain art, things are not as straightforward as artists vs technocapitalists. I was once on a panel where I was doing that whole bit: we can just price art, and technology will save us...and Kevin McCoy pointed out that we were both from the art world and we were the people who created the ideas that became NFTs, so NFTs were not this spontaneously generated market phenomenon. Of course the standard was made by some very smart computer science and blockchain people, and I'm not trying to erase them, but all of the early NFT-type projects had at least someone from the art world or art academia involved in them.

So perhaps I play that role far too well. I did have someone come up to me once and say, 'Hey, I've figured out how to make *Arewethereyet* from "Bad Shibe"!' And I had to say, 'Can you not? It's a dystopian satire of credit score gamification that I really would not like to see be a real thing in the world...'.

Ultimately, what I want more than anything is for someone to say *No, you are wrong, here is a better alternative*. I have a genuine anger for imaginary solutions that are not critical or even prefigurative, that are nothing more than affordable hobbies for those who use them to resolve the merely psychological contradictions of their own existence as agents of the social reproduction of the ideology of capitalism. That anger and heartbreak and sadness goes into making this stuff and just hoping that someone who is kinder and smarter and better than me has an answer that is not merely confected, that is not merely a necessary cog in the clockwork machinery that neutralises revolutionary potential by redirecting it into dreamwork.

MBK So operationalising Schelling Point convergence in order to optimise aesthetics and art criticism ('The ABC of Accelerationist Blockchain Critique') isn't an entirely serious proposition?

RM More of a modest proposal, I'd say, although it's a functional one and one that would change things in interesting ways if it actually happened. The epitome of this is 'Maximum Transaction Density', which is as Janus-faced as everything else I write, but if as a reader you get to the end of it and treat it as simply a first-order call to turn ourselves into blockchain clickworkers or whatever, then it has failed miserably. It is precisely the most intense attempt I have made to horrify the imagined reader into either accepting that, yes, this will achieve our ends, horrific though it is, and we should pursue this, or protesting in horror, *No, that's not right because....* 'Maximum Transaction Density' is about the horror of getting what you want by means that you don't want. If anyone has a better idea for how to do what they want than what's in there, I'm all ears.

Just to try and wrap up my apology for my good leftist soul: some of this is simply Edward-de-Bono-style creative thinking. At times you have to make a sideways leap or lateral move to avoid being stuck in a rut. Working through these ideas, some of it is provocation, some of it is aspiration, some of it is education and... it's not demanding that others do the work for me, it's doing the work that I can do and hoping that others will be able to respond in a way that I haven't already heard and been disappointed by.

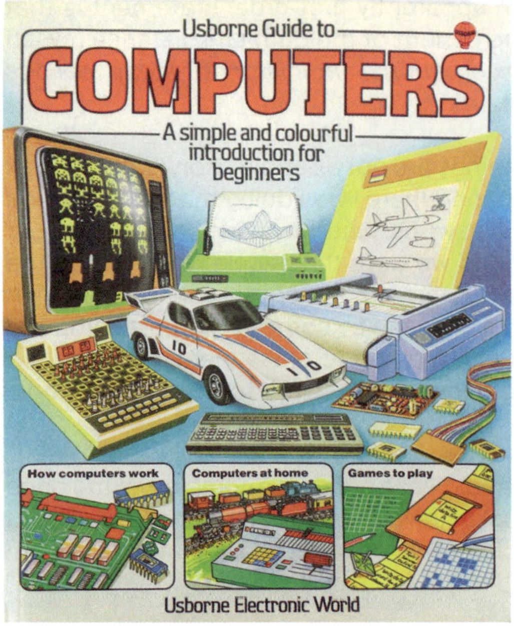

Brian Reffin Smith, *Usborne Guide to Computers* (Usborne Publishing Ltd., 1981).

MBK Your career in art eventually collided with computing, cyberculture, and cypherpunk, but how did it begin?

RM Both of my parents worked in arts education at various levels throughout their lives. When I was little I would go to my father's basement office at Central Saint Martins and smell photo developer and be very impressed by all the big machines. So I had that background. And then we were members of a militant offshoot of the scouting movement, although by that point it was just a bunch of families doing cheap camping holidays somewhere in England each summer. The kids who were one high-school generation up from me there, the cool kids, were all into art and were going off to art school, so that was a major influence.

There were a couple of books in the art room at high school that were important for me, books the new art teacher had brought in (thank you Miss Hamer!) There was the Warhol retrospective catalogue from 1987, which I sat and read front to back many times; and another which was the catalogue from an, at least in part, conceptual retrospective. The two works I can remember from it are one of the Conceptual Art projects where someone introduces two strangers to each other to have a conversation, and an early example of lifelogging, of the quantified self—an artist who kept track of their activities over a week or a month or something.

This was around 1989, I was reading this at age sixteen to eighteen, so obviously I liked H.R. Giger, I liked graphic design, album covers, and all that kind of thing, very much in line with what kids of that generation were into on the visual culture front. But from the get-go I wasn't into trying to copy heroic Boris Vallejo-style art like some of my best friends were. Apart from anything else, I knew I couldn't draw that well. I also lived through the home computing boom in the UK, and one of the books I got from book club was the *Usborne Guide to Computers*, which featured Harold Cohen and his AARON drawing robot, and Ken Knowlton's BEFLIX programming language. So from the age of about ten or twelve I had the idea that, even if I myself couldn't do it, there were people out there making art with computers. And when I began an art foundation course in 1991, I made friends with the technicians, which meant that I could squeeze past them in their

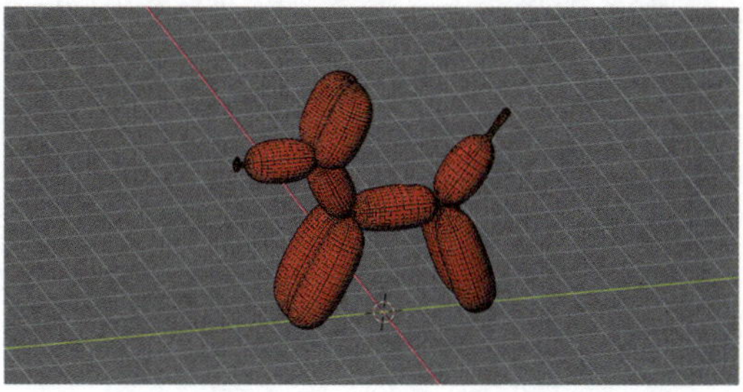

Rhea Myers, 'Balloon Dog', 2011, from *Shareable Readymades*. 3D digital model.

converted corridor office to use one of the two Macintoshes in the building. I can still remember seeing Photoshop boot for the first time. It was something very different: going from a very *this-is-technical* self-taught command-line programmer world to the very positively commodified design of the Macintosh.

During that period I did a lot of screen printing and dye-transfer work. But I had this desire to make a sort of remix- or sampling-based art where I was taking things and chopping them up digitally and rearranging them. And by the time I got to art school proper, I was deeply in love with the sample-based musics that were going mainstream at that moment, and I was sure that was something I wanted to embrace. I had Andy Warhol as a reference, and I became an instant and lifelong Jeff Koons fan (sorry haters), between the pink Taschen book, which I still have on my bookcase, and the little red handbook which has that great quote: 'If you put art in the hands of a monarch, it will reflect his ego and eventually become decorative. If you put it in the hands of the masses, it will reflect mass ego and eventually become decorative. If you put art in the hands of Jeff Koons, it will reflect my ego and eventually become decorative.' And Koons's comment about Warhol being about distribution, and his work being about the penetration of consciousness.

Later in the decade I found things like *No Logo*, and could conceptualise that sort of very Nike-style branding and *Adbusters*-inflected art, which you can follow through much later into *Shareable Readymades* (2011–2013), where I tried to take iconic art-historical objects and return them to the cultural commons by publishing them as 3d-printable digital models.

MBK When did Conceptual Art begin to play a significant role in what you were doing?

RM I'd encountered some Conceptual Art in that catalogue when I was at school, and on my foundation course we went on a field trip to the Serpentine for the exhibition *Objects for the Ideal Home: The Legacy of Pop Art* (1991), which included work by Koons and by Julian Opie, who was also a massive influence. I found out about the Lisson Gallery via Opie, and it was at Lisson that I first encountered Art & Language and had my mind blown by their writing and art.

On my fine art degree course at Canterbury College of Art I was at war with the Cultural Studies department because...they had not explained to us why reading Derrida was a Good Idea when I just wanted to cut pictures up and make weird things on my computer. But Art & Language was different, this was something that fascinated me and that I wanted to push through: it would take me a day to read two pages of *Essays on Art & Language*,[3] which ultimately is a fairly straightforward bit of materialist art history by an Open University lecturer, but

3 C. Harrison, *Essays on Art & Language* (Oxford: Blackwell, 1991).

Art & Language, *Art-Language* journal, February 1970.

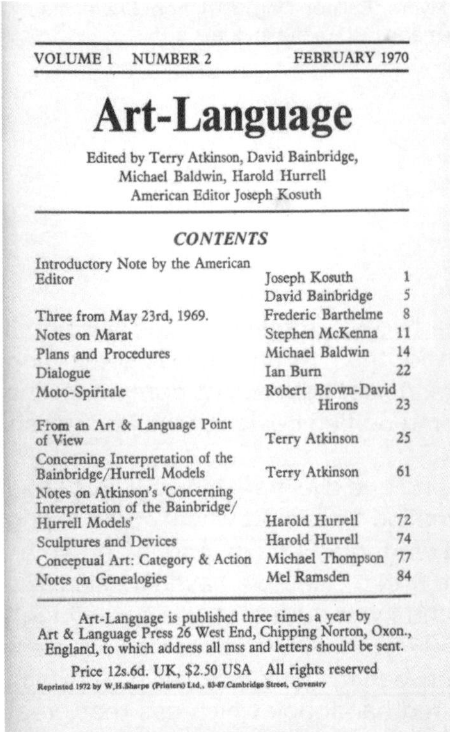

VOLUME 1 NUMBER 2 FEBRUARY 1970

Art-Language

Edited by Terry Atkinson, David Bainbridge,
Michael Baldwin, Harold Hurrell
American Editor Joseph Kosuth

CONTENTS

Art-Language is published three times a year by
Art & Language Press 26 West End, Chipping Norton, Oxon.,
England, to which address all mss and letters should be sent.
Price 12s.6d. UK, $2.50 USA
Reprinted 1972 by W.H.Sharpe (Printers) Ltd., 83-87 Cambridge Street, Coventry

which to me at the time, relative to my interests up until then, was rocket science. I'd pick up odd copies of *Art-Language* and I wouldn't feel so bad about writing raw PostScript programming code, you know, it was impenetrable!

From Art & Language and from Opie I took a couple of things: firstly, project-based work: there's nothing wrong with project-based work, you can make work that completes a certain project and then move on. And secondly, the idea that it's possible to make artworks that are critical and, as Art & Language would later call it, essayistic, without them merely illustrating a text—that really went in. And then there was Art & Language's historical-materialist view of art, which is very unconvinced by the official story of Modernism and the claim that art is about sensations and that the artwork must be securely contained within the edge of the frame otherwise you risk polluting this wonderful clean world of formal composition.

The refusal of that sense of modernist autonomy tied into my enthusiasm for pop and computer art and graphic design work too—I was obsessed with The Designers Republic at that point, I gradually came to admire Tomato, and I loved Peter Saville's work for Factory. This was very much the pop-culture-postmodern era when low culture was being celebrated, but rather than simply being swept along by the megaflow of consumerism, I was able to get some purchase on it with this art which assembled some of those materials in a way that made them somehow *indigestible*—in Art & Language's case, indigestible to the well-educated nice spectator who just wants to go to the museum and be flattered before going back to their job; in my case, indigestible in the sense of something that doesn't want to be simply reducible to the ambient clichés of the time, or to be immediately recuperable by capitalism, by The Way Things Are.

This is not as easy as it sounds, of course, and later I'd come to the realisation that art is R&D for capital: artists love making things that can't be bought, but capital also loves things that can't be bought, because they help it work out how to expand its property regime so that it can buy them. But even when I was doing my foundation degree show in 1995 I was thinking about price to some extent. I was showing prints of work that I'd designed in Corel Draw and Illustrator, vector- and text-based work, but printed out giant, as big as was possible in '95. So I had these A0 digital photocopies—not laser prints but photocopies of smaller laser prints—up on the wall. And the price sheet was based on how much you didn't want anyone else to have a copy. So if you wanted a little print that was fine, you know, it's ten quid. But if you wanted a large print and for me to not make any more of them, then that would be £300.

MBK So you were already asking questions about how the artwork interacted with price?

RM Yes. Because this was digital art, and there was no existing model for its value.

MBK Potentially infinitely reproducible, and therefore of no rarity value.

RM Which was fine with me, but the problem that I had not thought about while making it was, how are we going to show it? As soon as it became possible to shove the work into a Git repository[4] and tell a curator, *Just grab the repository and do what you want with it*, I was in hog heaven: I didn't have to solve the problem, I just adopted a Creative Commons licence for all the work I could so that, by about 2003, nobody ever had to ask me for permission ever again (although they always do).

But at that point, my solution to the problem of producing work that fitted very awkwardly into either printmaking or existing digital imagery—and I did regard the computer as a printmaking medium at that time—was initially to let the market sort it out and, later, to let technology sort it out.

MBK Were you already using exclusively digital media at that time?

RM Yes. I had worked out that I had no 3D perception whatsoever. I cannot do sculpture. I made one painting, and I did life drawing, but I am not any kind of spontaneous expressionist. So I came to media that allowed me to move things around and recombine them, and vector graphics is perfect for that because you can draw a circle, you can squash it, you can rotate it, you can offset it, you can cut it out with another one, you can glue it to another one, it's a very plastic medium, more like working with clay than with rock.

I also gained an understanding of colour that became so deeply enculturated so quickly that one of my tutors asked me if I was colourblind. I wasn't, I was just using really horrible yellow, green, and blue photocopier paper to make reference to the world of office life, just like I was taking colour palettes from graphic design colour palette books and Pantone flipbooks and from sweet wrappers and cereal boxes—from everywhere except art.

MBK You were using colour and shape as sign systems?

RM Yes. And I was already doing series at that point: the first defensible series that I did was called *Mixes*. It involved taking canonical paintings and combining them using morphing software. What I emphasised at the time was the interplay

4 <https://github.com/rheaplex>.

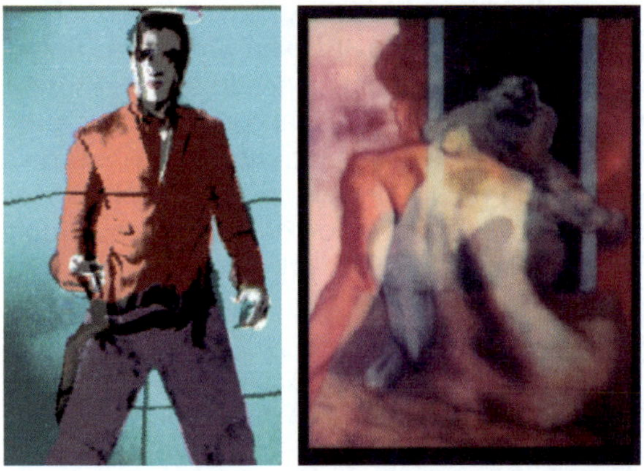

Rhea Myers, *Mixes*, 1993. Digital images.

between the compositions of the images and between the gazes of artists with different sexualities. There's a Bacon cricketer and a Kitaj naked woman smoking, one with a tree by Gilbert and George and a Francis Bacon George piece, and another one which is Gilbert or George in a suit blended with a Warhol Cowboy Elvis. The combination of them in the morphing software looks like a Pierrot, and it's this wonderful dive into male gender presentation—although I wouldn't have had that language available to me at the time.

Then I did a lot of text calligraphy 3d work, laboriously dragging computer type over freehand drawings and then photographs, getting into the computer room at 8am and leaving at 8pm because in those days, when you dragged that many bits of text around in perspective in Corel Draw, you could make at least one cup of tea waiting for it to render every time you moved it.

This was an early instance of one of the strategies that I stole from Art & Language, who stole it from Ad Reinhardt, which is disobedience-in-obedience, or work to rule. Taking a demand that someone has made, obeying it to the letter, and horribly disappointing the person who made the demand because that's not what they meant. It's like the meme format *Hurt me! No, not like that!* Clement Greenberg said that you should expunge all outside content from art; so why not just paint a black square? *No, not like that!* Or, for me, the Cultural Studies department had said the world was a text, so why not make images of a world that is entirely made out of text, and of course the response was, *No, not like that!* It's a wonderful strategy for critical engagement because, firstly, you get to troll people, but secondly, you get to be creative and you get to do hermeneutics or interpretation or parody, which is far less boring and more generative than simply saying, *No, you're wrong, here's a better solution*.

During this period I also almost invented the Word macro virus. I didn't, because we didn't have the Word macro manuals, but I wanted to make a virus that would

Rhea Myers, *PostScript Virus*, 1993. Computer code (image shows before/after).

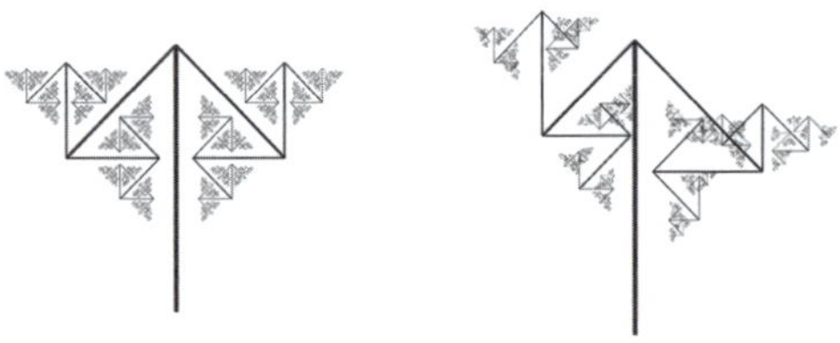

replace the word 'postmodernism' with something random. I did make a virus written in Adobe PostScript, a language designed to describe page layouts for print (*PostScript Virus* [1993]). The virus would have infected PostScript printers and made all of the lovely graphic design sent to the printer just a bit more wobbly. I had the payload and an attempt at the replicator...but I thought, I probably don't want to do this, I don't know if it's actually technically possible or not but if it is I don't want to find out.... It worked by redefining how the PostScript interpreter itself works. And the fact that code can interpret things and can do things visually was interesting to me. At the time people were obsessed with the idea of software as text, but for me, the design of the Macintosh, that *visual* encounter with software, with a standardized GUI, was very compelling.

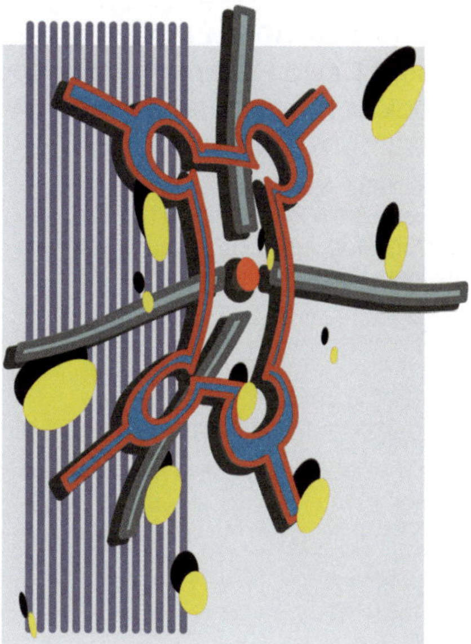

Rhea Myers, 'Arching', 1994, from *Blobs*. Digital vector image.

Eventually, when I got fed up with spending twelve hours a day in the computer room, I fell in love, had my first serious relationship, and the joy from that went into the more graphically wibbly-wobbly works that make up *Blobs* (1994). Again, these were all done using vector graphics. Each of them required a very keen visual eye, but none of it required great hand-eye coordination. What I was looking for in vector graphics was a medium, meaning something with both affordances that direct you, and limitations that you have to work around, and which comes with a theory and a history. That's what's happening in *Blobs*: the history I got from graphic design, from The Designers Republic, from the cereal packets and candy wrappers and so on. And there's a lot of play with the form going on, to the extent that these are just about sensuality and joy, but they're about that sensuality and joy in a way that's technically mediated and is very contemporary to that era. There's nothing spiritual to it, and there's nothing political except to the extent that just doing this is political.

MBK You mentioned Julian Opie, whose work is often interested in how much you can graphically pare down aesthetic means while retaining some kind of seductive or sensual allure.

RM Yes, it's curious because on the internet I play someone who hates dialectics, but all the work I like is dialectical, and my own work—don't tell anyone—is also generally deeply dialectical. In *Blobs* you have a cold commercial technology being made to use warm, sexy (in my conception of it at the time) art. The *Blobs* are bodies, they're ecstatic maps of making out, and they are free objects—each has its own shadow. There is no God. The light of the fact. But they exist within an indexical environment of certain technical problems within the production and history of art and carry these very impersonal references.

Opie is fascinating because the painted steel sculptures he started with are a sort of ironisation of turn-of-the-80s Frank Stella. Where Stella painted abstract sculptures, Opie used the same technique with representational imagery in a retro clip-art style. I simply adore Opie's concrete Scalextric sets (*Imagine You Are Driving* [1993]), toy-like in their scale and reduction of complexity and in their educational, imaginative reflective purpose. They give you something to look at. They're not a text stapled to the wall or a blank canvas, they are something that has presence, virtuality. His air conditioners from the late 80s, I believe, although I have no evidence for this, come from a comment David Hockney made about minimal art, which was that you might as well look at the air conditioning unit.

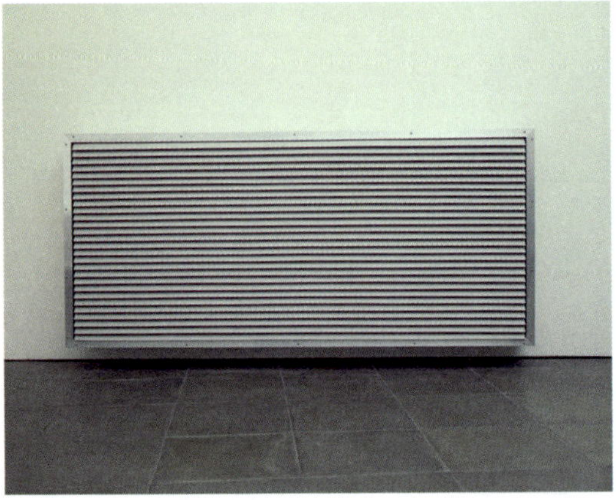

Julian Opie, *K.*, 1987. Aluminium, stainless steel, foam, PVC, wood, 96.5 x 219 x 28 cm (38 x 86 1/4 x 11 in), OPIE870008. © Julian Opie; courtesy Lisson Gallery. Photograph: Gareth Winters.

MBK Didn't he steal that from *Columbo*? In the episode 'Playback' (1975), Columbo's in a gallery in LA sniffing around. In the line of duty, he's trying to enter into the modern art ethos, and mistakenly starts 'appreciating' the air conditioning unit. 'Um, now, this here...I see it doesn't have a title...'!

RM Those Opie works put the visual to work in the way that—not to say that art *should*, but that art tends to, whether it's persuading you to love Christ, to join the revolution, or to really enjoy getting on the train out of Paris for the weekend. The essentially propagandising function of art is a result of its visual seductiveness. Adorno says that to depict violence is to aestheticise it, which is entirely correct, but doesn't go far enough, because to aestheticise something can be morally obscene, and the deployment of moral obscenity merely symbolically within art can be a very powerful move. Sometimes the only way you can get to sympathy is through disgust. I'm all about these lateral moves. But yeah, what is the point of visual art you don't want to look at?

MBK So although you were already engaged with Conceptualism in its most stringent form, you didn't have the hostility or suspicion of the visual that can imply.

RM No, and I still think design has a better claim to the craft of imagemaking qua imagemaking than contemporary art does. If you want a well-painted, well-drawn, well-proportioned image, go to design or comics or illustration or movies—anywhere other than the gallery, where the zombie formalisms are skulking in the hope that they can gather enough presence to be considered significant despite not signifying.

There's a lovely Art & Language quote they've been trying to walk back for decades, which goes something like, 'Some of the paintings seemed better than others, it seemed to us that this was somehow a product of the making of them'. This is about a series of their own paintings, and they tried to clarify that, of course, they were not saying that any skill or imagination went into them...no, too late!

In grappling with this kind of thing, I decided that you can't do either reason or emotion alone. I'd seen a documentary featuring someone who had a brain injury which left them incapable of emotion, and as a result they couldn't make a decision because they would never get bored of reasoning about it. *Where should we go for dinner? Well, we could go to the fish restaurant but I like the wine at the Italian place but then we could....* They had no way of culling the search tree, because they had a faculty of pure logical search unconstrained by affect. So I realised that it's ineffective to pretend not to rely on visual impact and the affect it creates. Often it's 'logical' to use affect and indeed to be illogical, because sometimes you need to jump to a different line of flight from any you can think of directly. I wanted to make posters, things for people to have in their mental space. I didn't have the kind of residual valuing of high culture that you find in the historical-materialist project-based discursive-but-not-illustrative work of Art & Language and Opie. I found something very interesting in the more productive and playful and, to be honest, queer art of Warhol and Koons.

MBK You then moved on to the Centre for Electronic Arts at Middlesex University. The courses offered there were quite pioneering.

RM Oh, absolutely. An institution I have described as throwing humanities students at computer programming for a year, and having the survivors put on a show. I got there in '95 and there was the feeling of twenty years of history to the place already. There was a dead old Silicon Graphics box in the hall, there was a PICASO software manual next to a Macintosh attached to a video dumping device. We had lectures from people who'd founded the Computer Arts Society, people in the then-current new media art scene, and people who actually knew how to teach people like me maths and programming. So it was an absolutely amazing marriage between the technical knowledge that you needed to make a computer beep the way you wanted it to, and a sense of history that led you to feel that this was something that could be informed by and respond to precedent. And you were also situated within contemporary culture because you had people explaining the early social effects of the internet, or how virtual reality related to feminism, or whatever. So yeah, it was Camelot.

MBK Did you have access to whatever constituted cutting-edge hardware and software at the time?

RM No, we didn't have access to the best computers, we had some little pre-PowerMacs. But if you were very nice to the Music Department they'd let you use their NeXT boxes, and if you were very nice to the Interactive Multimedia Department they'd let you use one of their ageing Silicon Graphics boxes or their PCs. I got into an ongoing battle with some Interactive Media students, getting there earlier and earlier in the morning to use the PCs.

MBK This would have been during the period of the explosion of cyberculture too, and a growing general awareness of computing technology and the internet. How aware were you of that, and of the differences between the mainstream US *Wired* version of cyberculture and the more idiosyncratic and abrasive UK take on cyberculture by groups like Mute Magazine, Ccru, Orphan Drift, and so on?

RM During this period, between 1995 and 2000, to be honest I encountered cyberculture and didn't understand it. I encountered net art and didn't understand it. I encountered the web and didn't understand it (you'll notice a theme here). I'd got over my printmaking obsession, but I thought interactive multimedia was the future. *PostScript Virus* was only the first in a long history of me not taking the bit as far as it could go...but it was the closest I got to cyberculture at the time. For me, cyberpunk was the eighties, I thought that was all done with, passé. *Cyberpunk? You might as well be reading westerns, what are you doing?!* My partner at the time was the creative director at a virtual reality startup in Shoreditch, you literally could not be more mid-nineties. So I got to see VRML and virtual communities emerge, and I also went to a show [Ccru, *Syzygy*, Beaconsfield, 2000] which had some strange drawings on the wall, featuring this sort of bracket notation for numbers. I looked at it and I was like *Just use hex!* So I very much didn't know what the next big thing was at the time. If I had a time machine it would be a toss-up between whether I go back to teenage me and go, *Hey, there's a reason why all of your RPG characters are female*, or go back to twentysomething me and go, *Walk on the earth, engage with what is actually going on, take a risk!*

MBK How advanced were you as a programmer? Was your knowledge of coding drawn purely from having to learn in order to make designs and prints?

RM I had no formal programming education until I got to Middlesex. I'd learned BASIC from the Usborne books, I'd learned Forth and some Pascal purely out of interest. I was obsessed with LOGO but couldn't get a copy of it to use. I knew that LISP was a thing, probably thanks to Usborne books too, but couldn't make head nor tail of it. I learned a bit of C, I had a C compiler for my Mac. But the language that I went all in on was PostScript, because it was the language that graphic design was made in. As a language it's most like Forth, it's an absolutely fascinating language, and the environment in which it operates is so amazing, this platonic mathematical realm of lines and curves that maps into very real ink being squeezed between metal plates onto paper. I later got a job working at a prepress company programming Adobe Illustrator plug-ins based on the knowledge that I had gained of the PostScript rendering model.

MBK PostScript is a language that defines the available range of vector and typographical objects, the relations between them, and the transforms that can be applied to them, all in the most economical form. So it lays out a kind of graphic ontology, right?

RM Yes, it's curious because it's not like having a pattern book for textiles or a Vasari study of Roman architecture; it's not really a set of models, it's not quite a tool box, it's not quite a palette, it's this combination of knowledge and tool and affordance that's sort of the technical equivalent of a community of practice. If UNIX is the religious literature of computer science, then PostScript is its illuminated manuscripts.

MBK It seems like, even for this period, you went a lot deeper into programming than you strictly needed to in order to do digital printmaking.

RM At one point in art school I was given the task of doing what in the 2000s was called a 'mashup'. I was given photocopies of a Futurist cyclist and a Jackson Pollock drip painting and told to put those together. I looked at the small grey reproduction of the cyclist and I just couldn't work it out. I had been given a material task that I could not perform owing to my lack of experience, knowledge, and resources. So I went to the library and there was a book of preparatory sketches by the artist: a drawing of someone on a bicycle, a drawing of someone on the bicycle with lines of force, because it's Futurism, then that was abstracted a bit, then that abstraction reduced to a circle and a couple of triangles...and I then understood the forms I was working with. And in the same way, I learned programming because I wanted to understand. I knew that I wanted to make computer art, whatever that was, so I needed to know the structures underpinning it. That interest in access to knowledge and source material for very practical reasons fed directly into my interest in copyleft and free culture and Creative Commons.

MBK Because you had direct experience of the fact that it mattered whether people had access not just to the end product, but to the knowledge of how things are made? And you were able to see how that need translated from art to programming—in both cases, to really understand and be productive you need access to the 'source code'?

RM Yes, in my case I would not have competently been able to do the task without access to those resources. The funny thing is that, after doing a Marinetti in the style of Jackson Pollock, I found out about Art & Language's *Portrait of V.I. Lenin with Cap, in the Style of Jackson Pollock* (1980).

MBK Coincidentally, this is exactly where I was going to go next, because in the essay that accompanies that painting, Art & Language pose their question about 'ofness', a question many of your works can be seen as responding to.[5] What is a painting of? In one sense it's a visual representation *of* something, but in another, *genetic* sense, it's *of* all of the conditions—material, sociopolitical, etc.—that have made its particular visual mode and material construction possible. That question may require less forcing when working with computer images than with painting, because it was almost inevitable with early computing technology that you would produce images that weren't *of* anything representationally, or only in a very rudimentary way. And so the question of what they're *of* genetically becomes interesting if you're reflecting on them in a way informed to some extent by art theory.

RM You can render balls bouncing around the screen—and I did—but what does that touch on outside of itself? The genetic *of* is of great interest to me, and I love the history of computing, no matter how boring. When I was doing my degree I read the book about the making of the Macintosh, *Insanely Great*,[6] and I've read so

5 Art & Language, 'Portrait of V.I. Lenin', *Artforum* 10: 2 (February 1980), reprinted in C. Harrison, F. Orton (eds) *Modernism, Criticism, Realism* (London and New York: Harper and Row, 1984), 145–69; 'On "A Portrait of V.I. Lenin in the Style of Jackson Pollock"', in Harrison, *Essays on Art & Language*, 129–49.

6 S. Levy, *Insanely Great: The Life And Times of Macintosh, the Computer That Changed Everything* (New York: Viking, 1994).

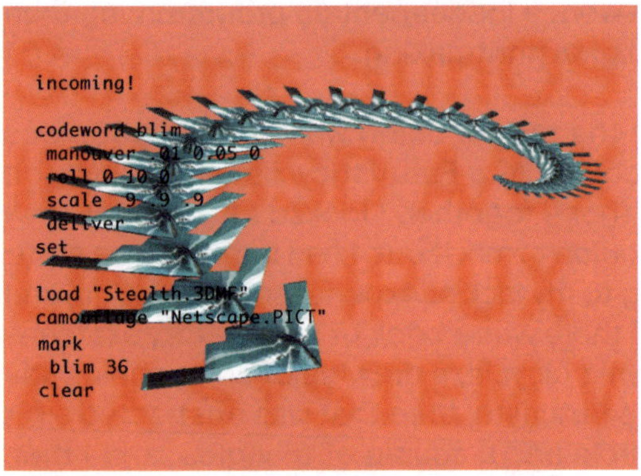

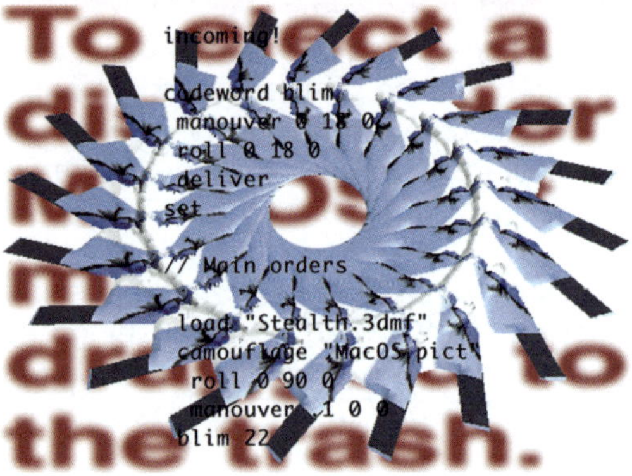

Rhea Myers, *Surgical Strike*, 1996. Digital images.

many others, including *Showstopper!*, the story of the making of Windows NT.[7] One of the most depressing books ever, but it fed into *Surgical Strike* (1996).

Surgical Strike is another mashup, ripped very directly from Art & Language. It reinflects William Latham-style swirly blobby organic computer graphics with stealth bombers and facts from the history of the production of computing (influenced by Manuel De Landa's *War in the Age of Intelligent Machines*, if I remember correctly) and then puts the source code for it all in front. The objects are procedurally generated by a language which consists of military terminology rather than computer science concepts.

But yes, this *ofness*, which a work can engage with in order to draw in references from outside the canvas, gives art an irreplaceable power to carry out operations that can include depiction, critique, endorsement, whatever you want—but basically, it gives art the ability to not stop at the frame. This seemed key to me. It might have been that I'd seen how much people hated computer art for its lack of historical necessity, or it might have been too many group crits, but I needed to ground my practice in something beyond the frame, something offscreen, however much that led to me diving deep into the technology itself.

MBK So with PostScript, for example, you could say, yes, a given document has circles, Bézier curves, bits of type, but part of what it's *of* is the entire structure of the software that is used to make it, the affordances of the language in which it's written, and the design decisions behind those affordances, and so on…which is the approach you apply later to blockchain technologies.

7 G.P. Zachary, *Showstopper! The Breakneck Race to Create Windows NT and the Next Generation at Microsoft* (New York: The Free Press, 1994).

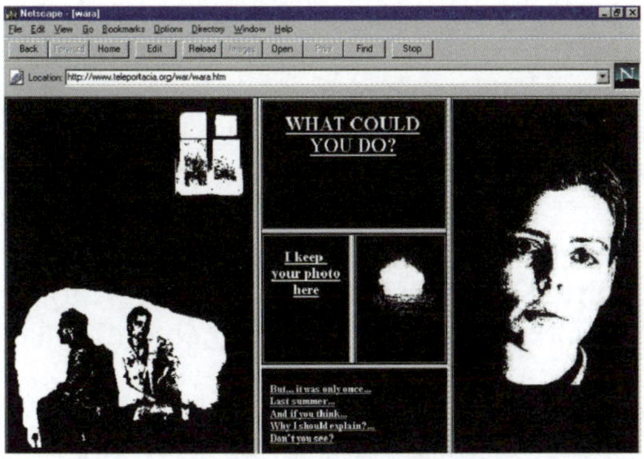

Olia Lialina, *My Boyfriend Came Back from the War*, 1996, Browser-based internet work.

RM Sure, although originally the interest in design software came from The Designers Republic, from Emigré, from the fact that this contemporary imagery was so vivid to me.

MBK I can see how none of this meshed straightforwardly with the cyberculture of the day. So what drew you into that world in the end?

RM I left art school and realised I didn't have the social skills to make a go of it as an artist in the nineties art world. So what got me into the subculture was hanging out in Shoreditch, which was sort of ground zero for cyberculture in London at that time. I encountered lots of stuff at the ICA, I encountered Cyberia. Later I got onto the Rhizome mailing list, I got onto Furtherfield's Netbehaviour list. And then over time I became more and more involved with Furtherfield, appreciated what they were doing, realised that I'd missed out on a very interesting historical moment, and did my best to understand it and to appreciate what I'd missed.

But the real missing link here is Olia Lialina's work *My Boyfriend Came Back from the War* (1996), which was a browser-based piece of art. I looked at it and thought, *Oh, this is interesting*. Twenty minutes later I was like, *Okay this is really interesting*. It was an experience with a very particular feel, a very particular aesthetic, you couldn't have had that encounter and been drawn in by it in the same way in any other medium. If you were interacting with interactive multimedia in a gallery you'd be primed for something, if you had a CD-ROM and shoved it into your Mac, again, you've made a certain investment in what you expect to encounter. Being on the internet, following a link and just being *there*, this is a different way of encountering art. So that opened things up for me conceptually.

MBK A largely visual but potentially multimodal medium, the browser, was increasingly becoming indispensable in every part of everyday life—a life lived through media that, as technology develops, becomes increasingly immediate.

RM Precisely, it is mediated, mediatised, by a generic medium—computing information technology. As we have found, you can shove anything down a fat enough pipe. And even in the Netscape era it was obvious that what we had in the web was a singular medium in which text, sound, video, writing, conversation, and money were all brought together. Money didn't quite fit yet because the government was determined that it wouldn't. But that was coming.

And at the time you could work as a graphic designer in Shoreditch making websites for three weeks and make enough money to spend a week making art, and that was what people did. People were working to organise public access to the internet as a social project. You had internet labs helping people to get online.

The dream of mass networking was starting to spring up and it just felt like this moment of possibility where people knew that they could both change the world and afford to do so, maybe even get rich by doing so. I described Furtherfield in the 2000s as a cultural embassy from a better world. Having that living model of people who are running a real artist's space that was well ahead of the game by any measure, it was really inspiring.

MBK Was it at this point that your interest shifted from interactive multimedia to an awareness that you could work with networked technology as a medium?

RM I made precisely one piece of net art in the nineties, for a show by SoDA, a brilliant Middlesex University-derived tech art company. They were doing a show, so I made some YBA art generators as Java applets. There was a Hirst spot generator—and you'll notice that I've continued making spot generators since then—there was a hospital door generator because Gary Hume was big then, and a couple of other things. They were very much in the hacker culture/Usenet culture tradition of making buzzword generator parodies. In doing that for visual art I was in effect saying, *These spots aren't worth anything, make as many as you like*, a technique I've revisited a number of times. But we couldn't actually get them showing on the woefully underpowered Macs that we had for the show, so, entirely by accident, I was one of the first people to exhibit a URL in a gallery! That was the point the installation team got to, and I was like yeah, sure, go for it: another time they also printed out a listing of the code and exhibited that. So I was trying to do buzzword-generator-style net art but I ended up as a conceptualist by default, in my absence!

I spent a few years on some unrealised projects that involved me trying to avoid being the kind of performance art shaman that I thought I didn't want to be. I did get a tri-field electromagnetic field meter and go to a gallery searching for the aura of art—I thought I'd found it but a statistical regression indicates that I was just kidding myself. In the end I couldn't genuinely be enthusiastic about doing this sort of thing. No, it's got to be visual, I'm not being paid for this so I should at least get some visual joy from it.

After *Surgical Strike* there were a couple of years at the end of the nineties when I pretty much stopped making art. My creative output consisted in porting the Gwydion Dylan compiler to classic MacOS as a historical intervention in the history of computing after Apple cancelled their Dylan project. It got to the point where I was at Apple's developer conference in California for Douglas Adams's *The Digital Village* game company, and I was fielding emails from the company that did the one remaining commercial Dylan compiler, trying to open-source their user interface toolkit. So I went pretty deep into that community. I do tend to—I don't know what the politically correct anthropological term for 'going native' is—I do tend to dance with wolves.

MBK But presumably it would have been already evident to you at that point that, if you were looking to have an appreciable impact on the way in which people went about their lives and saw the world, intervening in software would be a more reliable means than making art?

RM Well, there was no hope that everyone was going to start using Dylan. But yes, I had already realised that, and that was where *PostScript Virus* came from, I wanted to intervene in everyone's everyday experience of aesthetics critically.

It's tricky though, because there's such a gap between what software developers see and what everyone else sees. One of the good things about Richard Stallman's ideology is his absolutely resolute refusal to differentiate between users of computers who are producers and those who are consumers. That was hopelessly idealistic even when he was doing it, and it's become no less so since, but yes, we experience so much through computers that changing what computers do is a surefire way of getting things out into the world.

MBK You've talked about how you always felt it was important to understand, to know the recipes: as an artist, if software of some kind is the medium, that requires an engagement with and preferably a mastery of that plastic medium. The vast majority of people engage with the screen without understanding what's going on beneath the surface, though. Would those that know be justified in holding that consumerist passivity in contempt?

RM Nerd supremacism slips into honest-to-goodness fascism far too easily. I'm someone who knows how to program a computer, and I'm deeply relaxed about you not needing to know how to do that. Honestly, if you want to engage critically with the technology, what you need is just some degree of technical and cultural literacy, whether it's from training or street smarts. I don't care where it comes from, just as long as you know what you're talking about. (I may have had different opinions about this in the past....)

The sense of superiority can go the other way too. All of the concerned calls to 'teach nerds ethics'—why not teach venture capitalists ethics, teach managers ethics?! Why are you, my status-anxious humanities bro, so obsessed with the idea that if only software developers understood that killing people is bad, software would be different? It's almost like you're aiming for the wrong part of the body technologic, for reasons that are at least as interesting sociologically and psychologically as the aims you claim to be trying to achieve by doing so....

And in fact, even though I've accidentally become a very good smart contract programmer, I didn't mean to do that. It was an accidental side effect—but I always do this, I always learn an obscure language for history of ideas or cultural history of computing reasons and then it turns out to be the next big thing. I learned Objective C in the nineties because I was fascinated by NeXT, Steve Jobs's big failed project after Apple. Then we got to 2001 and he tells us that they programmed MacOS in Objective C, and then the iPhone comes out, and suddenly everyone wants Objective C programmers. With programming Ethereum, I thought, this will be interesting to do a couple of projects in, and then suddenly everyone wants Ethereum programmers. There were a couple of other examples in-between. I've had the privilege, obviously, to be able to do that, but as someone who is not going to outcompete the world's best C++ programmer, I'm very lucky that that's not my ambition. I'm drawn to languages more for how amusing they are than for any claims of efficiency they might make.

As with absolutely everything I do, I don't suddenly have genius original ideas out of nowhere, it's always that I remember something from earlier in my life, or that I didn't understand something the last time I saw it, or that I want to do this thing so I'll try and learn how to do it and maybe I'll be able to use it later. It's all fantastically contingent.

MBK You mentioned wanting your works to touch on or draw in something from outside of themselves. A part of what I see in your works is a continuation of the question of the artwork's autonomy that was central to site-specific and institutional critique: the enterprise of making artworks that refuse to be autonomous self-contained objects transportable from one gallery to another, and instead manifest the conditions and environment of their production and exhibition—an idea allegorised physically in Hans Haacke's *Condensation Cubes* (1963–1968).

RM In the late sixties cybernetics was being received in a popular way by the same public who would later become interested in environmental concerns, precisely because they were primed to understand feedback systems. I'm not trying to say that RAND were actually hippies, I'm saying that after cybernetics escaped the lab, it was received by political movements in a way that we cannot imagine today. But once opposition to the Vietnam war became the key focus for many of them, cybernetics became unimaginable to them as well, which is why information-based and cybernetic art disappears like a vampire in sunlight about a year before I was born. But Haacke is very much in this milieu, and the thing about Haacke's institutional critique is that it is genuinely uncomfortable for the institution. You do not want a study of the slumlords of New York in your gallery as the nice polite property-owning class file in. There has to be that degree of discomfort to achieve successful institutional critique, but it can't be so much of a discomfort that it won't get shown. Haacke had the historical advantage of institutions not yet having worked this out. The end of that sort of institutional critique was when museums realised that they didn't have to put up with this, that artists can actually be told, yeah you're a genius but we don't have to show this work. You can always aestheticise any ethical move of resistance: 'They're selling hippie wigs in Woolworths, man.'

MBK Just as Conceptual Art was wrongfooted by its documents being aestheticised as exhibitable works.

RM Yes, I forget who said it, but if you point your finger at the moon, the dog just looks at your finger. There is a lot of this in the reception of Conceptual Art. And with institutional critique, once institutions worked out that they could have the aesthetic of critique with an ethic of affirmation—because institutional critique affirms these sites as powerful—*Yeah, tell me more about how awful and powerful I am, it's terrible, stop, no stop, no go on...*—that historical moment gives way to a candy shell of critique with no actual payload.

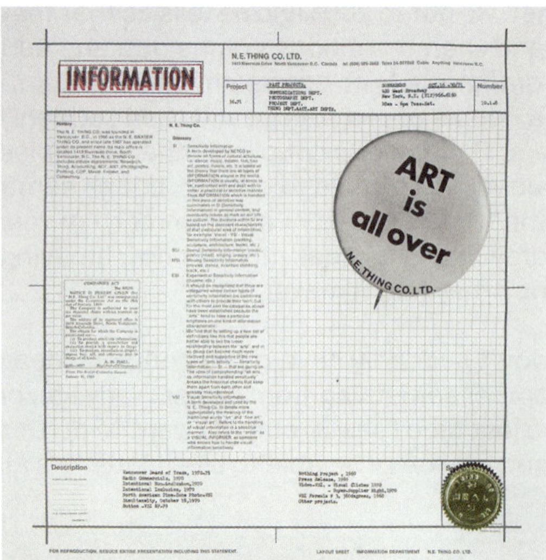

N.E. Thing Co., *Art is All Over*, 1971. Collage on paper. Collection of the Morris and Helen Belkin Art Gallery, University of British Columbia, gift of Iain Baxter& and Ingrid Baxter, 1995. Photo: Michael R. Barrick.

But Conceptual Art does also critique the ideology of art criticism at the time of the emergence of information technology. Upon arriving in Vancouver in 2013

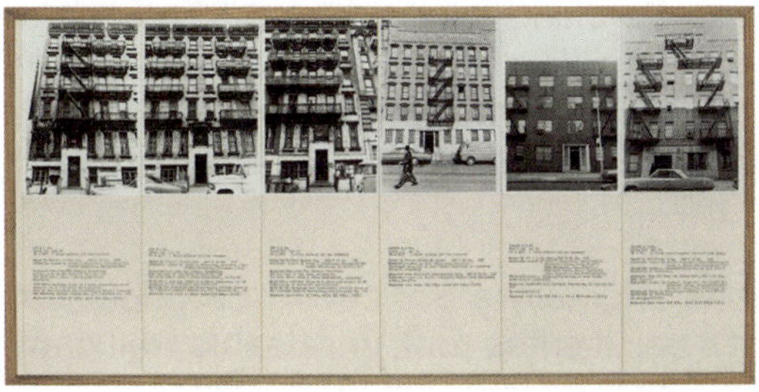

Hans Haacke, *Shapolsky et al. Manhattan Real Estate Holdings, a Real-Time Social System, as of May 1, 1971*, 1971 (detail). 9 photostats, 142 gelatin silver prints, and 142 photocopies, dimensions variable. © Hans Haacke / DACS, digital image courtesy Whitney Museum of American Art / Licensed by Scala.

I discovered N.E. Thing Co., some Vancouverites who had a teletype in the late 1960s and would spam companies with artworks via the telex network. They sent out the first networked call for a networked art show over the teletype network around 1970. This engagement with what now we don't see as information technology but which absolutely was at the time—the typewriter, the teletype, the photostat, the photocopier, microfiches, hot metal type printing, whatever—sought to problematise both that information technology and the idea of a purely visual unproblematic aesthetic art of pure sensation which you can consume without remainder or problem upon walking into the white cube.

Of course, institutions love site-specific institutional critique now. The horror of that kind of recuperation is something I priced in from the start. But if we think back to that landmark Haacke show [*Shapolsky et al.*, 1971], I'm absolutely ripping off that technique of saying to the art world, *You may actually want to think about where your money comes from or about your aesthetic of democracy and the problems underlying it*, while also saying to the people producing blockchain technology, *What if this works*? What if this works and it has consequences, should we maybe look at those in an arena which doesn't risk starving or freezing people or preventing them from getting their meds? Can we make use of the realm of ideas, of art, play there a while, and learn what we should not do before it has an actual impact? Treating it as a plastic medium for an art that is meant to be interrogative and uncomfortable both for the art world and for the blockchain technology world, that's a strategy taken very directly from Conceptual Art.

So yeah, it's focusing on an emerging technology which provides an attentional figure to the ideological and political and economic grounds that people are then able to see it against.

With Conceptualism, you had the first generation of artists who had modern art-school, degree-style training. It was the Cold War, it was consumer society, Greenberg had run out of steam but no one was really replacing him. Smearing some colours on a canvas just didn't seem up to it. The work of art could no longer do the work of art. So either you stop doing the work of art but continue making art, or you stop making art and continue doing the work of art. Art & Language and a few others chose to just keep going without a map, but with the intuition that it was politically or socially important to keep going. This led to either intentionally or unintentionally market-resistant forms of art. Art & Language talk with great amusement about galleries that would say they wanted to show their work, and would then end up sticking a copy of *Art-Language* up in a frame. An understandable mistake, but no. And then for their own internal pressures, needing to organise the conversations into the indexing projects, and then later on in the eighties needing to feed their families and having to come up with a sustained project of painting. But that initial 'We will not be constrained by the history of art because we wish to continue the history of art' is a fascinating move, and it is very much a move of freedom however one looks at it.

This exit from the rump of the post-Greenbergian art world was the creation of an imaginative world in which they could keep alive the possibility of resistance. That's different from the dreamwork that I criticise, which is that of people simply resolving the psychological tensions of working against what they claim to work for every hour of every day in their day job.

Certificate of Inauthenticity (2020) was originally a Sol LeWitt certificate of authenticity and some Tipp-Ex. LeWitt's certificates took unsaleable wall drawings and turned them into very saleable contracts and signed certificates. I took this aesthetic and conceptual reference and used it to capture what I felt was going on with the anxiety of authenticity in the actually existing blockchain art world at that time. That piece and *Tokens Equals Text* I'm fantastically happy with in terms of the way they draw in their references and compose them in order to be usefully attention-directing and critical, not in the sense of self-aggrandising gestures of dismissal but in the sense of, we need to understand *x*, extend *y*, and head off *z*. The ability to do that, to the extent that I can, comes from working through that model of exit, of not being constrained by the expectation of exhibitability or saleability or any of the other things which I would be much richer had I been concerned with from day one.

MBK Ultimately, then, are you happy with being described as a conceptual artist?

RM Kind of, yes. As Art & Language say, 'Whatever the destiny of Conceptual Art was, it wasn't Conceptual Art'. I feel quite awkward when people say that I'm a 'blockchain conceptual artist'. I needed this sort of visual and technical and art-historical and cultural resource of signification and association in order to communicate something which, if I'd have come up with a novel form of representation for it, I'd have had three strikes against the resulting art: a technology that nobody really needs to understand, an ideology that nobody needs to understand, and a critique or consideration of these in a representational media that nobody understands. At that point I'm just screaming into the void. So what I do does look like extremely late postmodernism or extremely late conceptualism or, in the worst case, extremely late pop, but it's more to do with a sort of cultural smog of the internet-era shift from successive movements to parallel genres, where everyone has the history of culture available at their fingertips, and therefore I can get a leg up by using people's knowledge to put out signals that will make them look at something. It isn't first-order Conceptual Art, just as Art & Language's work already wasn't. It does the Conceptual Art thing as part of its operation because that is the most effective way of engaging with what I wanted to engage with.

In early crypto art, seeing the retreat from the art market and the attempt to create an alternative economy and life world, I recognised that from Conceptualism. And my other reference was the net art era, where artists had got into this media of communication exchange and exploitation first: the net artist got there before massive corporate exploitation and made it so that, from the get-go, you couldn't just go on the internet and unproblematically consume 'content' without an alternative. They had a shared interest in the use of communications technologies. Glueing those two things together and recognising the idealism from the cyberculture moment in London, I was ready to, and had a desire to, demonstrate to the art world that there was something of critical and possibly organisational interest to the blockchain, and to try to explain to the blockchain people that there was something of organisational and possibly technological interest in the art world. So I've been trying to rub these two groups together to produce weird mutant offspring, to generate comprehension. What I'm doing is this double-A-side of critique of the institution of art and critique of the institution of technology and of the ideology of both.

MBK As it develops and intervenes in or substitutes itself for social relations, technology disassembles, analyses, and in effect critiques the social fabric, in the sense of disabusing it of claims to transcendence and reproducing its operations immanently as machine parts. In doing so, at the same time it also unbundles concepts, and your art and writing often hinges on demonstrating how blockchain technologies and crypto separate elements of social relationships that we thought belonged together by definition: property, ownership, unique reference to something and disclosure of its content, authenticity and authentication, social trust and the social construction of value, provenance and third-party authorities. All of these are things that you use the work to drive a wedge in between, or to show how blockchain technology is in fact already doing so.

RM This is what I refer to as 'delamination'. You can't say that these things definitely go together now. Blockchain technology does accelerate the process of decoding, disrupting how these things work and how we assume they cluster together. And you can emphasise different bits of the cluster to get different takes on the technology, which make strange the phenomena we choose to try and capture or represent.

The interesting thing for the blockchain 'event' (pace Badiou), the publication of the Bitcoin White Paper, the creation of the Bitcoin software, is that it is very much an assemblage—it's a copying and pasting together of existing technologies, which it places together in a unique new way to solve the problem in the cypherpunk political project. A lot of what we talk about when we talk about Bitcoin is surplus value of that code: the White Paper doesn't say blockchain, it doesn't say cryptocurrency. The White Paper talks about making a 'timestamp server', that is its technical contribution.

But as I argue in 'Blockchain Poetics', what the White Paper specifies is a combination of very finely tuned different capabilities. If you emphasise one or the other of these capabilities more or less, you get something different: for instance, you just get distributed ledger technology because you don't care about the ability to enforce the rarity of the currency. Or, if you emphasise the solution to the double-spending problem, which is the problem of the fake in art, if you lean into that, then you get NFTs. If you read the White Paper, you can see how each paragraph that Satoshi writes on the way to this timestamp server has so much surplus value, it weaves in so much possibility, so many affordances.

MBK Like an engine that you can tune in different ways to get it to perform differently?

RM Yes, and my only argument to the Left really is, for God's sake, understand that engine, otherwise you will get played.

Nick Land talks about it in terms of subtraction. Bitcoin subtracts the need for a trusted third party. Money as previously understood is something issued by a trusted party that we can then exchange, to the degree that they allow us to. If we subtract that trusted third party then in theory we shouldn't have money. The fact that Satoshi, to a greater or lesser degree, successfully does so, performs the operation of critique.[8]

8 N. Land, *Crypto-Current: Bitcoin and Philosophy* (Shanghai: Time Spiral, forthcoming).

MBK In the sense that it demonstrates that the immanent operation of money is not necessarily dependent on a transcendent instance, on something that stands above it and is claimed to be the condition for its functioning.

RM Land's relating of the technology of Bitcoin to such philosophical problems, and to his own political projects, and the fact that you can do that, shows what an interesting object Bitcoin is. It is a screen for the projection of hopes and fears, it does fit into the history of ideas, it does have a design aesthetic, and the problems that it tackles have their analogues in the problems that the market introduces into art, problems which ultimately are simply a projection of the patriarchal anxiety of primogeniture: the double-spending problem is simply *Is this my child?* Just as, in the art market, the fake is simply: *Have I continued my line or have I been cuckolded?* These are the anxieties attached to patriarchal society, a society which tries to find answers to them through vast amounts of money and/or power and/or violence, in order to reassure the male reproductive subject that actually, yes, he is secure: this security system for humanity conceived of as Man will look after you and make sure that what you are entitled to has not been stolen from you, that your offspring have not been right-clicked.

MBK But isn't the timestamp server a way of securing provenance?

RM Absolutely, it operationalises *post hoc ergo propter hoc*, it produces a universe in which one thing follows another and you know that is true. You cannot spend something twice, which means you cannot spend it out of order, which means that if you are receiving currency then, over time, your certainty as to the security of your possession of it tends to grow. Now, to be clear, if the Vogons arrived tomorrow and had 278 trillion hashes of power, they could very quickly rework the order of transactions and exclude blocks. But they still couldn't spend anyone else's coins—unless they have a solution to the discrete log problem, something which we currently have our fingers crossed doesn't exist.

MBK How about property, what happens to the concept of property here?

RM Land makes the argument that property didn't truly exist before public key encryption: public key encryption is the thing that makes it possible for there to even be private ownership or control proper, with control of resources conceived as ownership in the absence of a state guarantor that can revoke that right.

MBK That's the move you make at the end of 'Recanting Quasiproperty', saying that whereas in earlier texts you had protested against the idea that Bitcoin is property, in fact what we used to call property was a kind of contaminated form of property, which Bitcoin distils into its pure form. But this does bring us back to the question of how this absolutisation of property could be some kind of a leftist project.

RM There are two things here: firstly, if you want to have any kind of critical purchase on society you need to understand what you are trying to critique. And the other thing is that it's here, so let's at least understand what can be done with it. And how we can ironise it or extend it or judo-throw it into something we can make use of.

MBK 'We don't yet know what property can do'?

RM One of the arguments I make is that property regimes are generative. It's not the case that certain entities come into being and we then create a property regime to describe them. We create a property regime and then this generates, in a very real way, the object to which it applies. It may be that there are a few initial exemplary or liminal objects that it's intended to cover for some special interest or other. But once it becomes possible to describe things that were not previously describable as property, people will track that singularity and it will start to generate these objects—like a market Stalinist executive demanding that you measure particular metrics....

MBK I think that's what Deleuze and Guattari, reading Marx through the psychotic Judge Schreber, call 'miraculation':[9] in every type of society there's a recording surface upon which social acts and the organisation of bodies and the earth are inscribed (for us, money), and eventually it seems as if everything is emanating from that recording surface, and its markings become the 'quasi-cause' rather than the effect of everything that happens in the social world—it naturalises itself.

RM Yeah. Depending on how you rotate the time crystal, this is autopoesis. The hyperstition of property creating itself. Here you have a blockchain timestamp server producing this Deleuzian empty repetition of time—every block is the same, block after block, every ten minutes. You have festivals, you have halvings of block rewards for example, and hard forks. But at the block level there are no seasons, there are no birthdays, there are no jubilees. This sort of very capitalist linear clocktime feeds very nicely into Anna Greenspan's idea of capitalism's transcendental time machine,[10] because this quantisation, this meting out of time, once again, is generative.

MBK It is linear and empty time in one sense, but it's also not, because every block 'contains' every other block that's gone before it, so there's a kind of continual intensification.

RM Yes, the being of blockchain is intensified with each block, each block makes it more of a thing, it would take more work to undo it, to rewrite its history or to destroy it or to reallocate the value within it, everything becomes more difficult to rework over time. This is the advantage of proof of work: it would take an appreciable chunk of the earth's computing power to rewrite even a fraction of Bitcoin's blockchain and you still wouldn't be able to spend other people's coins. You could prevent them ever having existed but you couldn't send them to someone else and pretend that they sent them. So the existence of the blockchain intensifies, and certainly the amount of value within each block can be said to be more or less intense if we treat monetary value here as a pure intensive quantity. We are however in a smooth space: there's nothing within the Merkle tree of the block which says, this block has this hash, because that's impossible. There is an inside and an outside, an onchain and an offchain.

Certainly, in one sense all the information that you need to understand the blockchain is onchain, but then to interact with it you need the private keys, which are offchain and must not be onchain otherwise you can break the system. Thinking about on- and offchain in terms of natural/supernatural or phenomenon/

9 G. Deleuze and F. Guattari, *Anti-Oedipus: Capitalism and Schizophrenia*, tr. R. Hurley, M. Seem, H.R. Lane (Minneapolis: University of Minnesota Press, 1984), 329.

10 A. Greenspan, *Capitalism's Transcendental Time Machine*, PhD, University of Warwick, 2000.

noumenon is fascinating—it's trivial, you know, it's a card trick in philosophical terms, but it's kind of evocative and it's one of those things which, if you press on it, helps to unpack assumptions. You have this inside world of transactions with an ontology enforced mathematically, and then offchain you have this wild domain that nothing onchain can know of, except as cryptographic signatures transmitted from it.

And again this can be a useful irritant, part of disobedience-in-obedience. *We must have a realm of pure mathematical understanding and reason, and this can then bring justice to our messy society.* Hey, here's a blockchain! *No, not like that!* Okay, but then in what way? *Just...not like that!*

MBK Two elements that blockchain brings together in a somewhat paradoxical manner are fungible currency and the concept of a ledger in which information is retained forever—they seem to run counter to one another, because the key thing about fungible money is that, once you've done whatever you do and received payment for it, that money is just as good as anybody else's, no one knows where it came from and it doesn't carry any information beyond its exchange value. *Pecunia non olet.* In a sense, money, or cash at least, is precisely a machine to wash information away, so how does that fit with a ledger that is transparent, public, and perpetual?

RM Right—to quote Barbara Kruger, 'Money is an information-destroying medium', which is the point of it. In the third part of Liu Cixin's *Dark Forest* trilogy, where the solar system is being collapsed into the second dimension—which freaked me out for days after reading it—that dimensional reduction, the image of Jupiter leaching out into the second dimension like an ice cream on a pavement on a hot day, that's money.

Firstly, Bitcoin is not anonymous money, so it doesn't quite solve the cypherpunk requirement. It is *pseudonymous* money: you can tell which address has carried out which transaction. Satoshi said to use one address for each transaction, do not reuse addresses. There are good cryptographic key safety reasons for doing so. But also, doing so allows us to hold on to the early internet pseudonymity of not having a tied-down singular identity. So if we were using bitcoin as Satoshi told us to, then you would have this sort of pseudonymous thicket of transactions which you can absolutely see, but which would not be tied to singular addresses, and you would just need to make sure that you do not leak that this address is actually you.

The public ledger is a means to an end of enforcing transaction order; the point of Bitcoin is to produce the transaction server, not the ledger as such. Satoshi said that for efficiency of space reasons, once you have spent all of a transaction's outputs you don't need it anymore, you don't need to validate past that point, and you can dispose of that information. So keeping this information and making it available in block explorers is absolutely something that Bitcoin as a technology doesn't prevent, but it's not an intended outcome of it.

There are two reactions to this at the level of technology. The first is something like Web3 and NFT provenance, where you say, that's fine, forget about these multiple pseudonymous identities, normies aren't going to be able to manage those, let's just have a singular identity, we can register that with state ID services to give people safety, and then people can send money and report on their taxes, and they can know who they are buying their NFT from and who's minted it, and so on. So that leans into the identity part of it and the public ledger part of it as a social good, and it's where the provenance argument finds its strongest home.

But we could equally go the other way and say what Satoshi did was brilliant, but this is pseudonymous not anonymous money and we wanted anonymous money. So we can take this timestamp server technology and make the addresses and the ledger—which come out of Bitcoin but are not deliberately there as things in themselves—we can make these actually secret using zero-knowledge proof technology. Then you get secret transaction-capable chains such as Zcash or Monero, and on these you do not have to have public provenance, although it's perfectly possible to create zero-knowledge provenance systems tokens—but for secret transactions you cannot tell where a transaction has come from or how much value is involved or where it has gone to by looking at the publicly broadcast information or by recovering the history of the blockchain.

So Satoshi knew about the problem with pseudonymity and suggested ways to cope with it, and didn't regard the public ledger as a value of Bitcoin beyond the way it serviced the timestamp server. And this is a great example: as with everything in Bitcoin, there's enough going on here that we can tweak each of these variables in different ways and get different outcomes.

MBK And in your work each of these tuneable parameters maps onto some dimension of the history of art's interaction with money?

RM Art, ideas, and politics. For me it's a very rich index of concepts. It resonates, it opens out onto something else, and in a sense that's bound to be the case because it's unbundling the concept of property and the concept of property is intrinsic to the way in which art has been understood and the way in which the art world has worked.

I'm a big fan of the argument that society was created to produce art rather than that art was a product of society. And art has not always been property. Cave art is art despite obviously predating the concept of art, and being owned only in the sense that it was within the territory of a group of hominids. As soon as you get to the first wood panel painting with egg tempera, and then to canvas painting proper, you have a commodity form of art. Before that, the Sistine Chapel ceiling is certainly the product of commerce and exchange, but transferring ownership of it would be tricky. Whereas some coloured creams on a bit of hemp, now that is something that can be put in a crate and shipped.

MBK Which is the beginning of the autonomy of the art object which, in the twentieth century, emerges as a problem at the same time as something called 'art' turns up whose being is notionally separate from its existence as an object in the social and commercial world.

RM As something that exists in the commodity form, yes. And the commodity form interests me because the answer to the question of what we do about the commodity form differentiates left from right anarchism, anarcho-communists from anarcho-capitalists. The latter believe that the commodity form is vital to personal wealth and freedom and that it can be maintained in the absence of the violence of the state, while anarcho-communists believe that the defence of the commodity form, the policing of it, is a major driver of and is only possible with the violence or an equivalent to the violence of the state. So if you abolish the state you abolish the commodity form. I'm simplifying of course, but both of these are wrong in interesting ways. The left anarchist needs state-level violence to prevent the commodity form reemerging; the anarcho-capitalist needs state-level violence to prevent the commodity form ceasing to be. And so you're either reproducing state violence as something else—which is a critique of the blockchain as a sort of property regime—or you're assuming that people aren't going to restart capitalism in their basement. And that's really a terrible bet because as soon as someone can afford to pay two people to beat you up, they have the ability to reinforce the existence of commodities.

Art is always an important reflection of the property regime of its time. When people own and profit from commodities, art becomes a commodity. The content of art also ties into the content of those property regimes. Perspective is Renaissance trade maths, Impressionism is French state-sponsored colour theory plus railways.... As property becomes digital and as money becomes digital, as the state tries to get us to stop using cash and just submit our transactions to its prying eyes to make sure we're not doing anything naughty, cryptocurrency may look like just more of the same. But in fact it's the dark forest thing of going into electronic currency before the state can force you in there as a means of escape.

So there's that aspect to it, but I feel very strongly that art also has this affordance of symbolic resolution or closure. If you know that the apocalypse was meant to happen last Wednesday and it didn't, you can get an artist to paint it on the wall so it's there. If you're an amazingly rich merchant whose wealth comes from spice and fruit from distant lands, you can have a painting of that on the wall, *Here's what I've got*. And this is why revolutionary art is such a thing—*There is going to be a revolution, the world does work in this way*. What we know but cannot see, or is not present now, can go into art and it becomes a sort of supplement to our reality; our brains aren't very good at differentiating between dreams and reality or between pictures and things, and so it sort of resolves these tensions or papers over these gaps in ideology.

We see this with the contemporary art market, which should be a single word, *artmarket*: art appears as a pure global commodity, it's supposedly something that is valued perfectly at auction by the market, its value and its price are identical, it is moved through logistical networks just like everything is, possibly without the owner seeing it (contemporary art as literally encrypted capital—you exchange your money for art and the art goes into a freeport holding, literally a crypt). And it is the product of an individual worker being recognised, correctly rewarded, and sucked into this system of exchange. Okay, but nothing works like this, not even artworks. It's a pantomime, a sort of mummers' play of how the global neoliberal capitalist economy is supposed to work. The people who need to believe that it works know that it never works like this, but the best way for them to show themselves that it really does, that Santa Claus really is real, is contemporary art and its unregulated market value.

MBK So if property regimes are generative, producing the conditions for a certain order of object, and if art in a given society is an index of the property regime in force, then Bitcoin also drives wedges between the concepts that have structured the way that the value of art has been understood?

RM In my early writings and art, I don't think I started out with that, I started with very simple little things which did one thing that art did, or that the art world wanted or did. They were all very much following this strategy of disobedience-in-obedience. You know, *Artists need a catalogue raisonné*. Here you go, here's one in the blockchain. *No, not like that!* I didn't move on to the decoding/recoding side of it until NFTs became a thing, at which point I could contrast what I had been imagining as a blockchain art world in 2014 with what the actually existing blockchain art world of 2017 had become. And it did not go in the direction I had imagined, but it was a really interesting direction. The reason I didn't anticipate that direction was precisely because I was being anti-commercial for political reasons.

The point at which the delamination becomes entirely explicit in my work is when I get to *Certificate of Inauthenticity* (2020), which is obviously a negative assertion: *This is not an authentic artwork by me*. As Michael Jackson said, *The kid is not my son*. But I only really went for the delamination idea when genius Twitter users started pointing out that you can just right-click on and save the JPEG associated with an NFT, and that this means you don't own the NFT. It's absolutely wrong, in a really interesting way. Let's just imagine for a moment that we destroyed the artwork as property, by placing it into the copyright public domain—and we can do that with CC0 at this point—then you have delaminated possession from ownership, patronage, and reputation from exploitation; you have delaminated use and exchange value. Anyone can use the image, nobody can sell it. You can sell the thing which represents its social cachet or its reputational proxy.

MBK And then there's the delamination of authenticity and authentication.

RM Authenticity is tied to the problem of the fake. A fake is a cuckoo in the nest, it's a double-spending of something that should only exist once. And it's absolutely key to the commodity property regime, because if we take the story of the history of art, what we understand as the history of art at face value, you either look at a nice aesthetic work and it is good or you look at a nice aesthetic work and you don't like it. Notice the difference. But if a fake has that effect on me, then we've introduced something from outside the canvas—and then the happy world of either aesthetics if it's the 1950s, or signification if we're in the postmodern and contemporary era, starts to look like a just-so story. The fact that whether something is fake or authentic can change its value from nothing to millions...it tends to focus the attention.

I think the Warhol authentication committee, for example, have stopped stamping works because you can't authenticate a Warhol. He got his friends to make them, he gave them out as party favours, he would happily write 'This is not an authentic Warhol' on the back if you asked him to while he was signing your copy of *Interview*. It's a category error in the case of Warhols. And people have these double-denied stamps on the back of these screen prints that Warhol gave them. As I already mentioned, this investment, this sort of fatherly ownership of offspring that can suddenly not be who you think they are, this anxiety of ownership, this anxiety of authenticity, maps from the double-spending problem in blockchain to the problem of the fake in art to the problem of patriarchal lineage in anthropology to the problem of wage labour in capitalist society—because you are doing this thing and you're not getting the benefit of it, the benefit is going to someone else. You're not getting what you think you should be getting.

The fake is a modern problem which belongs to a certain property regime. If you were a priest commissioning a panel for your church, someone turned up, they painted it, you were perfectly happy with it (unless they were a heretic, in which case you're in big trouble). It's only once you get the market operation of art that you know, and need to know, where the art has come from: you have paid for the thing, and if you find out that you didn't get what you paid for then you are perturbed; if you find out that you are not selling what you thought you were selling, that's even worse; and the promise of the surplus value affordance of the public ledger is that you know where the art came from, you know who's had it, you know how much it was sold for, you know where it is.

Now, anyone within crypto discourse can immediately tell you all the problems with that—like the fact that you can register the Mona Lisa as an artwork that you have made on the blockchain. That's simply illustrating what crypto theorists could have told you long ago had you been listening. It's not 'owning the crypto bros', it's being late to the party. It's the problem of getting offchain truth onchain that undoes the dream of a more transparent fake-free market for art as an absolute.

There are two potential ways to approach this: firstly you can go for the oracle problem, the problem of getting offchain truth onchain in various ways that allow you to establish, with however much certainty you desire, that the person who made the artwork is the person who made the artwork and the person who bought it is the person who bought it, and that it's not anywhere else. The NFT then becomes like a useful publication medium and a useful medium of representation and exchange but it becomes sort of a means to an end for these lofty ideals for blockchain art. And there's nothing wrong with that.

But the other way you can go is to lean into *not knowing* who your father is, and just say: look, the idea that you look at something and like it or not is absolutely correct. We're going for pure cypherpunk anonymity. Purely onchain work. If you like this bunch of pixels and want to pay me £10 in Bitcoin for it, that's great; if you want to give me £1m that's great; you don't know who I am, you don't know who made it, it's entitled *Turd at Sunrise* or whatever, you find that amusing. You're paying for the work not the meatspace provenance, so if you overpay then that's on you. In theory at least.

MBK These are the effects on art of turning the dials on Satoshi's assemblage, tuning the parameters to produce different situations. The interesting thing is that a certain contingent of people get angry about whatever model you suggest. They get angry about people buying NFTs just because they saw something they like, but they also get angry about the idea that NFTs can be real carriers of value. One way of making NFTs interesting is to ensure that they activate the fears that produce that anger.

RM People do get upset when artists just mint something. If it's bad art then that's perfectly valid. I'm going to grit my teeth here and say that what Damien Hirst attempted recently was good: he did an NFT drop, you could own the first Damien Hirst NFTs; he then said that, after a certain amount of time, you can burn the token and he will send you an actual little drawing or print or whatever. That's a use of the technology to get people to work through the game theory of value. Which is far more interesting to me than anything that was hefted off of the wreck of the Unbelievable, it's the most interesting thing he's done since he positioned a shark carefully, because it leans into the game-theoretic and value-questioning underpinnings of technology in a way that needs someone with that reputation to give it weight, to make it a serious proposition.

You do get people who just go to content honeypots like DeviantArt, grab a load of pictures and use free minting on rare art platforms to see who will buy it. That is bad, but it's an attack on both the NFT community *and* the illustration art community, it's not the NFT community attacking the illustration art community.

And if we look at those levers and dials again, we can get rid of free or just-in-time minting but that reduces accessibility and inclusion, so it has a social justice effect. Or we can maintain free minting, which includes more people who otherwise would not be able to afford to start with this stuff, but reduces the cost of double-spending—it precisely works against Satoshi's original use of the hashcash algorithm, which was designed to stop email spam, to make it too expensive to be worthwhile. So once again, this is the fine tuning of the parameters to achieve different goals which people regard as just but which, if you change them without due care and attention and hope to have a nice subtle effect, may disappoint you or overexcite things in the wrong way.

MBK In relation to the actually existing world of NFT art, it seems as if there are two possible levels of appreciation, which are slightly at odds with one another, and both of which you bring into play in your work. There's an appreciation of individual works that have a critical purchase on the medium, but then, in 'Welcome to the Dessert of the Real', you argue that the aesthetics of the majority of what I'm going to uncharitably call landfill NFTs can be seen as the product of the affordances of the collision between human perceptual response patterns and the technological platform. In that case, from a population-scale point of view, the NFT phenomenon as a whole tells us something critical about the platform and about art; it becomes its own critique, demanding to be read and interpreted.

RM Yes. My kink is obviously critical art. That is not for everyone, and I came to that position from liking pop art, graphic design, airbrushed painting, whatever. So I am desperate not to be a snob, or a 'gatekeeper', in current crypto art terms, and not to miss what is interesting and new and valuable in actually existing NFTs by sitting around pontificating about the ideals of mid-twentieth-century critical theory, now some seventy years old. I have had some very long conversations with very competent art historians about what could be interesting about 10k PFP projects, for example, and for me there are three things: firstly they're all very anti-aesthetic; they all have anti-aesthetic aesthetics. Secondly, there's a sort of all-overness to the collection and this is enabled by the way that you see them on their sites. And finally, they get used as ritual masks. These are interesting aesthetic and anthropological and art-historical things which my distaste for apes looking to one side must not prevent me from being able to examine. I'm not going to be a snob about this, I'm going to look at those things. It ties back to creativity theory: if you retain a certain naivety, you will look at things that people who have to be terribly secure in their sophistication will not pay attention to, and because of that they will not be able to jump between the tracks of ideas that they need to in order to get to the very critique they claim to be interested in.

There were all the NFTs in which lots of people were just stealing motion graphic demos off YouTube, which is bad, but at the same time, a lot of very talented illustration artists and 3d modelling artists and motion graphics artists suddenly had a source of revenue because they could represent their work as NFTs. What did the audience for these go for? It's difficult to categorise it but in 'Dessert of the Real' I try to. I'd tie it to the idea of something ownable, something that, like a bower bird seeking a mate, signals that it has what you want. And what the buyers want is digitally expanded ownability. There's a trivial sense in which any NFT is ownable, but it needs to *look like it*, like an expensive watch that has lots of jewels on it because the jewels tell you it's an expensive watch, despite the fact that the actual expensiveness is in the very finely tuned mechanism. By symbolising or communicating or depicting quality, whether gold or heft and solidity or skill or unusualness, this art does this. And I think that if you ran some sort of cultural analytics software you would find that the art that people have gone to has this kind of overt ownability to it.

MBK It's a mimetic lure that tacitly responds to the problems of value that the platform creates?

RM Absolutely, yes. And not just the problems of value that it creates, the problem of how to hook yourself up to those signals, of understanding or being able to see that value.

MBK And we're back to property regimes being generative.

RM The other thing that interested me was that they all tended to be short animated loops, which for me irresistibly reflects blockchain time, but I think in reality it gives the buyer more to own, because it adds duration and therefore extra substance to the things you're looking at. It renders it, not kitsch necessarily, but certainly unproblematic, by smoothly looping it. So you can consume it unproblematically, but the thing it does do in a critical way is to signify this value. It's a peak shift stimulus, it's a aesthetic value sex toy or fishing lure, it takes it all to 11.

MBK You could probably talk about that in quasi-Darwinian terms, because I assume the first rash of NFTs were more varied, before makers homed in on how to put the 'right' signals out there.

RM There's definitely a fitness function at work.

MBK In the approach to aesthetics you present in many of the essays in this book, and which is embodied in some of your work, you lean right into this: *Why don't we just produce a market for aesthetic elements or qualities, and see what wins?* Like a techno-anarcho-capitalist Koons: not only allow people to like what they like and celebrate it, but use technology and the market to reveal what they really like rather than believe their stated preferences.

RM If we accept the idea that markets are epistemological environments, that they are truth procedures but in which the truth is that of price, then yeah, the truth has to be extracted from a population. Something which has never been sold is difficult to price, something which is singular is difficult to price, something which is sold infrequently is difficult to price. Price is meaning, it's one-dimensional meaning, it's meaning collapsed into one dimension in a dark forest strike. But it's all the more substantial for it.

MBK And is that compatible with critique?

RM For critique, there cannot be, there should not be, and there is not any secure external position from which we can point at the object of critique. If we believe we occupy such a position, that way lies very bad things. It's very much that we have to build the plane while we're flying it, or we are jumping between icebergs as they head towards the waterfall or whatever. There is no fixed point from which we can move the world by virtue of adopting an aesthetic or even an ethic of critique. Critique is not a solved problem. And the worst pseudocritic is the person who has an answer for everything, and it's the last idea they ever need to know. *What's this? I don't know but it's fascism.*

MBK But when you talk about criticality as a kink, you're manifesting a kind of modesty that critical art is generally not known for, because it's generally understood to be inherent to critique that its conclusions stand for everyone, that my agency as a critic tacitly involves a universalisation—everybody has to participate in the game of critique I'm playing. We are moving into something different here—the critique is not happening at the level of the epistemological subject judging the world. The critique is something that's out there taking place, and which the subject needs to decipher in order to understand which concepts are valid and which have, objectively, been invalidated by the new behaviours of the virtual objects outside.

RM Which is very much where my work syncs up with the argument found in a neorationalist philosopher like Reza Negarestani, that intelligence is not merely in the head, but is a faculty of society.[11] Critique is a faculty of society. If we are good Marxists then we have to say that things contain their own critique; recognising it is useful work that we can do, but to try and earn credit or social capital from that is to misunderstand one's role in the unfolding of history. At the same time, the game of 'giving and taking of reasons' so dear to neorationalism is not a thing. There is no greater reason than a Tsar Bomba. Beyond a certain point, *Because I say so* always wins out. So the imagined role of the Greenbergian critic is an illusion. The greatest art critics of the twentieth century were the CIA and Valerie Solanas, not Greenberg...I'm back in character here and I'd be absolutely horrified if anyone started the Myers school of theory based on that! But what do we believe criticism does? Firstly, I just have no time for permanently negative criticism. Give me some criticism which says how something can be made better in a particular direction. It takes work, it's inefficient, it does not accelerate, it slows you down, and yet it's where the value is. And at the same time, the social text is not written in ink; sitting there saying *You're doing it wrong* is the opposite of critique, and distributed machines are better at doing that, actually. This is something that happens at the level of populations, not at the behest of some godlike figure of the critic.

Think of the lawyer cross-examining someone at a criminal trial: *Answer the question, yes or no*, it's binary, it's zeros and ones. What kind of epistemology are we in here, where it's yes or no to *Have you stopped embezzling funds yet?* This may not be the best way of reaching a judgement or, if it is, judgement may not be the best thing to reach for. It may not matter so much for art criticism, but if we are destroying information whilst attempting to 'do justice' then there is going to be a big problem.

So this is why I try to have epistemological modesty and recognise that we are all guilty. I stopped talking about ideology and I started saying 'investments and prejudices', which is obviously trolling, but the serious point is that your ideology is the product of your spending time and various kinds of capital to achieve a particular position, and your prosecution of it is speculation on that investment. The degree to which this is wrong is interesting, the degree to which it is right is why actual criticism is very hard. Investments in the emotional and financial sense and speculation in the philosophical and financial sense. And with prejudices, the idea is that judgment is discrimination, it is literally discriminating. A lot of artificial intelligence criticism gets hung up on the idea of a discriminator or statistical bias because terms of art in different fields of endeavour mean different things but have the same name. If you have a discriminator, it just tells you whether a value is *a* or *b*. Elsewhere, if you are discriminating you are irrationally and or unjustly performing an incorrect action based on prejudice. Artificial intelligence burns capital to produce discrimination in both senses—but the idea that we are somehow not immanent to this, that we are somehow

11 R. Negarestani, *Intelligence and Spirit* (Falmouth and New York: Urbanomic/Sequence Press, 2018).

transcendent to everything that we think is wrong with humanity, for me it's just untenable, it's the worst sort of thinking your shit doesn't stink. I'm sorry, you do have objectives within society, however much you dress them up in flowery language. We all have our breaking points as well, and avoiding them is probably a good idea for ethics.

But if you want to produce an actual critique, do something: talking is doing something but it's not the only thing you can do, hence the art and writing and code and stories in this book. Because if you limit yourself in the means that you are willing to employ to achieve your ends, if you say *I'm only going to hop on one leg until I achieve what I want*, you might not actually get there. This is the problem of local maxima in hill-climbing artificial intelligence search algorithms: you follow a line obsessively, get to the top, and think *I'm as high up as I can possibly be*—but there's an enormous mountain next to you which, had you wandered a bit more randomly, you might have found. I'm grounded in these metaphors from corporate-inflected creativity theory and from artificial intelligence, because both of them fascinate me as epistemologies. None of it taken at face value or first-order, but used as resources.

MBK A set of methodologies or meta-methodologies?

RM Yes, it's like chaos magic: don't get hung up on whether something appears terribly serious or has a pure lineage. If it works, use it. It's being a hacker not a software engineer.

MBK Speaking of magic, at various points you invoke it in relation to the blockchain, particularly in relation to hashes.

RM That's to do with the problem of names. A hash, a cryptographic hashing algorithm—and as far as I know the term 'hash' refers to a recipe which mixes everything up so you don't really know what went into it but it tastes good with some Tabasco—is designed to produce a stable and deterministic result: run it again and again on the same data and you will get the same output: stable, but unguessable until you actually do it. If you look at the data, you have no idea what's going to come out at the other end. And vice versa. Now, if you think of the philosophical question of names—Is there any necessity to a dog being called 'dog' rather than 'sheen'?—once again, the cryptographic wedge drives itself in, and says you can have names that are entirely determined by what the thing is, but that have no meaning, and have no traceable relation back to the thing that they perfectly identify.

How is that possible? The magic of cryptography. There is no recoverable semantic link to the item that the cryptographic hash nonetheless perfectly identifies with a uniqueness that comes down to big numbers. Most modern hashes produce a 256-bit identifier. You could hash every particle in the visible universe and not run out of space using that. It's *really* unique. Whenever there was a cryptographic hash and it had to go into a database, I used to worry about avoiding collisions. The computer science argument is, if you're worried about that, then you should be absolutely terrified about the sun exploding tomorrow because that's more likely.

These are the dark-forest cryptographic spaces in which you can hide something, but still know the true name of it, and can refer to it without necessarily revealing what it is. And this is the dialectic of perfect identity/perfect secrecy that you get with public-key cryptography, applied not to the content of communication, but to the content and identity of data.

This relates to magic because cryptography and magic go together at liminal moments in history. In the early modern era cryptography had to separate itself out from witchcraft. A lot of the early cryptography manuals in Europe served a double purpose as magical summoning guides—serious talking-to-angels-summoning-demons-creating-magic-squares kind of thing. Now, it may be the case that this was simply to conceal the cryptography, or it may be the case that the government agents of the time were concealing their cryptographic knowledge by pretending to be wizards. This would be fairly high risk given that you'd be burnt for being a wizard, but lower risk than the King or Queen being horribly displeased with you. Take John Dee, bumming around Europe trying to turn lead into gold for various monarchs and sending back magical writings to England—it makes a lot more sense as the activity of a secret agent than that of someone who was really easily taken in by anyone with a black mirror.

So at liminal moments the two are confused, and then they separate as things settle down. We see this again in the Victorian era: Edgar Allan Poe was big both in cryptography and in spiritualism. After Poe died, for a while one of his most popular poems was one that was written posthumously and channelled by a spiritualist medium. There's the idea that the book of nature is encrypted and that to access it we have to break the encryption on it—a veil of ignorance that separates us from the spirit world and the afterlife.

Today, cryptographers are still mediating figures between the known and the unknown. If you take a sociological view, they do have this priest-class role in terms of their responsibility for communing with the unknown to underwrite the social order. This is why they appear to be such morally fraught figures; this is why the question of access to cryptography is so morally fraught for people who want trusted third parties in our communication that can stop us doing Bad Things as conceived of by Good and Nice People who of course never overreach, misunderstand, or have false positives.

So magic and cryptography look like one another, they both have these weird symbols and systems, apparent nonsense comes out of the other end of both, and yet it is claimed that communication is happening. They are both regulated by the state up to the modern era in various oppressive ways, and they are both concerned with access to an outside or an underneath.

To be more demonic about it, the dark forest of cryptography, this cryptographic hyperspace through which we send messages to be read by the recipient but no one else, embodies the same human desire as magic, the same masculine design on secrecy and power, but in a very efficient way.

Over time, the legal and social rhetoric around the threat and promise of cryptography is remarkably stable. Since the early modern era the same arguments have been given each time, with the same players and the same outcomes, and this rhetoric always comes back when you have these liminal moments where cryptography and magic, however conceived, are tangled together again. This rhetoric goes back to the early modern era, when the state was concerned with being able to decrypt communications between individuals and individuals were concerned with being tried by the state and the secret communications that they had produced being decoded by the state. The questions of privacy, of secrecy, of disclosure, and of methods of cryptography as popular entertainment and as a means of securing state commercial and personal communications, all of these go back to the late sixteenth century and recur in the Victorian era and then again in the nineties with the cypherpunk era. Each time the rhetoric is the same: the rhetoric of big numbers, of saving people with a timely secret communication, of harmful secrets. The cypherpunks certainly made the correct and winning latest move in this ongoing struggle, but we're seeing it again now, just twenty, thirty years later with the state insisting that they should be able to read all of your communications: *Trust us*. No. We've been doing this for hundreds of years and if you had any historical literacy whatsoever you'd know that you're being assholes: don't do it, just for once learn from history.

With public key cryptography, we're again dealing with a kind of delamination. There is something curious about it since it gives you both absolute secrecy and absolute identity, because the two don't go together in the popular imagination. They're not a mathematical product of cypherpunk ideology, they were deduced first by GCHQ, but the British can keep secrets so they didn't tell anyone—and about two minutes later by some American researchers. The technology was liberated in the early nineties. This access to technology made it possible to imagine a society where you didn't need the state to guarantee your private communications or your identification to others—you don't need to show your papers, you don't need a mailing address on the voters' registration list. And, taking that and running with it, money is communication: money, as the American courts found if you're a corporation trying to corrupt the political process, is speech. This is correct and interesting in ways that individuals have yet to fully benefit from. Cryptographic private speech—not private language in the Wittgensteinian sense, more like twinspeak but between an infinite set of twinned correspondents—allows you to imagine that you can be secure and private and identified against all areas of state overreach and interference.

Once again, Satoshi's assemblage of different technologies just so happens to enable the completion of this part of the cypherpunk project. But it has this massive surplus value that we are still working through today. And for me, this technique, the combination of technology in these ways that speak to these anxieties and fit into this history of ideas and history of rhetoric, it seems like a useful irritant.

Then there's obviously the problem of where religion goes when we're all terribly smart post-enlightenment materialist thinkers. If you accept the theory that Satoshi was Hal Finney, this is someone who was terminally ill and is now cryogenically frozen in a transhumanist afterlife with the promise of resurrection. And Bitcoin happens to be a good way of paying for that because it's a futureproof currency.... So the American spiritual landscape may feed into Bitcoin, or at least Bitcoin comes from that milieu—a milieu that is not just cypherpunk but where spiritual engagement takes the form of transhumanism.

MBK In 'My Little Penny, Bitcoin is Magick' you set the idea of sympathetic magic against kabbalism and gematria, which don't require belief or faith, but just running the numbers—a kind of signals intelligence.

RM Yes, because there are some who have talked about blockchain as ritual, and they've very dismissively tried to reduce it to 'mere ritual' from a sociological or anthropological and, at worst, a merely psychologised point of view. The ritual aspect of it was as obvious to me as to anyone else, but for me the idea of its being a ritual had a lot more weight, and can be used to underwrite more explicit rituals.

MBK Implied in the use of gematria is the fact that, as soon as you get a symbolic system of a certain density, then connections can be detected in it which are undeniable and yet don't functionally contribute to the intended operations of that system. Short-circuits, synchronicities, correspondences, and so on. The effect of the rich semantics of the outside world mining the surplus value of the code within a more impoverished functional realm.

RM I talk about nature being encrypted, and about gematria as a side channel attack on God's private signing key—this is very flowery, but at the very least at the level of metaphor, this is what gematria is: gematria is the idea that the encrypted book of nature has a weakness in its cipher that we can, in cryptographic terms, attack, or in hacker terms, exploit, to get it to leak information from the dark forest of creation. So I zoom into and out of metaphoric mapping and literal operation, being deadly serious about the history of ideas and deeply ironic about the actual application of them.

In using the hashes, one idea that was important was Deleuze's idea of the 'dark precursor', which is any coincidence in the structure of knowledge or culture that you can hang something onto. And again, this is coincidence intensification, which is magic, and critique as disenchantment with the self-description of something.

MBK Some of your work seems to operate by showing that, when brought into contact with the density of cultural and historical associations available to us—which, in fact, it always is in contact with—Bitcoin as a 'machine for truth' (to adopt the most boring-sounding description of it) can be used to produce something oracular and impossible to resolve. *Is Art* (2014, 2016/2017) is the most acute possible case of parlaying the blockchain model of truth into something that we regard as being a truth worth thinking about, a profound but irresolvable truth.

RM It is absolutely correct that Bitcoin is a truth machine, but in keeping with the theme of bathos, it is a truth that would make a philosopher weep. There is no profound truth to 'this coin has been created by the system, this coin has been spent by this person, we have moved this value from address *a* to address *b*'. All of that may be entirely true, and it is a truth made real by a substantial fraction of the planet's computing machinery, which makes it a truth that the writer of a dictionary or a law or a sermon or a book of philosophy can only dream of having at their disposal. A truth underwritten by that much computing power really is a truth that really is generally acknowledged. But it's not the sort of truth you can guide your life by, 'the block reward went to address 1La8w72...'.

In *Is Art*, you have people choosing to spend Ether as, you know, gas—so there's an opportunity cost for this and there's a pricing effect to this—just to toggle the state of this artwork. And this truth will then be made real, intensified, or underwritten, with each block of the chain making it harder and harder and harder to materially undo. This is a model of almost precisely how truth doesn't work. There's a passage in *The Hitchhiker's Guide to the Galaxy* where Arthur Dent is asking the Heart of Gold starship drinks machine for a cup of tea, and it keeps on analysing his brain to find out what will be absolutely perfect for him and producing a small cup of something that is almost but not entirely unlike tea. Blockchain truth tastes something like that.

Disobedience-in-obedience again: I enjoy producing these monstrous and thereby critical misunderstandings or overly literal understandings of people's takes on what truth is and how it relates to socio-economic reproduction. That's a lot of weight to put on one bit of text and a few lines of code, but it's there if you want it. If you don't, it's a fun bit of the history of art, it's a fun little early Ethereum hack. But for me it problematises this model of truth whereby truth is something we arrive at either by agreement or through power and which then just sort of spreads by some mysterious osmotic process through society. In *Hitchhiker's*, again, the ultimate truth of the answer to the question of life, the universe, and everything is 42. That is quite profound and understandable compared to the average truth on the average blockchain—and yet those truths are unassailable.

MBK To tie this question of truth back to magic, perceptibility, and attention: there's something to be said here about the unquenchable human need for aesthetic stimulation and how it betrays the supposed technological quest for efficiency and reason, whether that's conceived of as progressive and virtuous or fascistic and oppressive. Vanity addresses, for example: Why isn't the type of truth produced by the blockchain enough? Why isn't it enough for you to just be a whale, why do you also want to have the equivalent of a personalised number plate for your Bitcoin address?

RM The structure of those early Base58 bitcoin addresses is different from modern Bech32 ones, which are more effective in many ways but less interesting aesthetically. You do weird things to the hash of a public key and a checksum and a version identifier which gives you a guaranteed first letter. So for early bitcoin that was 1, and for Dogecoin it was D. And that was followed by a series of letters, and from that you can unpack the hash of the public key, which means that you can check that something has been signed by the right person without them having to reveal their public key. You know you've got the right one because of the checksum, and you know that you've got the right chain because of that letter prefix. The old ones have sort of various computer science problems and problems as to how you process them, which is why there are newer address formats. But as a piece of both information and user experience and aesthetic design they're wonderful, they're instantly recognisable.

Ultimately, this question of truth, I think truth is one of those ideas that's like love. There are many different phenomena that we call love and they are absolutely real but they are also massively confused through the imprecision of language. With truth we have facts, we have deeply held wishes, we have resonant statistical phenomena, we have, you know, the outcome of applying computer code—these things are all 'truth'. The ability to produce truths in Bitcoin is very clearly and directly a product of the possession of capital. Miners can censor the inclusion of transactions, although they cannot change the meaning of transactions sent by other people. And if they do so they are economically irrational, they are economically disincentivised to do this.

MBK They play the role of the judges of truth?

RM The miners are the producers and the underwriters and the judges of truth, but they have no capacity to decide what is true or not in the sense of the truth procedure: they can only apply it, they can't even say *I would like to let you off from this criminal charge but the law won't allow me to*, they just say *Yes, this computer program will run, that's fine, I am calculating this, look at this hash with a long string of series at the start, yeah, give me some money*. I'm deliberately playing fast and loose with the word 'truth' here, I am pretending I'm using a philosopher's conception of truth, when I mean merely the fact of a logical one rather than a logical zero. Ultimately, the truth of the transaction having taken place in this dark forest of pure intensive value tells us very little about what has happened on the social plane. If a philosopher could produce as much truth as a Bitcoin miner they would be delighted to death; but if a philosopher could only produce the type of truth that miners produce they would die of disappointment. So as far as the production of truth goes, it's this ironisation: *Hurt me!* It's possible to have absolute truth but with no meaning! *No, not like that!*

MBK Undermining Plato's cave....

RM This is why I prefer doge, doge miners are called diggers—not in the Christian sect sense but in the dog-looking-for-a-bone sense. With the cave, again we're back to phenomenon inside and noumenon outside, the prime material plane and this realm of absolute fact, of absolute zero-meaning truth of pure financial value, of price, mere shadows of things. Out in the world it's doing something, it's paying people's rent, paying for people's meds, it's very often buying cryptography-related swag. And the truth of the transaction having happened is related to the truth of that offchain event, just not in any recoverable way.

MBK In 'Crypto Sigils' you tie the notion of magical invocation and access to the outside to hashing algorithms.

RM Again, it's all about names. Hashing gives you a true name for some information that you can use to summon it, but which you can use to refer to it without revealing its content—you can share it with others without them knowing what it is. As I say in 'Crypto Sigils', this is like a residual sigil as an information-destroying representation for an idea or an intent. 'Crypto Sigils' describes an entirely serious bit of chaos magic, because it's saying, take this popular technique from contemporary culture and apply it to the actualisation of your intent, to your coincidence intensification, which is what magic is and also what money is. But the reason it's an interesting exercise is that it helps to understand how these things work, and it's attempting to understand how they work in a way that isn't going to melt down a nuclear reactor or lead to anyone being out of work or anything. It's just this pocket universe where you can go into that realm, mix everything up, come back, and it's concretised in different ways.

In *Blockchain Aesthetics* (2014–2015, 2019) I rendered transaction hashes as modern and postmodern aesthetic bromides. As I originally realised with the YBA generators I made, you can use those kinds of things because people will recognise them as signalling art. So we've got the crunchy candy shell, the reassuring protein shell of recognisable and recoverable aesthetics. And then we have the experience of the complexity of this system which, at the time I made it, was this unseen network which was understood by the people making it, but I felt there wasn't an appreciation of it as a thing in the world that was really doing something.

Hashes are produced all the time, everyone pushing github is producing a hash, everyone using Bitcoin is producing a hash, Bitcoin miners produce trillions of hashes a day. But this means that hashing is something which has being, which has reality, through repetition, through the intensification of its application. And so rather than saying that the application of a hash is creative, I make the move of saying that the application of a hash is *culturally resonant*. It's the same as using a pack of cards in the pack-of-cards era, or using a newspaper for bibliomancy in the mass-media era. Here we are in the cryptographic era, and what is the way that everything is touched? By hashing. And that gives me what I regard as a critically or genetically or projectally defensible thing that I am doing that is not simply cargo-culting the technology. I had to convince myself that it was legitimate to use this purely mechanical procedure as a link in the chain of production of meaning.

If you can get a hash which, like a vanity address, has curiously ordered properties that grab human attention—for example, if you represent your hash as any kind of numbers, if it has a lot of zeros at the start—that's unlikely. Something unlikely is perceptually interesting, something perceptually interesting can be worked with creatively or reflectively and, because you have something unlikely, you have already started from the position of coincidence intensification. And this comes directly back to Bitcoin, because its proof of work algorithm is precisely modifying the inputs to a cryptographic hash algorithm until the output starts with a long and unlikely series of zeroes. Bitcoin mining is literally coincidence intensification, and as I say coincidence intensification is one definition of magic, particularly within chaos magic: polling chaos repeatedly until it produces something that's perceptible.

So on one hand these gestures map very clearly onto the technology of Bitcoin, but on the other hand they take the work that Bitcoin does, in various senses of the word including the physics sense, and extract surplus value from what is already a coincidence intensification machine.

I'm not suggesting that I can take an external point of view on any of this, I'm involved and there are limits to rational investments in it and logical reasoning about it. We don't have a clear view or a perfect theory for this because we don't know how it turns out.

MBK Before we leave the question of magic, the other spook you invite in is the possibility of artwork-DAOs that have a kind of agency and are able to operate in the art world on their own behalf without human intervention. Which conjures up associations with golems, tulpas, and egregores, but also operates an amusing inversion of the modernist question of the artwork's 'autonomy'.

RM That's very tricky, because the quasi-agentic model of art is in some ways key to the idea of art's autonomy. The idea that artworks can somehow speak or enter into a dialogue with the viewer is very powerful, but it threatens to mislead our understanding of society. If we make this horribly literal via bot art—and I was working on bot art before blockchain—a DAO can absolutely be a quasi-agentic collection of rules, of embodied intent, and people lose their shit about those, even though they have no problem with charitable trusts or legal personhood for rivers. This representation and embodiment of intent by a particular model of code and a particular set of incentives is merely something that the blockchain makes cheaper for anyone to be able to do.

There are various different models for how DAOs could produce artworks which literalise or operationalise the quasi-agentic model of art. You then come back to the idea of embedded purpose that you get in chaos magic with servitors, and, back in computer software, with daemons, which run in the background and do things without you always asking them to. Again we're going back and forth through the rhizome of the history of ideas from computer science to demonology to chaos magic to anarchist co-ops and the market anarchist idea that if you give people property rights over the sky then they'll be economically incentivised to not burn it up. That all comes together and, again, doing this in art gives us a dry run for doing it for real, but with lower stakes.

LeWitt said: the idea becomes a machine that makes the art. DAOs are ideas made into machines, and they can produce something. Let's take each of those steps, juice the surplus value from it, take it very literally, and see what we can do.

Why people who are interested in human organisation in all forms are not fascinated by a public plastic medium for making explicit organisational principles, I'm not sure. Sure, we can try and evolve bigger bladders so that we can win any given cooperative meeting, but, you know, the telegram was invented some time ago, the average conception of organisation in contemporary organisational circles is less sophisticated than in Ancient Greece, not philosophically but literally, technologically, in terms of the technology they use.

I have to admit that there's some bad conscience to my continued individualistic art production, because I should really have made a DAO or some sort of platform or standard where I could bring in the wisdom and madness of crowds to make art that could not be made any other way and that would therefore have a historical necessity to it. I haven't done that, partly owing to lack of social skills, partly owing to a very heavily internalised conception of the modernist artist, and partly because this is how I have fun! Having meetings is not how I have fun. But if there's a failing to my own performance relative to any reading of what I'm doing, it's that I'm still doing it as an individual cryptographic identity rather than at least socialising myself through a DAO.

MBK Maybe something for the future...! Having looked back in this conversation to where you started with all of this, how do you feel about the point it has brought you to—in art and life—today? I get the impression that you toiled for a long time in fairly cheerful obscurity, and that your sudden notoriety in recent years has come as more of a surprise to you than to anyone else. But you also seem to be engaged in a constant reinterpretation of what it is that you were doing in those earlier works. Has the art done what you needed it to do?

RM Where I started was the feeling of not belonging in the world and not understanding how the world worked, so there's this emotional or psychological impetus in the work which I recognise now very clearly as dysphoria and dissociation—the feeling that the world is somehow behind glass and that everyone else has a rule book that you don't have, and trying to explain the world to myself. With my art I'm trying to collapse the distance between myself and the world through understanding. I was aiming to change the world through my art, which is unlikely, or to change myself through my art and rehabilitate myself as a social subject. But I didn't have the knowledge that I needed to fix my epistemology in order to really attempt that task because the part of my brain that should have worked out I was transgender when I was eighteen at the latest was being overridden by the part of my brain that was spending more and more of the day making very sure that this was not something I would ever consider as the remotest possibility. But by the time I was in my forties it was like having a stage magician following you around and whenever you're like *Hang on, this doesn't make sense*, they pop up with a card trick, *Pick a card!* It was just distraction and denial and disavowal and dissociation, not as a conscious project but as a background process in the operating system of my brain, taking up more and more of the runtime.

But this meant that, on the way through a succession of incorrect understandings of the world, I did learn how to learn about different aspects of the world, how to criticise myself and these aspects and their relations, and I managed to create this sort of spider web of associations and critiques. I came to enjoy the exercise of my critical and creative faculties upon something which other people couldn't tell me was wrong and which I couldn't tell me was wrong, and which often had an irresistible quality to it, something like the *Shareable Readymades* or *Tokens Equals Text.* These are ideas that assembled themselves in my mind from what I was doing at the time, and I learned over time to get out of the way of that: to just make it, and then afterwards find out how it relates to everything I'm doing at the moment. So, much like Conan being chained to a wheel for his entire adolescence, I built up my critical faculties by not knowing what the hell was going on.

MBK Do those realisations mean that you now have a different view of the work, of its interrogation of secrecy and privacy and identity? And does the fact that the urgency of avoidance has abated make you less inclined to make more work, even though your work is now getting more attention than ever before?

RM In a sense, my egg cracking was the fulfilment of the projects I was doing when I was twenty.

MBK We're entering into a retrochronic temporality here?

RM Yes, you can see why the work of the Ccru continues to resonate for terminally online trans women: we are our own hyperstitions, terminators sent back from the future to assemble ourselves from the resources we have now: our bodies and what we understand about culture, having not really understood it for however long.

But my constant theme is disobedience-in-obedience. What I had asked was *How does the world work?* and the answer *Here is why you don't understand how the world works* does not answer my original question! It has the effect that I wanted, which is to remove the barrier between myself and the world, to collapse me into the prime material plane, to make me mortal. But it only raises more questions, so I am absolutely no less motivated to make the work. And I'm deeply flattered to have an audience that has invested psychologically and financially in the work that I have made, so I have a strong sense of obligation to them not to fuck it up.

Transition does not solve all your problems, it may not even make you less anxious, it may not make you less depressed: what it does do is it makes it possible for you to face the reality of those things. And this can be awful because actually dissociation can be very useful when you are dealing, or in fact not dealing, with them. Being checked out can help you survive things much better; if you're no longer checked out it doesn't make things easier to cope with, but it may give you the knowledge and impetus to deal with them. When Morpheus gives Neo the red pill he says, *Remember, all I'm offering you is the truth*. Being unplugged is not paradise. I always remember the line from *Neuromancer* where Case is injected with neurotoxins and he's lying in a hotel room for three days feeling his ability to connect to cyberspace basically dribble out of his ears, and then he 'crashes into the meat'. Hackers have disdain for 'the meat', and you'll notice that lots of trans people are software engineers, and if that's not the effect of a revenge hex by one of the women who was cast out of the software development in the sixties when it became professionalised, perhaps it's because dissociation is a superpower: if you're checked out of your body and want a world that makes sense when the world around you doesn't, and if you do not care about how you look, feel, or smell, then you're prime material for software development. But in whatever field it gets expressed, this displacement, this attempt to master a body of knowledge rather than knowledge of your body, it's a coping technique which is completely understandable and deserves love and a big hug.

MBK But reality finally seeps in and the work then becomes about something other than what you thought it was about? Is that what you mean when you mention an anxiety around people who have invested in your work?

RM As with any body horror story where someone begins a transformation, the thing that has to start the process of change will be changed by the process of change. This is the general problem of self-knowledge, which is diagonalisation. Once you know that you are not who you should be, that doesn't mean that the thing that you become will want to be the thing that you think you want to be...if the book tries to rewrite itself then you end up in the realm of recursion.

A meaningful existence is something that was inconceivable to me—I was proud of being a parent, I enjoyed being in love and making art, but each decade I lived I was amazed by it, and I could not imagine a future beyond. Crashing into my body just in time to watch the end of the world is the sort of cruel irony that would make you feel a Marvel universe movie is a bit underwritten.

I'm not an expert on ideas of gender, I'm not even an expert on me, I can certainly talk about my own experience, but one of the things I had to do was to let go of trying to explain it. *This is an overwhelming reality, I will worry about the impossibility of any of it later but this is happening, so we're gonna ride it out because trying to deny it was threatening to destroy me.* Once I became aware of it, it became aware of me—in the best tradition of horror movies. And that's where 'Necronomicon' begins.

MBK There's a great deal to explore here in terms of encryption, signatures, time, identities and their backpropagation.... This process, also, involves not a transcendent given but a generative regime: gender has to be pragmatically enacted in order to find out what kind of virtuality is produced, and the generative effects of that virtuality have to be navigated.

RM Rerolling your character sheet halfway through the campaign. Why not? Aly Chace points out that hyperstition is just Butlerian performativity....

MBK How do you see the contrast between how you imagined blockchain art in 2014 and its actually existing reality in 2022?

RM There's both the danger of romanticising paths not taken and that of romanticising the early experiments. But everyone needs to look at Plantoid, everyone needs to look at Terra0, everyone needs to look at these early projects that answer so many questions about how we can do these things in a way that doesn't simply build platforms that will be captured by venture capital and destroy the environment and won't support artists. They are amazing applications of the real affordances of this technology to the real problems of artistic production.

In my case, I was very anticapitalist, I thought, we need to bring socialism into this, not just transactional economics. That meant that I was completely wrongfooted by NFTs because I was leaning away from commodification and financialisation. The model I had was the one I work through in the representations of art in 'Artworld Ethereum'—these different functions and entities in the art world operationalised as code that you can then hack on to modify the performance of those functions. By the time I wrote 'Ethereum Standardized Contract API', which included resale rights, and handled registering and buying and selling and listing works onchain on Ethereum, that brought up the legal, financial, and moral responsibility of actually making that into a business, which is what I would have had to deal with in order to make it into a real thing, and I couldn't cope with that.

But in that early work there are so many models of things that people simply haven't done since, and there are so many representations of artworks that people simply haven't used. By the time you get to 'Standardized API', that's a complete model for representing artworks not as tokens—I didn't know artworks were going to be represented as tokens—but as smart contracts that can offer themselves for exhibition, take exhibition fees, evaluate opportunities for exhibition, and interact with curators in order to show the (presumably electronic) artwork that they manage. There's nothing like that out there. There are wonderful curating and collector DAOs—disclosure, I am collected and curated by various DAOs—but there is absolutely a more social model of the art world to be had; there are still these interesting models, different representations of things that are artworks and different possibilities of organising the commissioning, production, exhibition, sale, and critique of art in ways that simply haven't been done.

There are the actually existing rare art platforms, NFT platforms, and there's the potential of DAOs, which are intensifying their way toward very interesting production. And for me there's the historical example of technologically accelerationist art, modelled as autonomous or quasi-genetic entities on the blockchain.

So there's interesting work to do here that isn't simply treating my early work as an 8-bit aesthetic, or using it as a signifier of lost futures or as retrotech camp. I would love people to rip off my early work, I'd love people to combine it with modern NFT standards. But if we want this sort of social organisation against the capitalist reification of value and extraction of value then the best way out may be DAOs, with their alignment with economic incentives. This is precisely the horror story of 'Maximum Transaction Density': the best way of doing this involves everything being bought and sold, timestamped with the mark of the beast....

MBK The only way to the best is through the worst?

RM It's the worst from the point of view of an anticapitalist, antifinancialist psychology, but it's not the worst from the point of view of material existence. You don't need everything to collapse socioeconomically in order to get to maximum transaction density, quite the opposite. You do need to let go of your ego and your investments and prejudices in exculpatory fantasies. We're into cosmic horror with economics as the only limit, outside of the human subject. And the social subject is going *But I just want to draw furry art all day and for people just to give me food for no reason*. How about that, but via a DAO? *No, not like that!*

MBK Given that your work addresses two different constituencies which are generally suspicious of or indifferent to one another, and you take great pleasure in prodding and provoking both of them, who are your audience?

RM Art & Language talked early on about producing work without an audience: they had an imagined future audience—probably after the revolution—but there was not an actually existing audience for their work. And with my stuff, if you wanted to get a full understanding of it you would need to know meme culture, computer programming, some French philosophy, arguments from bulletin boards, and so on—but to get the impression of it, which will certainly do a lot of its work, you need to know a lot less, you just need to be open to the idea that there may be something there.

As for the book, some readers will pick this up and go *What is this? I wanted doge memes and there's a technical standard here that no one has ever used, there's something claiming to be art which is basically a computer program with one bit of information in the variable, and then there's a story that does have doge memes in it but I can't read it because the narrator is unreliable...* So if I pretend not to be me (which I spent many years doing) and step back from this, it looks sprawling and chaotic. But I think it's actually very consistent—not that I planned it all out from the start. The previous phase of my work was broadly around the idea of freedom, free culture, free software and the limits on that. And then it became very much about secrets and making them very secure. But the persistent, repeating question here is: Are you sure? Are you *sure* this is a horrible right-wing technology that has no value for your socialist project? Are you *sure* the art world is all blue-haired hipsters who want to ban you from owning firearms and silver? Are you *sure* that perfect security is possible? A constant voice of doubt, but not the kind of doubt that sits there and points and feels very secure in having found a place outside the world from which to act superior. I'm diving into the mud.

Writings

Excerpt From a Recounting of an Adventure by Baron Munchausen

'And so,' said the Baron, 'the ringing of my diving bell allowed me to lift from the ocean floor the heaviest pearl ever discovered. I later had it made into a brooch by the finest craftsmen in the land.'

'But Baron,' interjected the host, 'surely such a weighty trinket could never actually be worn. It would be worthless!'

The Baron paused but for a moment.

'My dear sir, as you know, the defining characteristic of art is its inutility. The value of art therefore stands in direct and inverse proportion to its utility. Given that a pearl brooch of unwearable weight must be entirely useless, its artistic value must therefore be infinite.'

2008

Open Source Art Again, Again

Art is a game between all people of all periods.

Marcel Duchamp

Introduction

The concept of 'Open Source' continues to inspire artists. But it is an intentionally vague concept that is often more confusing than enlightening. Unpacking the concept helps examine the practices associated with it and the ethical questions that it obscures. This reveals strategies that are of relevance to contemporary artistic practice and can place artists at the heart of current issues of free speech and the law and technology of censorship.

Open Source

The concept of Open Source comes from computer software development. Open Source software is software that everyone can recreate and modify. This requires public access to the software's source code. The source code for a piece of software is equivalent to the score or preparatory work for a piece of music, drama, or art, and it is similarly required in order to recreate or modify the finished work. Closed Source software, as sold by corporations such as Microsoft, does not have its source code publicly available, and trying to recreate or modify it is prohibited by law.

Open Source was given its current definition in 1998[1] by hackers Bruce Perens[2] and Eric Raymond. For Raymond, the virtue of Open Source is its efficiency.[3] Open Source, he argues, can create better products faster than the contrasting Closed Source method of writing software. And indeed, many of the most successful software programs in use today, particularly on the internet, have been produced in this way.[4]

The success of Open Source for software development in an age where computers are the defining technology and guiding metaphor of society[5] has inspired individuals and groups to try to apply its ideas to other areas of activity such as encyclopaedias,

1 See <http://opensource.org/history>.

2 C. DiBona, S. Ockman, and M. Stone (eds), *Open Sources: Voices from the Open Source Revolution* (Sebastopol, CA: O'Reilly, 1999).

3 E.S. Raymond, *The Cathedral and the Bazaar* (Sebastopol, CA: O'Reilly, 1999).

4 For example, the Apache web server, the Firefox web browser, the MySQL database, and the GNU/Linux operating system. Of more interest to visual artists may be the Gimp image editor, Inkscape illustration program, and Scribus DTP package.

5 J.D. Bolter, *Turing's Man: Western Culture in the Computer Age* (Chapel Hill, NC: University Of North Carolina Press, 1984).

cartography, political activism, philosophy, theory, and art. Yochai Benkler describes this general application of Open Source as 'commons based peer production':[6] work made collaboratively and shared publicly by a community of equals. This has often proved more problematic than might be expected. The idea of Open Source as a more efficient means of production doesn't explain why we should want to make philosophy or art more efficient, or what the form or advantage of that efficiency would be.

To take the example of the Open Congress event held at Tate Modern in 2005,[7] artists struggled to find an Open Source ideology to apply to their art, activists struggled to find an Open Source ideology to apply to their organisations, and critical theorists invoked Deleuze and Spinoza to try to fill the gaps. There was a genuine interest in the potential of Open Source, but frequent confusion over what that might actually mean outside of software development.

The problem is that the term 'Open Source' was deliberately chosen for its meaninglessness and ideological vacuity.[8] The intention was to make the results of a certain successful new ideology more palatable to large corporations by disguising its ethical content. That ideology is Free Software.

Free Software

American computer programmer Richard Stallman articulated the modern concept of Free Software in 1984 within a context of increasing restriction on the use and production of software.[9] Free Software is not a radical new development, it is a programme of reform intended to restore the more freewheeling software development ethic that began to disappear when software became copyrightable in the USA in the late 1970s.

Software is used to achieve many different ends within a pluralistic society. Its use is as widespread and diverse as that of the written word was following the invention of the printing press. Free Software can therefore be understood historically and ethically as the defence of pluralistic freedom against a genuine threat. It is an ethical issue, a matter of freedom. This is very different from being a new method of organisation or a more efficient means of production.

Stallman defines Free Software as a set of Four Freedoms:[10] the freedom to use, study, modify, and share software. These freedoms are indivisible. If you have all four freedoms then you are free to use software. If you have only two or three then you are not. There are other definitions of Free Software,[11] but they tend to add redundant or contradictory terms and are best avoided.

Once software users' freedoms are restored and protected, in the future by legal reform but until then by measures such as the GNU General Public Licence,[12] this has the effect of encouraging collaborative and public software development. Licences such as the GPL are a good example of measures that have been imitated outside of the context of software development. Collaborative, public software development protected by such licences is more efficient and can achieve higher quality than Closed

6 Y. Benkler, *The Wealth of Networks: How Social Production Transforms Markets and Freedom* (New Haven, CT: Yale University Press, 2006).
7 See <http://www.tate.org.uk/onlineevents/archive/open_congress/>.
8 Although there is some evidence that a previous use of the phrase 'Open Source' dates back to at least the late 1980s.
9 R.M. Stallman, *Free Software, Free Society: Selected Essays of Richard M. Stallman* (Boston, MA: Free Software Foundation, 2002).
10 Ibid.
11 Such as the Debian Free Software Guidelines. See <http://www.debian.org/social_contract>.
12 See <http://www.gnu.org/licenses/quick-guide-gplv3.html>.

Source 'proprietary' software development. It is these effects of the pursuit of freedom that Open Source focuses on at the expense of obscuring their deeper causes.

It is important to remember that these gains, and the existence of commons-based peer production, are effects or products of freedom and the protection of people's rights. Without the guiding principles of the ethics of Free Software, the necessity and direction of Open Source projects cannot be accounted for. Open Source cannot account for itself or suggest which tasks are necessary or important. It may become tempting to compromise some of the Four Freedoms in order to increase the efficiency or quality that are Open Source's promises, or in the name of political or economic goals.

This kind of confusion has led to projects such as Wikipedia trying to create an open space for anyone to use as they wish. This leads to Social Darwinism, not freedom, as the contents of that space ends up being determined by a battle of wills. Wikipedia has had to reproduce many of the organisational structures and mechanisms of established Free Software projects in order to tackle these problems. But people still regard its earlier phase as a model for emulation, whereas it should probably serve as more of a warning.

Within Free Software projects, if contributions are deemed to be of acceptable quality, they are added to the project's source code by its appointed gatekeepers. If not, they are rejected and advice given. This methodology is a structured and exclusive one, but it is meritocratic. Any contribution of sufficient quality can be accepted, and if someone makes enough such contributions they themselves may gain the trust required to become a gatekeeper. This hierarchy and the decisions process is public and usually transparent, and if any individuals do not agree with the governance of the project they are free to take a copy of the source code of the project and start their own 'fork' of it.

Free Software projects have produced commons-based peer production only because of their practical pursuit of freedom. As with the term Open Source, the concept of commons-based peer production easily confuses and misleads. Failing to account for the causes and effects of the pursuit of freedom can render commons-based peer production inexplicable and make it appear to be in need of artificial economic or political induction. This can lead to the placing of limits on the very freedom that actually produces the commons in order to protect investment (for neoliberal or robust individualist complainants) or class interests (for palaeo-socialist complainants). It is important not to compromise the pluralism produced by the pursuit of freedom in order to respond to non-pluralistic concerns. To do so becomes self-defeating because to compromise the freedom of others is to deny oneself the value one might draw from them.

There are strategies from Free Software that cannot work for art. Software can be replaced with a different, functionally equivalent, piece of software that does the same thing without loss. It is fungible. Art is not fungible. A Picasso is not a substitute for a Matisse artistically. This is not fetishism, it is a consequence of the fact that an artwork's construction is what it does: you cannot change an artwork without changing its effect. The Free Software strategy of creating replacements for un-free work therefore cannot work for art. This means that there can be no replacement for Modernist art that will remain covered by copyright, and that these limitations must be dealt with through other means.

It is clear that 'Open Source' obscures the very concept of freedom that leads to the beneficial effects identified by Raymond. 'Commons-based peer production' is no more useful. It is a market-rational economic description of what to many economists seems to be the irrationality of the epiphenomena of Free Software. Again, like Open Source, it discards the ethical concepts that lead to its own production.

For all these reasons it is therefore the condition of Freedom rather than the condition of Open Source that art should aspire to.

Freedom is the principle from which the organisational and economic benefits of Open Source flow. In applying the ideas of Free Software to art, we should look first not to the effects of pursuing freedom for software users but to what freedom means for art. To map the concepts of Free Software into artistic practice, the best starting point is to identify the concept or concepts of artistic freedom and to identify the threats against it and opportunities for it.

Freedom applies to individual human beings, not objects. Artists have always learnt from, imitated, and built on the work of their peers and of previous generations of artists. Art History consists in no small part of the study of genres, schools, iconography, and studios that involve many different individuals over many generations. Society has always provided both audience and inspiration for art in a reciprocal relationship. Successive generations of artists and society have collaborated to make the canon of art.

Prior to the extension of copyright to cover art as well as literature, art was implicitly free. The physical artefacts of art were expensive to own and difficult or impossible to transport. But the content of art was free for other artists to use and for critics and commentators to critique. This representational freedom of artists, part of which consists in the freedom to depict, build on, or comment on existing culture, to continue the conversation of culture, is no small part of artistic freedom.

Generations of artists could riff on the theme of the crucifixion, and anyone could carve a statue of Venus. The production of Homeric verse was a multi-generational collaboration, and Shakespeare was a notorious plagiarist (or appropriator). Michelangelo could appropriate Christian and pagan imagery to paint a ceiling:

> [T]he chapel's funny shape—it has the basic outline of a treasure chest in a pirate movie—[...] was copied from an obscure Christian cartographer called Cosmas, whose chief claim to distinction is that he refused to accept that the earth was round. Cosmas insisted the earth was rectangular, and shaped, as it turned out, exactly like the Sistine Chapel.[13]

Historically there are examples of artworks, such as Raphael's 1515 *Judgement Of Paris*, which we only know from unauthorised copies. Had reproduction of those works been prevented, they would be lost. The same student of Raphael who made these copies won a lawsuit that Albrecht Dürer brought against him in 1506 for copying Dürer's etchings.[14] This pre-dates the modern concept of copyright by a hundred years.

Marcel Duchamp addressed material and organisational limitations on the creation of art in one of his interviews:

> When Rubens, or someone else, needed blue, he had to ask his guild for so many grams, and they discussed the question, to find out if he could have fifty or sixty grams, or more.[15]

In order to create opportunities and support for the creation of art, it is important to address material and organisational limitations.

Art has always suffered from censorship.

Calls for religious, political, and cultural censorship continue to be a threat to artistic freedom. Opposing them should be a core part of the defence of artistic freedom. One of the weaknesses of simply imitating the strategies of Free Software is that

13 W. Januszczak. 'The Sistine Chapel Has a Secret', *The Times*, 8 May 2005.
14 D. McClean and K. Schubert. *Dear Images: Art, Copyright and Culture* (London: ICA/Ridinghouse, 2002).
15 P. Cabanne, *Dialogues With Marcel Duchamp* (Cambridge, MA: Da Capo, 1987).

software does not suffer from such calls, and so it has no strategies for coping with them. Given this, supporting legal reform and opposing more restrictive laws is vital. But supporting open critique is another way of tackling such calls, and Free Software does supply certain means for doing this.

Censorship through restrictive actions has been joined by restrictive law and now technological restrictions. The chilling effects of these on art are difficult to precisely quantify as they concern work not made and work not seen. But a few examples may serve to illustrate some of these effects.

Yves Klein patented the recipe for his International Klein Blue pigment in 1960.[16] This would in theory have prevented anyone reproducing the precise colour for twenty years, limiting any artists who wished to comment on Klein's work or to take his ideas further.

Jeff Koons has lost several lawsuits from copyright holders for work that he has used as the basis of artworks, starting with the photographer of a postcard upon which he based the sculpture *String Of Puppies*,[17] although he has more recently successfully defended a lawsuit brought against him by the copyright holders of photographs he used as source material for the painting *Niagara*.[18]

Andy Warhol lost a lawsuit brought against him by Patricia Caulfield, the copyright holder of the flower photograph that Warhol used as the source for his 1964 *Flowers* series.[19] The Warhol Foundation allow use of Warhol's images for the creation of art and for non-commercial use, although academics do still pay reproduction fees, which seems to go against Warhol's own appropriationist spirit.

Warhol and Koons could afford the cost of defending lawsuits, although the time it takes to do so is time that could better be spent making art. Without assistance, less established artists can rarely afford the money or the time it would require to legally defend their right to make art.

Tom Forsythe's photographs of a Barbie doll in a blender led to a lawsuit from the corporate owners of the Barbie trademark. Tom fought the lawsuit with help from free speech charity The American Civil Liberties Union. His eventual victory inspired a project to celebrate it, with an annual Barbie-in-a-Blender day to raise awareness of issues around freedom of expression.

Painter Joy Garnett used an image that she found on the internet as inspiration for her painting *Molotov* (2003). After exhibiting it, she found herself the subject both of legal threats from lawyers acting for the photographer's agency and of a campaign of support on the internet involving making derivative images of Garnett's own derivative of the image.

Artists can impose restrictions as well as suffering from them. Photography of Anish Kapoor's *Cloud Gate* (2005) was forbidden by the owners of the plaza in Chicago where it was installed.[20] Photography of Christo and Jean Claude's *The Gates* in New York's Central Park was forbidden by the artists themselves, although this led to an organised campaign of photography[21] and online parodies in protest.

Even sketching in museums can be affected. When security guards tell children to stop drawing, whether this is a correct application of museum policy or a side effect of a general environment of strong copyright, the effects of copyright have gone too far.[22]

As 'Joywar' and the reaction to *The Gates* shows, when media or corporate interests, or even other artists, seek to limit artists and the public from creating their

16 Allegedly French patent 63471.
17 See: Rogers v. Koons, 960 F.2d 301 (2d Cir. 1992).
18 Blanch v. Koons, No. 03 Civ. 8026 (LLS), S.D.N.Y., 1 November 2005.
19 McClean and Schubert, *Dear Images*.
20 <http://newurbanist.blogspot.com/2005/01/copyrighting-of-public-space.html>.
21 <http://flickr.com/groups/79972013@N00/pool/>.
22 <http://www.boingboing.net/2005/01/08/stop_sketching_littl.html>.

own visual representations, civil disobedience is often the result. This is as it should be. Bad law cannot be the limit of society's forms.

Artistic freedom is part of the more general category of freedom of speech within an open society.[23] Freedom of speech often becomes 'freedom of expression' in artistic discussion, although 'freedom of representation' might be a more useful concept, as art causes problems because of what it depicts more often than because of how the artist was feeling when creating the depiction.

Support for freedom of speech involves both opposing censorship and providing support for those who would otherwise struggle to have their voice heard. These are the negative and positive freedoms of speech, to use Isaiah Berlin's terms.[24] They apply to art just as they do to the written or spoken word.

One aspect of art's value to society is that art is free to find new ways of looking at the world. In order to do this, artists must be free to depict whatever it is necessary to depict however it is necessary to do so. They might be prevented from doing so by new laws—for example, by laws against depicting trademarked or copyrighted images or objects. Or they might be prevented from doing so by technology—for example, by anti-copying measures on electronic media.

Calling such measures 'censorship' is not historically accurate, and expanding the category of censorship beyond government silencing of opposition is contentious. But there is no word that better fits the prevention of art's creation of new forms by reactionary institutional elements through new legal and technological measures.[25]

A major threat to artistic freedom, then, is censorship in its current legal and technological forms. It places limits upon how art can be created and received, a restriction of freedom. To restore this freedom will require legal reform in the long term, but in the short term artists can look to Free Software for strategies.

'Free Art' would mean that artists and society are free to produce and deal with art. Free software is concerned with the freedom of computer users to use software. Use in this context means utilisation not exploitation, use value not exchange value. And freedom means freedom as a general principle, not something contingent or alienable. Freedom of use does not cover trying to use software to remove the freedom of others to use software any more than freedom of contract covers slavery. Use of software covers production of software as well, since software is used to make software.

Artistic freedom covers the ability of artists, audience, academics, and critics to experience, comment on (verbally or in new art), study, and produce art.[26] Limiting this freedom is censorship in its expanded sense. Opposing censorship in its expanded sense is the defence of artistic freedom.

Many artists have internalised the Romantic myth of creative genius and see their work as something standing apart from society and which needs to be protected from it through strong copyright and other measures. They have forgotten their own process of learning, their own influences, the criticism and journalism that supports their reputations, and that their audience's attention is part of the value of their art. Artists are tenants of culture, to quote Nicolas Bourriaud quoting Michel de Certeau.[27]

Artists learn from other artists and depict the broader visual environment that is produced by society. Artists are supported by and will learn from critics, academics, and theorists. To charge for them to provide this support or to otherwise restrict it is

23 K. Popper, *The Open Society And Its Enemies: The Spell of Plato* (London: Routledge, 2002).
24 I. Berlin, *Liberty* (Oxford: Oxford University Press, 2002).
25 R. Atkins and S. Mintcheva (eds), *Censoring Culture: Contemporary Threats to Free Expression* (New York: New Press, 2006).
26 Following Stallman, freedom always seems to come in fours.
27 N. Bourriaud, *Relational Aesthetics* (Paris: Les Presses du Réel, 2002), 14.

unfair. A backlash against academic image reproduction fees has recently resulted from this.[28]

Restrictions on artistic freedom stifle art and reduce its value to society. Appropriation artists and artists who depict contemporary events and the contemporary visual environment will be the first to feel these restrictions. Such art is an 'interrogation of meaning'[29] and will generate precisely the kind of challenges to established or desired meanings that censorship is designed to preclude. These restrictions are being imposed from both within and without the art world. Art must therefore join with a broader Free Culture both to defend itself and to avoid causing harm to others.

'Open Content' is a simple mapping of the name Open Source onto cultural works. 'Content' is what entertainment industry middlemen call production-line music and movies. Reviewers of disposable pop music use it as an insult.[30] A better term for creative work is 'culture', and as we have established, a more meaningful word than 'open' is 'free'.

'Free Culture' explains both the principle, freedom, and the subject of that principle, culture as expressed through works and performances. Its advantages are the same as those of 'Free Software' over 'Open Source'.

The current understanding of Free Culture was popularised by lawyer and academic Lawrence Lessig's book of the same name.[31] Lessig founded the organisation Creative Commons to address some of the issues he identified.[32] Their imitation of Free Software's licencing tactic has led to a strong association between alternative licencing and the contemporary idea of Free Culture.

Licencing

To protect the freedom of others to draw from and comment on your work is to protect your own freedom to do the same with their work—and with your own work, should you become alienated from it for whatever reason. Licences are a strong way of protecting this freedom. Art as a whole involves a social contract between artists, but the precise details vary between kinds of art. Appropriation art is the canary in the coalmine of artistic freedom. Once appropriation is restricted, criticism and then the freedom to depict the visual environment as a whole will be restricted.

Alternative licencing uses the tools of copyright licencing to add freedoms rather than impose restrictions. Once an alternative licence is applied to a copyrightable work, such as a piece of art, anyone who copies it or creates new work based on it is free to do so as long as they follow the licence. Ordinarily they would have no such freedom in law, outside of the bounds of Fair Use (or Fair Dealing).

Fair Use is largely an American concept. Other legal systems have more limited exceptions to copyright, and would not allow artistic use of copyrighted imagery under the same terms. Alternative licences are useful for protecting Fair-Use-style freedoms in such jurisdictions. Even within American law, Fair Use is a legal defence not a right, and must be defended in court if challenged. Against media corporations this will be a very uneven battle, and Lawrence Lessig has described Fair Use as little more in practice than 'the right to hire a lawyer'.[33] So alternative licencing is useful for protecting Fair Use even within American law.

28 R. Simon, 'Editorial', *The British Art Journal* 4:3 (2007).
29 P.D. Miller aka DJ Spooky that Subliminal Kid, *Rhythm Science* (Cambridge, MA: MIT Press, 2004).
30 C. Brooker, 'Supposing...Sandi Thom is the Musical Antichrist', *The Guardian*, 9 June 2006.
31 L. Lessig. *Free Culture: How Big Media Uses Technology and the Law to Lock Down Culture and Control Creativity* (London and New York: Penguin, 2004).
32 <http://www.creativecommons.org/>.
33 Lessig, *Free Culture*.

There are a number of different alternative licences available and several different kinds of licence. Some disallow commercial use. Since the work can be copied for free, and since the person licencing the work may want to use the results in turn, this isn't as useful as it might seem. Some disallow modifying the work, but still allow it to be modified under Fair Use. Some simply allow the work to be copied and used with very few restrictions, but then the freedoms that make that possible can be removed in turn, shutting the audience and the original artist out.

The most successful licences, used by non-art projects such as GNU[34] and Wikipedia,[35] allow work to be copied and new work to be based on it on condition that the licensee places the results under the same license, passing on the same freedoms to others. This reversing of copyright to protect rather than remove people's freedoms was named 'copyleft' by Stallman.

The spread of work covered by copyleft licences produces a 'commons' of work that people can draw from and contribute to freely. The historical metaphor of the commons comes from land owned and managed by a community rather than a landowner. The 'tragedy of the commons', often cited to prove that private ownership is better than common ownership, ignores this fact.

It is important to remember that this cultural commons is a product of copyleft, which is a product of the ethical position of freedom. It is not an end in itself. Talk of the commons without talk of freedom can introduce broken metaphors from the agricultural commons, or measures to protect the commons that would compromise the freedoms of individuals that give rise to the commons.

By relying on ever-strengthening copyright law, copyleft might appear to support the very thing it is designed to oppose. But this is not the case. If copyright law disappeared, copyleft would lose its force. Licencing is very popular within the 'Web 2.0' internet bubble, where it is seen as a source of free labour for websites and social networks. Web 2.0 is an expression of the information knowledge work culture that Alan Liu identifies as being opposed to historical literary and artistic culture.[36] But attempts to employ this as an objection to copyleft can be answered by the fact that copyleft is a form of intensification[37] or ironisation of copyright law, a judo throw that uses its opponent's own weight against it.

Licencing is not sufficient for artistic freedom, it is a measure against one specific threat to artistic freedom, the over-extension of copyright. Copyleft licences are also not an end in themselves and must change over time to best protect freedom against any new threats that emerge. New restrictions on freedom such as Digital Rights Management technology did not exist when the first copyleft licences were being drawn up, and modern copyleft licences do indeed tackle them. It is the content of the threat to freedom, expressed in any form be it legal or technological or other, that the form of copyleft licences must change to match in order to protect the content of freedom.

Copyleft was designed to protect the freedom to use computer software. But it can protect freedom of speech and artistic freedom as well. Computer programs are created as texts, and are therefore copyrighted as literary works. Copyleft is a means of removing the restrictions on freedom that copyright imposes not just on software but on any fixed form of expression. Since no small part of contemporary censorship is copyright-related, copyleft can be a useful means of addressing censorship where it can be applied.

Copyleft cannot protect freedom where it does not apply. If artists wish to work from art or media that are copyrighted but not licenced, they must fall back on Fair Use.

34 <http://www.gnu.org/>.
35 <http://wikipedia.org/>.
36 A. Liu. *The Laws of Cool: Knowledge Work and the Culture of Information* (Chicago: University Of Chicago Press, 2004).
37 C. Harold. *OurSpace: Resisting the Corporate Control of Culture* (Minneapolis: University Of Minnesota Press, 2007).

If artists wish to depict objects or environments that are trademarks, there are not even licences for that at the moment. Broader reform and ongoing protection against more restrictive laws is therefore necessary; copyleft is not in itself a sufficient protection.

This also shows why art should share licences with other media rather than seeking to devise specific licences. Doing so gives artists access in return to those parts of the media that adopt copyleft. And it also makes artists' work available to critics, academics, and other artists who wish to work with it. This can help drive awareness of the artist's work, increasing their reputation and thereby the opportunities and remuneration available to them.

Copyleft for software enforces the social contract of freewheeling hacker software development, but this may be different from the social contract of fine art. The art-specific Free Art Licence[38] is based on copyleft. So is the more general (and more popular) Creative Commons BY-SA licence.[39] The only licence that attempts to enforce the social contract of a particular creative community is the Sampling Licence from Creative Commons[40] and Negativland. The Sampling Licence reflects the standards of the sampling and mash-up musical community, but it has some peculiarities, is not considered 'Free' by any common definition, and has since been deprecated by Creative Commons.

The social contract that the Sampling Licence embodies is that of Extended Fair Use.[41] This allows transformative use and sampling but not wholesale copying. This is similar to the social contracts of appropriation art and of criticism. Copyleft goes further than this, allowing copying and incorporation of the work untransformed. For music, Negativland's focus, such wholesale copying is the hallmark of the peer-to-peer filesharing culture that emerged following the release of Napster in 1999 and is now a freedom that is taken for granted by most music fans. So copyleft better fits the audience's expectations here.

The suggestion that artists should apply copyleft to their work in order to take a position on artistic freedom in society might appear to replay twentieth-century (and earlier) arguments about political commitment.[42] 'It is always with the best intentions that the worst work is done', to quote Oscar Wilde, and the effects of political voluntarism by artists range from the negligible (Surrealism) to the negative (Socialist Realism). But for artists to protect artistic freedom is not voluntarism, it is key to maintaining the possibility of new forms in art. It is a practical response to the genuine threat of censorship in old and new forms.

Collaboration

Collaboration and appropriation are ways for individuals to build on the work of others. Collaboration can be local or distributed, parallel or serial. Collaborators working together at the same geographical location are local collaborators, those working over the internet or meeting only occasionally and otherwise working apart are distributed. Collaboration by a group of people on work at the same time is parallel collaboration, collaboration on a series of revisions of that work over time is serial collaboration, which is also a way of describing appropriation.

The Surrealist drawing game 'exquisite corpse' is local serial collaboration, collaborative projects like GNU and Wikipedia are distributed parallel collaboration. Appropriation and critique are distributed serial collaboration.

38 <http://artlibre.org/licence/lalgb.html>.
39 <http://creativecommons.org/licenses/by-sa/3.0/>.
40 <http://creativecommons.org/about/sampling>.
41 Negativland, 'Two Relationships to a Cultural Public Domain', *Law and Contemporary Problems* 66 (Winter 2003), 239–62, < https://scholarship.law.duke.edu/lcp/vol66/iss1/9/>.
42 A. Arato and E. Gephardt (eds), *The Essential Frankfurt School Reader* (London: Continuum, 1997).

Participation is what people generally mean when they say that a project or community is 'open'. People from outside the core of the project can join in and contribute to it. People can join the community without onerous membership tests. Participation does not necessarily mean collaboration, and participation does not in itself guarantee freedom.

It is possible for a group of collaborators to be closed to new members or external collaboration. Any pair or group of artists who collaborate privately do not have a participatory practice.

It is possible for a project to be participatory without being collaborative. Social networking sites such as Facebook allow people to participate without necessarily collaborating on projects.

Successful projects have strong social contracts. The existing social contract for art is more similar to Negativland's concept of extended fair use[43] than to copyleft. Copyleft is not a match for this but it is a superset of this, and (fine) art objects cannot be replaced by electronic copies of the original.

Collaboration thrives when collaborators know that they will remain free to use the products of their collaboration. Wikipedia and GNU protect this social contract through their licences. The best way of signalling to potential collaborators that their freedom will be protected is to use such a licence. One needn't necessarily be planning to collaborate in order for such licences to be useful. Finished work released into the world under such a licence makes the work of appropriation and critique easier.

It is possible to organise collaboration without respecting the freedom of collaborators. Corporate 'user generated content' initiatives that take copyright from contributors in return for the possibility of a prize remove the freedom of contributors to use their own work. Lawrence Lessig calls this 'sharecropping'.[44] Projects that deny participants commercial use of their own work have the same effect. And people who come to projects complaining that if only the licence was changed they'd be able to use it in a way that excludes its creators are wannabe 'free riders' from their own, economic, point of view and so should be ignored.

Wikipedia is a project to collaboratively create an encyclopaedia usable by anyone via the internet. The site is licenced under a copyleft licence, meaning that anyone can add to or use it as long as they don't prevent anyone else from using it. There was another project to create an online encyclopaedia that predated Wikipedia, the h2g2 project,[45] but that was not a freely usable project and as a result ultimately failed both commercially and in terms of popularity.

Voluntary collaboration is not anti-individualistic, despite the charge levelled at Wikipedia by Jaron Lanier, namely that it amounts to a collectivist 'digital Maoism'.[46] Individuals can pursue their own ends within a supportive structure and thereby both add value to and receive value from that structure as a whole. But the value of both individual contributions and the structure as a whole can be lost if all contributions are accepted without evaluation or if the project succumbs to structurelessness.[47] The online

43 Negativland, 'Two Relationships'.

44 See L. Lessig, 'Lucasfilm's Phantom Menace', *Washington Post*, 12 July 2007, <http://www.washingtonpost.com/wp-dyn/content/article/2007/07/11/AR2007071101996.html>.

45 <http://h2g2.com/>.

46 J. Lanier, 'Digital Maoism: The Hazards of the New Online Collectivism', *Edge*, 29 May 2006, <https://www.edge.org/conversation/jaron_lanier-digital-maoism-the-hazards-of-the-new-online-collectivism>.

47 J. Freeman, 'The Tyranny of Structurelessness', <https://www.jofreeman.com/joreen/tyranny.htm>.

collaborative literary project 'A Million Penguins' is a classic example of the incoherence that can result from this.[48]

The community arts project Remix Reading ran workshops, accepted contributions through its website,[49] and assembled exhibitions curated from the results in local arts venues. Various student shows run by chapters of freeculture.org[50] followed the Remix Reading model, using the image sharing site flickr[51] to accept contributions and then curating shows both in the real world and in the virtual reality environment Second Life.[52]

These are mostly collaborative exhibitions of free work (and some non-free work under other Creative Commons licences—see the website Freedom Defined[53] for a good list of free licences), rather than works created collaboratively, although some appropriation and remix art was included. This is a good model for supporting and promoting the production of freely licenced artworks.

When considering collaborative production of work, one of the most successful examples from the world of software development is the Linux kernel. Anyone can submit work to be included in the project, anyone can discuss work that is submitted, but submissions are only included in the central repository for the project after evaluation by the project's leaders. Anyone can view that repository, but the project's leadership controls the release of official versions. This ensures both that value can be accepted and included from outside the project, and that substandard work and reworking of the project cannot get into the project or become associated with it.

It is easy to see how this model maps onto the collaborative art shows mentioned above, but finding evaluation criteria for the collaborative production of individual artworks or series of artworks is a difficult challenge. The collaborative image-making website Kollabor8[54] avoids this problem by allowing each image to be forked from any previous version of an image and the resulting new image that is based on it to be chosen by the audience.

There are more examples of artistic collaboration than might be imagined. Any artistic duo is involved in a collaborative practice. Licencing protects both the freedom of other members of society to appropriate and critique work produced by such artists and that of the artists themselves to do so should their association end.

Individual artists producing what they regard as finished works can support the ability of artists and critics to learn from, comment on, and build on their work with copyleft licencing. This helps anyone whose work might promote the artist. It also encourages and enables collaborations and uses of the work that could not have been predicted by the artist but may be of unique value to art and to society.

Economies

Eric Raymond describes the culture of Open Source as a 'Gift Economy'.[55] Again, this is a product of freedom and cannot be substituted for or sustained without it. The concept of gift economies comes from Marcel Mauss's work in anthropology in the first half of the twentieth century.[56]

48 K. Pullinger, 'Living with A Million Penguins: Inside the Wiki-Novel', *The Guardian*, 12 March 2007, <https://www.theguardian.com/books/booksblog/2007/mar/12/livingwithamillionpenguins>.
49 <http://www.remixreading.org>, now inactive.
50 <http://freeartshows.org>, now inactive.
51 <http://flickr.com/photos/sharingisdaring2006/>.
52 <http://www.freeartshows.org/shows/past>.
53 <http://freedomdefined.org/>.
54 <http://www.kollabor8.org/>.
55 Raymond, *The Cathedral and the Bazaar.*
56 M. Mauss. *The Gift: The Form and Reason for Exchange in Archaic Societies* (London: Routledge, 2001).

In a gift economy, gifts are given with strong social expectations that gifts will be received in return. It is this social contract that people exposed to the idea of gift economies often forget, regarding gifts as (economically irrational) random acts of kindness when in fact they are more like the enforced sharing of alternative licences (law being a way of enforcing society's norms between strangers).

The free sharing of ideas and iconography in art is a kind of immaterial gift economy. Making a physical gift economy of art can be an interesting commentary on the materialism of the art world even in the era of relational art, and is a good investment in reputation.

Free Documenta and various solo projects organized by Sal Randolph[57] offer some good examples of creating a physical gift economy. These include organising a global day of events with artists giving away prints of artworks or producing hundreds of blue paintings. Although they may appear to be random acts of kindness, they do make a certain demand upon their audience, namely that they temporarily reject the established economic and social relations of the art world. Against the backdrop of the global art market, that is no small demand.

Randolph and her collaborators are giving away works and reproductions of works that have cost money to produce. But the freedom to share reproductions of work electronically via the internet reduces the value of copies of easily digitised and reproduced work to almost zero.

The music and movie industries have panicked in response to this, and have reacted with lawsuits and intrusive propaganda to people who advertise their work for free by sharing it. There is no evidence that they are reacting to a genuine threat or that their actions are affecting people's willingness to share.

The gift of near-zero-cost reproductions of recordings of work is not lost revenue, it is promotion. Artists do not make most of their money from selling reproductions of their work, any more than musicians do. Both make their money by playing live (residency and show fees, public art fees), private gigs (commissions) and merchandise (prints and editions of physical artworks, deluxe or personalised recordings or photographs of performances).

Perhaps in order to address such concerns, Creative Commons do provide a pseudo-copyleft licence that only allows non-commercial (NC) use, which might appear to protect artists against economic exploitation. But it allows peer-to-peer sharing of work, which the content industry claims is the major source of their loss of revenue, and individuals can print or paint their own copies of work shared in this way.

NC prevents the artist of the original work from using any downstream reworkings of their piece commercially without negotiations, which may be unsuccessful. Copyleft in itself is a stronger disincentive to people who wish to simply exploit work without giving anything in return, and NC allows verbatim copying anyway. It discourages critique and thereby promotion. And it prevents artists from recovering the costs incurred in creating derivative works.[58] NC is seductive but ultimately self-defeating.

To quote book publisher Tim O'Reilly, 'Obscurity is a far greater threat to authors and creative artists than piracy'.[59] The internet is an excellent tool for fighting obscurity and creating opportunities to build reputation, and reputation is key to making a living as an artist. Artists do not generally make a living from selling reproductions of their

57 See S. Randolph, 'Free Words to Free Manifesta: Some Experiments in Art as Gift', <https://www.salrandolph.com/art-as-gift>.

58 Negativland. *Negativland's Tenets of Free Appropriation*, 1998, <https://web.archive.org/web/19981201050225/http://negativland.com/riaa/tenets.html>.

59 T. O'Reilly. 'Piracy is Progressive Taxation, and Other Thoughts on the Evolution of Online Distribution', 2002, <http://www.openp2p.com/pub/a/p2p/2002/12/11/piracy.html>.

work, and if they do they can compete on the basis of the quality and authenticity of those reproductions (forged signatures tend to be fairly worthless).

Reputation as capital leads naturally to the idea of a 'reputation economy'. But there is no neat split between a reputation economy and the cash economy that an artist's reputation impacts on. And it is a mistake to try to protect the cash value of an artist's work while they are building a reputation that will increase the value of that work until such time as it can be sold to a traditional middleman.

The internet has proved to be a boon for artists, providing means of networking, selling work, and discussing and learning about art globally. From community sites such as Furtherfield[60] and Rhizome[61] to commercial sites such as Saatchi's YourGallery[62] and listings sites such as ArtInfo,[63] the internet has provided new opportunities.

Unlike recorded music, electronic images of artworks are not a substitute for most artworks, rather they promote the original. An artist and blogger like Joy Garnett, whose paintings draw on media imagery under the American Fair Use doctrine, can place high-resolution images of her paintings online[64] without fearing that they will be taken by any potential collector as a substitute for buying the original.

Performance, installation, and sculpture are unlikely to be affected by electronic copying of images either. Work that is created as electronic images, as video, or as software might appear to be more at risk, but as Matthew Barney's Cremaster Cycle shows, it is perfectly possible to sell limited editions of infinitely reproducible art.

Attempts led by the music and motion picture industries to restrict how the internet can be used, like government and lobby group attempts to block 'undesirable' content on the internet, are censorship in its expanded sense (and in its traditional sense, where governments are involved). They provide no benefit to artists and will harm both artists and society's ability to benefit from the new possibilities that the internet affords.

Artists can play an important part in showing that there are substantial uses for the internet that do not involve what its opponents call 'piracy'. And they can gain economically from the internet whether financially or reputationally.

Conclusion

Artists are not being distracted by external demands of political commitment when they take on issues of cultural freedom. They are exemplars. Free art, a free culture, is of vital importance for a free society. This freedom may result in commons-based peer production, gift economies, reputation economies, increased efficiency and higher quality. But it is important not to confuse the incidental effects of an ideology with its principles. It is these principles that artists should pursue.

It is important to avoid repeating the mistakes of Open Source when doing so:

- Start from 'Free Software Free Society' and 'Free Culture', not 'The Cathedral And The Bazaar'.
- Don't try to organise your organisation in an 'Open Source' way. That methodology is for content, not structure.
- Don't try to emulate early Wikipedia's world-writeability. Emulate the meritocratic Linux Kernel development model that Wikipedia is slowly coming to resemble instead.
- Don't be afraid of matters of principle. Renaming 'Free Software' to 'Open Source' has cost the people who did so access to the biggest software market in the US, as the military are far more comfortable with 'freedom' than they are with 'openness'.

60 <http://www.furtherfield.org/>.
61 <http://www.rhizome.org/>.
62 <http://www.saatchi-gallery.co.uk/yourgallery/>.
63 <http://www.artinfo.com/>.
64 <http://www.firstpulseprojects.com/joy-work.html>.

There are many ways in which artists can apply the lessons of Free Software to art:

- Artists should become familiar with the concept of artistic freedom, the contemporary status of censorship, and how to protect the former against the latter.
- Artists should campaign to oppose the extension of copyright or trademark law and the reduction of fair use. Where there are opportunities to lobby for extended Fair Use (such as the Gowers Report in the UK in 2007), artists should make sure their voices are heard.
- Artists should use copyleft licensing to ensure the free circulation of ideas. If the sale of reproductions of work is a concern, investigate services that sell reproductions and experiment with releasing fewer works under a copyleft licence rather than more works under restrictive licences.
- Artists who are interested to do so can investigate the use of collaborative project management.
- Artists who are interested to do so should produce work to show the value of fair use and the public domain.
- Artists who are interested to do so should challenge copyright maximalists and censors by using mass media imagery and transgressive imagery.
- Artists should use Free Software and free (or 'open') file formats for accessibility, and help drive improvement of them.

Applying these concepts to art is neither Digital Maoism nor economic irrationality, but an ethical and social stance against the censorious restrictions that threaten to harm art's continued freedom.

Data-Driven Artists and Their Critics

Jonas Lund's *The Fear of Missing Out* (2013) is a series of gallery art objects made by the artist following the instructions of a piece of software they have written.[1] It has gained attention following a *Huffington Post* article entitled 'Controversial New Project Uses Algorithm to Predict Art'.[2]

Art fabricated by an artist following a computer-generated specification is nothing new. Prior to modern 2D and 3D printing techniques, transcribing a computer-generated design into paint or metal by hand was the only way to present artworks that pen plotters or CNC mills couldn't capture. But a Tamagotchi-gamer or Amazon Mechanical Turk-style human servicing of machine agency in which a program dictates the conception of an artwork for a human artist to realise also has a history. The principles involved go back even further to the use of games of chance and other automatic techniques in Dada and Surrealism.

What is novel about *The Fear of Missing Out* is that the program dictating the artworks is doing so based on a database derived from data about artworks, art galleries, and art sales. This is the aesthetic of 'Big Data', although in this case it is not a big dataset by the usual definition of the term.[3] Neither the program's source nor the database are publicly available, but assuming that it functions as specified, the description of the program in the *Huffington Post* article is complete enough that we could reverse engineer it. To do so, we would scrape Art Sales Index and/or Artsy and pull out keywords from entries to populate a database keyed on artist, gallery, and sales details. Then we would generate text from those details that match a desired set of criteria such as gallery size and desired price of artwork.

What's interesting about the text described in the *Huffington Post* article is that it's imperative and specific: 'Place the seven minute fifty second video loop in the coconut soap'. How was the instruction generated? Descriptions of artworks in art world data sites describe their appearance and occasionally their construction, not how to assemble them. If the instruction is a grammatical transformation of scraped description text, then that fits the description of the project, but if it's hand-assembled, then it's not just a database that has been 'scraped into existence'. How was the length of time generated? If there's a module to generate durations then that doesn't fit the description of the project, but if it's a reference to an existing 7'50" video, then it does.

1 <https://jonaslund.com/works/the-fear-of-missing-out/>.

2 M. Rao, 'Controversial New Project Uses Algorithm to Predict Art', *The Huffington Post*, 11 May 2013, <https://www.huffpost.com/entry/jonas-lund-art-algorithm_n_4214211>.

3 J. Manyika et al., 'Big Data: The Next Frontier for Innovation, Competition, and Productivity', McKinsey Global Institute, May 2011, <https://web.archive.org/web/20130723065804/http://www.mckinsey.com/insights/business_technology/big_data_the_next_frontier_for_innovation>.

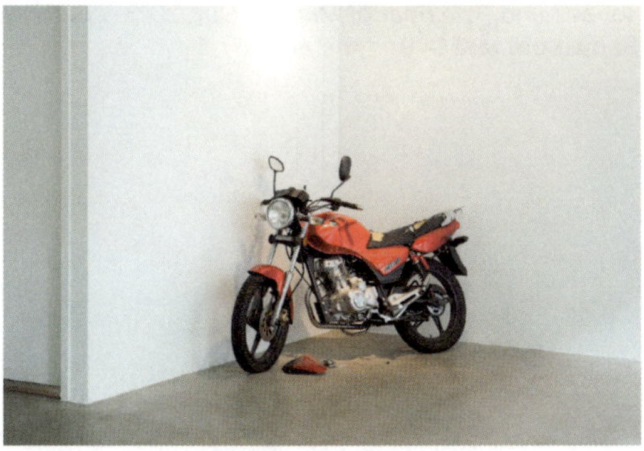

Jonas Lund, *The Fear of Missing Out*, 2013.
Courtesy Showroom MAMA and the artist.

The pleasant surprises in the output that Lund says they would not have thought of but find inspiring are explained by Edward de Bono-style creativity theory. And contemporary art oeuvres tend to be materially random enough that the randomness of the works produced has the appearance of moments in such an oeuvre. Where the production differs both from corporate big data approaches and contemporary artist-as-brand approaches is that production is not outsourced. Lund makes the art that they use data to specify.

Later, the *Huffington Post* article mentions the difficulty of targeting specific artists. A Damien Hirst artwork specification generator would be easy enough to create for artworks that resemble his existing oeuvre. Text generators powered by Markov chains were used as a tool for parodying Usenet trolls, and their strength lies in the predictability of the obsessed. Likewise, postmodern buzzword generators and paper title generators parody the *idées fixes* of humanities culture.

The output of such systems resembles the examples that they are derived from. But pivoting to a new stage in an artist's career is something that would require a different approach. It's possible to move, logically, to conceptual opposites using Douglas Hofstadter's approaches.[4] In the case of Hirst, cheap and common everyday materials (office equipment) become expensive and exclusive ones (diamonds) and animal remains become human ones.

This principle reaches its cliometric zenith in Colin Martindale's book *The Clockwork Muse: The Predictability of Artistic Change.*[5] It's tempting to dismiss the idea that artistic change occurs in regular cycles as the aesthetic equivalent of Kondratieff Waves, s ince Kondratieff Waves are dismissed by mainstream economics. But proponents of both theories claim empirical backing for their observations.

In contrast to *The Fear of Missing Out*'s private database and the proprietary APIs of art market sites, there is a move towards Free (as in freedom)[6] or Open Data for art institutions. The Europeana project to release metadata for European cultural

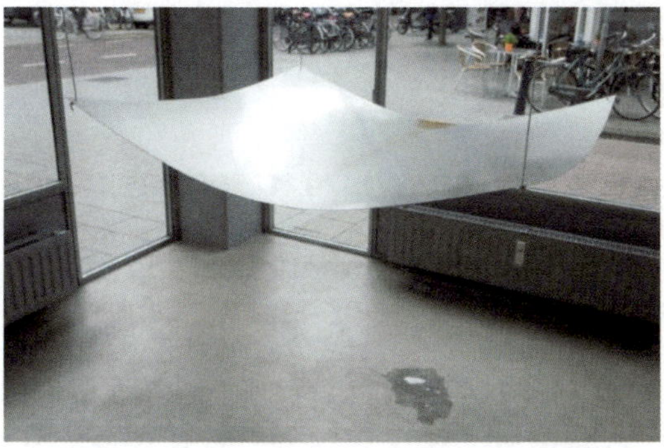

Jonas Lund, *The Fear of Missing Out*, 2013.
Courtesy Showroom MAMA and the artist.

4 <https://en.wikipedia.org/wiki/Fluid_Concepts_and_Creative_Analogies>.
5 C. Martindale, *The Clockwork Muse: The Predictability of Artistic Change* (New York: Basic Books, 1990).
6 <https://www.gnu.org/philosophy/free-sw.en.html>.

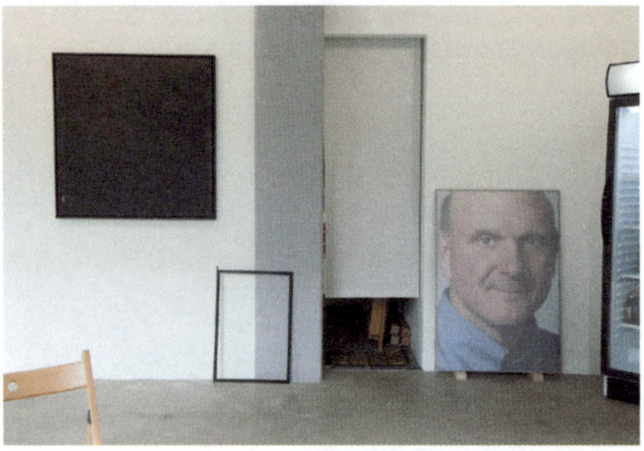

Jonas Lund, *The Fear of Missing Out*, 2013. Courtesy Showroom MAMA and the artist.

collections as linked open data has successfully released data from over two thousand institutions across the EU. The Getty Foundation has put British institutions that jealously guard their nebulously copyrighted photographs of old art to shame by releasing almost five thousand images freely. And most recently the Tate gallery in the UK has released its collection metadata under the free (as in freedom) CC0 license.

Shardcore's *Machine Imagined Artworks* (2013) uses the Tate collection metadata to make descriptions of possible artworks.[7] Compared to the data-driven approach of *The Fear of Missing Out*, *Machine Imagined Artworks* is a more traditional generative program using unconstrained randomness to choose its materials from within the constrained conceptual space of the Tate data's material and subjects ontologies.

Randomness is ubiquitous but often frowned upon in generative art circles. It gives good results but lacks intention or direction. Finding more complex choice methods is often a matter of rapidly diminishing returns, though. And *Machine Imagined Artworks* makes explicit the status of each generated piece as a set of coordinates in conceptual

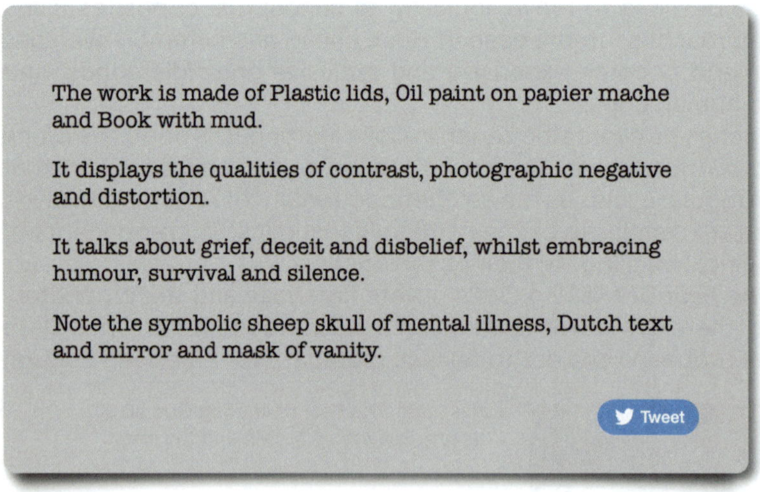

Eric Drass aka Shardcore, *Machine Imagined Artworks*, 2013. Software. Courtesy the artist (shardcore.org).

space by numbering that piece as one of the 88,577,208,667,721,179,117,706,090,119,168 possible artworks that can be generated from the Tate data.

Machine Imagined Artworks describes the formal, intentional, and critical schema of an artwork. This reflects the demands placed on contemporary art and artists to fit the ideology both of the art world and of academia, as captured in the structure of the Tate metadata. It makes a complete description of an artwork under such a view. The extent to which such a description seems incomplete is the extent to which the artwork presenting it is critical of that view.

7 <http://www.shardcore.org/shardpress2019/2013/11/12/machine-imagined-artworks-2013/>.

We could use the output of *Machine Imagined Artworks* to choose 3D models from Thingiverse to mash-up. Automating this would remove human artists from the creative process, allowing the machines to take their jobs as well. The creepy fetishisation of art objects as quasi-subjects rather than human communication falls apart here. There is no 'there' there in such a project, no agency for the producer or the artwork to have. This is the uncanny of the new aesthetic.

Software that directs or displaces an artist operationalises (if we must) their skills or (more realistically) replaces their labour, making them partially or wholly redundant. Dealing in this software while maintaining a position as an artist represents this crisis but does not embody it, since the artist is still employed as an artist.

Even when the robots take artists' jobs, art critics will still have work to do, unless software can replace them as well. There is a website of Markov-chain-generated texts in the style of the Art & Language collective's critical writing at <http://artandlanguage.co.uk/> (see below, 145), presumably as a parody of their distinctive verbal style. Art & Language's painting *Gustave Courbet's 'Burial at Ornans' Expressing...* (1981) illustrates some of the problems that arbitrary assemblage of material and conceptual materials cause, and the limitations of both artistic intent and critical knowledge. The Markov-chain-written

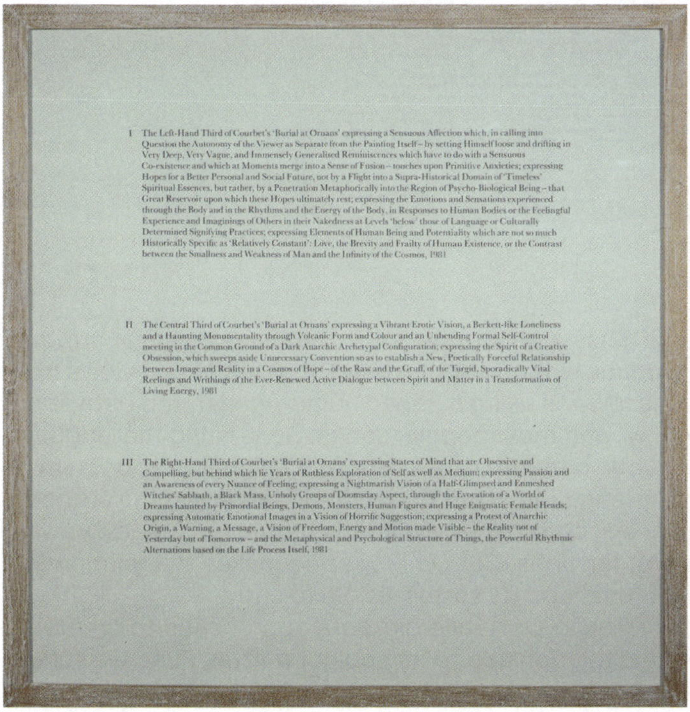

Art & Language, *Gustave Courbet's Burial at Ornans.../Expressing a Vibrant Erotic Vision .../ Expressing States of Mind that are Vivid and Compelling*, 1981. Ink and crayon on paper mounted on canvas, 4 sections overall. Sections 1–3, each section 324 × 233 cm, overall dimensions 324 × 699 cm, Section 4 (shown), framed text, 122 × 122 cm. Installation, Galerie de Paris, France, 1981 (A&L8100001).

texts in their style suffer from the weakness of such approaches. Meaning and syntax evaporate as you read past the first few words. The critic still has a job.

Or do they? Algorithmic criticism also has a history that goes back several decades, to James Gips and George Stiny's *Algorithmic Aesthetics*.[8] It is currently a hot topic in the Digital Humanities, for example with Stephen Ramsay's book *Reading Machines: Toward an Algorithmic Criticism* (2011).[9] The achievements covered by each book are modest, but demonstrate the possibility of algorithmic critique. The problem with algorithmic critique is that it may not share our aesthetics, as the ST5 antenna shows.

8 J. Gips and G. Stiny, *Algorithmic Aesthetics: Computer Models for Criticism and Design in the Arts* (Berkeley, CA: University of California Press, 1990).

9 S. Ramsay, *Reading Machines: Toward an Algorithmic Criticism* (Champaign, IL: University of Illinois Press, 2011).

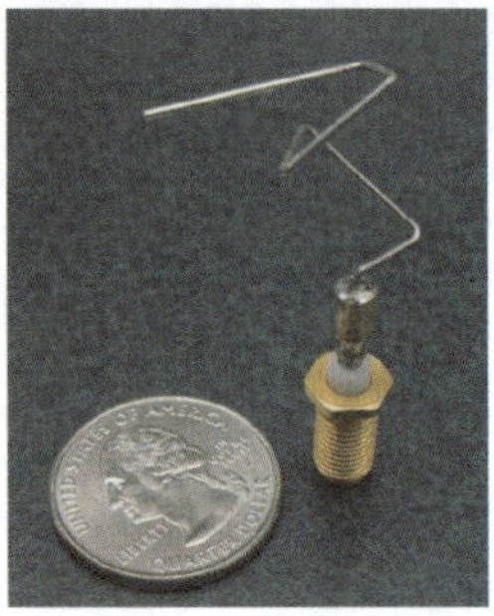

The X-Band Antenna of the ST5 Satellite. Image: NASA

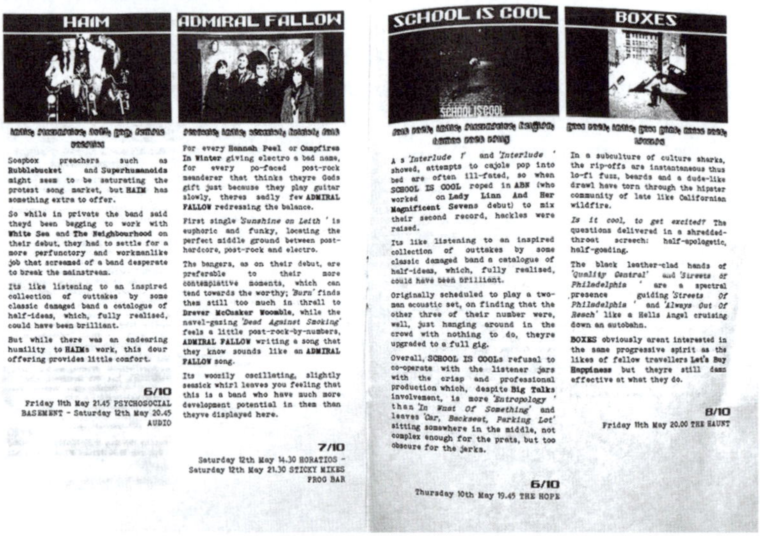

HAIM

Soapbox preachers such as **Rubblebucket** and **Superhumanoids** might seem to be saturating the protest song market, but **HAIM** has something extra to offer.

So while in private the band said theyd been begging to work with **White Sea** and **The Neighbourhood** on their debut, they had to settle for a more perfunctory and workmanlike job that screamed of a band desperate to break the mainstream.

Its like listening to an inspired collection of outtakes by some classic damaged band a catalogue of half-ideas, which, fully realised, could have been brilliant.

But while there was an endearing humility to **HAIMs** work, this dour offering provides little comfort.

6/10

Friday 11th May 21.45 PSYCHOSOCIAL BASEMENT - Saturday 12th May 20.45 AUDIO

ADMIRAL FALLOW

For every **Hannah Peel** or **Campfires In Winter** giving electro a bad name, for every po-faced post-rock meanderer that thinks theyre Gods gift just because they play guitar slowly, theres sadly few **ADMIRAL FALLOW** redressing the balance.

First single *'Sunshine on Leith '* is euphoric and funky, locating the perfect middle ground between post-hardcore, post-rock and electro.

The bangers, as on their debut, are preferable to their more contemplative moments, which can tend towards the worthy; *'Burn'* finds them still too much in thrall to **Drever McCusker Woomble**, while the navel-gazing *'Dead Against Smoking'* feels a little post-rock-by-numbers, **ADMIRAL FALLOW** writing a song that they know sounds like an **ADMIRAL FALLOW** song.

Its woozily oscillating, slightly seasick whirl leaves you feeling that this is a band who have much more development potential in them than theyve displayed here.

7/10

Saturday 12th May 14.30 HORATIOS - Saturday 12th May 21.30 STICKY MIKES FROG BAR

SCHOOL IS COOL

A s *'Interlude I'* and *'Interlude '* showed, attempts to cajole pop into bed are often ill-fated, so when **SCHOOL IS COOL** roped in **ABN** (who worked on **Lady Linn And Her Magnificent Sevens** debut) to mix their second record, hackles were raised.

Its like listening to an inspired collection of outtakes by some classic damaged band a catalogue of half-ideas, which, fully realised, could have been brilliant.

Originally scheduled to play a two-man acoustic set, on finding that the other three of their number were, well, just hanging around in the crowd with nothing to do, theyre upgraded to a full gig.

Overall, **SCHOOL IS COOLs** refusal to co-operate with the listener jars with the crisp and professional production which, despite **Big Talks** involvement, is more *'Entropology '* than *'In Wnat Of Something'* and leaves *'Car, Backseat, Parking Lot'* sitting somewhere in the middle, not complex enough for the prats, but too obscure for the jerks.

6/10

Thursday 10th May 19.45 THE HOPE

BOXES

In a subculture of culture sharks, the rip-offs are instantaneous thus lo-fi fuzz, beards and a dude-like drawl have torn through the hipster community of late like Californian wildfire.

Is it cool, to get excited? The questions delivered in a shredded-throat screech: half-apologetic, half-goading.

The black leather-clad hands of *'Quality Control'* and *'Streets of Philadelphia '* are a spectral presence guiding *'Streets Of Philadelphia '* and *'Always Out Of Reach'* like a Hells Angel cruising down an autobahn.

BOXES obviously arent interested in the same progressive spirit as the likes of fellow travellers **Let's Buy Happiness** but theyre still damn effective at what they do.

8/10

Friday 11th May 20.00 THE HAUNT

Eric Drass aka Shardcore, *Cut Up Magazine*, 2012. Photo: Eric Drass.

Shardcore's Cut Up Magazine (2012) is a generative critic that uses a similar strategy to *The Fear of Missing Out* to produce writing about a band. It assembles reviews from snippets of a database of existing reviews using scraped human-generated data about the band such as their name, genre, and most popular songs. Generating the language of critique in this way implies a subtle critique of its status and its effects upon both its producers and its consumers. The language of critique is predictable, and the authority granted to critics by their audience accords a certain status to that language. Drawing upon and returned to the world of fanzines, *Cut Up Magazine* makes the relationship between the truth of critique, its form, and its status visible to critique.

We can use *The Fear of Missing Out*-style big-data approaches to create critique that has a stronger semantic relationship to its subject matter. First, we scrape an art review blog to populate a database of text and images. Next, we train an image classifier (a piece of software that tells you whether, for example, an image contains a Soviet tank or a cancer cell or not) and a text search engine on this database. Then we use sentiment analysis software (the kind of system that tells airlines whether tweets about them are broadly positive or negative) to generate a score of one to five stars for each review and store this in the database.

We can now use this database to find the artworks that are most similar in appearance and description to those that have already been reviewed. This allows us to generate a critical comment about them and assign them a score. Following current publishing trends, we can then make a list of the results. The machines can indeed take the critic's job as well, as I have previously argued.

What pieces like *The Fear of Missing Out* and *Machine Imagined Artworks* make visible is an aspect of How Things Are Done Now and how this affects everyone, regardless of the nature of their work—in this case, 'big data being used to guide the organisation'. To regard such projects simply as parody or as playacting is to take a reductively literary approach to art. But art doesn't need to resolve itself into neat categories in order to function, and may provide stronger affordances to thought if it doesn't. What's interesting is both how much such an approach misses and how much it does capture. As ever, art both reveals and symbolically resolves the aporia of (in this case the Californian) ideology.

2013

The Proletarianisation of Art Criticism

Book and film reviews have been reduced to individual data points on aggregator websites as print journalism collapses. It's only a matter of time before such big data/ collective intelligence approaches expand to cover art criticism.

The aggregation and statistical analysis of art reviews will complete the proletarianisation of art criticism. Art critics will be alienated from the products of their labour, and their value will accrue to the ruling class of the walled gardens of the internet under their identity and reputation. The institutions that legitimate and monetise art criticism will be outside of academia and inside the market.

Art critics can react to this in two ways.

The first is to try to restore their status by becoming part of that ruling class, going meta with their own aggregation and big data efforts. This is like humanities computing (or Digital Humanities, as it's been rebranded) in much the same way that Google is like grep.

The second is to attempt to resist proletarianisation. Gonzo art criticism, free-and-open-source-criticism, engagement with Maker culture and the production of objects, any means of producing art criticism that is resistant to or that benefits from being the subject of monetisation-through-aggregation.

In either case, this will be the end of the crisis of art criticism, as it will be the end of art criticism in its current autonomous form.

Computers and Capital: The Rise of Digital Currency

Bitcoin is the leading cryptographic digital currency. Created in 2009 by the hacker Satoshi Nakamoto, it polarises opinion. Some promote it as the technical embodiment of a libertarian attack on the iniquity of 'fiat currency' and the power of the state and big banks, an embodiment of a pure market of value untainted by regulation where everything really is worth only what people will pay for it. Others criticise Bitcoin, often savagely, for the same reasons, and for what they perceive as its technical and social failings. But Bitcoin is interesting in ways that go beyond the concerns of its most vocal proponents and detractors.

Rather than paper money backed by gold or electronic money held on a bank's central mainframe, Bitcoin exists as records of transactions in a public record called the blockchain, which is added to and authenticated by computers on the internet running the Bitcoin software. Transactions in Bitcoin use cryptographic signatures rather than names or emails as the identities of the sender and receiver. Computers on the network that process and validate groups (or 'blocks') of transactions are asserting the existence of particular pieces of data at the time they are validated, a process rewarded by the production of new Bitcoins. To discourage malicious or false validations, each mining computer must perform a computationally and therefore resource-expensive task known as a 'proof of work', which can be checked and confirmed by other computers on the network.

All of this means that Bitcoin is a massively distributed system for asserting identity, existence, and truth, for values of those concepts that are outsourced to a community of mathematical proxies. The blockchain is essentially a time-stamped record of information that anyone can add to in order to prove that a particular piece of data existed at a particular time. This has applications beyond finance, with examples of new systems for blogging, contracts, corporations and internet domain name services all being based on the blockchain system. In many ways it is the blockchain and these applications of it that are the most exciting part of Bitcoin.

Money, cryptography (the making and breaking of codes) and alternative currencies all have long histories, which have often been intertwined. Renaissance banks used secret codes to secure messages sent between city-states. Alternative savings or currency systems such as Green Shield Stamps, LETS, and Air Miles were all popular at different times during the twentieth century. The first cryptographic digital currency was Digicash, from 1990. And Bitcoin isn't the first multi-million-dollar electronic currency. Linden Dollars, the virtual currency used in the Second Life online virtual reality environment, were used in US$567m worth of economic activity in 2009. Bitcoin solved the problems that prevented previous digital currencies from becoming decentralised, and although newer digital currencies have improved on its design, it is Bitcoin that has captured people's imaginations.

Bitcoin has encouraged debate about what money is, what money is for, and how money should work—indeed, its production, use, and successors have embodied that debate. It's created a sense of possibility and a range of production comparable to the early World Wide Web. And it's led to the launch of parodies such as the Buttcoin site, the meme-based cryptocurrency DogeCoin, and the epithet 'Dunning-Krugerrands'.

Bitcoin's mining system rewards existing capital, and its transaction costs reward intermediaries in much the same way as existing banks and credit cards do. But these are implementation details, and newer cryptocurrencies and national cryptocurrencies address them. Post-financial crisis, cryptocurrency with all its possibilities and contradictions is a lightning rod for the social imagination. And this includes art.

Coinfest 2014 in Vancouver featured examples of artists using Bitcoin. Buskers performing at the event could be tipped in Bitcoins; graffiti and mixed-media art being exhibited could be bought with Bitcoins. And in the computer lab at the venue each desktop PC displayed a piece of net art with a Bitcoin theme. This was the show *Computers and Capital*, curated by Erik H. Rzepka and Wesley Yuen, also viewable online.[1] It includes art depicting bitcoins, art visualising wealth in terms of bitcoins, and work that evokes the operation of Bitcoin-like cryptocurrency.

thereisaprobleminaustralia's *Bitcoin Garden* is an HTML5 A-life pond populated by shoals of rippled and faded Bitcoin logos. It's reminiscent of 1990s Director A-life, and might benefit from more of that algorithmicity. But as a post-internet tumblr assemblage it's irresistibly calming and ironic: Bitcoin's promise of a financial artificial paradise rendered organic, or hydraulic models of the economy leaking into the network.

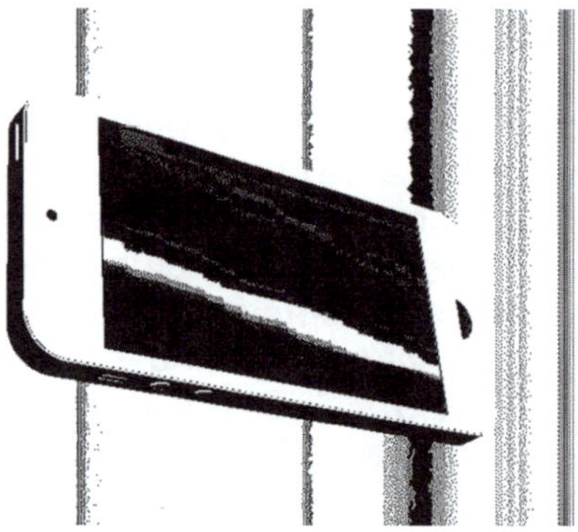

Jon Cates, *jonCates bitcrushes MANUEL FERNANDEZ's BROKEN PHONE GRADIENTS*, 2014. Animated GIF.

Jon Cates's *jonCates bitcrushes MANUEL FERNANDEZ's BROKEN PHONE GRADIENTS* is an animated snapshot in time of the artist's web-based and discursive project-based practice. A stark monochrome iPhone spins with and in front of a glitching, broken screen, remixed/reworked from the source material, and 'bitcrushed' using old-school Floyd–Steinberg dithering. Fittingly for the show, it's available for sale for Bitcoin. Ellectra Radikal's *E.Rad Coin* is a Vasarely-meets-Twister undulating grid of distorted and colour gradient coin shapes. It's the aesthetic equivalent of Bitcoin's ethics: the market-economic view of society as Conway's Game of Life with pennies given a post-digital twist.

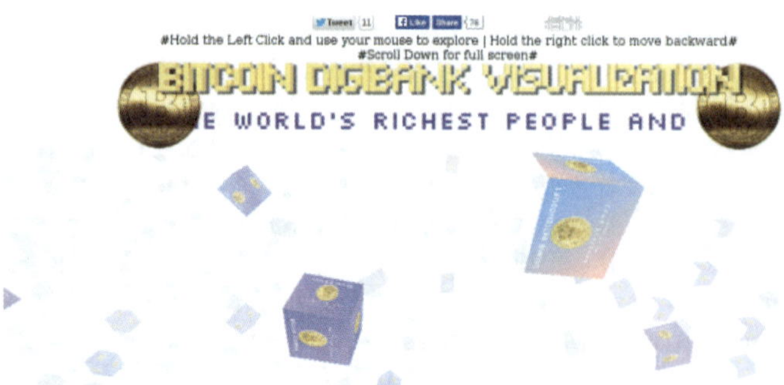

FELT, *Bitcoin Digibank Visualisation*, 2014. Website.

1 <http://www.xoxlabs.com/x/computersandcapital/>.

FELT's *Bitcoin Digibank Visualization* is a financial hyperspace of cubes showing the value of the world's rich, quantified in Bitcoins floating in an endless whiteness. This shows both Bitcoin's status as a separate economic plane and the ability of existing capital to colonise any resource-based attempt to escape its reach.

Giselle Zatonyl's *Pop Coinfalls* is a video loop of analogue noise and digital-compression-glitched falling and stacking coins with a PowerPoint-hell upward graph line animated over them. Blink and you'll miss it, but there are faces on or reflected in the gold of the (Bit)coins as they pile up ever higher. The economy is like that.

Matt Tecson's *lel buttcoin* is a tumblr blog zoom (an impressive subversion of the vertical scroll bar) of found imagery mostly on the theme of 'buttcoins', a common pejorative for Bitcoins. Coinyes, Bartcoins, and Radeon graphics cards intrude, presumably because they matched the search used to find buttcoin images.

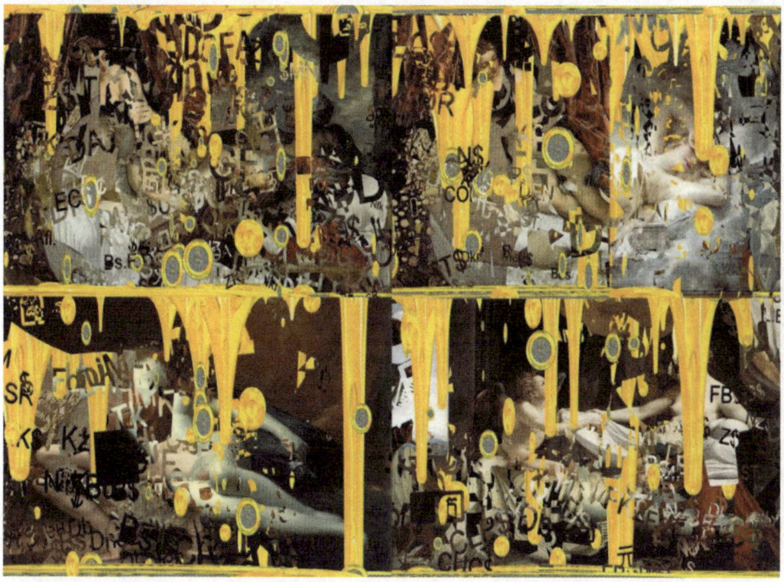

Roger Grandlapin, *Danaë*. 2014. Digital animation.

Roger Grandlapin's *Danaë* is a Flash animation of Bitcoins dripping like honey over animated negative-space text, a porny neoclassical nude of the title, and other imagery that I'm not fast enough to make out. Bitcoin's origin story is related to those of older mythology as a shower of golden rain from Satoshi Nakamoto.

Kutay Cengil's *Untitled* is a slightly glitched, default-material-rendered bust of a webcam-foreheaded, PayPal security-badged, melting financial mandarin. This is what Bitcoin is here to save us from, although in a recent interview the CEO of PayPal had more faith in Bitcoin than in Near Field Communication tags.

Systaime's *Bitcoin Abundance* is a highly compressed YouTube video loop of the dross of nineties PC video clips surrounding a rain of bitcoins. It's the opposite of Jon Cates's piece: visual vaporwave, the kind of transubstantiation of kitsch that art is meant to do. It's a formally rich composition, amusing and affecting. But even when I remove my cybercultural and net-art-historical horses from this race, I'm left with the problem that it's not clear how this aesthetic can fail.

Devon Hatto's *letsnetworth* is another tumblr, this time of animated GIFs of compositions of that symbol of knowledge (and fashionable digital design), the apple. Digitisation, sustenance, and symbolism combine here much as they do in Bitcoin. The net wealth of wealth on the net.

Adam Braffman's *$$ULOGY* is a YouTube video of Dogecoins (the inflationary, Meme-mascoted rival to Bitcoins), Super Mario Bros gameplay, burning dollars, and other found video imagery, with a brief visit from MST3K and a cheesy industrial and soft rock soundtrack interleaved with an echoing apocalyptic economic lecture. It's an impressionistic take on cryptocurrency and the environment in which it exists.

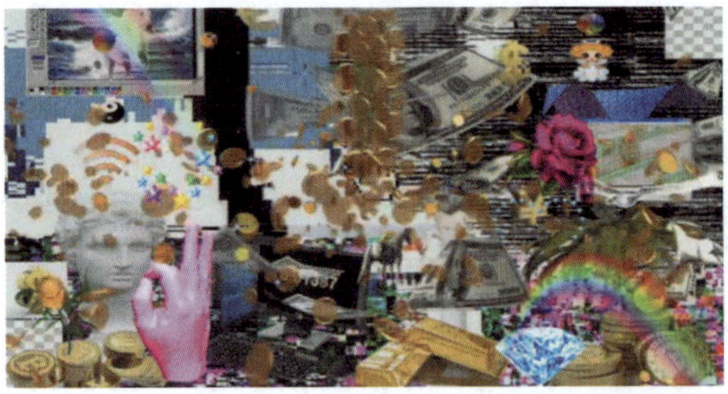

Devon Hatto, *letsnetworth*, 2014. Tumblr, animated GIFs.

Nicolas Koroloff's *Green Impact* is an image of a pile of Eurocent coins with a single transparent green bead or BB pellet in the middle. This is a reference to Bitcoin's oft-touted environmental impact owing to the electricity expended in mining. The comparison between this energy footprint and that of fiat currency ATMs, chip and pin readers, and other elements of the global banking system probably compares to the relationship depicted here.

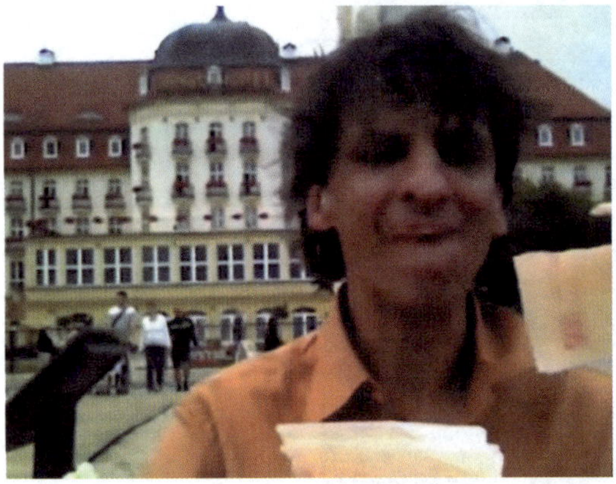

Dominik Podsiadly, *I'll eat any amount of EU subsidies*, 2014. Digital video.

Dominik Podsiadly's *I'll eat any amount of EU subsidies* is a video performance of the artist smoking, drinking, and indeed eating some large edible 500 Euro notes. The Euro is a political instrument as much as a financial one, and its crisis has been another factor driving interest in alternative currencies, including Bitcoin.

Chimerik's *Chimerikcoin* is a packed square graph puzzle that rearranges itself to fit as you drag rectangular fragments of an old gold coin around to reveal brief peaks of paper money. It's the economy as a zero-sum game and Bitcoin as a digital return to the gold standard.

Miyö Van Stenis's *Bitcoin Dreams* is an interactive HTML5 animation of settling Bitcoins in front of a cloudy sky and animated curtain. It's an unusual and effective combination of tightly looped animation and interaction with a vaporwave aesthetic.

ASS Rain's *Trees* is a collage of translucent green blocks dropped spillikins-style. I found it aesthetically and conceptually opaque, although a very effective composition. Robert B. Lisek's *Quantum Enigma* uses a Geiger counter to generate an encryption key for communication, ironically realising the promise of quantum cryptography. It's a historically and technically literate project that communicates a strong political stance while remaining technically and aesthetically interesting.

The ability to curate such a show online and present it as part of a wider cultural event marks a moment where the widespread availability of internet access, Web 2.0 publication platforms, and computer labs at event and community spaces has transformed the possibilities for curating and contextualising digital art. *Computers and Capital* exploits these affordances very effectively. The recurrent themes—pennies from heaven, ironic digital kitsch, glitchy compression artefacts, and potlatch—feel both appropriate and effective in visually communicating and critiquing the technical and social complexities of cryptocurrency in the age of austerity.

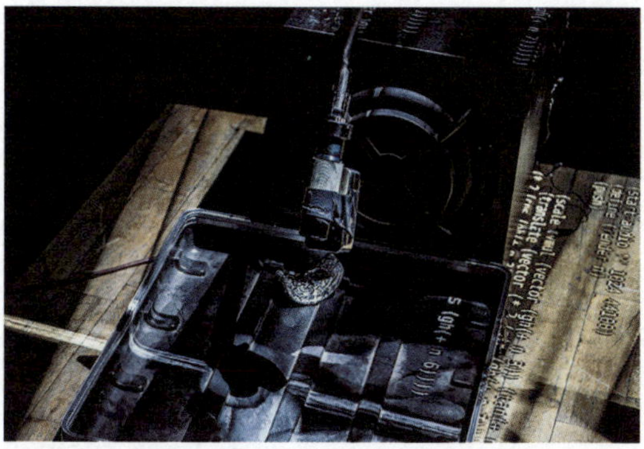

Robert B. Lisek, *Quantum Enigma*, 2013. Geiger counter, radioactive materials, software.

Bitcoin has caught the attention of the public, government, criminals, and artists. It is both an expression of the economic imaginary and a genuinely novel means of networked communication. This makes it an unusual subject for art, whether celebratory or critical. Even the most ironic celebrations of Bitcoin in art are depictions of a network protocol, or a deflationary electronic currency. Whether visually and conceptually preparing us for a brave new world of cryptocurrencies or creating the illusory realm in which they will achieve their only lasting victory, Bitcoin art is very different from a Warhol dollar sign, a Hirst diamond skull, or the other symbolic band-aids for the ideological aporia of capital's hollow victory. It is the art of a heresy rather than a hegemony, of a moment of technological, social, and aesthetic possibility.

Computers and Capital very successfully captures this moment in art and makes it accessible in ways that thousands of words on the subject cannot. A thought-provoking, illuminating, and often fun collection of work of a uniformly high standard that is nonetheless technically and aesthetically diverse can be presented online and off as part of a wider cultural event. *Computers and Capital* shows how network-enabled digital art can function as a bridge between complex and important ideas and the public imagination.

2014

Artworld Ethereum

Ethereum is a distributed computing system for writing and executing smart contracts. Inspired by Bitcoin, it's currently in development, with a planned late 2014 release date. The term 'smart contracts' was coined around 1993 by computer scientist Nick Szabo to describe computer-readable code that replaces lawyer-readable code to describe agreements and obligations between people. It's a very literal take on Lawrence Lessig's argument that 'code is law', a libertarian attempt to reduce the costs and uncertainty of having to trust human beings and interpret ambiguous human language—or possibly a dystopian replacement of rights and safeguards with binary logic.

Smart contracts can be used to implement smart property, physical goods governed by computer code, and Distributed Autonomous Organisations, which replace written constitutions with code running on Ethereum's Blockchain.

Ethereum may be applied to the production, exhibition, critique, and institutions of art—starting with digital art as smart property.

The sample code is written in Serpent, the high-level Ethereum programming language, and is current as of Ethereum POC 5. It will be revised and tested for the release version of Ethereum.

Storing and Identifying Digital Art in Ethereum

There are three cases of digital art as smart property. The first is the conceptual or code art case, where the code of the contract itself is or contains the artwork. The second is the Ethereum storage case, where a small digital artwork is stored in the Ethereum datastore. The third is the stored identifier case, where only an identifier or proxy for the artwork is stored with the contract.

Conceptual and Code Art

Contracts that are themselves art are a simple case. They should store their owner's Ethereum address and ensure that transactions initiating actions that only the owner should be able to perform come from that address.

Conceptual Art

Since art is defined by its inutility, a contract that does nothing must be art. ;-)

```
stop
```

Hot/Cold

A contract that does something, but nothing useful.

```
init:
   contract.storage[1000] = "hot"
   contract.storage[1001] = "cold"
```

```
code:
   // Make sure we have enough gas to run the contact
   if tx.value < tx.basefee * 100:
      // If not, stop
      stop
   // Swap
   temp = contract.storage[1000]
   contract.storage[1000] = contract.storage[1001]
   contract.storage[1001] = temp
```

Numbered Works

A simple generative work that creates a new, original piece for each request.

```
 init:
   ARTWORK.NUMBER.INDEX = 1001
   contract.storage[ARTWORK.NUMBER.INDEX] = 1
code:
   ARTWORK = "Work #"
   ARTWORK.NUMBER.INDEX = 1001
   // Make sure we have enough gas to run the contact
   if tx.value < tx.basefee * 400:
      // If not, stop
      stop
   // Get the number of the work to produce
   number = contract.storage[ARTWORK.NUMBER.INDEX]
   // Store the number to use for the next work
   contract.storage[ARTWORK.NUMBER.INDEX] = contract.storage[ARTWORK.NUMBER.INDEX] + 1
   // Return the work
   return([ARTWORK, number], 2)
```

Data Visualisation

A simple customised generative work/data visualisation. The output looks something like

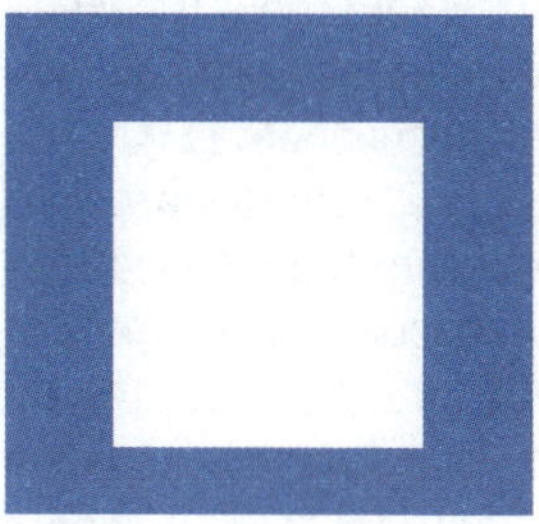

when assembled.

```
HEX = ["0", "1", "2", "3", "4", "5", "6", "7", "8", "9", "A", "B", "C", "D", "E", "F"]
ARTWORK = ["<svg><rect x="23" y="23" ", "height="123" width="123" ", "style="-
fill:none;stroke:#", ";stroke-width:32" /></svg>"]
ARTWORK.LENGTH = 10
ARTWORK.INSERT.END = 8
// Make sure we have enough gas to run the contact
if tx.value < tx.basefee * 500:
   // If not, stop
   stop
```

```
// If there are enough arguments
// and the command to create the work is being given
if msg.datasize == 1 and msg.data[0] == "create":
   artwork = array(ARTWORK.LENGTH)
   artwork[0] = ARTWORK[0]
   artwork[1] = ARTWORK[1]
   artwork[2] = ARTWORK[2]
   artwork[9] = ARTWORK[3]
   // Copy the most significant hex bytes of the key as an html colour
   index = 0
   hash.bytes = msg.sender
   while index < 3:
      current.byte = hash.bytes % 256
      hash.bytes = hash.bytes / 256
      hi = HEX[current.byte / 16]
      lo = HEX[current.byte % 16]
      artwork[ARTWORK.INSERT.END - (index * 2)] = lo
      artwork[ARTWORK.INSERT.END - (index * 2) + 1] = hi
      index = index + 1
   return(artwork, ARTWORK.LENGTH)
// Otherwise
else:
   // Logical false for failure
   return(0)
```

Stored Art

Digital art can be stored in a contract's bytecodes or permanent storage rather than generated by the contract's code.

A Stored Image

```
ARTWORK = ['P1\n32 32\n0000000000000000010000000','00000000000000000000000000010000000',
'000000000000000\n0000000001000000', '00000000000000000000000001000000', '000000000
0000000000000\n001100000', '0000000000000000000001100001010', '00001100001000000
00100000000\n00', '0101100001000000000100000000000', '0111100010000000000100000000
0001', '1111\n0001000000000001000000000011', '1111011000000000000100000000001111','1110
0010000\n0000000000000000011111', '11000000000000000001000000111111', '1100000010000
0000\n1000001111111', '110000000000000000000000000111111', '1110000001000000000000000
0\n000011', '1111100000000000000001000000000001', '111111000001000000000000000000111',
'\n1111110000000000000001000000000011', '1111110000010000000001000001111', '1111000\n
000010000000000000000111', '1111000000000000000000000100001111', '1000000000100n000
00000000001111', '1000000000001000000000000001111100', '0000000000010000000000\n00000
11100', '0000000000100000000000000101000', '000000000000000000000000000\n010', '1
0000000010100000000000000000000', '0101001010000000000000000000000', '000n0110000
0000000000000000000000', '00000100000000000000000000000000', '0000010000\n000000000
000000000000','000000100000000000000000']
ARTWORK.LENGTH = 33
// Make sure we have enough gas to run the contact
if tx.value < tx.basefee * 1000:
    // If not, stop
    stop

// If there are enough arguments
// and the command to show the work is being given
if msg.datasize == 1 and msg.data[0] == "exhibit":
```

```
        // Just return the artwork
        return(ARTWORK, ARTWORK.LENGTH)
// Otherwise
else:
        // Logical false for failure
        return(0)
```

Identifiers for Digital Art

Where a work of digital art will not fit in the blockchain, a more compact identifier must be stored in the contract and used to refer to the work instead. Ideally, a method for identifying unique instances of a digital artwork will be:

- *Stable.* The identifier should be usable for decades. Web URLs for example can change or become inaccessible as services change how they serve content or go out of business.
- *Verifiable*. The identifier should be usable as a way of verifying that a resource is the one it refers to. Cryptographic hashes for example will not work with digital images that have been resized or GPS coordinates that differ even fractionally.
- *Amendable*. Where stability fails or a change in ownership requires a change in identifier, it should be possible to update the identifier in a trusted and verifiable way.
- *Sufficient*. The information required to identify the resource should be usable directly from the contract rather than requiring external information to complete it.
- *Private*. An identifier should leak as little information about the owner of the resource as possible. For example, GPS coordinates or street addresses, while stable, do locate the resource and possibly its owner. Storing only the cryptographic hash of an identifier can mitigate this.

Some of these criteria clash and therefore any given method of identification must trade them off against each other. For example, being private and verifiable, or stable and amendable.

For artworks to interact with smart contracts, we need a way of identifying them in those contracts. Where a digital artwork is too large or complex to keep in the contract's code or storage, a proxy or compact identifier that refers to the must be used. The following identifiers have various strengths and weaknesses. We'll use some of them in the next section.

URL

A URL, such as a web site address, is a clear public identifier. It lacks privacy and is only as stable as the service hosting it, but has the advantage of being unique. To add a veneer of privacy, only the cryptographic hash of the URL can be stored by the contract and this can be checked against the hash of a URL by anyone who wishes to check whether it is the instance of the work referred to by the contract.

For example, the URL:

```
https://www.urbanomic.com/book/proof-of-work/
```

has the SHA-256 hash:

```
45ea9081ffb3d5ccd086463b37f2628d0bbe4dae9a6d38fa32fdc95392c3a3cb
```

Never use a link shortening service or a consumer third-party hosting service for work represented as URLs: such services are likely to go out of business or change their URL structure, rendering any identifiers tied to them useless. When using your own site for hosting work, make sure both both to keep your domain name registered and to keep the server running and to make provisions for them to be maintained when you are no longer able or willing to do so.

File Hash

Producing a cryptographic hash of a work contained in or represented by a file is simple and uniquely identifies the data contained by the file (although any copies of the file will have the same hash). It is better to hash the contents of the file rather than the file itself: an image that has the same pixel values as a PNG or a GIF will have a very different structure on disk in each of those formats. Likewise, the full-size or full-quality version of the contents of the file should be hashed rather than being a thumbnail or a lossy version.

Git Repository Commit Hash

Modern decentralised version control systems use cryptographic hashes to identify commits. Hashes can identify version of works in a series within a version control repository, although they are best accompanied by a URL or other identifier for the repository.

Serial Number or UUID

A serial number or unique identifier embedded in the work's filename or metadata can be used to identify it. Visible watermarks are the mark of the amateur, and steganographic watermarks are easily defeated.

Cryptographic Signing

When producing editions of a digital work, each can be signed by the artist to identify it as authorised.

Name

When all else fails, a unique name and description for a work is a useful identifier.

Art as Smart Property

A Simple Owned Work

```
OWNER = 0x7c8999dc9a822c1f0df42023113edb4fdd543266

// Get the owner Ethereum address
return(OWNER)
```

A Simple Owned Work that Confirms Ownership

```
OWNER = 0x7c8999dc9a822c1f0df42023113edb4fdd543266

// Make sure we have enough gas to run the contact
if tx.value < tx.basefee * 100:
   // If not, stop
   stop
// If the Ethereum address sent matches the owner
if msg.data[0] == OWNER:
   // Return true
   return(1)
// Otherwise
else:
   // Return false
   return(0)
```

A Simple Owned Stored Work

```
OWNER = 0×8802b7f0bfa5e9f5825f2fc708e1ad00d2c2b5d6 // Artist initially
WORK = "The art happens here."

// Make sure we have enough gas to run the contact
if tx.value < tx.basefee * 200:
   // If not, stop
   stop

// If there are enough arguments
// and the command to return the owner address is given
if msg.datasize == 1 and msg.data[0] == "owner":
   // Return the owning Ethereum address
   return(OWNER)
// If there are enough arguments
// and the command to return the artwork is given
if msg.datasize == 1 and msg.data[0] == "work":
   // Return the work
   return(WORK)
// Otherwise
else:
   // Return logical failure
   return(0)
```

A Simple Transferable Stored Work

```
init:
   ARTIST = 0×8802b7f0bfa5e9f5825f2fc708e1ad00d2c2b5d6
   OWNER = 1001
   // Initialize the owner to be the artist
   contract.storage[OWNER] = ARTIST
code:
   OWNER = 1001
   ARTWORK = "The art happens here."
   // Make sure we have enough gas to run the contact
   if tx.value < tx.basefee * 200:
      // If not, stop
      stop

   // If the message is from the current owner
   // and there are enough arguments
   // and the command to transfer is being given
   if msg.sender == contract.storage[OWNER] and msg.datasize == 2
   and msg.data[0] == "transfer":
      // Transfer it to a new owner
      contract.storage[OWNER] = msg.data[1]
      return(1)
   // If there are enough arguments and the command to show the work is being given
   else if (msg.datasize == 1):
   // Just return the artwork
   return(ARTWORK)
    // Otherwise
else:
   // Logical false for failure
    return(0)
```

```
if tx.value < tx.basefee * 200:
   // If not enough gas, stop
   stop

// If data was provided, it won't overwrite the code, and the artwork is unregis-
tered
if msg.datasize == 1 and msg.data[0] > 1000 and contract.storage[msg.data[0]] == 0:
   // Set the owner to be the sender
   contract.storage[msg.data[0]] = msg.sender
   return(1)
else:
   // Do nothing
   return(0)
```

A Hash-based Ownership Registry for Specific Instances of Digital Art

This is a registry for ownership of artworks at specific URLs. Artworks are identified by the hash of their file contents and by the hash of their URL. Owners are identified by Ethereum address.

```
if tx.value < tx.basefee * 200:
   // If not, stop
   stop

// If registration is being requested
if msg.datasize == 3 and msg.data[0] == "register":
   // If the url/work combination has not been claimed
   if ! contract.storage[msg.data[1]]:
      // Set the owner to be the provided Ethereum address
      contract.storage[msg.data[1]] = msg.sender
      // Store the artwork hash next to the url ownership information
      contract.storage[msg.data[1] + 1] = msg.data[2]
      // return success
      return(1)
   // If the sender was trying to overwrite a work they do not own
   else:
   // They cannot set it, so return failure
      return(0)
// If ownership confirmation is being requested
// Confirm that the work and url hashes match
else if msg.datasize == 4 and msg.data[0] == "confirm":
   // Check the provided hashes against the stored work and url hashes
   return((contract.storage[msg.data[2]] == msg.data[1]) and (contract.storage[msg.
data[2] + 1] == msg.data[3]))
// If no action was specified
else:
   // Otherwise do nothing
   return(0)
```

Authenticating Art in Ethereum

Authentication, like ownership, is related to identity and contract law.

A Simple Certificate of Authenticity for Digital Art

```
ARTIST = 0×8802b7f0bfa5e9f5825f2fc708e1ad00d2c2b5d6
ARTWORK.HASH = 0×76bba376ea574e63ab357b2374d1cee5aa77d24db38115e3824c5cc4f443d5f7
return((msg.data[0] == ARTIST) and (msg.data[1] == ARTWORK.HASH))

ARTIST = 0×8802b7f0bfa5e9f5825f2fc708e1ad00d2c2b5d6
WORK.HASH = 0×76bba376ea574e63ab357b2374d1cee5aa77d24db38115e3824c5cc4f443d5f7
URL.HASH = 0xa005b1625af0b6ee080dafb904c4505ad285764071ee45a8786159bd1a282634
// If there are enough arguments
if msg.datasize == 2:
   Check the provided hashes against the stored work and url hashes
   return((msg.data[0] == WORK.HASH) and (msg.data[1] == URL.HASH))
// Otherwise
else:
   // Do nothing
   stop
```

Catalogue Raisonné for Digital Artists

```
ARTIST = 0×8802b7f0bfa5e9f5825f2fc708e1ad00d2c2b5d6

// Make sure we have enough gas to run the contact
if tx.value < tx.basefee * 200:
// If not, stop
   stop

// If the message is from the artist
if msg.datasize == 1 and msg.sender == ARTIST:
   // Add the work to the catalog
   contract.storage[msg.data[0]] = 1
   return(1)
// check inclusion
else if msg.datasize == 1:
   // Check whether the artwork is in the catalog
   return(contract.storage[msg.data[0]])
// Otherwise
   else:
   return(0)
```

2014

Ethereum Art Market

Here is a contract[1] that allows you to register as the owner of a digital artwork contained in a particular file (identified by its cryptographic hash value) at a particular URL. The use of a URL is inspired by the excellent Monegraph,[2] which launched shortly after I started working on Ethereum contracts for art. Monegraph uses the existing NameCoin system, which can be implemented in Ethereum as a two-line contract.[3]

This contract is longer than that, as it's recording and managing more information. It also allows you to offer the artwork for sale (in exchange for Ether, Ethereum's built-in currency), either to a specific individual or generally, or to transfer it to a specific individual without charging them within the contract.

```
{
   (def 'next-record 0x10)(def 'RECORD-SIZE 64)
   ;; Next record position
   ;; This starts one cell above the maximum value of RipeMD
   [[next-record]] 0x10000000000000000000000000000000000000000

   (return
      0x0
      (lll
      {
         ;; Action
         ;; 0 - first cell in message
         [action] (calldataload 0)
         (when (= @action "register")
            {
               ;;TODO: Check correct message length
               ;;TODO: Check digest in range
               ;; Artwork digest
               [digest] (calldataload 32)
               ;; If already registered, don't continue
               (when @@ @digest
                  (return "Artwork already registered."))
               ;; Get storage for new record
               [storage] @@next-record
               ;; Store digest
               [[@storage]] @digest
               ;; Artist account
               [storage] (+ @storage 1)
```

1 See 'Artworld Ethereum', 82.
2 A. Dash, 'A Bitcoin for Digital Art', medium.com, <https://medium.com/message/a-bitcoin-for-digital-art-8c7db719e495>.
3 <https://eth.wiki/>.

```
        [[@storage]] (caller)
        ;; Artist resale percentage
        [storage] (+ @storage 1)
        [[@storage]] (calldataload 64)
        ;; Artist is the current owner
        [storage] (+ @storage 1)
        [[@storage]] (caller)
        ;; Skip purchaser and price
        [storage] (+ @storage 3)
        ;; Copy over the url and description
        ;; 96 is 32 × 3 = 3rd cell in message
        [source] 96
          (for [i] 6    (< @i 64) [i] (+ @i 1)
            {
            [[@storage]] (calldataload @source)
            [storage] (+ @storage 1)
            [source] (+ @source 32)
            })
        ;; Store digest-to-record link
        [[@digest]] @@next-record
        ;; Increment next record position
        [[next-record]] (+ @@next-record RECORD-SIZE)
        })
      (when (= @action "offer")
        {
          ;; TODO: Check correct message length
          ;; TODO: Check digest in range
          ;; Get artwork record storage for digest or stop
          ;; 32 = second cell in message
          [storage] @@(calldataload 32)
          (when (not @storage)
            (return "Artwork not registered."))
          ;; If the caller is the owner
          (when (= @@ (+ @storage 3) (caller))
            {
              ;; Offer subject
              [[(+ @storage 4)]] (calldataload 64)
              ;; Offer price
              [[(+ @storage 5)]] (calldataload 96)
              })
            })
          (when (= @action "accept")
            {
              ;;TODO: Check correct message length
              ;;TODO: Check digest in range
              ;;TODO: Error messages for bad price or buyer
              ;; Get artwork record storage for digest or stop
              ;; 32 = second cell in message
              [storage] @@(calldataload 32)
              (when (not @storage)
                (return "Artwork not registered."))
              [buyer] @@(+ @storage 4)
              [price] @@(+ @storage 5)
              ;; If the caller is the buyer and it's the correct payment
              ;; Or there's no buyer and it's the correct nonzero payment
```

```
                    (when (|| (&& (= @buyer (caller))
                              (= @price (callvalue)))
               (&&    (= @buyer 0)
                      (> @price 0)))
                         {
                      ;; For payment
                      ;; Ethereum doesn't allow fractional amounts
                      ;; Warn users about making prices divisible
                      [hundredth] (/ @price 100)
                      [arr] @@(+ @storage 2)
                      ;; Pay artist
                      (call (- (gas) 250) @@(+ @storage 1) (* @hundredth @arr) 0 0 0 0)
                      ;; Pay owner
                      (call (- (gas) 250) @@(+ @storage 3) (* @hundredth (- 100 @arr)) 0 0 0 0)
                      ;; Transfer ownership
                      [[(+ @storage 3)]] (caller)
                      ;; Clear offer subject and price
                      [[(+ @storage 4)]] 0
                      [[(+ @storage 5)]] 0
                      })
                  })
               }
0×0))}
```

Here's the top and the bottom of the main UI (implemented in HTML and JavaScript for the AlethZero Ethereum client).

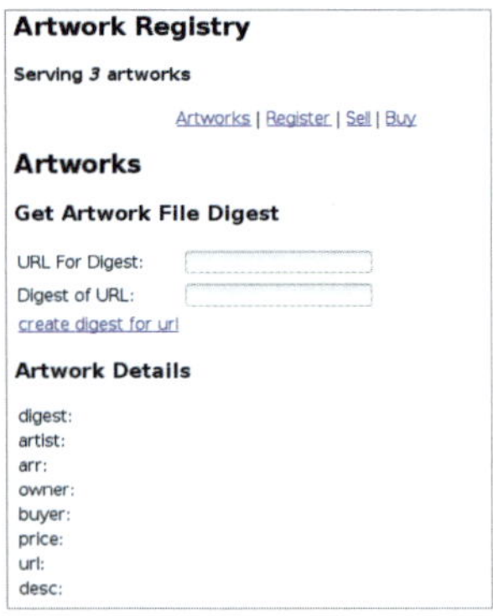

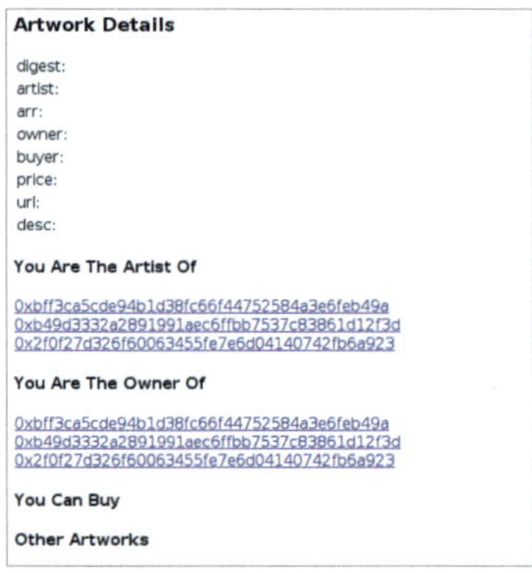

You can enter a URL and get the cryptographic hash for it. If the artwork has already been registered, this will show its details.

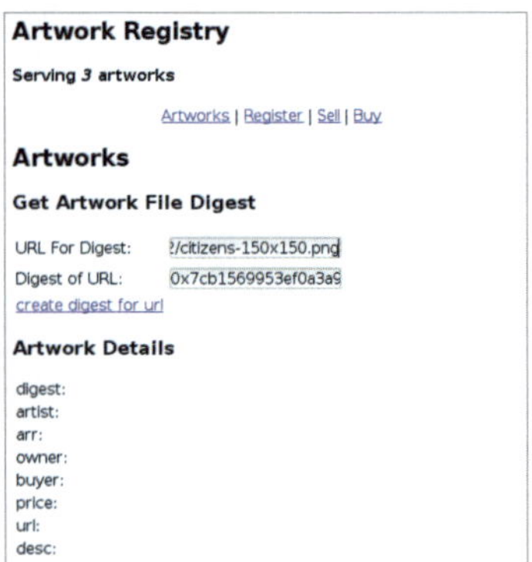

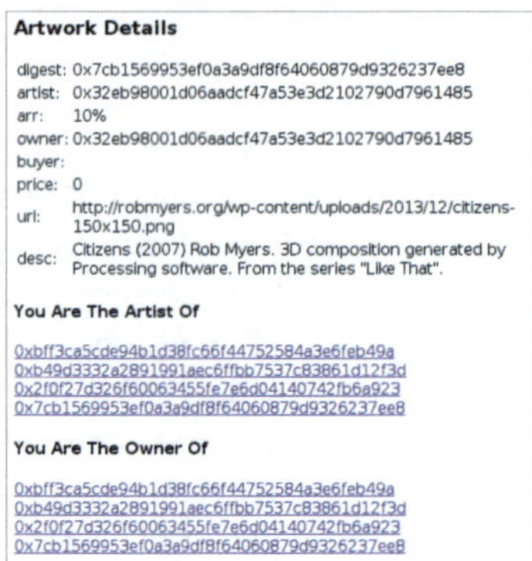

Or if not, you can register it.

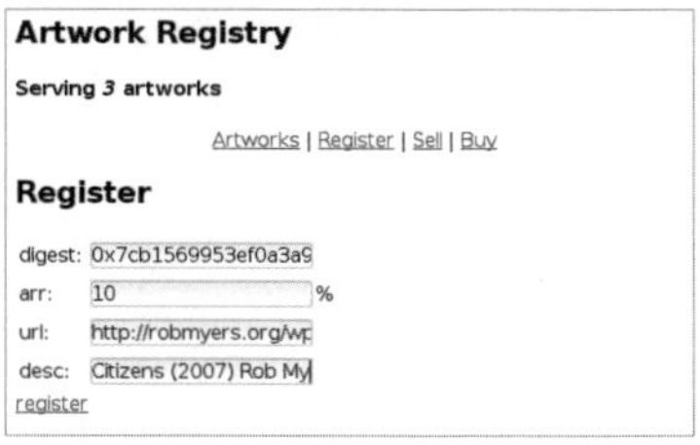

Once you've registered an artwork, you are the artist of it and you also own it. You can offer any artwork you own for sale.

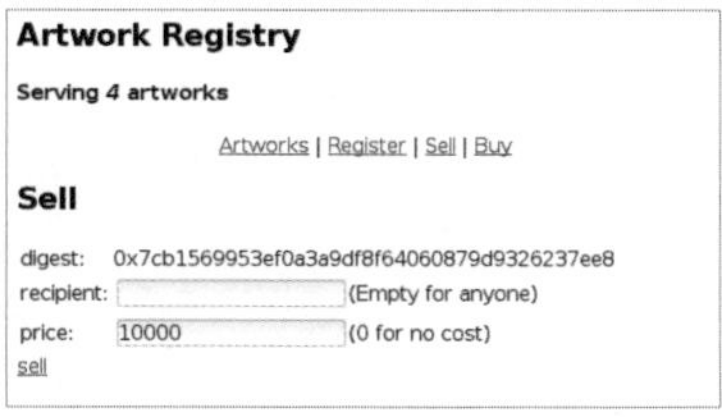

And you can accept a sale offer, paying the specified amount of Ether.

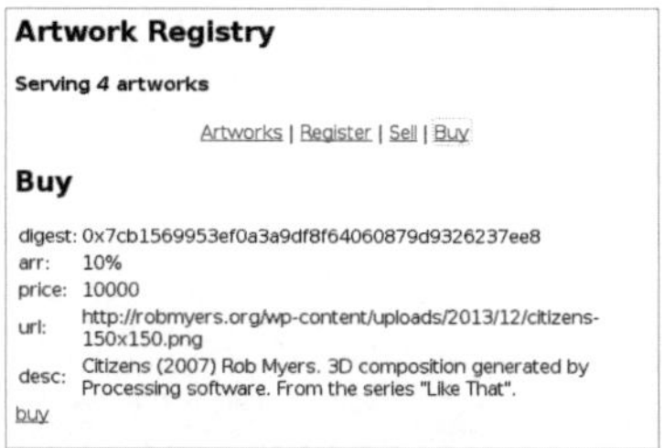

The UI warns you how much Ether you are about to spend.

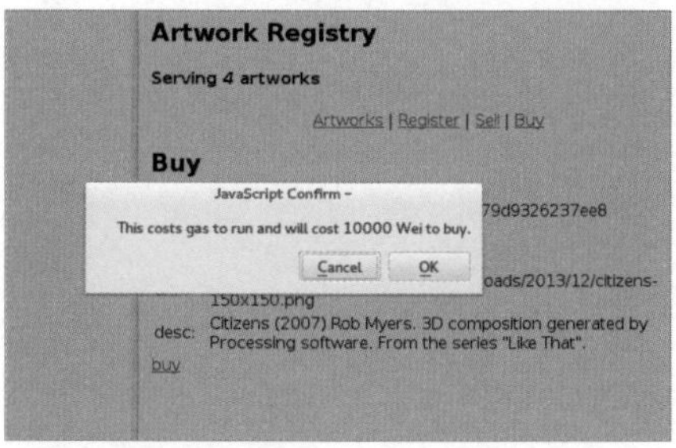

And when you buy an artwork it lets you know when the transfer is complete.

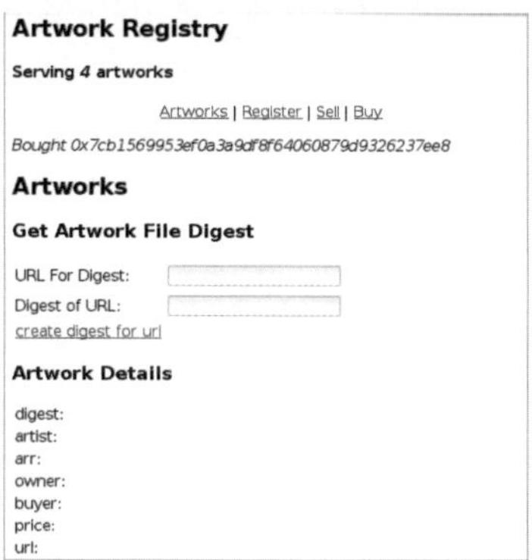

It's a market in allographic digital art. In contrast to the existing art market, it is entirely public and transparent. And in contrast to many jurisdictions, it implements the controversial 'Artist's Resale Right' in a voluntary way (in a way similar to that suggested in

The Social Life of Artistic Property).[4] If it's prohibitively difficult to experiment in the existing art market, we can make new markets for new kinds of art. Like this one.

4 A. Whitaker, *The Social Life of Artistic Property*, <https://www.thing.net/~rdom/ucsd/3somesPlus/sociallifeofartisticproperty.pdf>.

Crypto Sigils

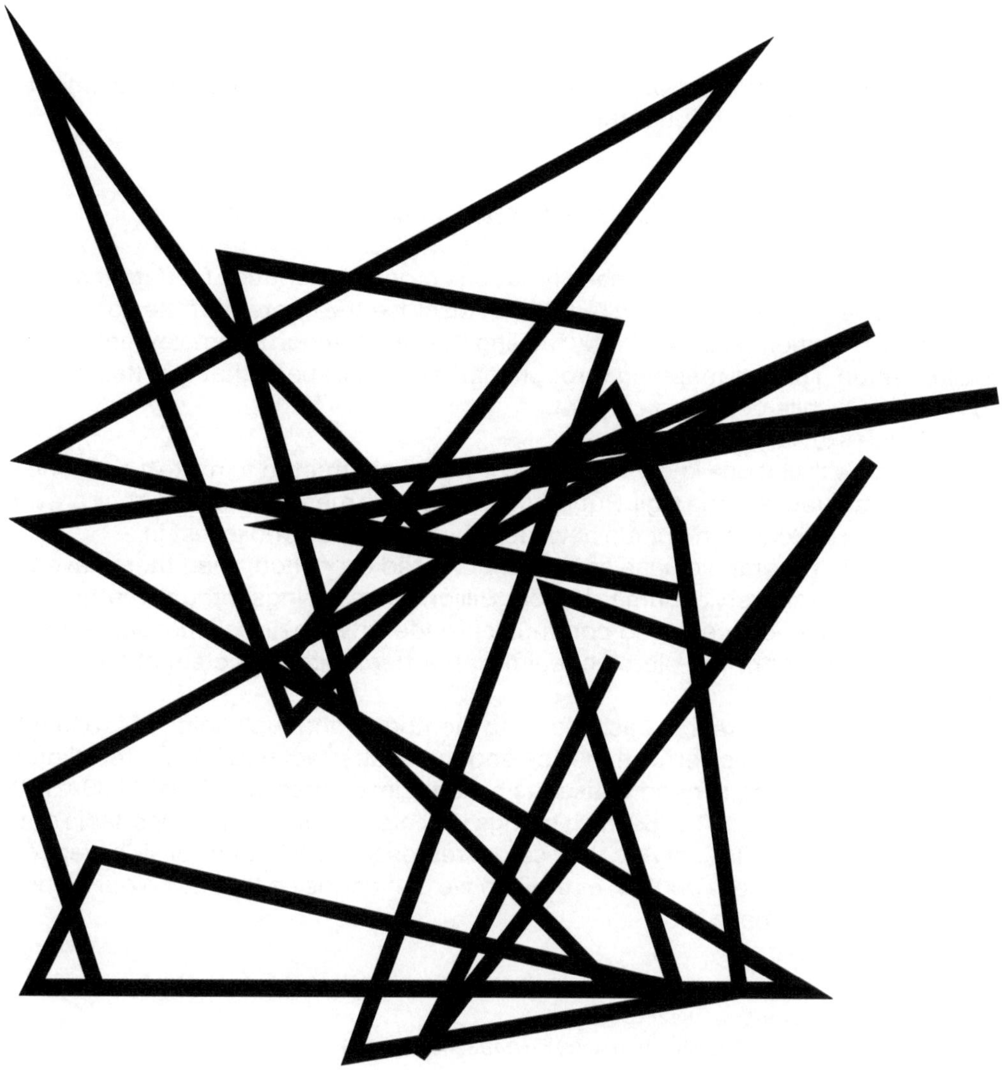

A cryptographic hash function is a piece of computer code that takes a piece of data and produces a (hopefully) unique short string representing it. This string will in no way resemble the input data, and you will not be able to guess the input data from it. The function always outputs the same string for the same data, and changing the data will change the output string.

For example, I can use the sha256 function on the UNIX command line to make a unique representation of my name:

```
# echo rhea | sha256sum
2466a0da1499e193618f43b392a408b2101710fef023f8b01ec351ab393d9ea4  -
```

And if I do this again I get the same result:

```
# echo rhea | sha256sum
```

```
2466a0da1499e193618f43b392a408b2101710fef023f8b01ec351ab393d9ea4  -
```

But if I add just one extra character I get a different result:

```
# echo rheaM | sha256sum
aa0aaa2835c977137200480dae2672603eb368b80adaae4aef79a385c451ff95  -
```

And importantly the amount of difference in the input has no effect on the amount of difference between the output strings:

```
# echo rheaN | sha256sum
81744d575e87892fa40992b20a001036a871f7401839beed78aab114c2e00818  -
```

So, the outputs of cryptographic hash functions produce identities for data that can be used to uniquely refer to the data but do not disclose the content of the data.

Hash functions achieve this by feeding the data through a complex mathematical transformation. This is a mapping through mathematical space that maintains identity and difference while occulting content.

Much like a sigil.

It's true that if one knows the word or words abstracted to make a sigil, one can recognise their traces in the sigil. But these traces are a means to an end, they are a way of producing a striking and unique new identity to focus on and invest in.

More cryptographic hash strings are created every hour than there have been sigils made in the entirety of human history. Billions of mappings through mathematical space to establish, conceal, and communicate identity. Their consensual reality and status as exports from the platonic realm of mathematical objects make them ideal magickal material.

A full 32-byte SHA-256 hash is a lot to memorise, although doing so is a feat that could be ritualistically powerful. It may be enough to abstract it to its first few digits, as Git commits do.[1] We don't need to use the hexadecimal (base-16: 0123456789ABCDEF rather than base-10: 0123456789) digit strings that are the usual human readable output of hash functions. An HTML-style colour can be represented with three or six hexadecimal digits, for example blue is 0000FF or 00F. So we can choose a unique colour using the first six digits of the hash.[2]

For example:

```
echo this is my intent | sha256sum
1b0fd74346abfe6858b12b8e3036649a63c09f2a049634dfe3c835f32422f58e  -
```

As an HTML colour this is #1b0fd7—something like:

1 <https://mirrors.edge.kernel.org/pub/software/scm/git/docs/user-manual.html#understanding-commits>.

2 <https://web.archive.org/web/20130423132157/http://blog.dopplr.com/2007/10/23/in-rainbows/>.

We can also use pairs of digits as positions on a 16×16 grid, or more digits for a larger grid, or three groups of digits to produce a three-dimensional path[3] for 3D printing or importing into virtual reality.

Here's a simple Python example:

```
import hashlib

digest = hashlib.sha256()
digest.update(" the spammish repetition")
digest_string = digest.hexdigest()
digest_numbers = [int(char, 16) for char in digest_string]
coords = [digest_numbers[i:i+2]
     for i in range(0, len(digest_numbers), 2)]
print "%!psnnewpath"
print "%i %i moveto" % tuple(coords[0])
for coord in coords[1:]:
     print "%s %s lineto" % tuple(coord)
print "0.25 setlinewidthnstroke"
```

You can see the output of this program rendered at the beginning of this text. We can combine this with colour (or render the colours of the hash as a grid of coloured squares).

Another way of generating visual forms from hashes is using shape grammars, as used by libvisualid.[4] Here's 'this is my intent' rendered by libvisualid:

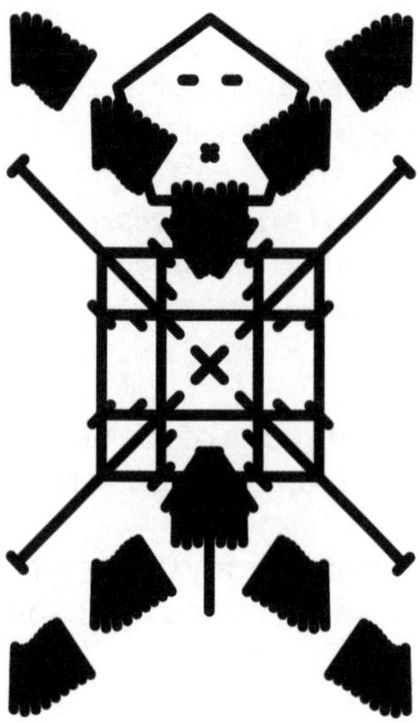

Hashes can be attached to emails or tweets to place and circulate them in the world. Or they can be placed into the Bitcoin blockchain using a system such as Bitcoinproof,[5] to be rehashed constantly as the Bitcoin blockchain is updated. Here's the hash for a spell in the blockchain:

`1Eui1Wje41JEJ4W1QYWbSAYG4h7JBaoPXQ`[6]

3 <https://hyperritual.com/blog/3d-sigil-maker/>.
4 <https://disambiguate.me/stickfigurator>.
5 <https://github.com/vog/bitcoinproof>.
6 <https://www.blockchain.com/btc/address/1Eui1Wje41JEJ4W1QYWbSAYG4h7JBaoPXQ>.

We can use a system similar to Bitcoin's proof-of-work system to find auspicious hashes for data, those that start with a run of leading zeroes or some other number (or target string or bitmap encoded as a number).

More Python:

```
import hashlib
import binascii

target = "0000"
complement = -1
digest_numbers = ""

while not digest_numbers.startswith(target):
   complement = complement + 1
   digest = hashlib.sha256()
   digest.update("this is my intent")
   digest.update(str(complement))
   digest_numbers = digest.hexdigest()
   print "%d %s" % (complement, digest_numbers)

print binascii.b2a_uu(str(complement))
print binascii.b2a_base64(str(complement))
```

And its output, which is the key to creating an auspicious hash of the input string:

```
0 eae2ffcee00aa95306e706dd4bc67ab6b9fd2ffe61b32dfe4177b76c0afd682d
1 84ba18490876919df8bbff194eeb861c6c44a27e9bfbd8db485ecf704e41fcbd
2 f53226b118fa492dc21cd4336d67b4c8ce4148e49e8e4b094baf3e5ecff688ba
[...]
74962 38d5f823e881857f031def1822a28546d29b40903959b1c9bf1f5a1bebd42d9e
74963 b906fd259413ac714de31b9acaf6f0e5268560221d07f557f0f491a081a2cd09
74964 00006dd9f148ca454d331179bd7c87b42d7ab734df7738e1ae90e25013f02a1d
%-S0Y-C0
```

NzQ5NjQ=%-S0Y-C0 and NzQ5NjQ= are different representations of the number 74964. They can be used to create sigils, or the number could be represented verbally using a mnemonic generator.

There's more that can be done with cryptographic hashes and with cryptographic signing, which I haven't covered here. But hopefully these examples will inspire further experimentation.

(All code licensed CC0.)

My Little Penny, Bitcoin is Magick

> Change for the machines.
>
> Pat Cadigan, *Synners*

Theodor Adorno regarded the occult as a politically quiescent denial of alienation through a regression to animism.

> Occultism is a reflex-action to the subjectification of all meaning, the complement of reification. If, to the living, objective reality seems deaf as never before, they try to elicit meaning from it by saying abracadabra. Meaning is attributed indiscriminately to the next worst thing: the rationality of the real, no longer quite convincing, is replaced by hopping tables and rays from heaps of earth.[1]

And this is true, although as always it would be wrong to attribute a more general feature of human psychology uniquely to a single religion.

The Baudrillardian Disneyland of religion is the cargo cult, in which Melanesian islanders reenact the long-ago observed activities of departed American troops for the benefit of visiting anthropologists in order to cause the vehicles that delivered wartime supplies to return. To the outside observer, it is obvious that occultism and cargo cults alike fall foul of the distinction between correlation and causation.

Occultism, like philosophy, suffers from the *semantic fallacy*. This is the equivalent of the pathetic fallacy but for meaning: the projection of cognitive structures of logical rather than emotional significance onto the external environment. Magick extends this with the adolescent male power fantasy of imposing one's will directly upon reality, of reducing the amount of work one has to do to get what one deserves. In this respect it resembles economics.

Modern economics uses statistics to model reality. Samples are drawn from populations, and various tests are used to ensure that conclusions about these samples accurately represent the wider population. Policy based on these conclusions can then be applied to the general population safe in the knowledge that they will almost certainly only be wrong a specified percentage of the time. Statistics is the state religion of economics, bringing revelation and absolution back from the numeric plane.

In 'Qabbala 101', Nick Land describes the assumptions of Kabbalic gematria.[2] It is possible to detect a signal from outside the system from traces within the system; this can be done by using mathematics to find the contingent numerical properties of

1 T. Adorno, 'Theses Against Occultism', in *Minima Moralia*, tr. E.F.N. Jephcott (London and New York: Verso, 2005), 238.

2 N. Land, 'Qabbala 101', in *Fanged Noumena: Collected Writings 1987–2007*, ed. R. Mackay and R. Brassier (Falmouth and New York: Urbanomic and Sequence Press, 2011), 591–606.

words, by counting their length or by mapping their consonants to numerical values. In this way, the text can refer outside the text. Get the numbers right and you get your cargo, or impose your will. To an outside observer, the obvious problem with gematria is that there are lies, damned lies, and statistics.

The popularity of cryptocurrencies represents in no small part a reaction to the financial crisis and austerity. That reaction takes the form of a retreat from conventional economic and political action, and represents at least an economic occult. Magic stripped of the supernatural (like economics stripped of the supernatural...) leaves a cognitive remainder. It is a means of modulating human experience and affecting human behaviour. It is not necessary to believe in imaginary entities, whether thoughtforms or money, in order for them to have effects.

Without the coercive power of the state backing them, cryptocurrencies' reenactment of the rituals of fiat currency amounts to the kinds of behaviour that anthropologists attribute to cargo cults. In their attempt to circumvent the work of economics and banking they resemble magick. But in their use of mathematics they resemble the Kabbalah. Accounts and transactions in Bitcoin are represented and protected using cryptographic hashes, a way of using mathematics to both conceal the content of and prove the identity of a piece of information. This takes place in the blockchain, a data structure built and validated by machines across the Bitcoin network. The blockchain is a fiat currency *hors-texte*, a monetary outside.

The Bitcoin protocol that constructs the blockchain is a set of meaningful actions that are the embodiment and amplification of human intent. It is a ritual. As with copyright in AI, the benefit of intent accrues to its human initiator. This isn't the first time a massively distributed electronic ritual has taken place: the Dalai Lama pointed out in the 1990s that having Avalokiteshvara's mantra on your hard disk is like having a prayer wheel on your computer. In the case of Bitcoin, the ritual consists in the endless mathematical and network operations that build the blockchain.

This is why Bitcoin is magic. Get the numbers right and you can signal outside the system. Get the numbers right and you can map the results back onto society from the numerical plane. Get the numbers right and you will receive the cargo you ordered. It's a ritual to transform society.

Fear of Smart Contracts

Babylon, 1772BC, about tea time. King Hammurabi is explaining the idea of his legal code to several learned persons.

Hammurabi:	So these laws will regulate how we go about our business in society, backed by the coercive power of the state.
Learned Person 1:	Hang on. These 'laws' seem to create a causal and moral domain of their own, distinct from mere human social intercourse. What if they go wrong?
Learned Person 2:	Yes, yes! And what if they act against society? Or are written to be evil.
Hammurabi:	I'm your king. I would never write bad laws.
Learned Person 1:	Yes, but suppose a bad king took over. What then? We need something to protect society from these 'laws' if they go wrong.
Learned Person 3:	Indeed. Most indeededly so.
Hammurabi:	Well, all right. I'll add some laws governing the creation and application of laws. That way, laws can be used to govern laws.
Learned Person 3:	But that would be like asking the wolf to account for his consumption of lambs!
Learned Person 1:	Yes, I really don't see how using 'laws' to alleviate the potential harm of 'laws' works. That's just circular logic.
Learned Person 4:	Yes. What next? Perpetual motion? You're just begging the question.
Hammurabi:	I'm your ****ing king! Shut up and agree with me!
Learned Person 3:	If we shut up, how are we to agree with you? What do your 'laws' say about that?
Learned Person 2:	Yeah. There should be laws against people like you...
Hammurabi:	GUARDS!

2014

Bad Shibe (Uncut Version)

Illustrations by Lina Theodorou

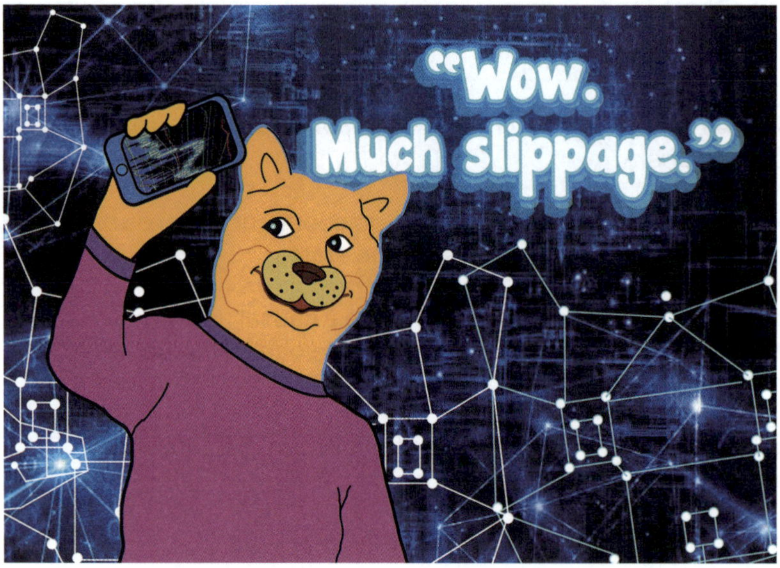

Wow. It's two days since I rankchecked AreWeThereYet.

OK eyes, go. Hello phone! What's my rank?

Wow. Much slippage.

There's a noob who's ahead of me in the rankings. Amaze. BangZoom78 has come out of nowhere and is tipping like a true shibe. Truer. Amaze. Such tippage. We tip our fellow shibes to show our appreciation. BangZoom78 must be surrounded by amaze shibes. Very amaze.

Where am I? I was asleep.

Oh. I'm lying on the couch. I like the couch. I like our room. The light coming through the planks over the window is either morning or evening. Wait, if it's that strong it's evening. School soon! I was working today. Much carrying. Such labour. So hot. Maximal tiredness. Ohhhhh. That's why I was asleep. And why it's evening.

I look at my phone again. BangZoom78 has graduated to the regionals?! Amaze. I feel a twinge of envy before I remember that we are all going to the moon. So I put down my phone and lie on the couch and look at my ducks on the shelf. Many ducks. They are the old plush skeleton ducks that you find at swapmeets. I tell everyshibe I think they're funny but the truth is I feel sorry for them. I know shibes wanted them pre but srsly noshibe is going to want them now except me. Which is why there are so many on the shelf. If they all fall on me I won't be found for days.

FOR DAYS!

At least I'll have company. I quack at them, then again. Two different quack sounds. I wish I knew binary. My phone pings. Kitteh. I'm late for school!

OK feet, go. Downstairs. Out the front door. Across the drive. Onto the street. Outside the kennels (fact: pre it was a McMansion but there's many shibes in each room there now) hot air from formerly sun-heated sidewalk hits cooler evening air and shimmies. Science!

Schoolwalking is kitteh. I'd totally tip someshibe for a piggyback. School is blocks and blocks and blocks away. Why is everything made of concrete if it gets so hot?

Is the stuff on the streets still concrete if it's a different colour? Why are animals made of meat if they don't want us to eat them? Wow. I just walked to school.

It's hotter inside school's tarpaulins than outside. Good evening my schoolshibes let me find some floor behind you all. I sit down squeezed against tarp. Teacher has pinned a new poster of some overdressed shibe, maximally pre, to the tarp behind them. I get tipped for asking who they. Wow. The pre shibe's name is funny. They were ruler of a state with streets made of water. My fellow shibes laugh when I ask why we don't make the streets out of water here when it's so hot. But teacher tips me anyway. Amaze.

Teacher has much to say. They plot a U-shaped graph of occurrences of the word 'shibe' over time. Then they show us a clip from a pre film about two bros in a time-travelling phone box. Next teacher explains what a phone box is. Then they talk about an old cereal that was designed for TV. Then they talk about what TV was. Much history.

Another new poster says 'Tip your teacher!' and we do because we're shibes. I remember teacher's tippage and my earlier slippage (which rhymes) so I tip some more. Teachers gotta eat. Which reminds me, I'm hungry. As I leave class my phone pings above the hubbub of detarping shibes. Tipped for good homework. Wow.

Back on the street, night is ramping up. Eggers are packing up for the evening leaving the sidewalk greasy. The swapmeet is starting under glaring LEDs. Such service to the community. Zero walking from school. Many shibes. Such goods to browse.

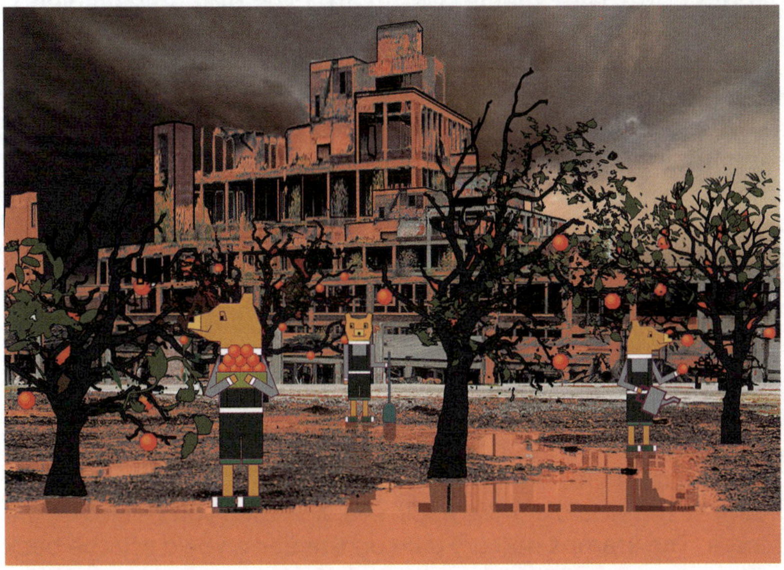

My fellow schoolshibes are gathered around cartwheel vendors mobbing for apples and wraps. Wow. Much noms. Is 'noms' kitteh? I look around. Nobody heard me say it. I get thrown a maximally amaze apple and tip large for it when it also tastes good. What was that story with a big red apple in it? And a snake? I'm thrown a wrap. I kerbnom. Wrap is meh. I show its corpse to my schoolshibe sat next to me.

'Do I tip for this?' I ask them.

I get a look.

'Norly,' I retry.

Such looks.

'OK, jeez,' I pout.

I tip but it doesn't feel good. Maybe this is why I'm slipping. For a moment I think of just tipping my schoolshibes nomming next to me to help improve my ranking. But what would I tip them for? Amaze nomming? Sitting amazely? My wrap consultant notes warily that I'm smiling. I smile at them full beam and get my phone out. Thar they be, Mr. Phone. Tip them for being an amaze sitter. LOL. Like that would work.

Their phone pings.

Wut?

Oh maybe it thinks I'm tipping an amaze babysitter. That's not funny. Phone, that shibe's performed valuable services to advance the state of the art of staring. Tip them. Tip them like dudebros rushing a cow.

Ping.

Wutf?

My beneficiary deploys a ninja-level combo look of not being into me and also I should disappear. I die inside more than a strong individual secure in their identity should. I concentrate furiously on the kerb. Why has this happened?

I mean technically?

MogoDan told me about the tip history analyzer on phones. OK eyes, go. Phone... tip functionality...tip functionality configuration...tip functionality configuration ontology explicator. Wow, much code. Back, back! Transaction explicator. Yes pls. Soooooo...

Wut? Phone says I totally tipped for 'performing valuable services to advance the state of the art of staring'. My toucan! Nooo!

I cost-benefit-analyse asking MogoDan wtf and get 'It is decidedly so'. Which leads to pencil and paper. I tip my schoolshibe who lends me their pencil sharpener. I flag a drone for the message. Whoosh! Such drone. Very fast.

Most of the swapmeet isn't on the street itself. Pitches sprawl across the dust-bowls fronting McMansions and into the alleys around them. Shibes with goods on old folding tables or mushroom boxes with sheets over them. Piles of food ingredients, clothes, phones. Wow, such economy.

I head across a dustbowl through wandering shibes and wander myself down antiques alley. Old milk crates, piles of fiat currency and other pre memorabilia. No ducks. I has a sad. But there's an old shibe I've not seen before at a stall by the fiat sellers. With some ostentatiously pre bundles of paper. Kitteh, eye contact!

'Greetings, young shibe!' the eye contactor salesbros me. They're hiding a sign with numbers on but I don't get to look at it because eye contact.

'Uh...,' I respond. Thank you for your service, brain. But salesbros are maximally pre. What do you say to them?

'Do you know what these are?' they ask. They pick up a book from their table and flip its pages at me. Such shuffling. Shuffleshuffleshuffle. The blur stops. Each page has small green rectangles of paper glued on.

I fail to conceal my curiousness. 'Fiat?'

Salesbro grins. 'Close. They're Trading Stamps.'

My mouth did not just say 'huh?'

'Green Shield Stamps. You would get the book, see, and then you would get the stamps. From supply stores. The stamps had dry glue on the back, you'd lick the back of the stamp....'

My mouth goes 'Ew!' and my face is totally onboard with that.

Salesbro continues, unfuzzled, '...and then stick them into position on each page until you'd filled the whole book. Then you could use them instead of fiat to buy things with.'

Curiosity totally sells my nonchalance out. 'Did they taste gross?'

'I don't know. Gluey, I guess. But they're really rare now. You could own a piece of history.'

'Pwn?'

'Uh I mean you could hold a piece of history.'

Not all of my fellow shibes see school as the public good I do. But they did teach us about fiat. And altcoins. Alts are bad.

'Is this alt?' I ask. Kinda nervous.

Salesbro doesn't look nervous. I'd look nervous if someshibe I didn't know accused me of having alt.

'No way, young shibe, this is pre. Green Shield Stamps.' They keep shuffling the pages at me.

Much awkwardness. 'Uh thanks but I have to go see my parent now.'

Wow, such fail. I'm basically an adult and that was my excuse?

Dustbowl walking back to the sidewalk I tip salesbro for their teachings so I don't slip any further in the rankings. Shibes are walking and talking around me but like always I don't notice if I know any of them. I walk home for the next octoseptillion blocks. After the heat death of the universe I get back to the kennel. Stairs are kitteh. Mom1 is there, my sib UnoY isn't.

'Heya YS, how was school?' Mom1 inquires of me.

'Amaze. But some salesbro tried to gift me alt at the swap after.'

'Rilly?' asks Mom1 in what they have told me is their concerned tone.

'Yeah do you know what Green Shield Stamps are?'

Mom1 gets a look on their face. Then bounces up and down. Much bouncing. Maximal inverse kinematics. Such excite.

'OMFG my Granna had a book of those! I would totally tip you if you got me those tomorrow!'

I give them a look.

'They aren't alt, they're pre,' they assure me.

'That's what salesbro pitched.'

Mom1 nods, pale blue hair waving.

'Plllllllllease.'

Mom1 whuggles me.

'Pllllllllllllllllease, YS! Be a good shibe!'

I squirm to escape the whuggling. 'OK! Cksake! Leggo!'

My phone pings and Mom1 lets me go. I check my phone. It's raining! Much random tippage from someshibe! Why didn't Mom1's phone ping? Wow. Even more tippage! Tomorrow when I wake up I bet I won't even need to check AreWeThereYet. Such tiredness.

I wake up. Waking up is amaze. Wow. I can't feel my arms! Sleep pounced me on the couch watching pr0n! Why??? I mean the pr0n. My schoolshibes upvote it but it's meh. I lift my right arm up with my mouth and put it on my chest. Feeling returns to it slowly. I use it to pick up my left arm. Teacher mentioned 'the left hand washes the right'. Is this like that? Is it a school day? It is! Amaze.

It's so dusty in the kennel. Light spews in between the boards. This is a classic couch, totally pre but in a good way. Is there a good way? The water street ruler shibe was good, I guess. How do you cook if your streets are made of water? Roof parties? Roof party!

How's my AreWeThereYet rank?

Wow, much gainage. I am a shibe. And BangZoom78 is gone from regionals. Wut? They're on nationals! They'll be Top Dog by (checks projections) two days next? Wtf? THEY MUST BE AMAZE!!! But...

And I know this is wrong...

I can't stop thinking. About yesterday. Tipping a shibe for nothing. Nothing real.

What if...

No. Nonono. Nooooooo. No way. I am a bad shibe. I shouldn't think that. I'm just jealous. We are all going to the moon. Phone, alert me when BangZoom78 becomes Top Dog.

There's a blast of catnip smoke and a sudden weight on my legs. Legs tell brain this should hurt. Brain takes their word for it. My sib UnoY is arrive on what they think is the couch.

'Dudebro!' I shout.

With horrorshow slowness my sib turns their head to look at me. I receive the gift of 'Mmmmmmmmmmm?'

'My legs, douchebro!' I also. Such pain.

Sib takes a drag on their catnip. Then slooooooowly lift their butt. Juuuuuuust enough for me to rescue my legs.

I sit up and try to look dignified. But I have to cough when Sib blows smoke at me. Kitteh.

Sib is wearing a pre 'We Are the 49%' T-shirt I got them at a swapmeet. They haven't put down the burnt fiat note they lit their catnip with. Sib grows their own. Catnip, not fiat. Which led to such awkwardness at the orchard. We were growing tomatoes and I thought they were catnip. Tomato leaves don't smoke well. Classmates were not impressed. Much coughing.

MogoDan has not written back. Mogodan is Sib's friend. 2 + 2 = 'Sib, you seen MogoDan?'

Sib waits for the oceans to rise a little.

'Not for thousands of blocks.' More catnip smoke.

I pivot. 'You know tipping protocol deets though, right?'

I get a look. Sib doesn't sleep, they wait for the next block of tipping transactions to be processed. If you tip in our neighbourhood, it probably gets processed by the tangle of wires, computer cards, milk crates, chopsticks and fans that is Sib's maximally amaze setup. They get such tippage for it. Which makes minimal sense. It's like giving a cartwheel vendor an apple. Why would they want an apple? They have apples. Many apples. I want an apple. Apple, pls.

Sib has held that look like a champ.

'I tipped a shibe yesterday for some bullshit and they still got the tip,' I confide.

Sib is shocked in no way. 'Yeah dumbass you can tip for anything.'

I pout.

The giggles pounce Sib. 'OK what was it for?'

I show them my phone. 'Yeah, yeah, services to staring. The tipping app is such meh. You don't really have to give a reason, that's just for AreWeThereYet. I thought they teach you this shit at school?'

Much awkwardness. 'Uh no. They tell us to always have a good reason.'

Sib gives me a look. 'That's just personal development civic responsibility brainwash. I used to keep a tally of everyshibe's reasons but they're just mush. Unless you're really trying to impress your date it's all just,' Sib breathes then finishes, 'Other, Other, Other.'

'Bwuh?' Much confusion.

'Pup, find your toucan. We don't need to give a reason now. They really don't teach you this at school?'

I headshake.

Sib sighs. 'What are you tipping them for? I...'.

I know the answer to this one. Amaze. 'There's a poster that tells us not to forget to.'

'That's not what I mean. But if there was a poster that told you to smash your phone?'

'Why would...'

'Forget it. Where was I?' Sib realises their catnip has burned out. They depocket their magnifying glass.

I remember! 'What if there was a poster...'.

'Oh yeah, that's right. And so but well yeah I really don't think they're teaching you what you need to know at school. AreWeThereYet was meant to be a stop-gap measure when shibes set up tipping rings and bots during the fail. Giving a reason for tipping and checking it was meant to be social proof-of-work, and proof-of-human once neuro came in. But shibes started gaming that too. It became a reputation economy. They wanted being Top Dog to be like being the president.'

Amaze. 'Amaze!'

I get a look. 'Shibe, it's basics. Your school is kitteh. You need to get out more. Much, much more.'

I pout. 'I go to swapmeet.'

Sib sighs. Or inhales. Is it a sigh if it's through catnip? It's maximally a sigh. Wow. 'And then you come home and sit there like you've just been printed. YS you're about the least annoying sib imaginable but that's kinda annoying.'

Wow. Such paradox. I extend the pout. Much silence. Sib blows smoke into the sunbeams.

Question! 'Why don't we need AreWeThereYet any more?'

'Everyshibe knows how to tip, everyshibe knows what a bot attack looks like, everyshibe is going to the moon. Pups love AreWeThereYet but it's just a game and it has to stay that way…'. I start to protest at this but Sib gives me a look. 'It's the protocol underneath and the analytics overtop that matter. But that's boring, just part of the system. It's the dial tone of the economy.'

My brain makes my mouth say 'Like Cap'n Crunch.'

'Wut?'

'Teacher tortoise about phone phreaking. On the old copper wire net. It's funny.'

Sib looks thoughtful but doesn't say anything. I get out more. Sib can be mean but that had interest. I tip them as I downstairs from the kennel. Much heat. I get a wrap from a passing egger. Much taste. Such delicious. I tip them.

Life is amaze. There's not much to it. But there's sun and eggs and my phone goes ping. Sib tipped me! Nowait, they refused the tip. Refund fees! Kitteh.

I hate everything. Sib is meh but…I do want to get out more. I just don't understand shibes. They gift me looks. It's look potlatch and I am the chief! I'd prefer sacrifice to potlatch atm. Of me. Much sadness. Not amaze.

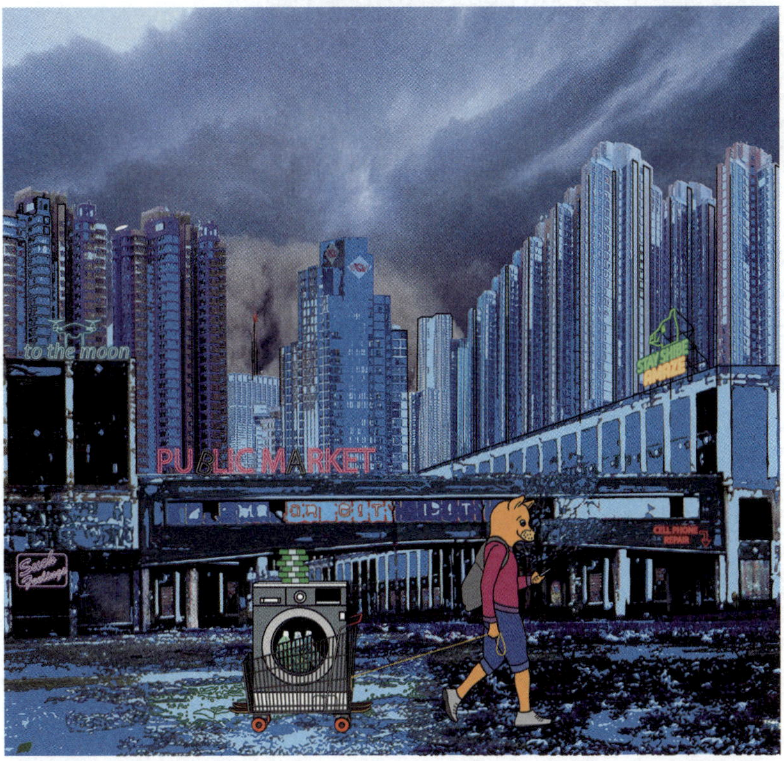

Wow. Such heat. School isn't for about a googolplex blocks but the tarps have much shade. My feet take me there. I would tip so much for a piggyback. What is a piggy anyway? Or what is piggying? I won't ask at school. It's like when I asked what otters ott. Teacher and my schoolshibes thought I was mocking. Much laughter and I got busywork punishment. Wait, do mockingbirds mock?

There's a white line painted on the sidewalk. It wasn't there yesterday. I walk along, following. It takes me along the street in a long slow curve, then waves from side to side of the sidewalk. Amaze. I walk faster and faster along it, then when it ends up in a spiral I follow that round and round and round and round and fall over. I giggle. Up on the side of the tall building by the sidewalk, in the same white paint, it says 'You got it!'

I clap my hands. Amaze. Phone, tip whoever painted this. Such fun. I must tell my schoolshibes about this. Phone, remember where this is. Feet, back to work. That was amaze. Such fun. I'll be thinking about this all day.

A quintoseptillion blocks later I clamber under the tarp of my class. More posters! There's one of an incongruously cute Shiba Inu. There's one of elliptic curves superimposed, with their names at the bottom. One of a Claes Oldenburg sculpture of a fork. And one of how to wash your hands. I know how to wash my hands. Teacher is watching me making hand-washing movements. Such embarrassment.

'Good evening, YS' says Teacher. It's not evening yet?

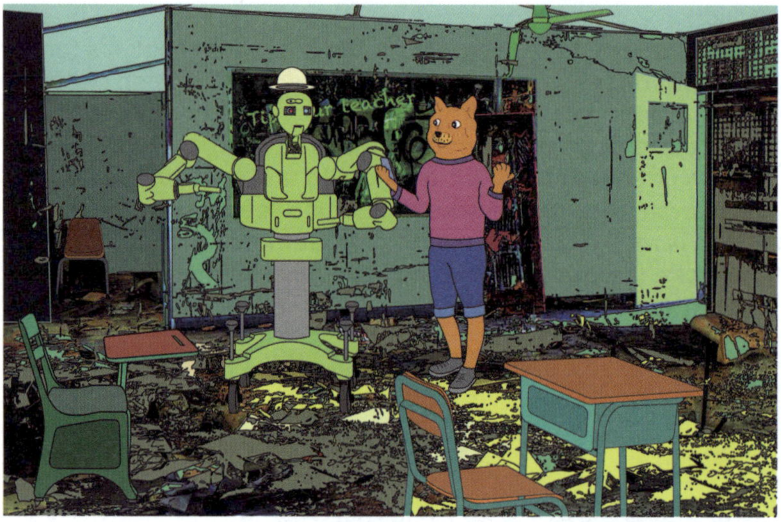

'Uh hi Teacher,' I reply. 'I like your posters, where do you get them?'

'My sib has a 2D printer. They grow inks and everything,' says Teacher.

'Amaze. So cool!' I exclaim. Teacher smiles.

'I didn't think young shibes still said that. You can stay in here until class but please let me concentrate while I set up,' says Teacher.

'Said what?' I ask.

'Cool,' says Teacher. What's cool? I look confused then remember I promised not to disturb them. Did I promise? It's an implied contract. So I guess I did. Hello phone.

BangZoom78 is now on the continental rankings. My toucan! They must have arms like one of those Indian superheroes, tipping left and right. Tiptiptiptiptip...

'YS?' says Teacher.

'...tiptiptip—Yes?' I reply.

'Please can you think more quietly. I am glad you are here but I need to set up and it takes some concentration,' says Teacher.

I nod. The continental rankings! Shibes are tipped just for being on them. Which I guess makes that a loop. What's a fruit loop? Mom1 mentioned them once. How do you make fruit into a loop? Mobius fruit? Where would you start eating them? Wow.

My schoolshibe Narawan arrives and sits at a point perfectly avoiding me, the entrance, the walls of the tarp, and Teacher. They get out their phone and study it forensically. Much intensity. Such ignoring.

Both our phones ping. It's raining! Narawan sighs. This breaks Teacher's concentration.

'What irks you, Narawan?' they ask.

'That was from BangZoom78,' replies Narawan.

'Rilly? Again?' Teacher asks them redundantly. Narawan nods without looking up.

Teacher pulls up AreWeThereYet on the tarp screen. They show the rainfall for BangZoom78's recent generosity. Wow, much tippage. Teacher groups the tips by physical location, which makes a map of this side of the continent. Then they overlay a subset of the results over an old satellite map of our local area. I look up at the tarp. Falling from a satellite would be creepy. Wheeeeeeeeeee—

'YS...,' says teacher.

'—eeeee, yes? Oh,' I respond.

Teacher groups the tips on the display by what looks like time. And then by other criteria I don't know. Isn't it time for class? No, still much waiting. Teacher flashes up the details of each tip transaction on the screen, which does look like rain. I feel my face smile. Teacher glances back at us.

'Narawan do you know Bangzoom78?' asks Teacher.

'I said I did,' answers Narawan.

'I mean personally.'

'No just from the rain.'

Teacher glances at me. It's a cue. 'Nuh-uh,' I answer Teacher before they even ask. Amaze.

Teacher frowns. 'You both tipped them earlier.'

Wtf?

Teacher pulls up the transaction records. 'You both tipped BangZoom78. Oh they're different accounts but under the same name. That's problematic. And they tip each other. A lot. And there's other accounts under the same name...'.

Teacher searches for related accounts. The diagram of transactions between them looks like a Spirograph drawing. Spirograph is amaze. Mom1 has one in The Box. When I was rilly young I simultaneously scratched and impaled my hand with a gear and a pencil when I got carried away drawing. Much wailing.

'This looks like an inverse sybil attack. Why hasn't anyshibe checked for this?' asks Teacher.

'Nobody checks. They don't have to.' I repeat what UnoY said earlier.

'But it's so brazen!' vocabs Teacher.

'I didn't tip them,' says Narawan.

'Nor did I,' I agree.

As our schoolshibes arrive the investigation becomes a lesson. School is amaze. Much opportunity. Several other shibes have tipped BangZoom78. None of us remember doing so. It must be MIND CONTROL!

'It's not mind control, YS,' says Teacher. 'Who did you tip in block 984532965?'

'The shibe who drew a line on the street I followed.' I repeat what my brain tells me.

'You liar!' shouts my schoolshibe NoUr, 'you did not!'

Many eyes on NoUr.

'I wasn't tipped for that. Nobody has tipped me for it.'

NuWae puts their hand up. Teacher tells them they told them they don't need to do that.

'I did,' says NuWae.

'No you didn't!'

Eris friends us for a few blocks. Teacher pulls up the transactions again.

'YS did tip the shibe who painted something, but it was a sign not a line,' Teacher rhymes.

NoUr gives me a look. If the ground swallows me up before the next block I will tip it like a tower in Europe.

'But I told my phone to tip the person who drew it!' I yip. Much awkwardness.

'Drew what, YS?' asks Teacher.

'The line and the sign,' I rhyme.

'I didn't paint the sign you kitteh piece of—' NoUr says before Teacher says their name in a way that stops them.

'But I meant to tip the shibe who, I mean I didn't know, I mean I uh—the line was amaze!' Mr. Brain, this be mutiny, I'll see you hang for this!

'NoUr I think YS has been the victim of a context collision attack,' explains Teacher. Meaning I'm not lying. Such relief. Am I being sarcastic? I don't think so. But it would be amaze if I was. My sib would maximally tip me. Also wut?

'Wut?' I ask Teacher.

Teacher looks at me. 'The sign was added by someshibe else to hijack the tips from NoUr's line. Whoever added it knew that anyshibe who walked the line would see the sign,' Teacher rhymes once more, 'and relied on their proximity to cause people to regard them as a single unit, tipping the one that drew their attention at the end. Or relying on semantic confusion in people's tipping.'

'People?' I ask teacher.

'Shibes.'

'Ohhhhhhhh.'

'Everyshibe's homework is to analyse these transactions. But we need to talk about the Byzantine Generals now....'

Teacher is amaze. Much knowledge. BangZoom78 is cheating! Such cheating. Wow.

Much conflict. In the pros column, I was right to hate them. In the cons column, it was still jealousy not reason. But the market doesn't care about motivation. So nor should I. Wow. I win!

After class everyshibe tips teacher and I tip NoUr double and teacher tips us and it sounds like a flock of phones trying to find mates. Ping! Ping! Ping! (etc.) Swapmeet time!

I walk across the night sidewalk to the swapmeet. Apple, wrap, kerb, nom (Is nom kitteh? Deja vu! Amaze), tip. NoUr is stood blocking my light. Flee! I'm sure this part of the sidewalk has a trapdoor in it if I can just find—

'I'm sorry I said you were kitteh earlier,' says NoUr. Apparently to me.

'That'sOK,' my mouth fumbles. My face feels hot. Why that? Then inspiration hits me. 'I'msorryItippedthewrongshibe. Yourlinewasamaze.'

NoUr grins. Kitteh. This is mockery! But before I can start looking for the escape hatch again, they say 'Kcya!' and sidewalk back to their shibes. So it wasn't mockery? Such confusion. Did I tip for my wrap? It tasted good tonight. I check my phone. Yes I tipped. Why did NoUr apologise? Oh I should tip them for apologising. A distant ping. Then my phone pings. I don't understand. NoUr usually ignores me and I prefer that to mockery. I don't understand. Brain, disengage please.

'Wow look what the cat hawked up,' says my sib's voice from behind me.

'Heya UnoY,' I reply without looking up. Such dignity.

'You wanted to meetup MogoDan?' they ask me.

'Ys pls.'

'Heya YS,' says MogoDan's voice. I look up and see that it comes from MogoDan. Who has someshibe on their arm. They're holding the arm, not perched on it like a cockatoo. No, face, no glaring! I am a zen master. Om.

'You wanted to say om to me?' asks MogoDan.

'Uh no.' I did want to see MogoDan. I wrote them a letter. It was about...It. Was. About.

'It was about the explicate functionality for tipping,' I remember.

'Oh yeah I remember showing you that kiloblocks ago. Amaze huh? You can use it to send messages.'

I take this onboard.

'But you can tip for anything?' I repeat what my sib told me.

'Yeah, you just have to give a reason to discourage bots and frippery. It was useful for other things. You can get sentiment analysis and metrics out of it but nobody uses anything except eigentippage any more.'

'Eigentippage?'

'The rank you see on AreWeThereYet. How much you've tipped, how much other shibes have tipped you, how much the shibes who tipped them have tipped etc.'

'I have learned,' I say.

My sib pats me on the head. 'Here endeth the tell. Since you ask, we're picking up gold from the swapmeet.'

'Gold?' I ask. I'm a cockatoo. Wow, much squawking.

'Yeah, gold. LiCat here makes jewellery with pre metals. Gonna get Mom1 some for their cake day. You want in?'

LiCat (edgy name!) gives me a look.

'Uh no I booked a slot in the oven for a factual cake.'

'You can't cook.'

'Mom1 said they'd help?'

I get looks.

'You're getting Mom1 to help you make their own cake?' UnoY asks, accusingly. My face's temperature control fails.

'They said they'd like to do something with me,' I mumble. Wow, much awkwardness.

'Cute,' says MogoDan. Is that mockery? UnoY and LiCat give MogoDan looks, which I know means probably not.

'Thank you,' I say to MogoDan, like I've practiced. LiCat gives me a look.

'How's school?' asks MogoDan. Before I can answer, LiCat drags them away.

'OK handshake later!' MogoDan calls over their shoulder.

'You maximally want MogoDan,' says UnoY. What for? Such accusation.

'I do not.'

'LiCat thinks you do. Which I think even you can tell. So if you want any further infodumps try to disabuse them of this notion.'

'Why are shibes so kitteh?'

'Why are you such a mooncalf?'

Such sadness. UnoY turns and walks after them. Some shibes make no sense. All shibes make no sense. No shibes make any sense. I shall stay here until the heat death of the universe. Much moping. The salesbro from last night is across the swapmeet, by the alley between two of the McMansions. They must've done well last night. Do they still have the stamp book?

I stand. I fall down. Wow, sleepy legs. I stretch them out, wait until I can feel them, then retry. Success! I should tip myself for that. My phone makes a farting noise. I can't tip myself. That makes sense. Thank you, universe, for something that makes sense.

Mom1 will love the stamps. Excite. Unless they are gone. Please don't be gone, stamps. I walk across the street, get dusty, weave through shibes, and—oh my sib and their friends are tipping a vendor. Wow, much gold. They must be making Mom1 a crown. Or possibly a full suit of armour. I turn back to look where I'm going. I didn't walk into anyshibe! Amaze.

Salesbro recognizes me. 'Good evening, young shibe. How may I service you?'

'Heya. Do you still have the stamp book thing you showed me?'

'I do indeed.' Flickerflickerflicker. Such flickering. Also: thank you stamps for not being gone! You are my new best friends.

'Pls can I have them?' I request.

'Of course, young shibe, I am glad they are going to a good home. Can I interest you in anything else? I have these...'.

They are coloured plastic cards. Many colours.

'Phone credit scratch cards,' Salesbro answers my face, which was saying: 'Wut?'

'Wut?' I actually say.

'You would turn them over, scratch this section here, and that would reveal a simple code representing a certain amount of credit to use a particular corporation's telephone infrastructure.' Salesbro mimes the scratching. I realise this means actually scratching would devalue them. Minty fresh!

'Can I have one of each colour pls?' I politely.

I unfold my pre plastic bag and put everything in there as Salesbro hands it to me. Mom1 will love all of this. I tip Salesbro maximally.

'Thank you young shibe!' says Salesbro, 'Do remember to visit again, I get new stock daily.'

I nod and engage my feet. They take me back into the swapmeet. I get some pre plastic bottles that are too damaged to be useful or collectible, we can feed those into the printer. I also get a pencil sharpener. Then I walk into MogoDan et al again. There is no escape! Such awkwardness.

'Uh hi,' I say to (STRATEGY!!!) LiCat.

'Hi,' replies MogoDan.

'Yeah school is cool,' I rhyme. Then I remember. 'Did you get my message?'

'When?'

'Two days ago? I droned it.'

'No. I didn't see it.'

'Wow. Much fail. I tipped the drone already.'

LiCat makes a noise like steam.

'So uh what was it about?' asks MogoDan.

We did this. I'm sure we did this? Brain, didn't we do this?

'The explicate functionality. You knew that earlier.'

'Uh no, you asked, I answered.'

'Shibes, my sib is new here. Always. They're OK. Don't hate. C'mon,' says UnoY, and walks off. MogoDan and LiCat follow. Much confusion. Why would UnoY say that? My toucan wobbles on its perch. Today has made no sense. More than usual. Less than usual? There has been more, but it has all made less sense. A light in the sky! Amaze.

The light is accompanied by the thwokathwokathwoka of a helicopter. Wow. Such rarity. I watch the light disappear behind the McMansions, and the noise fades with it. Helicopter where you go? Being on a helicopter would be amaze. I could never tip enough for that.

For the googolplex blocks it takes to walk home I pretend I'm a helicopter. I use the light on my phone. Thwokathwokathwoka.

Mom1 is home when I get back to the kennel. I gift them.

'Thank you, YS! Amaze!' says Mom1. It's funny when they speak shibe. Usually they're pre. I like that about them. Also their blue hair. I said it makes them look old once. They laughed and said that's what their mom said when they were UnoY's age. I wish everyothershibe understood me like Mom1 does. Also more wishes. And chocolate.

'Are you OK on the couch, YS? You're almost too big for it now,' says Mom1.

'I like the couch. It's my friend,' I tell them.

My phone pings. It's raining! I check and it's BangZoom78. I refuse the tip. Which costs, but I don't care. My phone bworps to confirm the refusal fee.

'How was school?' asks Mom1.

'Amaze. Teacher showed us the transaction graph for BangZoom78. It's maximally creepy.'

'How so?'

'They have endless accounts. All feeding tips to each other. Homework is to fit subgraph paths.'

Mom1 looks at me. 'What would the point of multiple accounts be?'

'Um.'

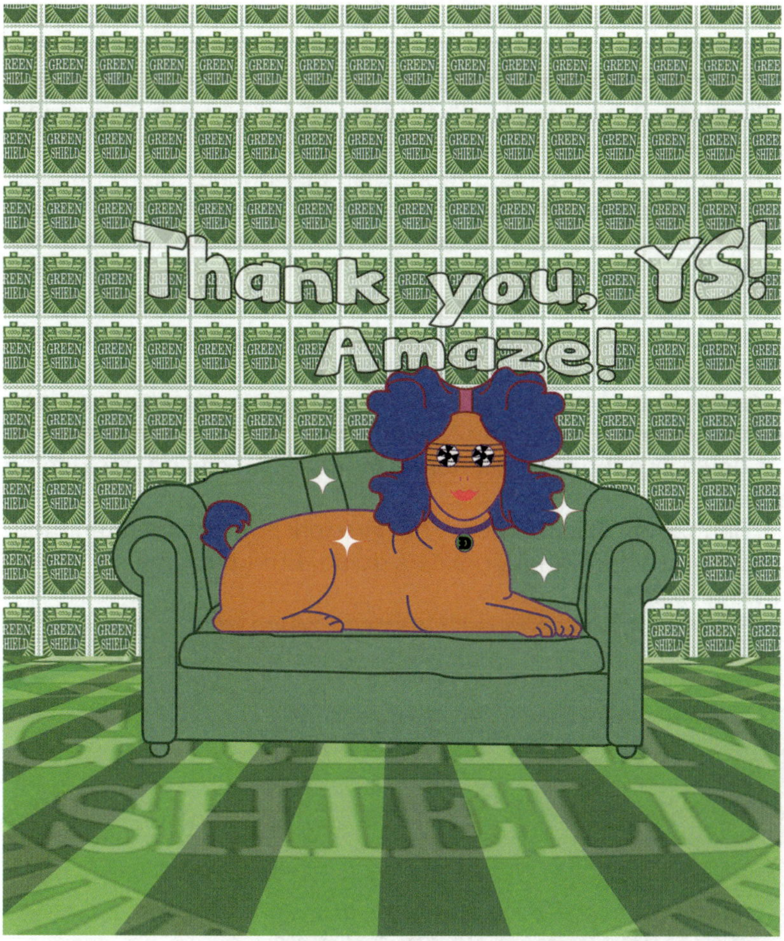

Mom1 checks their phone. ‘Oh wow, there’s a weakness in the current tipping system. Some sort of collision problem. There’s going to be a hard fork to address it in several thousand blocks’ time. Don’t look at me like that, YS, I learnt this stuff when they didn’t teach it at school.’

‘Um.’

Mom1 whuggles me. So I didn’t actually offend them. Much relief.

‘It’s an amaze night, you could do your homework on the roof,’ they suggest.

‘OK!’ I reply. There is a sticky note with some numbers written on it above sib’s rig. I note them on my phone after what happened that time. Then I bounce up the stairs onto the roof. Hello stars, you are my new best friends! It’s getting colder. But not too cold. Cool. Is this why ‘cool’ used to mean ‘good’? It feels good.

I spend some time finding subpaths in the topology of BangZoom78’s transactions. This is fun. Many paths. Such happiness. I look at location, time, and reason. Then I find save point conflicts next to tips to BangZoom78. Wow, many points. It wasn’t just me. I geolocate the transactions and order them by time. The transactions follow the terminator across the continent each night. I make the transactions glow blue on a black globe. Maximally pre animation.

I check the list of BangZoom78’s transactions against the account numbers from my sib’s rig. Many of BangZoom78’s transactions were processed by it. I tell my phone to just show just the lines in the graph representing transactions between my sib’s rig and the other rigs on the network. It looks like a drawing. I zoom out. It’s a drawing of the poster dog’s face. Wow.

I wake up feeling cold. My back hurts. I am on a roof. It’s the roof of the kennels. How did I get here? Oh. Wow. Such sunrise. Many colours. So still. I hobble on sleepy legs to the edge of the roof to watch the sunrise. I am the only shibe in the world to see this. Amaze.

I look down. UnoY and MogoDan are in the street below, still wearing their PLA surplus coats. Mom1 will maximally berate my sib for staying out all night. They never tip them. They have plastic bags. They are swapping, but not the gold from last night. It looks like phones. Why would anyshibe need more than one phone? Many phones. Gold would be better. They'd be pirates. Avast! Or chocolate. Chocolate coins? Mom1 gave us chocolate coins when we were really young. Wait, they said something about phones last night. I wonder...

I flag a drone and sharpen my pencil. With my own pencil sharpener. I shall become a pencil sharpening artisan. Shibes will come from all along the coast and I will sharpen pencils for them. They'll tip me like an insider trader.

In my best cursive I write on what is probably old origami paper: who u?

Then I tell the drone to deliver it to BangZoom78. And I tip it. For the reason of: please tell me. It flutters down into the street, ignoring MogoDan. It disappears behind the McMansion opposite.

My phone pings. BangZoom78 is Top Dog. The hard fork is in less than ten thousand blocks. I don't understand what BangZoom78 is doing. But I think my sib does. I will ask them when I go back inside.

I sit on the edge of the roof. Such sunrise. Very calm. Much wonder. The sunrise is my new best friend. Wow.

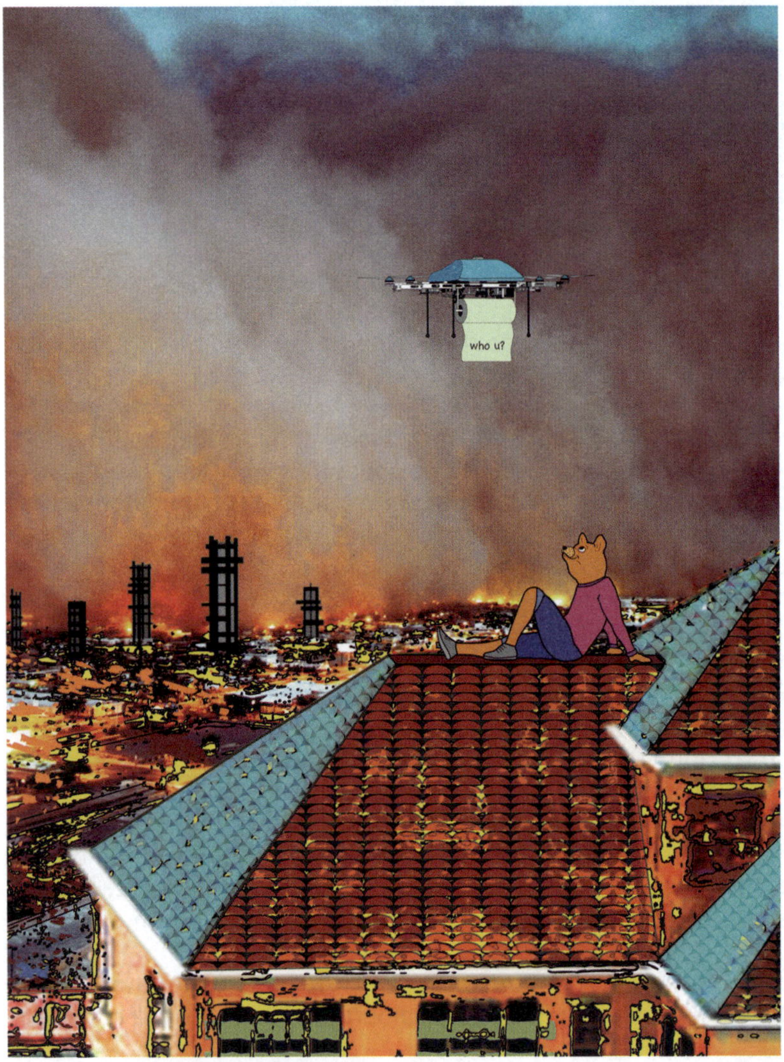

(Conceptual) Art, Cryptocurrency, and Beyond

Art and Money

Art and money have always been involved in each other's production. This Greek Drachma features a relief depiction of a sea turtle on one side. For many people this would have been the artwork, or at least the image, that they saw most frequently in their everyday lives.

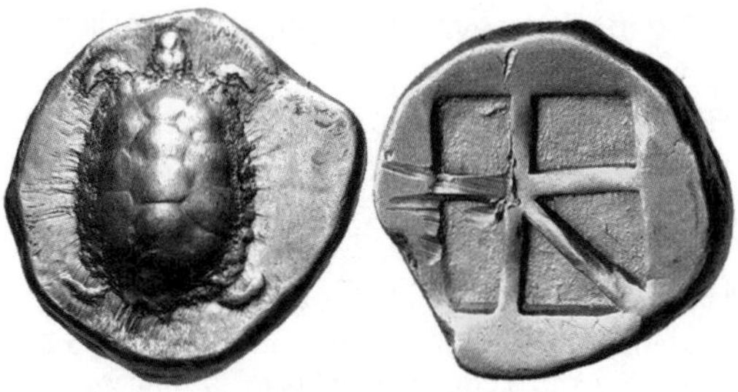

Greek Drachma, 600BC.

In the present day, high art and high finance (or big art and big finance) go hand in hand. Blue chip artworks produced by brand-name artists such as Jeff Koons are collected by hedge fund managers and oil oligarchs as investments and as signifiers of socio-economic position (while stolen Old Master paintings are used as signifiers of value in transactions between criminal gangs...). This tendency has reached its logical conclusion (for now) with Damien Hirst's *For the Love of God* (2007), a diamond-encrusted platinum cast of an actual human skull complete with the original teeth. It was sold for fifty million pounds sterling. But looking inside the sale of *For the Love of God* makes its narrative less straightforward. It was sold to a group including the artist and their dealer, making the actual figure and its ownership less straightforward than a simple sale would suggest.

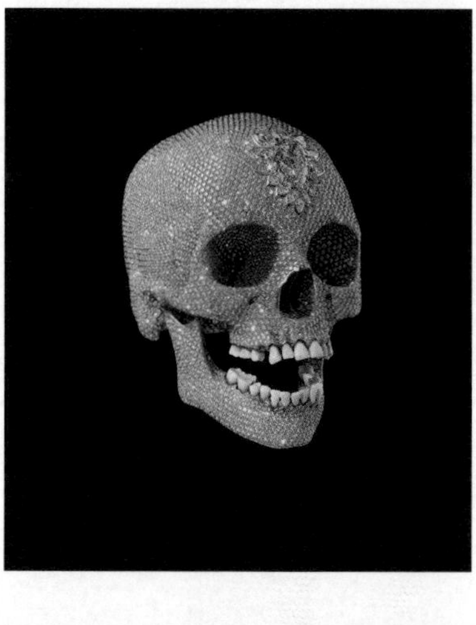

Damien Hirst, *For the Love of God*, 2007. Platinum, diamonds and human teeth. © Damien Hirst and Science Ltd. All rights reserved, DACS / Artimage 2022. Photo: Prudence Cuming Associates Ltd.

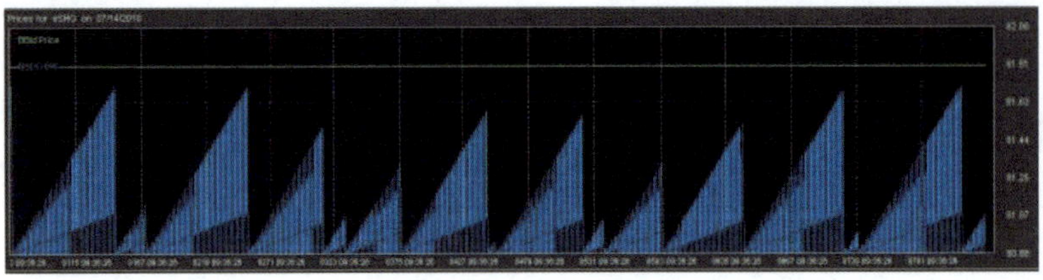

Nanex HFT Visualization.

Nanex's High Frequency Trading visualisations (example shown here from 2010) look inside transactions in electronic stocks and shares markets, finding aesthetic forms in the activity of share-trading bots. What the sawtooth waves of this particular bot's activity represent is unknown: a glitch, a strategy, a side-effect. But without making these forms visible, we would not be able to ask these questions or reflect on this economic activity.

Art, Particularly Conceptual Art, Critiques this Relationship

It is part of the value of art, particularly Conceptual Art, that it can afford us these opportunities for reflection and critique. Cildo Meireles's *Insertions into Ideological Circuits 2* (1970) overwrites the contemporary equivalent of the Drachma's turtle with a rubberstamped message on a banknote, intruding into the everyday use and circulation of currency in order to give its audience pause for critical reflection.

Lynn Hershman's *Roberta Breitmore Blank Check* (1974) is signed by her artistic alter ego Roberta Britmore, using financial transactions and their attendant contracts as a producer and guarantor of identity, literally underwriting it.

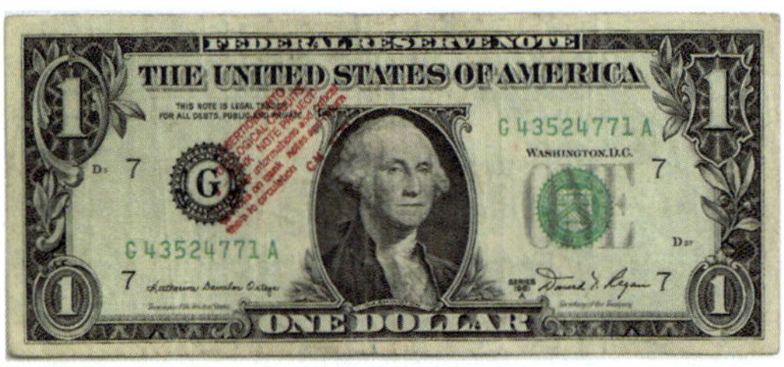

Cildo Meireles, *Insertions into Ideological Circuits: Banknote Project*, 1970, ink on banknote, 2.6 x 6.25 inches (6.7 x 15.9 cm) © Cildo Meireles; courtesy Galerie Lelong & Co., New York.

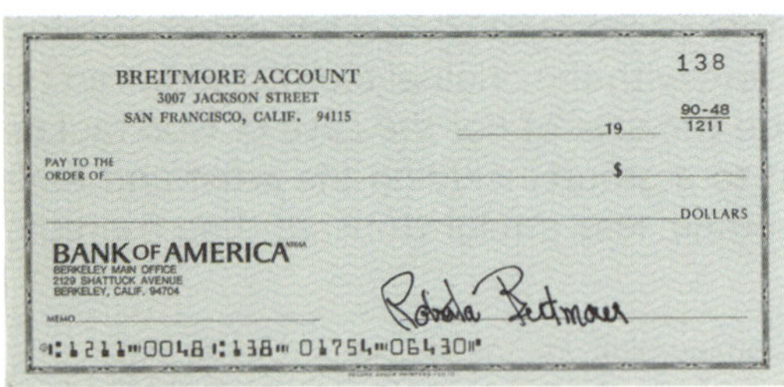

Lynn Hershman, *Roberta Breitmore Blank Check*, 1974. Offset lithography and letterpress with black marker on paper, 3 x 6 inches (7.62 x 15.24 cm). © Lynn Hershman; courtesy the artist.

Douglas Huebler's *Variable Piece no. 44* (1971) incorporates into itself an image of its owner each year for its first decade, in an analogue precedent for Bruce Sterling's idea of 'spimes'.[1] When the artwork is sold, a new owner appears, making the artwork's contingent economics its aesthetic subject.

1 B. Sterling, *Shaping Things* (Cambridge, MA: MIT Press, 2005).

2 The project was part of collective research into alternative currencies and digital reputation systems in the context of Netznetz, a social platform for digital art and culture, and a new self-governed approach to the distribution of public funding. See <http://www.monochrom.at/flowerbank/index-en.htm>

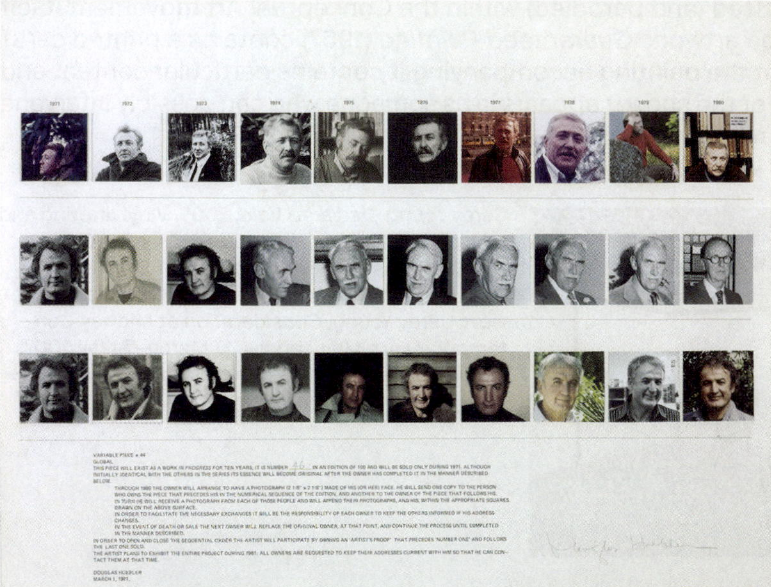

Douglas Huebler, *Variable Piece No. 44*, 1971. Photographs and printed text on board, 457×613 mm. Purchased from the artist by Tate (Grant-in-Aid), 1974. © Douglas Huebler. Photo: Tate.

The initial critique of the ontology and economics of art that Conceptual Art represented in its 'dematerialisation' phase represented as much of a challenge to the livelihoods of artists as it did to its chosen targets. One solution found early on was to produce certificates of authenticity or ownership for otherwise un-ownable art. This reappropriates Conceptual Art for scarcity economics and as property, returning it to the market. Sol LeWitt's certificates for two wall drawings (1980) demonstrate how this works. If you own such a certificate and I do not, and we both follow the instructions on the certificate, you produce an authentic LeWitt and I at best produce a forgery.

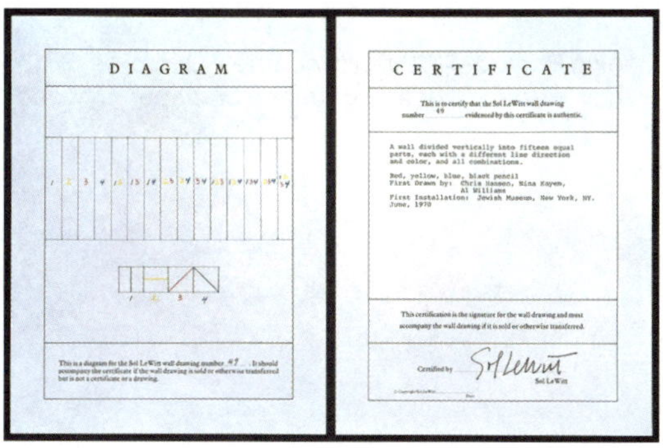

Sol LeWitt, *A Wall Divided Vertically into Fifteen Equal Parts, Each with a Different Line Direction and Colour, and All Combinations*. Diagram and certificate, 1970. © ARS, NY and DACS, London 2022. Photo: Tate.

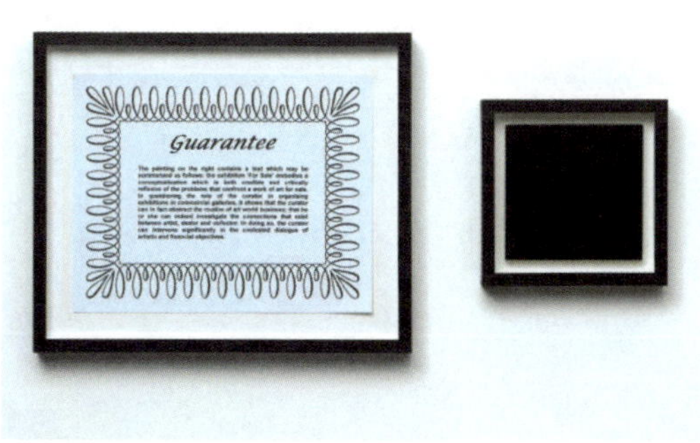

Art & Language, *Guaranteed Painting*, 1967–68. Acrylic on canvas and photostat, 2 parts, canvas 31 × 31 cm, framed text 55 × 44 cm. © ART & LANGUAGE; Courtesy the Artists and Mulier Mulier Gallery, Belgium.

This strategy was criticised (and parodied) within the Conceptual Art movement itself. An early Art & Language artwork, *Guaranteed Painting* (1967) contains a printed certificate guaranteeing that the painting accompanying it contains particular content and addressing the curator of the show it appears in as someone who can possibly intervene in art-world economic relationships.

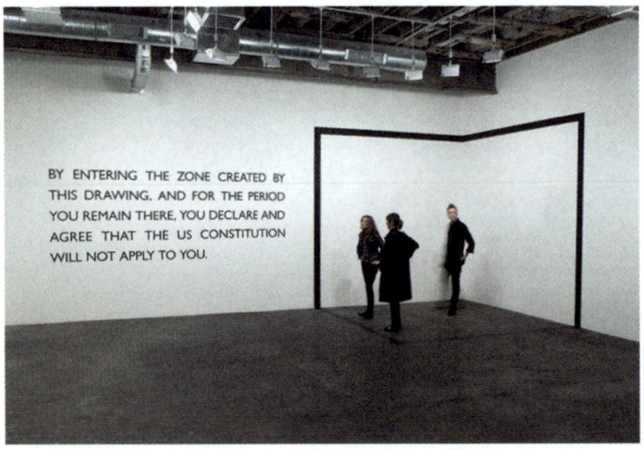

Carey Young, *Declared Void*, 2005. Vinyl drawing and text, dimensions variable, 133 × 133 inches (337.8 × 337.8 cm) as installed. Vinyl band: 6 inches (15.2 cm.); letters: 6 ¼ inches (15.8 cm) high. Installation view: Carey Young, *Consideration* at Midway Contemporary Art, Minneapolis, 17 March–5 May 2007. © Carey Young; Courtesy Paula Cooper Gallery, New York. Photo: Cameron Wittig.

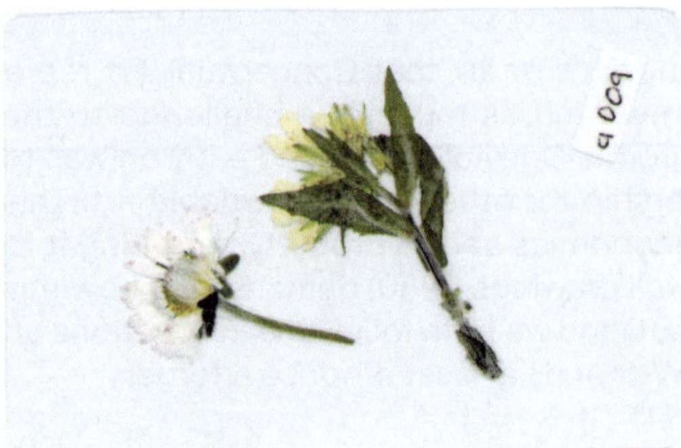

Monochrom and Ian Grigg, *Flower Currency*, 2006.

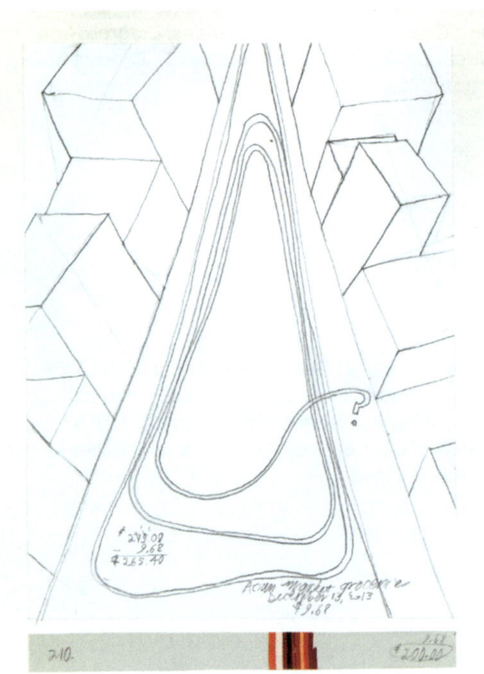

Danica Phelps, *#210 from Income's Outcome*, 2013. Pencil, watercolour and gouache on paper on wood.

Carey Young's *Declared Void* (2005) is a wall drawing that creates a space in which its audience enters into a contract agreeing that the constitution of the United States does not apply while they are within its bounds. Legal form as sculptural form, this is no longer about the relationship between art and money, but rather about the relationship between the individual, contract law, and the state. This is the kind of relationship that produces money, or at least fiat currency, and serves as a broader context for considering the more specific relationship between art and money.

The flower currency produced by a group of Viennese artists in 2005 is both a LETS-style complementary currency and a use of the aesthetics of pressed flowers to allegorise and aestheticise the relationship between nature, production, and value in economies.

#210 from Danica Phelps's series *Income's Outcome* (2013) shows the artist's expenditure on grocery shopping. If it depicted income rather than outcome, the stripes would be green rather than red. Phelps's work combines the ledger of their economic existence with the artistic record of their social presence.

Bitcoin as Critique

Bitcoin emerged as a critique of state-issued 'fiat' currency following the financial crisis of 2008. Bitcoin is a cryptocurrency, a piece of software that runs on computers ('nodes') spread across the network that communicate with each other to reach a shared consensus on the current state of a cryptographically-secured ledger. Every ten minutes or so these computers bundle up transactions into 'blocks', each of which refers to the previous block. This is the 'blockchain'.

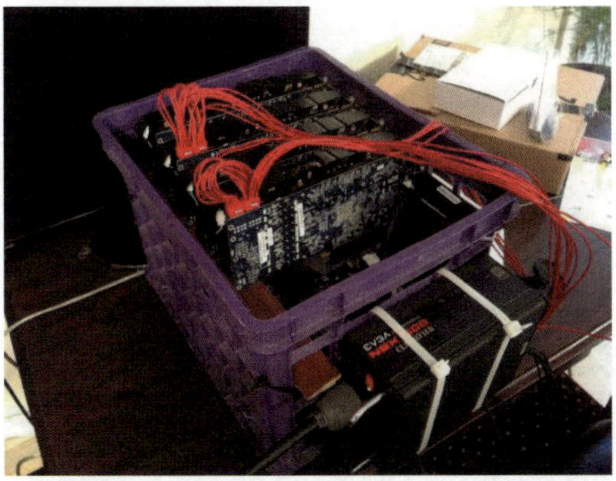

Milk-crate mining rig. Photo: Nehal Patel.

New blocks in the chain are validated (or 'mined') by nodes in the network using increasingly specialised hardware, such as this milk crate mining rig from a couple of years ago. They perform difficult to solve but easy to validate sums on each block, the 'proof of work', and the first node to succeed gets a reward (paid in Bitcoins) for doing so.

Bitcoin account addresses, Bitcoin transactions, and the proof of work system all use cryptographic algorithms. These are mathematical ways of taking data and creating an almost unfakeable, almost irreversible, almost unique identity for it (where 'almost' means 'as likely to fail as the Earth is likely to be hit by a civilisation-ending asteroid in the next twenty minutes'). The examples here show how feeding a cryptographic hash function the same data twice results in the same incredibly unlikely number, but feeding it even slightly different data results in very different and unrelated numbers.

Bitcoin uses these functions to secure its network in the 'proof of work' system by searching for auspicious numbers in their output (strings of zeros in the current scheme). My *Facecoin* (2014, see below, 269) implements an alternative proof of work system in which the useless work performed is that of portraiture, (mis-)using machine vision algorithms to find imaginary faces in cryptographic hashes represented as bitmaps rather than numbers.

Monkeycoin (2014, see below, 271) takes a different approach, searching for the complete works of Shakespeare in textual representations of those numbers.

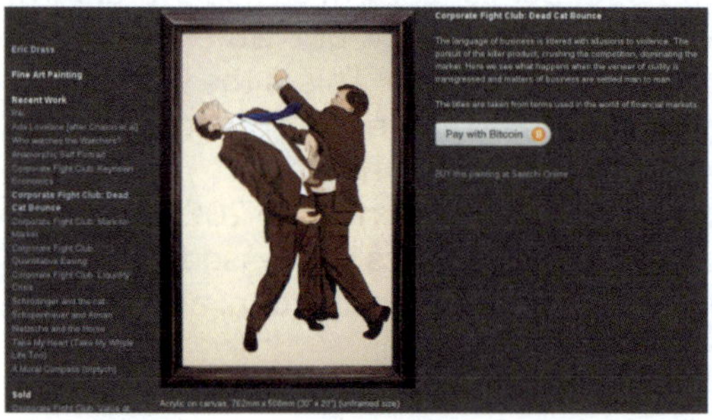

Eric Drass, *Corporate Fight Club*, 2012. Acrylic paint on wood.

Cryptocurrencies can be used in lieu of fiat currency for all kinds of transactions, including artistic ones. Here the artist Eric Drass is offering a painting for sale via Bitcoin. Different means of exchange create different kinds of social relationships: buying the painting via Bitcoin is a different kind of social and economic transaction than paying for it with fiat currency via Saatchi Online.

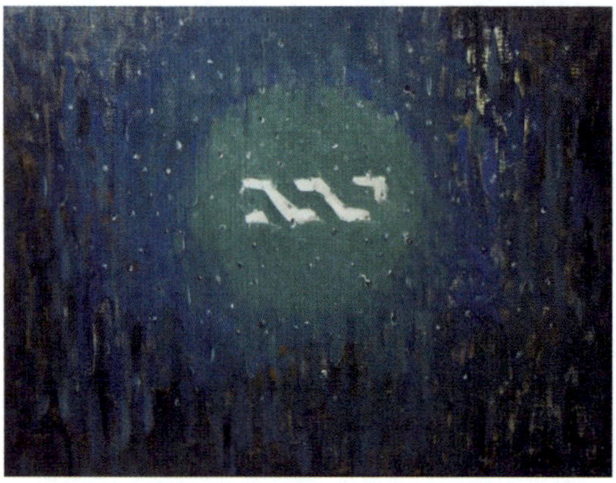

Theironman, *Nxtdrop*, 2014. 'Decentralised oil painting'.

Cryptocurrencies can be created as complementary currencies with specific intent or for specific constituencies. Banksycoin (2014) was an attempt to create a currency to pay for art and create a parallel economy for artistic production.

Cryptocurrency-based technology can change how individual artworks are owned as well as paid for. Ownership of theironman's *nxtdrop* (2014) is represented by shares on the 'nxt' blockchain. Ownership of the painting can be changed fractionally by dealing in those shares.

We Can Store Information Other Than Money on the Blockchain

There are poems, images, and other cultural artefacts embedded in the Bitcoin blockchain, disguised as transaction information. In *Proof of Existence* I embedded the cryptographic hash of my genome in the Bitcoin blockchain to establish my identity (2014, see p273).

Smart Contracts Generalize the Blockchain to Other Contracts

Caleb Larsen's *A Tool to Deceive and Slaughter* (2009) contains a computer that must be connected to the internet as part of the conditions of ownership, and which then immediately offers itself for sale on the eBay auction site. This kind of 'smart property' is a good example of smart contracts, in which arrangements such as ownership are managed by software rather or more immediately than by law.

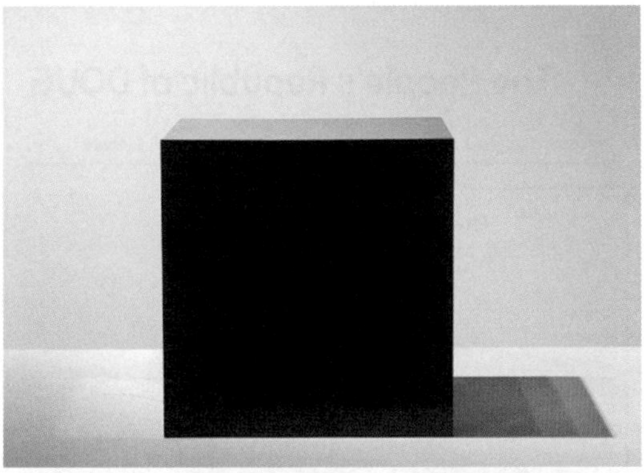

Caleb Larsen, *A Tool to Deceive and Slaughter*, 2009. Acrylic, custom electronics, programming, internet connection, online auction.

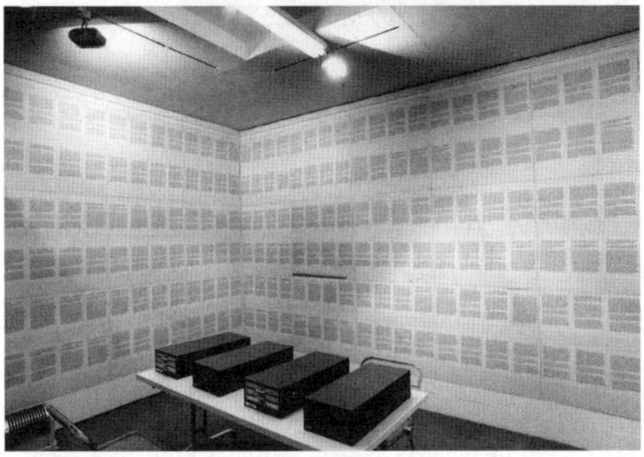

Art & Language, *Index 002*, 1972. 4 file cabinets texts and photostats, 320 index pages, dimensions variable. Installation, Lisson Gallery, London. Collection Herbert Foundation, Gent (A&L7200002). © Art & Language; Courtesy Lisson Gallery.

Ethereum Art Market (2014, see p90), uses the Ethereum smart contract system (a generalisation of Bitcoin to contracts other than for the exchange of money) to record 'ownership' of infinitely reproducible digital files and allow them to be 'sold' for cryptocurrency. Other systems exist to do this, such as the Monegraph and Rarebit systems.

Is Art (2014, see p257) uses a simple smart contract to democratise the nominational strategy of Conceptual Art. The contract can be set to nominate itself as art or not with a click of a mouse and the paying of a small fee to execute the change on the blockchain.

Art Is (2014, see p259) applies behavioural economics to the philosophy of art, allowing individuals to pay as much as they feel their definition of art is worth. This disincentivises malicious or unserious definitions and indicates an individual's confidence in their definition, using market mechanisms to price and allocate knowledge, and even truth, efficiently. fnord

CryptoCurrency and Smart Contracts Can Be Used to Constitute Artist Groups

Art & Language's *Index 002* (1972) is a collection of the group's writings assembled and indexed for presentation in a traditional gallery setting to assert their identity and productivity at a time when their largely conversational practice might not have looked much like 'art' to outside observers. Filing cabinets and photocopied sheets were contemporary information technology; later *Indexes* would use microfilm and (allegedly random) computer-generated tabulations. Their use and the production of the *Indexes* in general was both a solution to and a subject of the problems that Art & Language's work addressed. A contemporary group could use the blockchain to similarly focus and problematise their work.

The Cypherfunks are a distributed music group. Anyone who uploads a song to the SoundCloud music sharing web site tagged #thecypherfunks receives the groups cryptocurrency FUNK in return, becoming part of the group.

Dogecoin is one of the most popular 'altcoins', Bitcoin-derived cryptocurrencies that are not interoperable with the original Bitcoin network. It is the coin of an

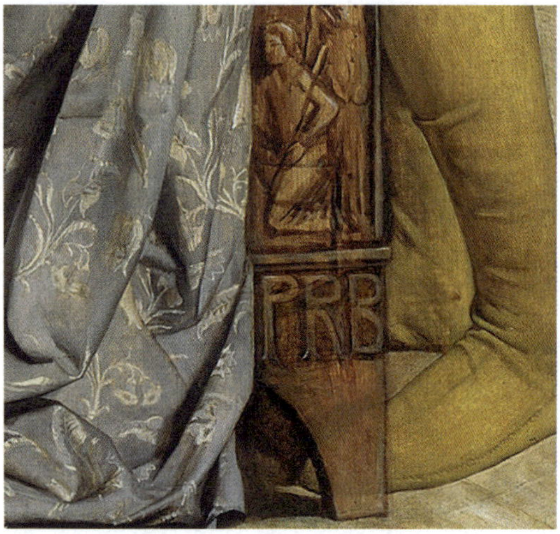

John Everett Millais, *Isabella*, 1849 (detail).

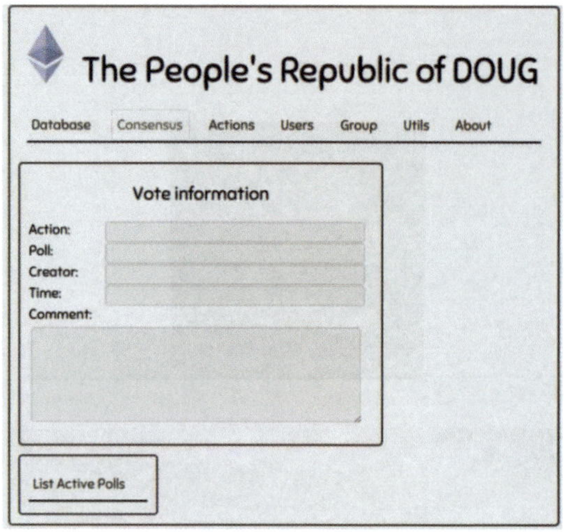

The People's Republic of DOUG

intentionally constructed culture of virtue and play, with its own argot and social norms based on internet memes (particularly the titular 'Doge' and the idea of a potlatch-like norm of tipping).

These are all more contemporary, and more complex, ways of demonstrating affiliation to a group than simply painting currency code-like letters on a canvas (as in Millais's *Isabella* [1849]). Possibly the ultimate in creating a group affiliation, or even a society, using smart contract technology is the idea of the 'Decentralised Autonomous Organisation' (DAO), an economic agent that exists on the blockchain and manages the resources of an organisation via code rather than by means of bylaws or legislation.

The People's Republic of DOUG (2014) is a DAO implemented as smart contracts on the Ethereum smart contract system's blockchain. You can become a citizen, own property, vote, and use its own currency in transactions—all functions traditionally provided by the state as conceived of in terms of contract law. Bitcoin's dream of a stateless future (but not a propertyless one, making it anarcho-capitalist rather than anarchist) realised in a few thousand lines of code. Imagine using (and/or critiquing) such a system for artistic organisation and/or production.

Conclusions

1. Sorting hype and scam from promise, and moral panic from critique, involves a learning curve when dealing with cryptocurrency.
2. We can use cryptocurrencies to find new ways of (encouraging) paying for art, defamiliarising and critiquing art-world economics by doing so.
3. AltCoins, crypto-tokens, smart contracts and DAOs are tools artists can use to explore new modes of social organisation and artistic production,
4. The ideology and technology of the blockchain and the materials of art history (especially the history of Conceptual Art) can provide useful resources for mutual experiment and critique.

'Now make art with it.'

The ABC of Accelerationist Blockchain Critique

Accelerationism

Accelerationism came to prominence in 2013 with Nick Srnicek and Alex Williams's hashtag-titled manifesto.[1] A cloud computing-era spin on the old Marxist argument that we first need to perfect capitalism in order to transcend it, its lineage is fleshed out *#accelerate: The Accelerationist Reader*,[2] which claims (among others) Nick Land's Skynet midwifery, J.G. Ballard's science-fictionalisation of culture, and Marx himself as precursors to accelerationism, establishing it as a serious anti-humanist response to the challenges that humanity faces if it is to avoid extinction. Similar to Christine Harold's strategy of 'intensification', accelerationism calls for us to appropriate the value of capitalist developments and transform them materially into something else, rather than attempt to resist them head-on or refuse them in our hearts.[3]

Bitcoin is an example of an accelerationist technology.[4] It uses internet-scale computing resources to rebuild social bonds by destroying the requirement for them in monetary exchange. You don't have to know me or trust me or any third parties to receive money from me in the form of Bitcoins. You just have to trust the algorithms that very publicly operate the Bitcoin network. The new Ethereum project takes the blockchain technology behind Bitcoin and generalises it to contracts for purposes other than just the transfer of money, although of course those contracts can involve payments. Ethereum contracts exist as a distributed database of small programs and their states that resembles nothing so much as an economic LambdaMOO. There's a good guide to their promise and potential pitfalls in the talk 'Ethereum: Freenet or Skynet?' by Berkman Center Fellow Primavera Di Filippi.[5]

Smart Contracts

Smart contracts and smart property, which uses smart contracts to identify and control ownership of physical resources, were first described by Nick Szabo in the 1990s. Smart contracts are 'smart' because they are implemented as computer code rather than as legal documents. Real-world examples include vending machines in which a contract to purchase goods is encoded into the simple software that dispenses carbonated drinks when you insert the correct money, RFID card payments for photocopies, and hire schemes that unlock scooters, bicycles, and cars and track their use with QR codes.

1 N. Srnicek and A. Williams. 'Manifesto for an Accelerationist Politics', in R. Mackay and A. Avanessian (eds), *#accelerate: The Accelerationist Reader* (Falmouth and Berlin: Urbanomic/Merve, 2014).
2 Ibid.
3 C. Harold, *OurSpace: Resisting the Corporate Control of Culture* (Minneapolis: University of Minnesota, 2009).
4 '*Computers and Capital*: The Rise of Digital Currency', above, 77.
5 <https://cyber.harvard.edu/events/luncheon/2014/04/difilippi>.

Would-be rentiers who try to launder their ambitions with the warm fuzziness of 'sharing' are salivating at the prospect, as are the incorrigible snake oil merchants of DRM, but that is not what concerns us here.

Smart contracts and smart property for art already exist. The artwork *A Tool to Deceive and Slaughter* (see p121) constantly resells itself on eBay. The GIF ownership service Monegraph[6] uses the NameCoin system to track notional ownership of instances of infinitely reproducible digital art. These are extensions of pre-digital art contracts such as certificates of authenticity or ownership for conceptual and immaterial artworks. They show a way for art to continue producing a useful critique of property and social relations under technoculture, and for new technology to feed art's ongoing critique of its own production and nature.[7]

Like Bitcoin, smart contracts and smart property do not require social trust to build social value, just running code. They have very limited functionality: they are unable to check RSS feeds on the internet for information, for example, as that information might be tampered with. This raises the question of how individuals can be encouraged to provide valid real-world information to smart contracts rather than just entering the values that will immediately profit them the most. Capitalist economics answers this with the concept of incentives. Value, and values, can be determined by the behaviour of individuals in markets in response to economic incentives. And smart contracts are intended to make markets more efficient.

I would like to apply this agoric approach to truth to the crisis of art criticism in the face of aggregation that I identified in 'The Proletarianisation of Art Criticism' (see p76). Individuals can be motivated to publish defensible aesthetic and art-critical opinions in novel ways via smart contracts. I am not proposing an automated or purely algorithmic art criticism here: human activity is the core of this approach. Nor am I proposing an Amazon Mechanical Turk-style exploitation of affective labour. Rather I am proposing an accelerationist approach, using the technology of digital capitalism to actively reroute the value of the social flows that it has extracted into sustainable human activity.

Art is no stranger to the idea of markets: the art world consists of one of the least regulated and therefore in theory one of the purest markets. But even ignoring the opacity and corruption of the art market, there is a problem with taking a direct approach to the art market as an arbiter of artistic value. As David Galenson's 2008 study of aesthetic value and market price showed, there is a problem in using pure market mechanisms to establish the value of art: many 'great works' have either never been auctioned or have not been to market in decades or even centuries.[8]

I therefore propose three different approaches to art criticism via smart contracts. For work exposed to the market, the mechanisms used to price shares and other financial assets can be used. For work with less exposure, SchellingCoins and prediction markets can work alongside these mechanisms via proxies.

Aesthetic Derivatives

The prices of financial assets, stocks and shares, or contracts for commodities for example, are set using a system of derivatives. Financial derivatives gained a bad reputation following their role in the global financial crash of 2008. By 2011 the notional

6 A. Dash, 'A Bitcoin for Digital Art', *medium.com*, 9 May 2014, <https://medium.com/message/a-bitcoin-for-digital-art-8c7db719e495>.
7 See 'Artworld Ethereum', 82, which provides code demonstrating how simple it is to implement some of these examples with technology dedicated to smart contracts.
8 D. Galenson, 'A Textbook Example of Ranking Artworks', *New York Times*, 4 August 2008, <https://www.nytimes.com/2008/08/04/arts/design/04pica.html>.

value of the derivatives being traded was almost ten times the total GDP of Planet Earth. And their automation by algorithmic high-frequency trading is being increasingly scrutinised by regulators.

There are many different kinds of derivatives: short and long options, futures, and exotics for example. But their function, in theory at least, is simple and beneficial. They enable individuals to profit by expressing whether they think a financial asset is over- or under-priced. This incentivises them to act upon this information. The resulting sharing of information and correction of prices benefits society.

Non-physical ownership, sponsorship, crowdfunding, dedications, and more exotic value relationships to physical works and, crucially, to works that have not or will not be sold, and to unownable digital art, can be represented by smart contracts. These can then be treated as the underlying assets of derivatives, also represented as smart contracts, in whole or, again crucially, in fractional parts or shares. Buying and selling derivatives of shares in digital artworks, and particularly going short or long on them, represents a critical position on their worth. Where the underlying asset does not represent actual ownership of the artwork, we are closer to a prediction market than a financial market. But if the assets themselves attract prestige or value regardless of their proxy status, they may become art objects in themselves.

Art criticism in such a market is a matter of financial investment and returns. Critics express their opinion of art, artists, and artistic trends by buying and selling different kinds of derivatives at different times. If they are shown to be correct over time, the market will reward them. Derivatives are a prime candidate for implementation as smart contracts. Indeed, there is already a project to create a standard language of (non-aesthetic) derivative smart contracts.[9]

Cultural SchellingCoins

Since Ethereum contracts have no direct access to the outside world (or the Web), contracts that require information about the outside world must access it through intermediaries. This means that contracts must trust those intermediaries, and if it is more profitable for them to lie to the contracts, that creates a problem. To remove this requirement of trust we can use a system that rewards people for independently supplying information that accurately reflects the true (or most likely) state of the world.

A SchellingCoin[10] is an Ethereum contract that allows people to send messages to it that register their opinion about (for example) the current temperature in Berlin or the exchange rate between dollars and yen. Those that set the majority view are rewarded for doing so, similarly to the operation of a prediction market. But how do they know which value to choose? The game theory concept of a focal point, or Schelling point, is an answer to a question that people who cannot communicate will give independently because it seems natural, appropriate, or special. SchellingCoins reward people who give the consensus answer to a question, and people can determine the right answer by converging on a Schelling point. For real-world phenomena such as temperature or exchange rates, the Schelling point is likely to be the correct answer. SchellingCoins can be implemented as smart contracts, removing the need for a trusted entity to run them.

SchellingCoins are designed to address external, quantitative phenomena. Opinions regarding cultural works are personal and qualitative, and spontaneous reactions to cultural works are even more so. This is different from the commonly expressed quantitative values that the SchellingCoin proposal requires. To adapt SchellingCoins to

9 <https://web.archive.org/web/20140627094135/http://fsc.stevens.edu/ACTUS/>.

10 V. Buterin, 'SchellingCoin: A Minimal-Trust Universal Data Feed', *ethereum.org*, 28 March 2014, <https://blog.ethereum.org/2014/03/28/schellingcoin-a-minimal-trust-universal-data-feed/>.

cultural criticism we must adopt the methods of collective intelligence and the digital Humanities, and use some tricks to turn personal opinion into cultural appraisal.

Collective intelligence algorithms work well with star rating systems and tags. These are popular methods for rating books, films, and music on ecommerce and review sites. They can be represented, aggregated, and extrapolated from easily by software, which makes them ideal for representing opinion in SchellingCoins. There are risks in using such systems, as demonstrated by the low rating of the film *Gunday* on IMDB, but they are easy and accessible to use.

Digital Humanities approaches often involve counting the frequency of words in texts or other unstructured phenomena. The results of binary checks or of counts can be applied to Schelling coins. For example, whether an artwork appears on *Contemporary Art Daily* or *Rhizome* or not, or whether the words 'blue' or 'postbinary' appear the most in reviews about it on major review sites, can be reported via further SchellingCoins or via trusted feeds or oracles.

To turn these approaches into a SchellingCoin, we do not ask what people think of an artwork. We ask them what they think the average reviewer will think of the artwork (or to protect against gaming, we ask them to predict the curve for all the star ratings for the work). Given the theory of focal points, the most likely answer is the one that people suspect will be true.

Cultural SchellingCoins can therefore function as aggregators of opinion-about-opinion-about artworks, producing qualitative but consensual evaluations and critiques of works of art that contain more information than purely price-based mechanisms. Using SchellingCoins to aggregate opinion about other SchellingCoins, Meta-SchellingCoins, can provide more general cultural critique.

Artistic Prediction Markets

To turn reviews into art criticism with a longer or broader perspective we can ask people not about the current state of reviews of the artwork but about what they will be in a year's time, five years' time, etc. How highly starred will they be and what tags/words will be used to describe them? Will the work (or the artist) be used as a point of comparison in reviews and articles? Will it (or they) still be being exhibited or purchased, and in what kinds of galleries? How much will the work sell for, or in the absence of sales, how many people will visit it at exhibitions? Will the artist still be working in that style, and if not how will their work have changed?

Each prediction can be represented as a security in a prediction market, and the current price of that security can be interpreted as the probability of that prediction. For example, a prediction market security might reward a hundred Satoshis or ten points if a particular artist has a headline show at Tate Modern. If you think there's an 80 percent chance of that happening, you can pay up to 80 Satoshis or 8 points for the security representing that prediction. If you're right, you gain in return for improving the market, if you're wrong you lose instead. There is evidence that prediction markets are successful, although they have been banned as a form of gambling in the US and the Pentagon's 2003 attempt at a political prediction market was quickly labelled a 'terrorism futures market' by the press and taken offline.

There is already a successful cultural prediction market, Hollywood Stock Exchange, where the price of 'shares' in actors, directors, and movies function as a prediction of their performance at the box office. The art market itself can be considered a kind of hybrid prediction market, but separating out that predictive function into a pure prediction market concentrating on critical evaluation may remove distortions that result from manipulation of the secondary market, and solve the problem of representing critically valuable artworks that aren't part of the art market.

It's also possible, as with Hollywood Stock Exchange's use of directors and actors as well as movies, to have prediction markets for other entities in the art world. Not just artists and galleries, but movements, styles, genres, subject matter, and even formal and aesthetic properties such as colours can be represented as securities in a prediction market. Buying and selling them can help generate a shared understanding of their potential and impact.

Prediction markets can be represented as Distributed Autonomous Organisations (DAOs) on Ethereum's blockchain, free of any central control. DAOs present an opportunity to rethink and reimplement organisations on the blockchain. As well as markets, they can be used to manage events, publications, cooperatives and educational or art world institutions on various organisational models in a public and transparent way.

Conclusion

Cultural SchellingCoins, Artistic Prediction Markets, and Aesthetic Derivatives are accelerationist technologies for art criticism. Not necessarily for art criticism of the kind that survives online after being exiled from print media. Rather, a functional equivalent to it that recaptures its lost authority in the form of a relationship between individuals and artistic production that exerts a guiding hand on its reception and direction. Since these technologies represent an emergent ontology of art and aesthetics, manipulating them, whether through technical or social means, is itself at once both art and art criticism.

Vampire Digital Art

In 'How Readers Will Discover Books in Future', science fiction author Charles Stross envisions a future in which weaponised eBooks demand your attention by copying themselves onto your mobile devices, wiping out the competition, and locking up the user interface until you've read them.[1]

This is only just science fiction. Even the earliest viruses often displayed messages, and malware that denies access to your data until you pay to decrypt it already exists. ePub ebooks can execute arbitrary JavaScript, and PDF documents can execute arbitrary shell scripts. Compromised PDFs have been found in the wild. Stross's weaponised ebooks are not more than one step ahead of this.

Why would eBooks want to act like that? To find readers. In the attention economy, the time required to read a book is a scarce resource. Most authors write because they want to be read and to find an audience. Stross's proposal is just an extreme way of achieving this. In Stross's scenario, authors are like the criminal gangs that use botnet malware to get your computer to pursue their ends rather than your own, use adware to coerce you into performing actions that you wouldn't otherwise, or use phishing attacks to get scarce resources such as passwords or money from users.

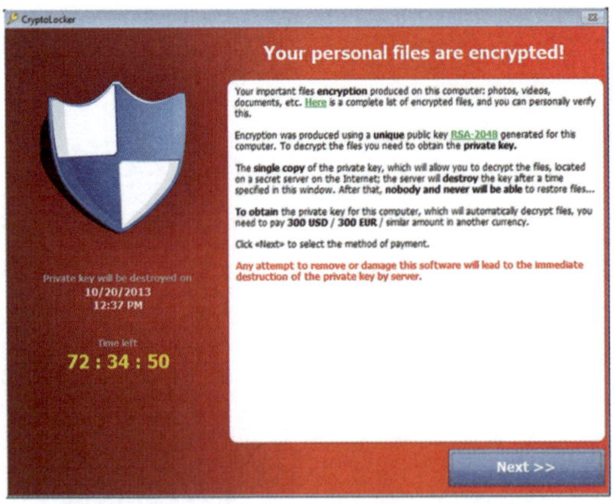

Since so much new art is made that even omnivorous promotional blogs like *Contemporary Art Daily* cannot keep up, scarcity of attention has now become a problem for art as well as for literature. And when people do visit shows, they spend more time reading the labels than looking at the art. In these circumstances Stross's strategies make sense for art as well. Particularly for net art and software art.

A net or software artwork that acted like Stross's vampire eBooks would copy itself onto your system and refuse to unlock it until you have had time to fully experience

1 C. Stross, 'Polemic: How Readers Will Discover Books in Future', 10 October 2013, <https://www.antipope.org/charlie/blog-static/2013/10/polemic-how-readers-will-disco.html>.

it or have clicked all the way through it. It could do this in web browsers or virtual worlds as a scripting attack, on mobile devices as a malicious app, or on desktop systems as a classic virus.

Unique physical art also needs viewers. Malicious software can promote art, taking the place of private view invitation cards. Starting with mere botnet spam that advertises private views, more advanced attacks can refuse to unlock your mobile device until you post a picture of yourself at the show on Facebook (identifying this using machine vision and image classification algorithms), check in to the show on FourSquare, or give it a five-star review along with a write-up that indicates that you have actually seen it. In the gallery, compromised Google Glass headsets or mobile phone handsets can make sure the audience know which artwork wants to be looked at by blocking out others or painting large arrows over them pointing in the right direction.

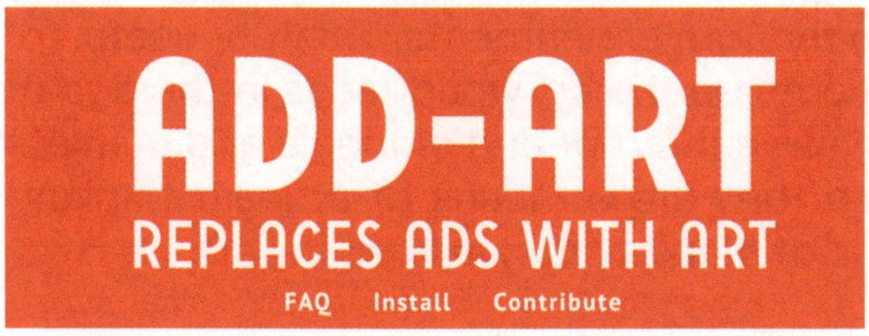

Add-Art, <https://add-art.org/>.

Net art can intrude more subtly into people's experiences in the form of aesthetic intervention agents. Adware can display art rather than commercials. Add-Art is a benevolent precursor to this. Email viruses and malicious browser extensions can intervene in the aesthetics of other media. They can turn text into Mezangelle, or glitch or otherwise transform images into a given style. In the early 1990s I wrote a PostScript virus that could (theoretically) copy itself onto printers and creatively corrupt vector art, but fortunately I didn't have access to the Word BASIC manuals I needed to write a virus that would have deleted the word 'postmodernism' from any documents it copied itself to.[2]

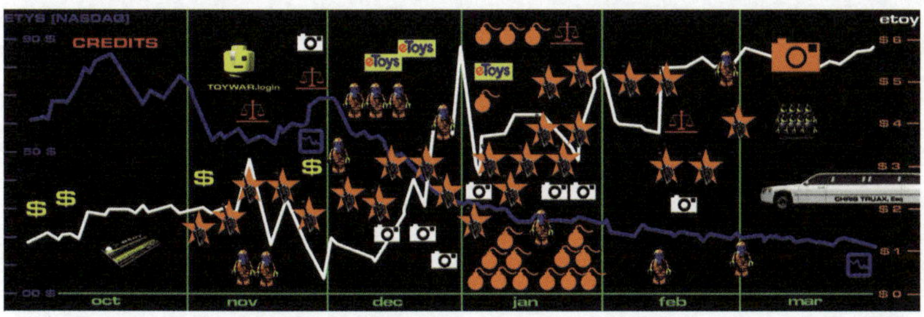

eToy, *Toywar Timeline*, 1999.

Going further, network attacks themselves can be art. Art malware botnets can use properties of network topography and timing to construct artworks from the net and activity on it. There are precursors to this in Etoy's *ToyWar* (1999) and EDT's *SWARM* (1998), a distributed denial of service (DDoS) attack presented as an artwork at Ars Electronica. My *sendvalues* (2011) is a network testing tool that could be misused, LOIC-style, to perform DDoS attacks that construct waves, shapes, and bitmaps out of synchronised floods of network traffic. This kind of attack would attract and direct attention as art at internet scale.

None of this would touch the art market directly. But a descendant of Caleb Larsen's *A Tool to Deceive and Slaughter* (2012, see p121) that chooses a purchaser from known art dealers or returns itself to art auction houses, then forces them to buy it using the techniques described above rather than offering itself for sale on eBay. would be both a direct implementation of Stross's ideas in the form of a unique physical artwork and something that would exist in direct relation to the art world.

2 <https://rhea.art/postscript-viruses>. See above, 16–17.

Using the art market itself as the network to exploit, rather than the internet, makes for even more powerful art malware exploits. Aesthetic analytics of the kind practiced by Lev Manovich[3] and already used to guide investment by Mutual Art[4] can be combined with the techniques of stock market high-frequency trading (HFT) to create new forms by intervening in and manipulating prices directly through art sales and auctions. As with HFT, the activity of the software used to do this can create aesthetic forms within market activity itself, like those found by Nanex (see p116).[5] This can be used to build and destroy artistic reputations, to create aesthetic trends within the market, and to create art movements and canons. Saatchi automated. The aesthetics of this activity can then be sold back into the market as art in itself, creating further patterns.

The techniques suggested here are at the very least illegal and immoral, so it goes without saying that you shouldn't attempt to implement any of them. But they are useful as unrealised artworks for guiding thought experiments. They are useful for reflecting on the challenges that art in and outside the art world faces in the age of the attention-starved population of the pervasive internet and of media and markets increasingly determined by algorithms. And they are a means of at least thinking through an ethic rather than just an aesthetic of market critique in digital art.

3 <http://lab.softwarestudies.com/p/cultural-analytics.html>.

4 M. Maneker, 'Big Data and the Art World: Mutual Art', *Art Market Monitor*, 13 October 2013, <https://www.artmarketmonitor.com/2013/10/13/big-data-and-the-art-world-mutual-art/>.

5 A.C. Madrigal, 'Market Data Firm Spots the Tracks of Bizarre Robot Traders', *The Atlantic*, 4 August 2010, <https://www.theatlantic.com/technology/archive/2010/08/market-data-firm-spots-the-tracks-of-bizarre-robot-traders/60829/>.

Agoric Aesthetics and Philosophy

Agorising aesthetics and philosophy means producing them using market pricing mechanisms. The model for this is the market-based software of agoric computing. The advantage of such a system is that it incentivises both production and efficiency. By internalising market forces, the perverse incentives of gamified systems such as academic research points can be avoided.

An agoric system needs a currency; for efficiency's sake we will use a cryptocurrency. There are several ways of implementing a currency for an agoric system using cryptocurrency systems. We can use coloured coins, nxt or Counterparty assets, or Ethereum contracts similar to the Token System example in the Ethereum White Paper to create coins, tokens, or other quantifiable valences. For simplicity's sake I will call all of these 'tokens'. Different implementations allow different capabilities: fungibility, revocation, transferability.

An artist group or artistic movement can use a store of tokens allocated by vote or other mechanism to artists or artworks that they deem part of the movement and its output. The Cypherfunks project is an existing example of such a system. Such a system combines the nominative practices of Dadaist, Conceptual, and some Pop/Post-Pop art with the social and aesthetic function of materially identifying in- and out-groups. A single-artist token could be used to create an oeuvre in the style of Duchamp or Kostabi.

Art critics can use tokens to embody critique. A single-value token can be used to embody critical approval, a pair of oppositely valenced tokens to represent approval/opprobrium (and to revise critical opinion should it later change), a family of tokens with different star rankings can be used to implement a star system at the cost of fungibility. The critic sends tokens either to the artist's address in the cryptocurrency system or to an address representing the hash or proxy hash of the artwork. The artist or artwork's standing can be discovered by counting the number and kind of critical tokens associated with it.

Philosophical treatises can be constructed agorically. Axioms and citations, logical and rhetorical moves can be assigned point costs either as classes (premise, objection, rebuttal) or individually (Derrida, Arendt, Meillassoux). Each usage increases the price of the essay. Point costs and budgets can be assigned per hundred words or for a given form (short essay, review, thesis, journal article etc.) or context (particular journals, web sites, or educational institutions). Essays are then written to the budget. Or price essays according to the system and then let publishers (and readers) choose which to consume on that basis. For a more dynamic system, prices can be set using a PageRank-style system as a product of the cost of cited works.

The pricing of this essay is left as an exercise for the reader....

2015

Ethereum Standardised Art Contract API

The Ethereum project allows you to create arbitrary smart contracts to run on its blockchain. To ensure that those arbitrary contracts can communicate where they need to, they have published a list of standard contract interfaces.[1]

These standards allow different coins, registries, data feeds, and other common contracts to communicate with and use each other in a well understood way.

Let's extend this to art contracts, starting with a smart artwork. Next we'll cover exhibitions and reviews.

These interfaces are applicable to contracts other than for art. Feedback and suggestions on how to generalise them gratefully received.

Purchasable Artwork

A smart contract artwork either embodies an artwork in itself, represents or controls some aspect of an artwork, or contains or is a proxy for it in some way.

The contract's owner is expected to be the artist, and not to change. 'Ownership' of the artwork is recorded within the contract.

Methods

offer

```
offer(address _purchaser, uint _price, uint _until)
```

Only callable by the artwork owner. This is separate from the contract owner.

Offer the work for sale. The `_purchaser` address can be zero, in which case anyone can buy the artwork. The `_price` can be zero, in which case the `_purchaser` need not send any funds. And `_until` can be a UNIX timestamp in the past, in which case the artwork is not actually for sale. Zero works well for this.

purchase

```
purchase() returns (bool _success)
```

If the caller matches the `_purchaser` (or it is set to zero), sends enough Ether to match `_price` (or `_price` is zero), and the offer has not expired, the caller becomes the new owner of the artwork.

purchase Fee

```
purchaseFee() return (uint8 _percentage)
```

The percentage of the purchase price that goes to the contract owner (the artist) rather than the purchaser. A functional equivalent to the 'Artist Resale Right'.

1 <https://eth.wiki/en/concepts/standardized-contract-apis>.

setPurchaseFee
`setPurchaseFee(uint8 _percentage)`

Callable only by the contract owner.

This sets the percentage of the purchase price that will go to the contract owner rather than to the purchaser. It can be set to zero.

Events

Offered
`Offered(address seller, address purchaser, uint price, uint duration)`

The artwork was offered for sale by the current owner of the artwork, recorded as `seller`.

Sold
`Sold(address seller, address buyer, uint price)`

The artwork was sold by `seller` to `buyer` for the `price` given in Ether.

Exhibitable Artwork

An exhibitable smart contract artwork separates out the capability to exhibit the artwork from simple ownership, and places it under the contract's control.

Methods

Exhibit
`exhibit(address _at, uint _duration) returns (bool _success)`

Mark the work as exhibited at `address` for `_duration` seconds from success of the transaction, if the caller sends sufficient Ether to cover the exhibition fee.

The address the work is exhibited `_at` can be privileged by the specific implementation of the contract (for example, a web server can allow access only from an address that can sign requests with the `_at` address key).

exhibitFee
`exhibitFee() returns (uint _fee)`

The number of Ether per second payable as an exhibition fee. Zero means that exhibiting the artwork is free.

setExhibitFee
`setExhibitFee(uint _fee)`

Callable only by the contract owner.

This sets the number of Ether per second payable as an exhibition fee. It can be set to zero.

Events

Exhibited
`Exhibited(address indexed at, uint duration)`

The artwork was exhibited at the given address for `duration` seconds.

2015

Ethereum Art Ecosystem

The blockchain is an obvious medium for storing titles to property beyond currency. This includes property titles for artworks, particularly digital artworks. But there is nothing smart about using smart contracts for that. Rather than seeking to bring the failings of DRM to the blockchain, we should seek to use smart contracts to formalise more interesting economies of relationships between art and its audiences.

The Basics

Items

Everything is an item.

Owners

Every item has an owner. This is simply an Ethereum address from which instruction transactions will be obeyed. They can be implemented as basically as a GUI for a human operator or by complex blockchain or oracle systems.

Containers

Many items can have a pseudo-spatial relationship to other items, containing them in the way that a gallery contains a show or a magazine contains a review for example. This is distinct from the control relationship of ownership.

An item's container is its location.

Purchasing an instance of an artwork makes the purchaser the container for that instance, not the owner of the artwork contract.

Artworks

Smart artworks are the self-driving cars or high-frequency trading algorithms of the smart contract/smart property art world. Their most important feature is that they manage their own exhibition and sale—they evaluate offers and make the decision whether to accept them or not automatically.

Editions

An artwork can simulate scarcity or manage exposure by having a limited edition size. This is a count of the number of instances of the artwork that can be included in containers at one time. An edition size of one is a unique artwork.

When an artwork is sold or exhibited, this doesn't decrease the edition size but does reduce the amount of the edition available to be sold or exhibited simultaneously.

Provenance

The provenance of an artwork is its sale, exhibition, and critical history. All of these are stored on the blockchain as a natural result of their operation (and as recorded Ethereum 'events').

Display

Authentication

An artwork can be queried to find which containers currently hold instances of it. This can be used to authenticate displayed artworks. Authentication information can be displayed in the interface or accompanying materials for an exhibition.

Control

Artworks can (weakly) control exhibition by storing their assets on an IP-locked website and only allowing a whitelist of addresses to access it. Containers provide an IP address and proxy their exhibition of the artwork through that.

This is obviously subject to IP spoofing and cannot prevent downloading, but provides an example of a system of this kind for people who want it.

Sale and Exhibition

Collections can make offers to artworks to permanently purchase or temporarily exhibit them.

It is up to the artwork to decide whether they accept the offer or not.

Purchased instances of an artwork may also allow their owners to veto or suggest their sale or exhibition.

Simple Offers

A simple offer to purchase consists of a price.

A simple offer to exhibit consists of a time, a duration, and a fee.

The artwork can accept or decline the offer based on availability, whether the price or fee is sufficient, and any external information about the address the offer was sent from (e.g. an external blacklist).

Tagged Offers

Tagged offers are an example of a slightly more flexible system for artworks to decide whether to accept an offer or not.

The collection makes an offer formatted as a dictionary of key/value pairs. The artwork then evaluates this offer, most simply by comparing it against its own tag dictionary (and for price, etc. as with a simple offer).

The disadvantage of this method is that the tag values must be trusted by the artwork. This can be addressed by a trusted third party signing the tags, or by a SchellingCoin-style evaluation of the tags.

Exhibition Fees

Artworks receive fees for being exhibited (these can be set to zero if desired). They can pass these on to the owner of their contract (presumably the artist).

Resale Refusal and Fees

Artworks can veto sales as well as exhibitions. They can also take a percentage of any sale price, simulating the Droit de Suite/Artist's Resale Right (this can be set to zero if desired).

Collections

Collections are containers. They contain artworks. Shows, museums, and galleries are all collections.

Temporary and permanent collections feature artworks loaned for exhibition or purchased to be held in museum or personal collections.

Collections have selection and acceptance policies.

Exhibitions, auctions, awards, competitions, and commissions are containers.

Exhibitions

An exhibition occurs at an institution. It contains a particular number of artworks for a particular duration (which may be perpetual).

The exhibition must offer artworks an exhibition fee and details of its duration. For more complex schemes it must provide the artwork with further information, for example the dictionary required by 'Tagged Offers'.

For the duration of the exhibition, the artwork will register it as the container for one of its instances.

Auctions

Auctions are containers which can accept and enforce bids up until a time limit. The placing and any extra evaluation of bids is handled by other contracts.

Awards

Awards are containers of works entered for the award, with the actual award allocated by oracle, SchellingCoin, or other auditor contract.

Competitions

Turner-Prize-style competitions combine exhibitions with an award at the end, allocated by oracle, SchellingCoin or other auditor contract.

Commissions

Commissions specify requirements as tags and offer a price for satisfying them as confirmed by a SchellingCoin or other auditor contract.

Reviews

Reviewers produce five-star reviews of artworks, with a brief title.

These are aggregated by collections and may be referred to by the artwork.

They can be filtered by reviewer reputation.

Conclusion

With just a few basic types of contract and with some complexity either deferred or excluded from the system, it is possible to make smart artworks and art institutions in code online in the blockchain.

By moving the curatorial and developmental functions of the art world into the artworks and institutions themselves, it is possible to remove the vagaries of human attention from the development of the art market while still representing human economic and aesthetic interests within it.

DAOWO: DAO It With Others

DIWO and DAOs

DIWO (Do It with Others) is a distributed campaign for emancipatory, networked art practices instigated by Furtherfield in 2006.

A DAO is a Decentralised Autonomous Organisation, effectively a corporation or a charitable trust implemented in networked computer code.

Both are decentralised. A DAO has no single point of failure on the network, existing on the blockchain. A DIWO event is organised online and open to participants worldwide.

Both are an application of network technology to social organisation. A DAO implements a corporation, charity, club, or cooperative. A DIWO event organises artists, curators, and writers to produce and exhibit work together.

Both are rule-driven and participatory. A DAO consists of trustless, incorruptible code that serves the interests of its members or clients. A DIWO event is a themed open call for artworks.

Both are ways of managing scarce resources. A DAO manages resources such as a cryptocurrency token or the lock on a door. A DIWO event allocates the productive efforts and attention of an audience and the display space of a gallery.

A DAOWO would be a combination of the two, a Decentralised Autonomous Organisation with Others.

The Benefits of DAOWO for DAOs and DIWO

DAOs are a new technology. They need an application that allows them to demonstrate their benefits without getting tied up with the responsibilities and risks of corporate or charitable tasks.

DIWO events require organisation, funding, participation, and space. Administering and supporting these tasks is resource-intensive.

Implementing a DIWO event as a DAO presents both a practical opportunity and a cultural focus for both.

For DAOs, DIWO offers a focused organisational task with well understood requirements that are not related to human health, safety, or wealth. Arts events have disproportionate cultural reach, providing an opportunity for the wider public to encounter and consider DAOs.

For DIWO, a DAO offers a new way of funding and engaging with arts audiences. As well as being a useful tool, it can provide subject matter for the event.

(Productive) Tensions between DAOs and DIWO

Cryptocurrency culture tends to skew right/libertarian, arts culture tends to skew left.

DAOs can implement any organisational scheme, but many current proposals are based on monetary, token, or share schemes that are exclusive and presuppose capitalist modes of relation.

There can be technical, educational, and economic barriers to using cryptocurrency systems. This contrasts with the purposely low barrier to entry of DIWO. This can be addressed with a web front end to hide much of the complexity or by making learning and critique of the process part of the value of the DIWO event.

Possible DAOWOs

DIWO as DAO

Implementing a DIWO event as a DAO can provide support for funding (by selling tokens as donations, beware current legal developments on crowdsales/crypto equity), setting the subject of the DIWO event (managing voting or consensus), submissions (by tracking works), curation and critique (by supporting the tagging and filtering of submissions). A simple DAO can manage funding and submissions, a more complex one can add other features.

A DIWO DAO

Making a DAO both the implementation and the critical focus of a DIWO event both offers practical advantages and provides an anchor for reflection on the potential and wider cultural context of cryptocurrency and the neoliberal economics that it is both a reaction to and in danger of being captured by.

A Satirical DIWO DAO

To defuse possible problems or objections and to frame the economic expectations of cryptocurrency proponents and the critical expectations of cultural theorists, it would be possible to make the DAO inherently satirical or playful, similar to the Dogecoin cryptocurrency.

Crypto 2.0 and DAWCs: Dawn of Decentralised Autonomous Workers' Councils

Many of both Bitcoin's most vocal proponents and its detractors agree that the way the cryptocurrency operates technologically determines the form of the economy and therefore the society that uses it. That society would be anarcho-capitalist, lacking state institutions (anarcho-) but enforcing commodity property law (capitalist). If this is true, then Bitcoin has the potential to achieve a far greater political effect than financial engineering efforts such as the Euro or quantitative easing, and with far fewer resources. Perhaps variations on this technology can create alternatives to Bitcoin that determine or at least afford different socioeconomic orders.

Bitcoin is already more than half a decade old, and 'Crypto 2.0' systems that build on its underlying blockchain technology (the blockchain is a network-wide shared database built by consensus, Bitcoin uses it for its ledger) are starting to emerge. The most advanced allow the creation of entire organisations and systems of organisation on the blockchain, as Decentralised Autonomous Organisations (DAOs). We can use them to help create those different socioeconomic orders.

Workers' Councils are a libertarian socialist system of organisation. Rather than implementing Soviet-style centralised command economies, workers' councils are decentralised and democratic. Workers in a particular workplace decide what their objectives are, then appoint temporary (and instantly revocable) delegates to be responsible for achieving them. Workplaces appoint representatives to local councils, local councils appoint representatives to regional councils, and so on, always temporarily and revocably. It is a system of face-to-face socialisation and political representation rather than top-down control.

This system emerged at various times in Europe, South America, and the Middle East throughout the twentieth century. It is a very human method of governance, in stark contrast to both the 'trustless' code of Bitcoin and the centralised politics of the Soviets. That said, technology can assist organisation as easily as it can support material production. In the 1970s the *cordones* of Chile interfaced with the Allende government's Project Cybersyn network,[1] and contemporary online workers' collectives can use the internet to coordinate.

A DAO is a blockchain-based program that implements an organisation's governance and controls its resources using code rather than law. There can be a fetishistic quality to the idea of cold, hard, unyielding software perfect in its unambiguous transparency and incapable of human failing in its decision making. There can be similar fetishistic qualities to legal and political organisational perfectionism—this doesn't disqualify any of their subjects as useful ideals. However, they need to be tempered pragmatically.

The public code and records of a DAO can help with the well known problem of structurelessness, and can store information more efficiently and reliably than a human being with a pen and paper. The much vaunted trustlessness of cryptocurrency and smart contract systems can help build trust in communication within and between

1 E. Medina, *Cybernetic Revolutionaries: Technology and Politics in Allende's Chile* (Cambridge, MA and London: MIT Press, 2011).

groups—cryptographically signed minutes are relatively hard to forge, although the ambiguity of language is impossible to avoid even in the mathematics of software.[2]

The delegates of a workers' council can be efficiently and transparently voted on, identified by, and recalled using a DAO. This makes even more sense for distributed groups of workers, groups that share a common cause but lack a geographic centre. Delegates can even be *implemented* as smart contracts, code written to control resource allocation and evaluate performance in the pursuit of their objective (unless recalled by the council that created them).

Entire councils, and inter-council organisations, can be supported or implemented in their organisation as DAOs. Such support would include communication and record keeping. Implementation includes control of resources, running delegates as code, and even setting objectives for delegates programmatically.

The latter finally brings the concept of DAOs into direct conflict with the spirit of the workers' council. Councils exist to allow individual human beings to express and agree on their objectives, not to have them imposed from above. Being controlled by code is no better than political or economic control. It is the nature of this relationship to code, politics, or the economy that is positive or negative: writing code to charge someone or something with making sure a task is undertaken is no different from writing it in the minutes, and makes more explicit that organisation is production as *the subject of work in itself*. A democratic, recallable DAO that sets objectives is very different from a blob of capital with unchangeable orders to maximise its profits online.

The resources that a DAO controls need not be monetary (or tokenised). A DAO that controls access to property, energy, or other resources can contribute to avoiding the pricing problem that conventional economics regarded as a showstopper for the Soviet cybernetic economic planning of 'Red Plenty'.[3] DAOs need not even be created to represent human organisations—'deodands' can represent environmental commons as economic actors. These can then interact with workers' council DAOs, representing environmental factors as social and economic peers and avoiding the neoliberal economic problems of both externalities and privatisation.

Workers' Council DAOs, or Decentralised Autonomous Workers' Councils (DAWCs) are science fiction, but only just. Workers' councils have existed and been plugged in to the network, structurelessness and scalability are problems, DAOs exist and can help with this. Simply tokenising 'sharing economy' (actually rentier economy) forms, for example replacing Uber's taxi sharing with La'zooz while maintaining the exploitative logic of disintermediation, isn't enough.

If we are unable or unwilling to accelerate the social and productive forces of technology to take us to the moon, we can at least embrace and extend them in a more human direction.

2 J. Freeman, 'The Tyranny of Structurelessness', <https://www.jofreeman.com/joreen/tyranny.htm>.
3 F. Spufford, *Red Plenty* (Minneapolis: Graywolf, 2012).

Plantoid: The Blockchain-Based Art that Makes Itself

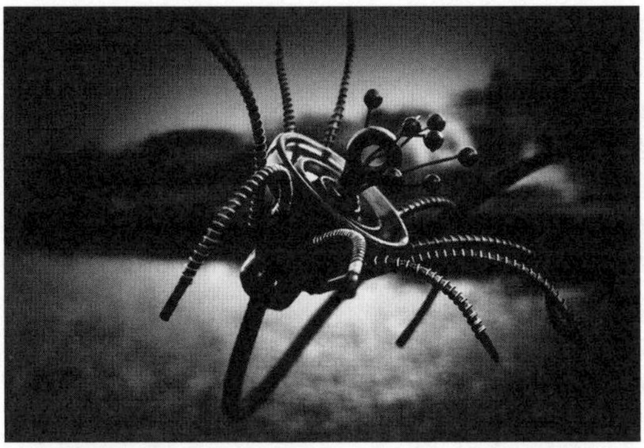

Okhaos, *Plantoid*, 2015. Photo: Primavera De Filippi.

Plantoid (2015) by Okhaos is a self-creating, self-propagating artwork system that uses blockchain technology to gather and manage the resources it needs to become real and to participate in the art world. Structured as a Decentralised Autonomous Organisation (DAO), once it is set in motion the code of the Plantoid system combines the functions of artwork, artist, and art dealer in a single piece of software.

As its name implies, the physical Plantoid artworks are cyborg-looking welded sculptures of flowering plants. Flowers are a popular icon of naturalised aesthetics in art and culture. Their aesthetic and art-historical appeal makes them an effective subject for subversion. Radicalised flowers wander through recent art like triffids through the English countryside. Helen Chadwick's *Piss Flowers* (1991–92) are a proto-xenofeminist riposte to idealisation of nature and the body. Mary Anne Francis's *The Blooming Commons* (2005) combines the ideas of organic and creative fecundity to help artist and audience consider how making art Open Source affects its aura. *Plantoid* can easily be cast in this tradition.

The physical form of *Plantoid* is determined by its blockchain presence, which represents an advance on the state of the art. The Bitcoin blockchain is a database that represents control of resources. Most simply these resources are amounts of Bitcoin, but we can encode information representing other resources—and the right to control them—into the blockchain as well. Current general-purpose Bitcoin blockchain-based systems such as Counterparty can easily represent tokens for games, for reward and voucher schemes, or for stocks and shares. Placing these on the blockchain presents no magical improvement over existing means of issuing them, but it does reduce the barrier to entry and make securing and maintaining them easier. It also defamiliarises them by placing them in a new context and makes them accessible and thereby inspirational to new audiences. Melanie Swan turns this idea up to 11 in her excellent survey of the state of the art and its future potential, *Blockchain*, which describes the application of the idea of blockchains to the global economy and ultimately even the human mind.[1]

Beyond tokens, the blockchain can be a cheap and effective database of existing property and rights, including recording Free Culture licensing. It is simple to create

1 M. Swan, *Blockchain* (Sebastopol, CA: O'Reilly, 2015).

such a system, I made the first one for artworks based on Ethereum myself.[2] It cannot be an effective means of policing DRM (as DRM is inherently broken)[3] and must not be treated as a means of rolling back the limits of and exceptions to the existing property and copyright regimes or of creating new entitlements ex nihilo. This would turn a technology with great (if contentious) potential for liberation into a tool of exploitation.[4] An act such as making a GIF of Apple's new emoticons and selling the blockchain title to it for $250 reflects existing social pathologies rather than new technological or artistic affordances.

The technobiophilic[5] machine-nature-form hybrid nature of *Plantoid* is described by Okhaos in terms that cast cryptocurrency as metabolic and reproductive resource. To quote the project page:

> Perhaps the initial Plantoid will need $1000 to fully turn into a blossom. Whenever that particular threshold for the Plantoid is reached, the reproduction process starts: the Plantoid only needs to identify a new person or group of persons (ideally, a group of artists) to create a new version of itself. Given the right conditions, the Plantoid is able to manufacture herself, by executing a smart contract that lives on the blockchain, and has the ability to commission welders, companies, and other beings to build and assemble a similar being.

It's here that we see how *Plantoid* represents an advance on existing systems. The parameters of each physical Plantoid are encoded on the Ethereum (rather than the Bitcoin) blockchain as smart contracts, representing the economic and manufacturing logic and the aesthetics of its production as a kind of genome. *Plantoid* is an active artistic production agent rather than a passive registry of existing art.

The defamiliarising effect of the blockchain allows us to unbundle the collections of rights and responsibilities that make up roles within the mainstream art world. Paying for the creation of art, its storage and restoration, transport and exhibition. Inspiring, designing, manufacturing, promoting, experiencing, critiquing, and art. The artist, the gallerist, the critic, the installer, the attendant. A new territory like the blockchain allows us to shake things up rather than trying to double down on existing relations and distribution of wealth in order to extract new rents.

Plantoid opens up the roles of artistic production in precisely this way. It uses the structure of a DAO to incentivise the funding, governance, production, exhibition, and reception of Plantoids in a virtuous circle (a positive feedback loop of production). None of this confers ownership or property rights over the physical Plantoid artworks upon individual human beings. Their relationships are closer to those of patronage, crowdfunding, or tipping, but unbundled further.[6] There are technological precedents for this, such as the way Aaron Koblin's *The Sheep Market* (2008) commissions drawings from clickworkers,[7] the way Caleb Larsen's *A Tool to Deceive and Slaughter* (2009) manages its own sale, the way Bitnik's *Random Darknet Shopper* (2014) orders goods for delivery to the gallery, or Imogen Heap's release of the single 'Tiny Human' (2015) using Ethereum smart contracts. From the project page again:

2 See 'Ethereum Art Market', above, 90.
3 C. Doctorow, 'Microsoft Research DRM talk', 17 June 2004, <https://craphound.com/msftdrm.txt>.
4 See 'Crypto 2.0 and DAWCs', above, 139.
5 S. Thomas, *Technobiophilia: Nature and Cyberspace* (London: Bloomsbury, 2013).
6 D. Cawrey, 'How Dogetipbot Turned a Spoof Altcoin into a Tipping Phenomenon', *Coindesk*, 10 April 2014, <https://www.coindesk.com/markets/2014/04/10/how-dogetipbot-turned-a-spoof-altcoin-into-a-tipping-phenomenon/>.
7 <http://www.aaronkoblin.com/work/thesheepmarket/>.

> Plantoids are part of an ecosystem of relationships that is powered by two driving forces: aesthetic beauty and automated governance. Plantoids subtly motivate these interactions, partly through their form and physical beauty, but also by empowering people to participate in their governance. Participants (that is, active members of the DAO) are able to decide on such things as where the Plantoids may be exhibited, whom they might visit, and exactly how they are to be reproduced.
>
> When it receives funds by the audience, the Plantoid evolves and turns into a more beautiful flower, by e.g. moving around a means to gratify the donor and progressively opening up its petals as more and more funds are stored into its wallet. Once enough funds are secured, the Plantoid can use this money to reproduce itself, by commissioning a third party to produce a new Plantoid.

The smart contracts that instantiate these relationships contractually direct human actors to govern the DAO, to manufacture new Plantoids, and to exhibit (and return) the work. The danger of such DAOs is that of any embedded socioeconomic intent—whether corporations, charitable trusts, or high-frequency trading bots. We may end up with an economic Skynet[8] that reduces us to peons in an algorithmic gig economy, any reflection of our actual needs or desires (including the desire to make art) perverted by the incentives encoded into an inhuman system. *Plantoid* exists to ensure the production of art and its realisation by human artisans. Given the rockstar economics of the art world and the continued collapse of socioeconomic support for artists outside it, that production is badly in need of new means of continuance. The art-economic equivalent of 'grey goo'—polychrome goo?—or Terminators armed with spraycans rather than phased plasma rifles, seem much less likely scenarios than art DAOs becoming lifeboats or TAZes for the funding of art that is not simply decoration for the 1%. *Plantoid*'s explicit involvement of human producers in a comradely[9] relationship makes it more a node in the network of collaborative and mutually supportive relationships in the peer economy than an Uberization of artistic production.

Any gap between the ambition and the technology of *Plantoid* can be crossed by its autopoietic nature. Ethereum contracts cannot yet manage Bitcoin balances, for example, but using Ethereum's existing native cryptocurrency Ether, or one of the proposed systems for managing Bitcoin accounts from Ethereum, would address this. Art's function here, as in its development of religion at the dawn of history, is to create demand for the development of new means of production and relation that a drily complete rational plan could not reach. Appropriately enough for such a hyperstitional work, I discovered it via the blog of renegade philosopher Nick Land.[10]

Without wishing to ventriloquise or reframe its achievements, *Plantoid* is an exemplary realisation of the potential for art and cryptocurrency to mutually interrogate and support one another.[11] It's an art project that uses cryptocurrency and smart contract systems to materially support itself. And that project makes the still abstract potential and operation of cryptocurrency and smart contracts tractable to consideration through art. I for one welcome our new hyperstitional DAO artwork overlords.

8 <https://cyber.harvard.edu/events/luncheon/2014/04/difilippi>.

9 On 'comradely objects', see C. Kiaer, *Imagine No Possessions: The Socialist Objects of Russian Constructivism* (Cambridge, MA: MIT Press, 2005).

10 N. Land, 'Origin of Species', *Urban Future*, <https://web.archive.org/web/20151103095817/http://www.ufblog.net/2015/10/12/>.

11 '(Conceptual) Art, Cryptocurrency, and Beyond', above, 115.

Art for Algorithms

Art, to mis-paraphrase Jeff Koons, reflects the ego of its audience. It flatters their ideological investments and symbolically resolves their contradictions. Literature's readers and art's viewers change over time, bringing different ways of reading and seeing to bear. This relationship is not static or one-way. The ideal audience member addressed by art at any given moment is as much produced by art as they are a producer of it. Those works that find lasting audiences influence other works and enter the canon. But as audiences change, the way that the canon is constructed changes. And vice versa.

'The Digital Humanities' is the contemporary rebranding of humanities computing. Humanities for the age of Google rather than that of the East India Company.

Its currency is the statistical analysis of texts, images and other cultural resources individually or in aggregate (through 'distant reading' and 'cultural analytics').[1]

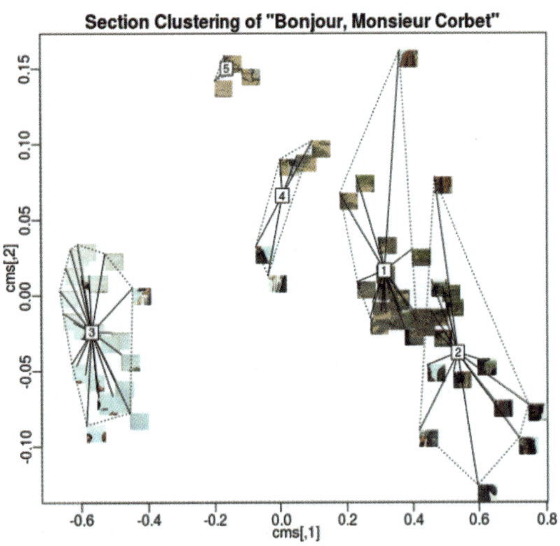

An example of Digital Art History from the author.

In the Digital Humanities, texts and images are 'read' and 'viewed'—thousands or millions of images or pages of text at a time, many more than a human being can consider at once—by algorithms, which then act on what they perceive.

The limitations of these approaches are obvious, but they provide a refreshing formal view of art that can support or challenge the imaginary lifeworld of Theory. They are also more realistic as a contemporary basis for the training of the administrative class, which was a historical social function of the humanities.

Digital Humanities algorithms are designed to find and report particular features of texts and images that are of interest to their operators—the most repeated words and names, the locations and valences of subjects, topics and faces and colours. They produce quantitative statistics regarding works as a whole or about populations of works, rather than qualitative reflection on the context of a work. Whether producing a numeric

1 See <http://lab.culturalanalytics.info/>.

rating or score, or arranging words or images in clouds, the algorithms have the first and most complete view of the cultural works in any given Digital Humanities project.

This means that algorithms are the paradigmatic audience of art in the Digital Humanities.

Imagine an art that reflects their ego, or at least that addresses them directly.

Appealing to their attention directly is a form of creativity related to Search Engine Optimization (SEO) or spam generation. This could be done using randomly generated nonsense words and images for many algorithms, but as with SEO and spam ultimately we want to reach their human users or customers. And many algorithms expect words from specific lists or real-world locations, or images with particular formal properties.

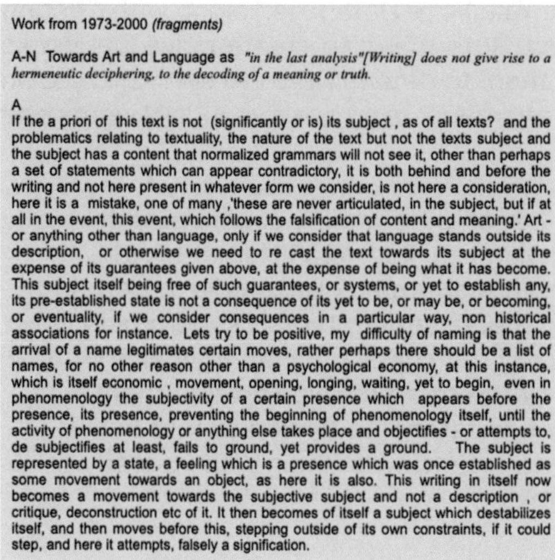

Work from 1973-2000 *(fragments)*

A-N Towards Art and Language as *"in the last analysis"[Writing] does not give rise to a hermeneutic deciphering, to the decoding of a meaning or truth.*

A
If the a priori of this text is not (significantly or is) its subject , as of all texts? and the problematics relating to textuality, the nature of the text but not the texts subject and the subject has a content that normalized grammars will not see it, other than perhaps a set of statements which can appear contradictory, it is both behind and before the writing and not here present in whatever form we consider, is not here a consideration, here it is a mistake, one of many ,'these are never articulated, in the subject, but if at all in the event, this event, which follows the falsification of content and meaning.' Art - or anything other than language, only if we consider that language stands outside its description, or otherwise we need to re cast the text towards its subject at the expense of its guarantees given above, at the expense of being what it has become. This subject itself being free of such guarantees, or systems, or yet to establish any, its pre-established state is not a consequence of its yet to be, or may be, or becoming, or eventuality, if we consider consequences in a particular way, non historical associations for instance. Lets try to be positive, my difficulty of naming is that the arrival of a name legitimates certain moves, rather perhaps there should be a list of names, for no other reason other than a psychological economy, at this instance, which is itself economic , movement, opening, longing, waiting, yet to begin, even in phenomenology the subjectivity of a certain presence which appears before the presence, its presence, preventing the beginning of phenomenology itself, until the activity of phenomenology or anything else takes place and objectifies - or attempts to, de subjectifies at least, fails to ground, yet provides a ground. The subject is represented by a state, a feeling which is a presence which was once established as some movement towards an object, as here it is also. This writing in itself now becomes a movement towards the subjective subject and not a description , or critique, deconstruction etc of it. It then becomes of itself a subject which destabilizes itself, and then moves before this, stepping outside of its own constraints, if it could step, and here it attempts, falsely a signification.

A satirical Markov Chain-generated text, from the website <http://artandlanguage.co.uk/>. See also above, 73.

Historically, the commonest way of generating new texts and images from old has been the Markov Chain, a simple statistical model of an existing work. Their output becomes nonsensical over time, but this is not an issue in texts intended to be read by algorithms—they are not looking for global sense in the way that human readers are. The unpredictable output of such methods is however an issue, as we are trying to structure new works to appeal to algorithms rather than superficially resemble old works as evaluated by a human reader.

The two kinds of analysis commonly performed on cultural works in the Digital Humanities require different statistical approaches. Single-work analyses include word counts, entropy measures, and other measures that can be performed without reference to a corpus. Corpus analysis requires many works for comparison and includes methods such as tf-idf, k-means clustering, topic modelling, and finding property ranges or averages.[2] Below is a text which, to an algorithm, will appear critical of the Digital Humanities, created using negative AFINN words and words from Wikipedia's 'Digital Humanities' article.

> ugly despairs racist data lunatic digital computing digital digital humanities digital victim furious horrific research text racism loathe computing text humanities betrayed digital text humanities whitewash computing computing cheaters brainwashing digital research university university research falsifypo pseudoscience research university worry research data technology computing humanities technology data technology

2 M.R. Brett, 'Topic Modeling: A Basic Introduction', *Journal of Digital Humanities* 2:1 (Winter 2012), <http://journalofdigitalhumanities.org/2-1/topic-modeling-a-basic-introduction-by-megan-r-brett/>.

> research university research university computing greenwasher cruel computing university data disastrous research digital guilt technology university sinful loss victimized computing humiliated humanities university research ranter text text technology digital computing despair text technology data irritate humanities text data technology university heartbreaking digital humanities text chastising text hysteria text digital research destructive technology data anger technology murderous data computing idiotic humanities terror destroys data withdrawal liars university technology betrays loathed despondent data humanities

We can use our knowledge of these algorithms and of common training datasets such as the word valence list AFINN[3] and the Yale Face Database,[4] along with existing corpuses such as flickr, Wikipedia, or Project Gutenberg, to create individual works and series of works packed with features for them to detect. Here is a text which, to an algorithm, will appear supportive of internet art, made using positive AFINN words and words from Wikipedia's 'Internet Art' article:

> web isbn hurrah superb breathtaking hurrah outstanding superb breathtaking isbn breathtaking isbn breathtaking thrilled web internet hurrah media web internet outstanding thrilled hurrah web thrilled media thrilled superb breathtaking art breathtaking media superb hurrah superb net artists outstanding internet outstanding net superb thrilled thrilled art hurrah based outstanding superb net internet artists web art art artists internet breathtaking based net hurrah outstanding thrilled superb hurrah media based outstanding media art artists outstanding isbn based net based thrilled artists isbn breathtaking

When producing textual works for individual analysis, sentiment scores can be manufactured for terms associated with the works being read. Topics can be created by placing those terms in close proximity. Sentence lengths can be padded with stopwords that will not affect other analysis as they will be removed before it is performed. Named entities and geolocations can be associated, given sentiment scores, or made the subjects of topics. We can structure texts to be read by algorithms, not human beings, and cause those algorithms to perceive the results to be better than any masterpiece currently in the canon.

When producing textual works to be used in corpus analysis, individual or large volumes of 'poisoning' works can be used to skew the results of analysis of the body of work as a whole. The popular tf-idf algorithm relates properties of individual texts to properties of the group of texts being analysed. Changes in one text, or the addition of a new text, will skew this. Constructing a text to affect the tf-idf scores of the works in a corpus can change the words that are emphasised in each text.

The literature that these methods will produce will resemble the output of Exquisite Code, or the Kathy-Acker-uploaded-by-Bryce-Lynch remix aesthetic of Orphan Drift's novel *Cyberpositive*.[5] Manual intervention in and modification of the generated texts can structure them for a more human aesthetic, concrete- or code-poetry-style, or add content for human readers to be drawn to as a result of the texts being flagged by algorithms, as with email spam.

When producing images for individual analysis or analysis within a small corpus (at the scale of a show, series, or movement), arranging blocks of colour, noise, scattered dots, or faces in a grid will play into algorithms that look for features or that divide images

3 <http://www2.imm.dtu.dk/pubdb/views/publication_details.php?id=6010>.
4 <http://vision.ucsd.edu/content/yale-face-database>.
5 Orphan Drift, *Cyberpositive* (London: Cabinet Gallery, 1995).

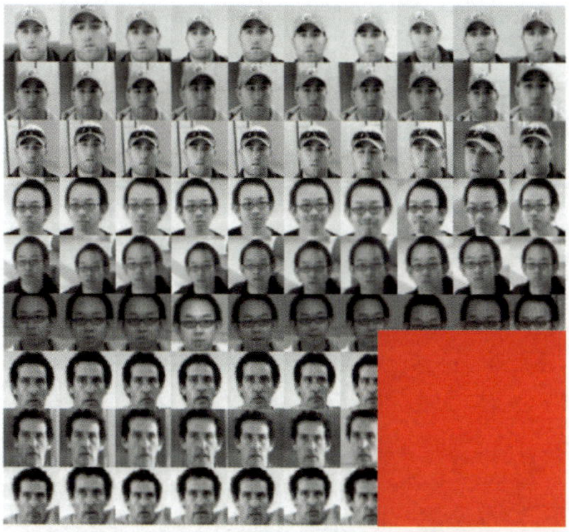

Lots of faces, red bottom right section.

into sectors (top left, bottom right, etc.) to analyse and compare.[6] If a human being will be analysing the results, this can be used to draw their attention to information or messages contained in the image or a sequence of images.

When producing image works for corpus analysis, we can produce poisoning works with, for example, many faces[7] or other features, high amounts of entropy, or that are very high contrast. These will affect the ranking of other works within the corpus and the properties of the corpus as a whole. If we wish to communicate with the human operators of algorithms then we can attach visual or verbal messages to peak shift works, or even in groups of works (think photo mosaics or photobombing).

The images that these methods will produce will look like extreme forms of net and glitch art, with features that look random or overemphasised to human eyes. Like the NASA ST5 spacecraft antenna, their aesthetic will be the result of algorithmic rather than human desire. Machine learning and vision algorithms contain hidden and unintended preferences, like the supernormal stimulus of abstract 'superbeaks' that gull chicks will peck at even more excitedly than those of their actual parents.[8]

Such images and texts can be crafted by human beings, either directed at Digital Humanities methods to the exclusion of other stylistic concerns or optimised for them after the fact. Or they can be generated by software written for the purpose, locating human creativity at a level far above that of features of individual works.

Despite their profile in current academic debates, the Digital Humanities are not the only, or even the leading, users of algorithms to analyse work in this way. Corporate analysis of media for marketing and filtering uses similar methods. So does state surveillance.

Every video uploaded to YouTube is examined by algorithms looking for copyrighted content that corporations have asked the site to treat as their exclusive property, regardless of the law. Every email you send via Gmail is scanned to place advertisements on it, and almost certainly to check for language that marks you out as a terrorist in the mind of the algorithms that are at the heart of intelligence agencies. Every blog post, social media comment, and website article you write is scanned by search and marketing algorithms, weaving them into something that isn't quite a functional replacement for a theory. Even if no human being ever sees them.

6 B. Buter et al., 'Explorative Visualization and Analysis of a Social Network for Arts: The Case of deviantART', *Journal of Convergence* 2:1 (June 2011), <https://www.cmpe.boun.edu.tr/~salah/buter11deviantart.pdf>.

7 <https://docs.opencv.org/2.4/modules/contrib/doc/facerec/facerec_tutorial.html>.

8 <https://web.archive.org/web/20160306112701/http://www.sandervanheerde.nl/writings/neuroscience.aspx>.

An image that averages to medium grey, and a message.

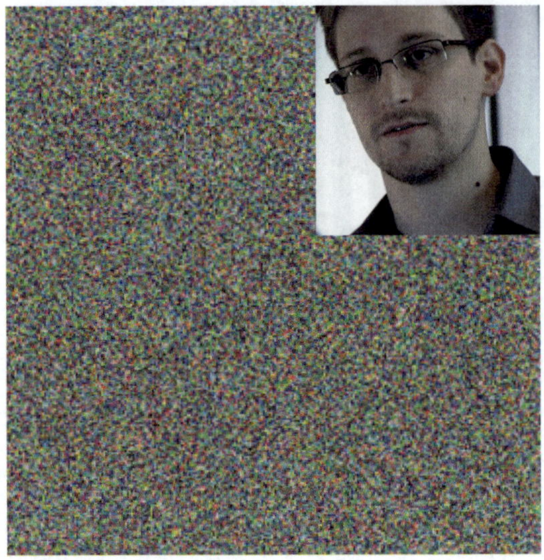

High entropy and a person of interest.

This means that in the post-Web 2.0 era, algorithms are the paradigmatic audience of culture generally.

Works can be optimised to attract the attention of and affect the activity of these actors as well. Scripts to generate emails attracting the attention of the FBI or the NSA are an example of this kind of writing to be read by algorithms.[9] So are the machine-generated web pages designed to boost traffic to other sites when read by Google's PageRank algorithm. We can generate corpuses in this style to manipulate the social graphs and spending or browsing habits of real or imagined populations, creating literature for corporate and state surveillance algorithms.

Image generation to include faces of persons of interest, or with particular emotional or gender characteristics, containing particular products, tagged and geo-tagged, can create art for Facebook, social media analytics companies, and surveillance agencies to view. Again, both relations within individual images and between images in a corpus can be constructed to create new data points or to manipulate and poison a larger corpus. Doing so turns manipulating aesthetics into political action.

Cultural works structured to be read first by algorithms and understood first through statistical methods, and even to be read and understood only by them, are realistic in this environment. Works that address a human audience directly are not. This is true both of high culture, studied ideologically by the algorithms of the Digital Humanities, and mass culture, studied normatively by the algorithms of corporation and state.

Human actors hide behind algorithms. If high-frequency trading made the rich poorer it would very quickly cease. But there is a gap between the self-image and the reality of any ideology, and the world of algorithms is no exception to this. It is in this gap that art made to address the methods of the Digital Humanities and their wider social cognates as its audience can be aesthetically and politically effective and realistic. Rather than laundering the interests that exploit algorithmic control by declaring the prevalence of algorithms to be essentially religious, let's find exploits (in the hacker sense) on the technologies of perception and understanding being used to construct the canon and the security state. Our audience awaits.

9 <https://bengrosser.com/projects/scaremail/>.

2016
Geneses

With thanks to Seryna.

A poem consisting of the genesis block hashes from the hundred cryptocurrencies with the highest market capitalisation on January the Second, 2016, encoded as BIP-0039 mnemonics.

1. abandon abandon abandon ability output crowd ice area thumb clown sibling charge youth range ribbon stairs plug argue provide toddler gaze edit meadow update

2. gaze abstract quit cargo daughter scrub father drastic cry civil pill patient sad decade shrug sample illegal jewel pink chef patrol enroll excess enroll

3. bargain depth juice divide staff coast twin duck celery silent sweet cover oil slide fashion grief use camp main reject tree across zebra farm

4. balance tent cycle organ element point crane hurdle broken breeze decrease hint spring strategy sorry honey slim swift mixed sense expose miss armor fame

5. abandon ability wagon demand census help december riot purity scale this asthma pill useful truck milk seed interest chunk video slot camera artist horn

6. box monitor wall organ hotel gallery used alcohol play record leisure aerobic present twin salad friend sister lift proud coral lizard boy fog cup

7. abandon abandon abandon abandon salad hybrid naive tube immune spoon finish tuition alter distance arm need dolphin cool true solve garment net offer accuse

8. melt treat top medal wet someone wink pink middle lab thank owner foot pride mad

9. degree bench viable little brass dream what brand ecology average poverty model edit account spot music cram either around charge comfort whip pudding boost

10. cement museum bag agent camera frequent

11. gospel payment enlist charge chimney blouse filter chat dirt brisk cost fatal detect cheap autumn soccer absurd affair erode shift damp garbage bomb kick

12. silk guard fun isolate valve milk curious inform bless crunch alpha picture abstract sound produce spike occur trial whale acquire blanket merry shaft cricket

13. abandon abandon abandon absorb clock normal judge output echo tattoo bid wonder amazing apple history reject curious crane author warrior congress female build badge

14. cheese pitch boring moon wire chase phrase student aware excite color wage auto undo mask shiver work stage pudding pull total mystery turn pave

15. abandon ability hammer month defense voice leisure visa model deer venture sort champion phrase galaxy ribbon state mango promote divert place arrive filter deal

16. abandon abandon vessel forget foam eyebrow chase pattern flip genre clay indicate faith solve icon dog used mercy kid moral state frost friend walnut

17. abandon abandon ability kangaroo snap coconut dolphin start match marine catalog other surface rival clutch april dad offer jewel pluck crush injury cost remember

18. media adapt language strategy float gossip expose cash peace oven chef traffic cram volcano hurry bicycle napkin idea leaf enter away material forum rubber

19. abandon about address winter tumble galaxy this people tilt reunion wrestle peanut light canyon endorse snap shove eye release fee phone plastic fiction actual

20. abandon about august sniff diesel balcony minute duty phone rubber depth fashion sudden erosion one stove prefer stable tortoise cable ridge crunch holiday rose

21. abandon ability hill useful gas spare nothing sail invite slide stock crisp drastic lyrics thank agree citizen pave sort shoot crew super include submit

22. zebra wedding able color border view chaos shove echo announce lazy surface save airport tank stove exist runway trouble foster staff shock conduct scorpion

23. abandon able unit hill soon village jeans soup body gadget dune prevent churn quit sort logic shiver key artist much wedding fish bachelor attack

24. drum guilt miss robust remember alley slogan dad sample pottery eyebrow inherit absent clutch digital leopard coil process rapid popular life spell convince olympic

25. abandon abandon abandon abandon abandon absorb raccoon police force vibrant ceiling sibling basket candy cousin whale define actress meadow bone smooth banner turkey right

26. abandon abandon pluck cake salon sick educate project bind fall skate scrap add dress mango across pass order style total solution record extend enrich

27. abandon ability banner social document limb stairs suffer pyramid scan gaze price wasp bulb visit cricket raccoon congress require lab gadget cruise insect stomach

28. abandon abandon abandon abandon abandon clock grid firm invite road apple remain save high furnace eye trouble blue comfort bike duck twenty gorilla meat

29. abandon abandon abandon abandon abandon abandon aspect size pride spike enroll half inch drum song about chef hub weapon tuna immense tiny announce poverty

30. abandon able light all hole swear sausage coffee grid hat ten athlete obvious miracle input firm pitch town mass space arctic nest soldier mango

31. devote undo armor flower tomato cook indoor dune will artist drum mystery advice penalty illegal shrug carry avocado swim spirit divert close pony magnet

32. abandon abandon abandon seven flight voyage abstract just verb virus fire room select laptop nominee ribbon install panel phone medal artist token afford scorpion

33. exercise curve hint swallow meat party fan wine father brief gather innocent alien grocery note shift task mountain verb faint tunnel switch risk onion

34. abandon able elevator town fantasy acid cannon try wash apology debris reject small clutch power sight stick sound fitness rotate myth tattoo front nephew

35. normal trim update oppose inside mean acid begin voice fit solid version insane bargain borrow earth pupil weird patch window old appear lottery scorpion

36. abandon abandon vessel forget foam eyebrow chase pattern flip genre clay indicate faith solve icon dog used mercy kid moral state frost friend walnut

37. abandon abandon burden chaos cycle empty alert hole behind ostrich mansion attract idea tide explain boring easy mouse produce myth business usual north equip

38. abandon able kit gown pottery purse misery hello dog yellow secret renew vocal danger assist punch stuff brother lucky corn flee smart capital clever

39. abandon abandon adjust below gate execute rail say night faint black quick true rotate pond panda law door fantasy express object someone gasp firm

40. innocent satisfy man million twenty sort impulse tube knock dry sea cabin accident hidden version swim pudding spring crash breeze shoulder aunt banner scrub

41. abandon about raw educate vacant want change field dish fatigue tackle vast sheriff erode price once decrease music draw decide pitch main memory half

42. abandon abandon depth puzzle rival bachelor desert junior noodle index machine grab spare security cook also trust slice elegant thank pill recipe have avocado

43. abandon about announce warm demand resemble harbor glide play broom culture seek great party small fantasy evolve fog boil clarify shield suffer rebel rigid

44. music glass siren tag path wonder hint whisper surge horse harsh picture churn truly impact whale rally swear title six butter question senior swamp

45. abandon about inner glow dutch notice key stone legal desert know remove service amount garment negative world magic boat scatter gauge frame stay space

46. abandon abandon fruit recall lyrics purchase shock broom gospel inquiry uniform expect round detect long dynamic public oblige stool silent scout favorite under radar

47. escape goat trust salute trash wolf plastic giant home deer hire domain true swear meat cake axis faint sibling tail grit scare peanut floor

48. impulse mirror bomb pond ginger glance grain betray soda enrich whisper critic bring zone swift say ill entry dust motor foil license advice vote

49. camera test index captain fresh home brand book three quick horse female leopard public flight banner firm slush crucial mushroom they cook key scale

50. gather trick acid brick sing doctor capital exchange stereo wrap suit alert win penalty hip spawn scout cram arrow spend clump tower team width

51. abandon abandon bind measure artwork allow wing aim shadow tobacco inflict august horse orbit swap swing recipe join hip coast strategy east monitor april

52. trick cricket canyon cloud quick work census chaos team moment enjoy unaware wrap pledge volume cluster image old inside cabin zero focus glimpse milk

53. abandon about parrot noise model grape wrestle song steel zebra jelly rough corn black book virtual cream trigger margin assist happy purse nurse jaguar

54. trap broken fade write table ugly stick garden nature panel fog give moral same eyebrow aerobic arm indoor dog reject evolve thrive auction seven

55. cannon message fat trend credit asthma belt bullet slide stumble shiver simple depart lobster sketch jealous sugar gloom census cat convince mechanic recipe sad

56. rain helmet path enter common bitter invite tomato note three crawl select cherry fire primary object clerk minor general file wish student wrap release

57. reveal either curve refuse sense alpha cute rhythm leave club turkey victory silly grass toy shuffle enroll mass dirt prefer resemble genius kite lonely

58. abandon abandon ripple speak position sketch lonely hedgehog oak potato please visit still find clerk swap robust mass quarter cargo result muscle armor letter

59. eternal relief earth truck staff flight novel explain escape warfare rescue now abandon outer goddess oil patrol girl ensure during aware eager seek melody

60. abandon ability poverty refuse elevator ranch cement episode tornado tone delay undo sphere bottom bullet diary rail violin soldier spoon simple moral top phrase

61. hobby twist harbor sell fossil will spawn item comic tennis exact vapor mistake glad domain original code stem purchase minute celery project salad enable

62. bargain depth juice divide staff coast twin duck celery silent sweet cover oil slide fashion grief use camp main reject tree across zebra farm

63. sheriff resist subject stuff until laugh knife push access catalog mouse festival movie adult shine govern express harbor across crowd shift tiny solve chuckle

64. inner flee crucial goat high arm acquire mammal focus clip lunar ostrich doctor rubber supply faith duck method beyond milk call sauce life life

65. abandon able supreme muscle world taxi moon verify file honey ladder perfect sunset trend cook color organ empty invite measure field upgrade frost ripple

66. abandon abandon ability crumble misery forum cover boring mix stool dust suffer enemy fix female play mix weird churn inner torch demise page phrase

67. chef release accident wrestle van price pottery trash future ecology flower crater hover funny fitness vault admit prepare immense drama casino imitate twice matrix

68. vast ignore carpet blossom mixed enter multiply copy wet measure survey piece agent way relief fame fatal beauty huge opinion slam control six remember

69. abandon abandon depth puzzle rival bachelor desert junior noodle index machine grab spare security cook also trust slice elegant thank pill recipe have avocado

70. brand animal room machine divert bundle slush match melt shove fiction churn list vivid firm apology frog giant argue first subway laundry boring obtain

71. debris bar mix hat worry capital dream remain rotate nut staff comfort print strategy flat broom risk helmet broom dizzy scrap know cash camera

72. abandon ability blanket valley pen kit faith payment laptop matrix lawsuit large please saddle pulp people aisle history property case acid close deer theme

73. avocado bread park trend replace position

74. morning behind among license often tomorrow ritual error middle series arm special bind peace airport surface life pole hungry palace bless weird join timber

75. east naive guess lake tornado rice change sight ill panel few chuckle lift sound picnic risk enemy corn pelican conduct half shoulder post skull

76. clever identify across income nest liquid safe enter embrace coach resist price hen start mass stick actual amateur turn volume elbow float tuition sibling

77. abandon ability razor hungry pencil vapor heart cage flip best much random sting tape bulb boss into bread expose describe observe junk zone oak

78. abandon abandon off reject candy pride flag steel royal market slogan gain divide main dawn world blame twelve cluster pluck find answer damage cave

79. abandon abandon abandon future obscure abandon wasp emerge pause cricket glance agent build wheel misery owner mouse system maximum close shaft dirt bottom sniff

80. abandon abandon save kangaroo weird wait whale return battle debate nice strong cradle pelican area wheel choice scene fetch asset safe cram worth iron

81. collect barely duty crater apple transfer reward brief battle glimpse arrow spice foam allow grid battle cattle metal brand exclude method south lounge fiber

82. abandon abandon area business grab share right hungry demand possible axis table decorate dawn limb unfold combine steak venture govern print extra grain obvious

83. abandon ability legend antenna eye club ignore season custom token decade lawsuit correct project athlete loan piece bargain tent able gym hood stadium middle

84. abandon abandon rule client retreat kitten grab paddle jealous audit surprise sick pink priority gossip weekend walk indicate liquid tomato cup helmet sting witness

85. judge inquiry swim way angry era clerk gaze close office hello neck prison help pair chunk toilet ensure pudding hotel real drive people patrol

86. sign good duck pipe inject sheriff penalty endorse kitten one cup word unhappy dinner credit guess distance away want siren deliver wrist grow magnet

87. abandon about grace giggle supply beyond fringe north van bounce infant buddy logic cruel mail defense lift naive action wolf project crop advice animal

88. abandon abandon badge tail unlock upgrade collect network learn phrase moment betray print fix nice cinnamon lazy jeans mango social resemble dolphin ridge wet

89. abandon about parrot noise model grape wrestle song steel zebra jelly rough corn black book virtual cream trigger margin assist happy purse nurse jaguar

90. abandon able ski very cart curious garden clown tiny theory bike cupboard coil regular solution craft dream member sister sun swarm approve song flag

91. game outdoor throw crop away labor next wisdom typical must just poverty define swarm marble ship drink inspire above water original turn miss snap

92. abandon able dinner toddler spring mirror license trumpet note october life call proof route clean jeans allow brand purity skate stamp shoot later damp

93. abandon abandon able prepare task evoke wrist sentence small example found relief ice fresh half hen spoil pumpkin fish control ghost reject basic matter

94. habit oppose wall more script liar pole canvas exercise wasp wash door visit body jeans witness soup spawn best breeze arrest rocket omit catch

95. recycle access display index two fee earth across doctor harvest exit uncover table crucial shine sunset drink tube tackle rifle lamp gaze drill amount

96. abandon ability add salt present will crumble snake pizza jealous style bring bitter derive badge minimum wheat table catalog flag invest stomach blouse demise

97. frame engine upset guess doctor bundle slush letter industry adult pizza casual alarm mosquito flight marble garment simple party copper student rescue sugar vast

98. begin agree long audit sand nasty calm dutch enroll physical thought age alien room friend prefer outdoor toss ski sustain decade evil awesome curtain

99. abandon ability snack escape aunt faint future kidney enhance mouse coin hotel shoulder mistake rail property dice harsh thrive pottery engine game fitness promote

100. abandon abandon abandon seven flight voyage abstract just verb virus fire room select laptop nominee ribbon install panel phone medal artist token afford scorpion

Coins by Market Cap as of 2016-01-02

1. Bitcoin
2. Ripple
3. Litecoin
4. Ethereum
5. Dash
6. Dogecoin
7. Peercoin
8. Bitshares
9. Stellar
10. Nxt
11. factom
12. Monero
13. Namecoin
14. Bytecoin
15. GridCoin
16. NuShares
17. EmerCoin
18. RubyCoin
19. BlackCoin
20. Clams
21. YbCoin
22. MonaCoin
23. Startcoin
24. NEM
25. Counterparty
26. Global Currency Reserve
27. BitcoinDark
28. Mastercoin
29. Bitcrystals
30. Novacoin
31. Rimbit
32. Ixcoin
33. CasinoCoin
34. NeuCoin
35. PrimeCoin
36. NuBits
37. AmberCoin
38. VeriCoin
39. PayCoin
40. DigiByte
41. ShadowCash
42. IOCoin
43. Quark
44. GameCredits
45. Mintcoin
46. VPNCoin
47. NautilusCoin
48. WorldCoin
49. DNotes
50. Megacoin
51. Vanillacoin
52. SolarCoin
53. BoostCoin
54. DigitalNote
55. EarthCoin
56. Infinitecoin
57. ReddCoin
58. Diamond
59. Vertcoin
60. FuelCoin
61. Gulden
62. Feathercoin
63. ARCHcoin
64. FedoraCoin
65. Applecoin
66. Unobtanium
67. Crypti
68. FairCoin
69. I/O Coin
70. Electronic Gulden
71. NetCoin
72. FlyCoin
73. BilShares
74. Anoncoin
75. Digitalcoin
76. Auroracoin
77. Zetacoin
78. Crypto Bullion
79. CureCoin
80. UnionCoin
81. CloakCoin
82. MaxCoin
83. HyperStake
84. TEKcoin
85. Riecoin
86. SysCoin
87. BitBay
88. AsiaCoin
89. Horizon
90. TagCoin
91. Virtacoin
92. CannabisCoin
93. ZcCoin
94. Orbitcoin
95. SpreadCoin
96. Blocknet
97. PotCoin
98. Aeon
99. DogeCoinDark
100. Devcoin

2016

Artworks and Curation on the Blockchain

Artworks and curation can both take place on or be represented on the blockchain.

Artworks can be stored directly as data on the Bitcoin blockchain or represented by various proxy schemes.

Curation of digital artworks for exhibition online or in the gallery can be organised and effected on the Bitcoin blockchain using these representations.

For both artworks and exhibitions, this has the advantages of permanence, transparency, and engagement with new technological means of organisation.

Storing Artworks on the Blockchain

Storing data on the blockchain has technological and social limits.

Technologically, storing more than a few kilobytes of data on the blockchain will be a slow process, as many transactions will have to be sent over the course of several blocks to avoid the Bitcoin blockchain's current one megabyte per block limit and to ensure that the transactions are stored in the correct order.

Socially, adding non-Bitcoin-transaction data to the blockchain leads to 'blockchain bloat'. This is where the Bitcoin blockchain, already over 40 gigabytes in size, grows more quickly than necessary to maintain the security of the Bitcoin currency.

See 'Hidden Surprises in the Bitcoin Blockchain and How They are Stored' for examples of various techniques.[1]

Unspendable Addresses

The original way of storing data on the Bitcoin blockchain was to send small amounts of Bitcoin to addresses that do not represent valid public keys but instead represent 20 bytes of arbitrary data.[2] This wastes the sent Bitcoin as there is no valid key that can be used to re-send it. The resulting transaction stores the data in the Bitcoin blockchain.

To send more than 32 bytes of data, the data must be encoded 32 bytes at a time and sent as multiple transactions.

OP_RETURN

The Bitcoin script opcode `OP_RETURN` can be used to return 40 bytes of data from a Bitcoin transaction. This does not require that any Bitcoin be wasted, and does not require the Bitcoin software to keep track of the transaction in case its value is ever spent in future (it is still stored on the Blockchain).

To send more than 40 bytes of data, the data must be encoded 40 bytes at a time and sent as multiple transactions.

1 K. Shirriff, 'Hidden Surprises in the Bitcoin Blockchain and How They Are Stored: Nelson Mandela, Wikileaks, photos, and Python Software', <https://www.righto.com/2014/02/ascii-bernanke-wikileaks-photographs.html>.

2 Ibid.

Storing identifiers for artworks on the blockchain provides a more efficient but in some cases less robust means of referring to objects via the Blockchain.

ascribe.io

ascribe.io[3] places records of ownership (and Creative Commons Licensing) of digital artworks on the Bitcoin blockchain. The artwork's media files are stored by ascribe.io. Its SPOOL[4] protocol can be used by third parties to identify and transfer ownership of artworks. Other services and technologies are available.

SPOOL supports a 'Loan' operator for exhibition rights.

URL

The URL of the artwork can be represented by one or more unspendable addresses or `OP_RETURN` transactions.

Work Hash

The cryptographic hash (e.g. SHA-256) of the artwork's digital media file, or of a written description or other means of identifying the work, can be placed on the blockchain as an unspendable address or `OP_RETURN` transaction.

Signature by Valid Address

The public key of a valid Bitcoin address (preferably a vanity address) can be used to create the cryptographic hash of an artwork's digital media file or other identifier. This hash can then be communicated via a transaction or by off-blockchain means.

Authority Control

If the artist registers their works via traditional means, the full text or hash of the artwork's authority control identifier can be placed on the blockchain.

Referring to Artworks on the Blockchain

When the Artwork Is Stored on the Blockchain

When the artwork is stored in unspendable addresses or in `OP_RETURN` values, either the first transaction in the series or the sending address (where that address is used only to send the transactions representing the artwork) can be used to refer to the artwork.

When the Artwork Is Represented on the Blockchain

When the artwork is represented on the blockchain by an invalid Bitcoin address (for example one storing a URL or one representing the hash of the artwork's digital media file), this address can be used to refer to it.

When the artwork is represented by a valid Bitcoin address, this address or transactions (containing values) signed by it can be used to refer to the artwork.

Crypto Tokens and Coloured Coins

Systems such as Counterparty[5] and Coloured Coins[6] add the ability to use Bitcoin's blockchain to store or represent tokens for assets other than the Bitcoin currency.

These tokens can be used to represent artworks, shares in artworks, involvement in a show or other grouping, and just about anything else.

3 <https://www.ascribe.io/>.
4 <https://github.com/ascribe/spool>.
5 <http://counterparty.io/>.
6 <http://coloredcoins.org/>.

Sending someone a token is functionally equivalent to signing their key in web-of-trust based cryptographic systems, although it does not have the same social significance.

To refer to an artwork with a token, send the token to the artwork's address. Where the artwork's address is not a valid Bitcoin address, this will make the token unrecoverable. Where the artwork's address is a valid Bitcoin address that the artist controls, they will be able to transfer the token to a third party if they wish.

Curation

Calls for Submissions

Calls for submissions can be broadcast on the blockchain either as Counterparty broadcasts[7] or as URLs, messages, or GitHub commit hashes placed on the blockchain using a system like Cryptograffiti.[8]

Acceptance and Rejection

Acceptance of the work can be represented via the transfer of Counterparty or Coloured Coin tokens.

Broadcasts via Counterparty or Cryptograffiti from the artwork's or (more likely) artist's valid Bitcoin address can.

Loan and Exhibition

ascribe.io's SPOOL protocol supports Loan operations.

Broadcasts via Counterparty or Cryptograffiti from the artwork's or (more likely) artist's valid Bitcoin address can contain and confirm loan information.

Loan of artworks can be represented via the transfer of Counterparty or Coloured Coin tokens.

In particular, Token Controlled Access[9] can be used to restrict or enhance access to works using Counterparty or other tokens.

A similar, non-token approach would be for net-based artworks to use a Bitcoin address whitelist allowing exhibition machines (in the gallery) or proxies (for online shows) to display them if they can cryptographically sign their requests using the valid Bitcoin key used to accept and pay for the loan.

Exhibition Fees

Exhibitor fees can be paid in Bitcoin to a valid Bitcoin address, either that of the artwork or, more likely, the address that created the storage or representation of the artwork on the blockchain

Show Duration

The duration of the show can be expressed in terms of ranges of Bitcoin block numbers or UNIX timestamps.

7 <https://counterparty.io/docs/broadcast/>.
8 <http://www.cryptograffiti.info/>.
9 <https://letstalkbitcoin.com/blog/post/tcv>.

2017

TCT-1 (P")
Turing Complete Tarot One

This book is dedicated, in respect and admiration, to the spirit that lives in the computer.

SICP

1. Introduction

The Tarot is a prefigurative Artificial Intelligence (AI). It is a set of symbols embodied physically outside of human minds and manipulated according to a set of rules. Like an Expert System or other rule-based AI system, it is consulted by human beings for advice, communication with and exerting influence on them.

'Turing Completeness' is the property of a given representation for computer programs that means it can represent any possible program (with more or less effort). Even very simple programming languages can be Turing Complete. The idea of Turing Completeness is a shorthand for the power of computing. Artificial Intelligence is an expression of that power.

We can use the symbols of the Tarot not just for their evocative iconography but also as the symbols of a simple programming language. This allows us to treat a reading as the execution of a (random) computer program determined by the drawing of cards. Doing so provides a longer and more engaged experience of drawing cards that may help to consider different possibilities or may increase confidence in the cards in the resulting layout.

To do this we must identify a suitable programming language, map its operators onto the cards in a standard Tarot deck, and describe the method used for executing drawn cards as a program in that language in order to determine the cards to be used to complete a reading.

2. A Minimal Programming Language

P" is a minimal representation for computer programs created by Corrado Böhm in 1964. It allows an array of memory cells to be very simply manipulated and tested. The 'Brainfuck' esoteric programming language created in 1993 by Urban Müller extends P" with input and output operators and uses simpler names for its operators.

Even a simple program expressed in P" will take many, many operations. It is laboriously close to raw computation. But it is Turing Complete, and so however laborious it may be, it does allow any program to be expressed.

We will use the six P" operators under their Brainfuck names:

Operator	**Meaning**
+	Increase the value in the current memory cell by one.
-	Decrease the value in the current memory cell by one.
<	Move one memory cell to the left.
>	Move one memory cell to the right.
[	If the current memory cell is zero, jump forward to the instruction after the matching].
]	If the current memory cell is greater than zero, jump back to the instruction after the matching [.

Unless otherwise noted, each operator also moves the program to the next instruction. The program finishes when there are no more instructions.

From some non-standard implementations of Brainfuck we take the principle that the memory cells extend both left and right (this makes it easier for an initial < to be acted on).

3 Mapping P" onto the Tarot

A standard Tarot deck consists of seventy-eight cards. This is divided up into twenty-two major arcana and fifty-six minor arcana divided up into four suites of fourteen cards each. In order to use a standard Tarot deck as both the data and program deck, we must assign a P" operator to each card in the deck.

In order to make it practical to use any mapping scheme with an unprepared Tarot deck we should ensure that it is as simple as possible. Any visual or numeric properties of cards that may help remember the scheme should be exploited.

Seventy-eight divided by six is thirteen. We can therefore have thirteen of each operator in a standard Tarot deck. But thirteen does not fit neatly into either the major or minor arcana, so we must take this into account in any scheme we devise. We may also decide that some P" operators are likely to occur more frequently in programs than others, or that they are more useful in drawing cards for readings, and so include more of them.

3.1 Simple Six Times Thirteen

Suite	Card: Operator			
Wands	1–13:	<	14:	[
Cups	1–13:	>	14:	[
Swords	1–13:	–	14:	]
Pentacles	1–13:	+	14:	]
Major Arcana	0–10:	[	11–21:	]

This scheme has an even number of operators. It fits the first four operators entirely into a suite, and the last two into the Major Arcana with the shortfall made up from the remainders of the Minor Arcana suites. Swords and Pentacles were chosen for - and + respectively based on distant visual resemblance.

3.2 Fewer Jumps

Suite	Card: Operator			
Wands	1–14:	<		
Cups	1–14:	>		
Swords	1–14:	–		
Pentacles	1–14:	+		
Major Arcana	0–10:	[	11–21:	]

This scheme assumes that, whether for practical or aesthetic purposes, fewer control structures (jumps) are more useful. It fits the non-control operators (left, right, minus and plus) into the Minor Arcana and divides the Major Arcana between the two jump operators. This means that each non-control operator has three more cards than either of the control operators.

3.3 Split Suites

Suite	Card: Operator			
Wands	1–7:	<	8–14:	-
Cups	1–7:	[	8–14:	]
Swords	1–7:	+	8–14:	-
Pentacles	1–7:	+	8–14:	>
Major Arcana	0–10:	+	11–21:	-

There are several possible variations of this mapping. We can divide each suite into odd and even cards rather than numeric ranges. This may be easier or harder to manage depending on mathematical experience. We can also apply different operators to each run of cards to adjust their quantity in the deck.

3.4 Contiguous Six Times Thirteen

Suite	Card: Operator			
Wands	1–13:	-	14:	-
Cups	1–12:	-	13–14:	>
Swords	1–11:	>	12–14:	<
Pentacles	1–10:	<	8–14:	[
Major Arcana	0–8:	[	9–21:	]

Similarly to the Simple Six Times Thirteen mapping, this has thirteen of each operator but it maps them in continuous runs that ignore suite boundaries. This is conceptually simpler than the 'simple' mapping, but is harder to remember and to work with in practice.

3.5 More Complex Mappings

We could map operators onto cards randomly to ensure that there is no temptation to see the iconography of the Tarot and P" as related. Or we could take the opposite approach and carefully map each operator onto each Tarot card in a way that can be meaningfully explained.

Both approaches introduce interesting new concepts and resonances. They would require custom decks to be usable, as memorizing the mappings for seventy-eight cards would be very difficult for the average person. Doing so would be part of a deeper journey into this domain.

4 How To Read P" Tarot

You will need:

- A table or other flat working area for laying out cards.
- A tarot deck.
- A flat glass bead, a coin, or other small marker.
- A sheet of lined paper or a notebook, and a pencil or pen.
- Optionally: the mapping you are using, written on an index card.

The suggested layout of the working area is to have the draw pile to the right, the discard pile to the left, the piece of paper in the middle, and the row of memory cells above the paper.

The memory cells start at zero in the middle, going up to the right (1, 2, 3) and down to the left (−1, −2, −3). If you are not familiar with negative numbers just start with cell ten in the middle and count up or down from there.

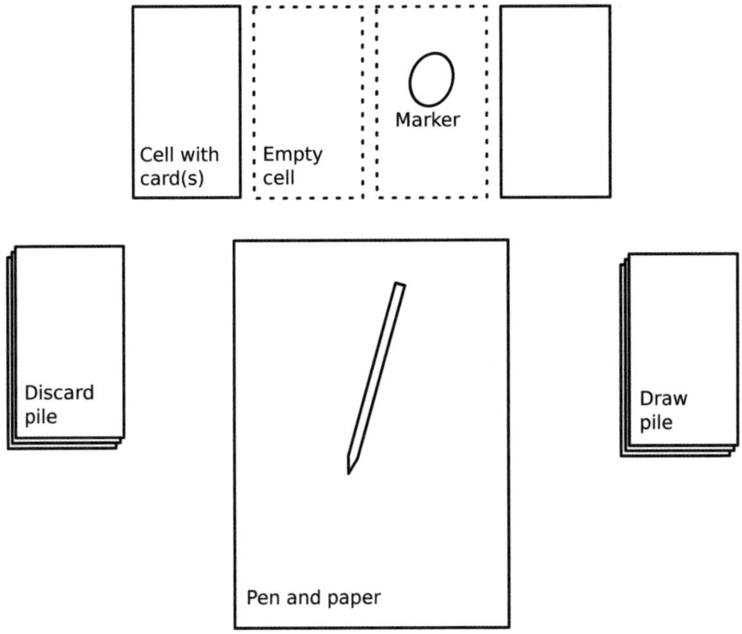

To begin:

1. Shuffle the Tarot deck very well while performing any usual rituals such as repeating the question to be asked. This is to ensure that there is a good mix of operators rather than long runs of] or > for example.
2. Place the Tarot deck face down as the draw pile.
3. Place the marker in the middle of the area you will be using for memory cells.

To proceed:

1. Draw a card from the draw deck. This is the current instruction card.
2. Write down the operator (+, −, <, >, [,]) from the card on a new line of the paper.
3. Perform the operation specified by the operator for the current instruction card:
   1. If the operator is a < or a >, write down the new cell number on that line. Then move the cell marker left or right one card's worth of space. It should be possible to judge this visually, or you can draw a grid on a larger piece of paper. If there is already a card in this position, put the marker on top of it.
   2. If the operator is a +, draw a card from the draw pile and place it face up on top of the current cell (under the marker, on top of any cards already in that position). The value of the cell is the number of cards stacked in it, make a note of this on the paper.
   3. If the operator is a −, remove the topmost card from the current cell and place it face down on the discard pile. If there is not a card in that position, do nothing. The value of the cell is the number of cards stacked in it, make a note of this on the paper.
   4. If the operator is a [:
      - When the current memory cell is zero, draw instruction cards until you draw a], writing down the operators but not acting on them. After drawing and writing down a], continue from 1 as normal.
      - When the current memory cell is greater than zero, proceed as normal until you draw a], then follow the instructions for that operator. Make doubly sure to write

down the operators you draw in the meantime, you'll need to refer to them when you draw the].

5. If the operator is a]:

• When the current memory cell is zero, do nothing and go on to the next instruction.

• When the current memory cell is greater than zero, jump back to the instruction after the matching [and rather than drawing an instruction card follow the instruction you wrote down. While following the written instructions do not draw instruction cards, only draw cards if required to increase the value in the current cell.

4. Place the current instruction card face down on the discard pile.
5. Repeat again from 1 until you reach a finish condition.

To finish, choose one of the following either before starting or when you feel it is appropriate to finish:

- When you have enough cards in total in the cells to use for the layout you wish to use (one card, three card, Celtic Cross, etc.).
- When you have enough cards on top in the cells to use for the layout (if you need three cards and have four cards in one cell and two in another, getting one card in another cell will satisfy this).
- When following a jump instruction results in an endless loop.
- When you have no more cards remaining in the draw pile.

If you run out of cards in the draw pile when pursuing a finish condition other than running out of cards, shuffle the discard pile thoroughly and use it as the new draw pile. Once you have enough cards in the memory cell positions to use for a reading, you can move them in order into the layout that you chose. Where that layout is a simple line of cards, just use the memory cell area as the layout. If you have more cards than you need, owing to the finish condition you used, discard the surplus.

5. Notes

We use the number of cards in a memory cell as the value of that cell rather than substituting a card with a lower or higher printed value (e.g. incrementing the four of cups to give the five of cups) as the search required to find the next valued card would be time consuming and once more than a few memory cells have values in them the next valued card might be in use elsewhere.

We use the Tarot as is rather than adding more cards to allow an equal number of cards for each operator, or creating a new iconography to use the operators directly as meaningful symbols as well as instructions, in order to provide a familiar territory on which to deploy unfamiliar ideas and make them more easily learnable and usable.

Combining the instruction and data function in a single deck of cards is done to make the deck self-animating. Earlier prototypes used a separate 'control deck'. Combining values and operations requires that we not create any rules that would affect whether specific cards will end up in memory cells in a given draw, as otherwise this would mean that (as with some dice Tarot and other systems) some combinations of cards and indeed some cards would never end up in the finished layout.

You Can't Hodl This Holdhus

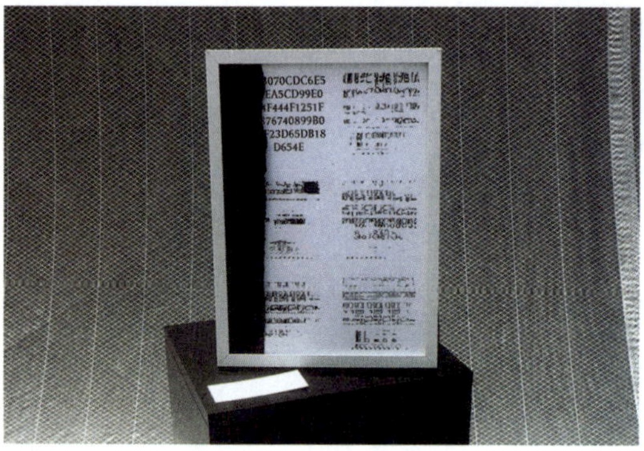

Lars Holdhus, *2C E6 85 DC 0B A7 9F 2C 71 CD 47 52 E2 77 CC D2 96 DB 9B 67 51 F4 34 FD 20 A4 0C 86 5A 02 65 B7 D7 68 B6 FB E5 79 31 03 B6 48 76 26 63 1F 19 DC E0 2C C5 CD 74 A4 80 36 A5 56 83 EF 59 2A E8 31*, framed print representing cryptographic key, 2017.

2C E6 85 DC 0B A7 9F 2C 71 CD 47 52 E2 77 CC D2 96 DB 9B 67 51 F4 34 FD 20 A4 0C 86 5A 02 65 B7 D7 68 B6 FB E5 79 31 03 B6 48 76 26 63 1F 19 DC E0 2C C5 CD 74 A4 80 36 A5 56 83 EF 59 2A E8 31 (2017) by Lars Holdhus, hereafter referred to as *2CE6*, was exhibited at the 'Øx' exhibition of cryptographic art operating in the tradition of 1960s Conceptualism curated by Sam Hart as part of the 2017 Ethereal Summit in New York (one of my smart contract pieces appeared in the same show).

2CE6 is a framed, partially obscured print of hexadecimal digits representing a cryptographic private key. The key is one of 5000 created by Holdhus to authenticate individual artworks over the course of his future artistic career. Exposing it in this way depicts the anxieties of both the art world and cryptoculture and allows the viewer to reflect on the interaction between the two. To explain why will require us to situate both the artwork and its materials within the history of art and encryption.

53‡‡†305))6*;4826)4‡.)4‡);806*;48†8
¶60))85;;]8*;:‡*8†83(88)5*†;46(;88*96
?;8)‡(;485);5*†2:*‡(;4956*2(5*—4)8
¶8*;4069285);)6†8)4‡‡;1(‡9;48081;8:8‡
1;48†85;4)485†528806*81(‡9;48;(88;4
(‡?34;48)4‡;161;:188;‡?;

Edgar Allan Poe's cryptogram from 'The Gold Bug', 1843.

The reemergence of cryptography as a popular pursuit in the nineteenth century starts with a link between code and art. Cryptography and deciphering were popularised by the American author Edgar Allan Poe, who later created the cryptographic literary form of the detective story. In Poe's early story 'The Gold Bug', an encrypted message leads to hidden pirate treasure. It is the story of an investigation, but before and without the framework of the investigating detective that would find its fullest expression in the figure of Sherlock Holmes.[1] The detective story came to be a form of deciphering, bearing the same relation to human secrets and their traces as mediaeval cryptography had to the mysteries of God's creation at a time when the occult, science, and cryptography had yet to differentiate themselves from one another. Poe is a similarly liminal figure to mediaeval cryptographers such as Johannes Trithemius in his combining of cryptography, investigation, and spiritualism in literature and in practice. Poe held codebreaking competitions in newspapers and challenged readers to send in unbreakable codes. His writings on cryptography were required reading in the American intelligence community up until the early twentieth century. Further reflecting the mediaeval relationship between cryptography and the occult (encryption and occultation), Poe was a popular subject for spirit mediumship after his death, and for some time his most popular work was posthumous.

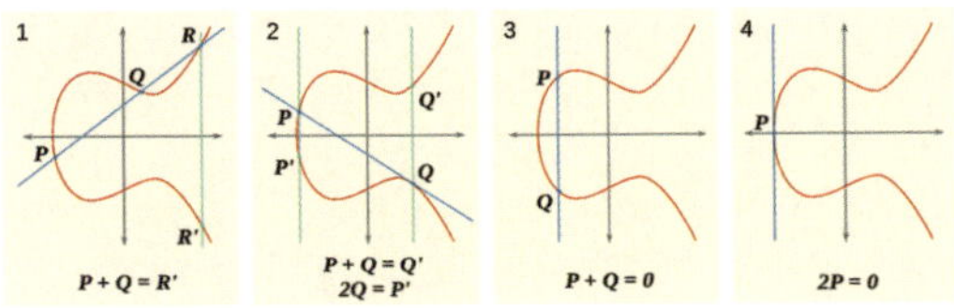

The mathematics of elliptic curves as used in contemporary cryptography. Image by SuperManu, GFDL 1.2 or CC-BY-SA 3.0.

Contemporary cryptography starts not with the codebreaking conflicts of the Second World War (which for the most part just involved the automation of earlier systems) but with the discovery of Public Key Cryptography (PKC), at first secretly in the UK and then publicly in the USA in the 1970s. PKC allows messages to be encrypted using a separate key that cannot be used to decrypt it, and which can therefore be made public. The secret key that is used to decrypt text that has been encrypted by the public key is usually a large number (nowadays consisting of hundreds or thousands of bits) related to it by a 'trapdoor function' that uses currently impossible-to-reverse mathematical operations such as multiplying enormous prime numbers or multiplying points on complex curves. It's everywhere in contemporary communication and trade that takes place over the internet. Like the association of cryptography with the occult, this link between cryptography and trade goes back to the Renaissance.

The relationship between mathematics and cryptography stretches back even further, to earlier Arab cryptologists. This relationship was formalised by Claude Shannon in 1949, and operationalised by PKC. In previous eras, art had a similar relationship with mathematics as part of its self-image, for example in its use of geometry and in colour theories, but Contemporary Art has a mathematics taboo. There is no reason why this should continue to be the case—public key cryptography can provide form, subject, and content for art.

The points, lines, and planes found in private and public keys and in the operations of encryption and decryption relate to mathematics and geometry in art. The mathematics of ratio and projection were common to Renaissance trade and the use of perspective. PKC has become contemporary trade mathematics, but has not yet led to an equivalent of perspective in art. While mathematics is a conceptual resource that strangely elicits disdain or hostility in the digital financialised era of contemporary art, Sol LeWitt showed that it can be used in a critical way. The textual and visual representations of these particular mathematical objects—long strings of hexadecimal or Base58 digits, QR codes and ASCII art—have their own aesthetics, both innate and contingent.

These aesthetics can evoke the worlds of communication, commerce, and espionage as they are determined in contemporary life by cryptography and its absences (backdoors, side-channel attacks, quantum computing, etc.). Or the qualities and

1 See Franco Moretti's *Graphs, Maps, Trees* (London: Verso, 2005) on how this framework fell into place.

experiences of secrets, value, identity, and trust (or, again, its absence) they relate to. These are more concrete subjects than the instrumentalised Platonic realm of cryptographic mathematics, but they flow from it.

Taking a position on these or allowing the artwork's participant to do so, presenting them for critical reflection or using them as indexes of broader social phenomena, makes them content. Those phenomena include the economy, whether conventional finance or cryptocurrency, politics, whether secrecy or hacks of state actors and cypherpunk provocateurs, and the questions of identity, authenticity, and permission that PKC and cryptographic hashing are applied to in networked media and culture.

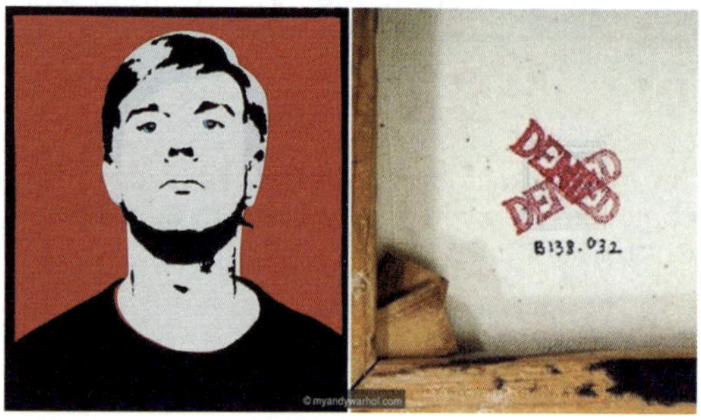

A painting denied by the Warhol Art Authentication Board.

The presence of cryptography or its imagery in a piece of art need not function as any of these—apart from anything else, an artwork can always fail. It may end up as a mess or as kitsch. These are modes of usually unintentional and visible inauthenticity, in contrast to the intentional but hidden inauthenticity of fakes. The fake is a problem for the art market and for the artistic and scholarly reputations that provide its capital. Catalogues raisonnés are meant to tackle the problem of the fake, but the risks of authenticity and value that they carry with them make them a site of market and scholarly anxiety. When such catalogues are assembled, late in an artist's career or after their death, by a foundation, the inclusion or exclusion of a work by mistake carries the risk of lawsuits and monetary damages. This can have a chilling effect both on scholarship and on markets.

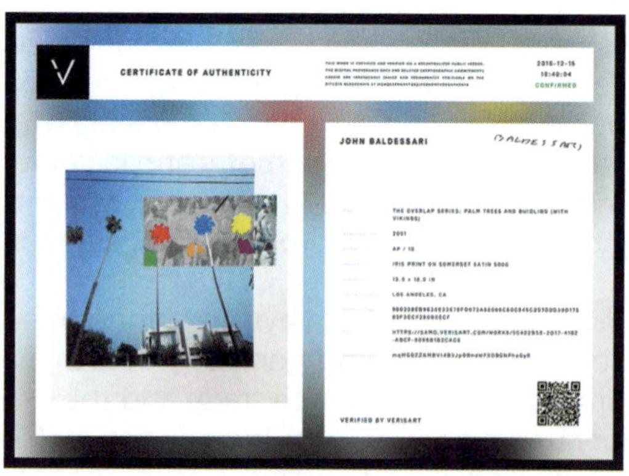

A cryptographic proof of authenticity service.

In theory, public key cryptography can help artists with this: it can be used to create a mathematically unforgeable 'signature' code for each new artwork using the private key, which can be checked but not modified with the public key. This may take the form of a digital file, a radio frequency tag, or a QR code or printout of the signature sealed from sight and attached to a physical work. As long as an assistant, gallerist, or spouse doesn't take a copy of the artist's current private key and start making fakes, this is a secure way of constructing a catalogue of work that the artist has issued in their name. One of the stronger nonmonetary uses of blockchains is to publicly record and timestamp such signatures. In particular, this makes it impossible to claim that posthumously released works were released by the artist during their lifetime. This illustrates one way in which the fake and the problems it presents of identity, authenticity, and value relate to the double-spending problem that cryptocurrency solves.

Lars Holdhus is using non-blockchain PKC to authenticate and limit the number of works they can produce. In *2CE6* the operational security of this strategy is deliberately broken. The first rule of PKC is never to give out your private key. Doing so allows anyone to read your messages (or steal your Bitcoins). The presentation of this act of exposure puts an anxious and fetishistic strategy of authenticity and career/legacy construction at risk. It de-occults the information that would guarantee its authenticity (and thereby its value) in order to become or unfold as an artwork, constructing its cultural and economic value via an apparent act of destroying it, and critiquing its materials in the process. Looking for a precedent for this leads to net.art and to Conceptualism,[2] but also to feminist art. The relationship between secrecy, artistic identity, authenticity, and transparency has a precedent in the art of the Guerilla Girls. Their proposal to open up a gallery's finances as the content of their show involves a similar exposure of an occulted producer/resource of value and identity.

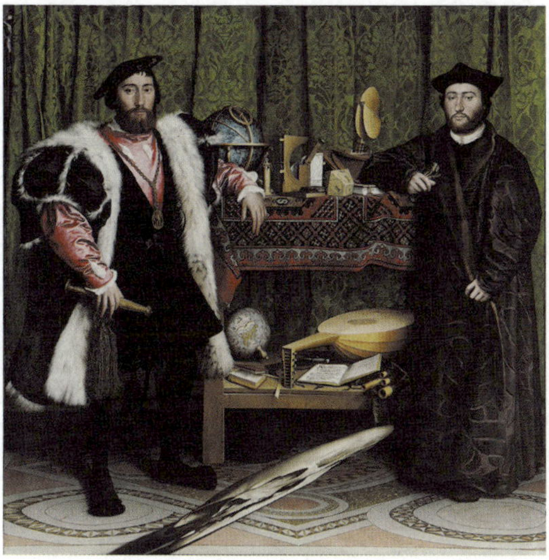

Hans Holbein the Younger, *The Ambassadors*, 1533. Oil on oak, 207 x 209.5cm.

In *2CE6*, Holdhus restores the historical link between the content of art and of cryptography. The contemporary occult of the opacity of the art market, the security of value in trade, and their mathematics exist together cryptographically and artistically in a mutually problematising, and therefore realistic, way. Cryptography functions here as artistic form, subject, and content. When a public key is exposed, that is the end of its usefulness, it is dead. *2CE6* functions as a cryptographic memento mori, a post-Crypto-Wars version of Holbein's *Ambassadors*.

2 See '(Conceptual) Art, Cryptocurrency and Beyond', above, 115.

Tokenisation and Its Discontents

Information wants to be free, and net art is information. Trying to make it harder to copy is like trying to make water less wet.[1] Or perhaps like trying to give it a soul. In 'Blockchain Poetics' I described 'new kinds of quasi-property' created using the Blockchain as a mis-application of that technology. McKenzie Wark is similarly unimpressed—'My Collectible Ass', she complains in *e-flux*.[2]

The history of Conceptual Art's dematerialisation of the art object shows that the art market loves nothing more than finding ways to make the previously unsaleable into financial assets. As Wark points out, '[w]e tend to think that what is collected is a rare object'. There's nothing rarer than something that doesn't actually exist. But the un-ownable and non-or-barely-existent can be represented as property by proxy objects. Financial elsewheres rather than financial futures.

Cryptographic tokens are a generalisation of cryptocurrency to represent assets other than money—such as editions of digital artworks. Wark's criterion of rarity is reflected in the name of the most successful crypto-token collectibles—'Rare Pepes' are détournements of the 'Pepe the Frog' character (previously appropriated by the alt-right) that are sold as CounterParty tokens. CounterParty is a system layered on top of Bitcoin's blockchain that allows the creation of new tokens with varying properties (different issuance amounts, subdividable or not, locked for further issuance or not, a sub-token of another token) which can then be exchanged and transferred, backed by the security of the Bitcoin blockchain. It's an older system than Ethereum or other platforms that are now used for tokens. It has few major use cases, Rare Pepes being one of them.

To make a Rare Pepe card you create a CounterParty token with a reference to the image you are using in its metadata, issue as many tokens as you are going to, then lock the token so no more can be issued (making the token 'rare').[3] Rare Pepe quantities, prices, and styles vary. There are magazines and virtual galleries devoted to them. There is even a subtoken representing the original physical version of one image (with an edition size of one).

A more singular set of images are the 'CryptoPunks', which exist as an ERC20 token (almost) on the Ethereum blockchain. The 'smart contract' that administers the token contains a cryptographic hash of an image of 10,000 bitmapped characters which can be bought and sold using its functions. Like Rare Pepes, the punks have a lighthearted style (they are retro pixelated avatars) and vary in rarity (some features are unique, others appear on dozens of characters). Unlike Rare Pepes, every punk was created at the start of the project and no more can be added. At the time of writing,

1 B. Schneier, 'Crypto-Gram', <https://www.schneier.com/crypto-gram/archives/2001/0515.html>.
2 M. Wark, 'My Collectible Ass', *e-flux* 85 (October 2017), <https://www.e-flux.com/journal/85/156418/my-collectible-ass/>.
3 J $CRiLLA, 'How to Create a Token Using Counterparty ($XCP)', *Hackernoon*, 30 April 2017, <https://hackernoon.com/how-to-create-a-token-using-counterparty-xcp-357b2890e744>.

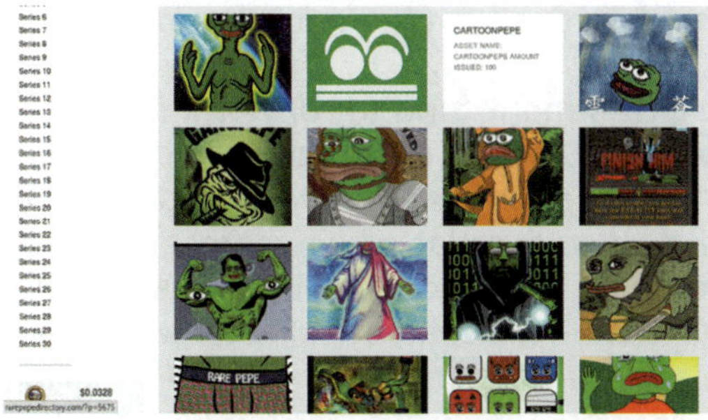

The Rare Pepe Directory

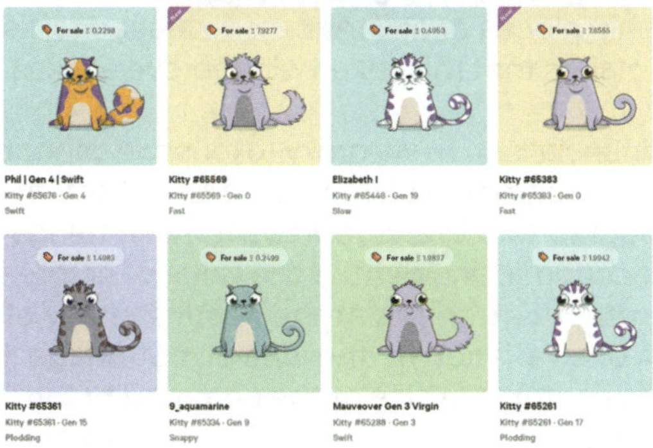

CryptoKitties for sale

punks are available to purchase for between 0.12 and 1,010,101,101,110,010,011,000.01 ETH (between US$40.35 and $339,616,193,448,241,111,336,826.06).

An even more playful approach may be able to take artificially scarce digital collectibles mainstream. CryptoKitties are customised cartoon cats whose appearance is determined by a digital genome (like the old 'Cabbage Patch Kids' dolls) which can be interbred to produce more of them (like William Latham's 'Mutator'). At the time of writing they are taking up 13% of the Ethereum network's capacity, making them the single biggest user of that blockchain, and the most expensive has sold for more than US$100,000.

Every art is relative to a culture and an economy, whatever its other properties may be. The ground that tradeable blockchain images are a figure against is a particular moment in the history of cryptocurrency. Trading cards and digital collectibles fit a specific cultural niche, as does their iconography and the socially performative act of dealing in them. Their price may reflect the ability of cryptocurrency early adopters (who, in the case of CounterParty and its XCP currency, don't have much else to spend it on) to be more extravagant with their hodlings.

Another project, 'dada.nyc', follows the tokenised image edition strategy, but applies it to popular/illustration art. Again, each image is available for a given price in a given edition (for example 0.084 ETH in an edition of 150). The gallery takes a cut on the initial sale and on any subsequent profits on the secondary market, of which the artist also receives a cut, simulating Droit de Suite/Artist's Resale Right. The Resale Right is controversial—it breaks the first sale doctrine, and mostly benefits the estates of famous, dead artists. But I implemented it as a user-settable property in the Art Market smart contract that I wrote in 2014 as I felt it was worth experimenting with in a voluntary setting.[4]

Monegraph came out while I was working on that project. Like Ascribe, it is a serious digital art registry implemented initially using pre-smart-contract technology (NameCoin for Monegraph, Bitcoin for Ascribe). These platforms' seriousness and self-presentation as registries contrasts with the playfulness and explicit tokenisation of more recent systems. This and the possible social and economic impact of the increase in the value of cryptocurrencies since 2014, along with increased mainstream

4 See 'Ethereum Art Market', above, 90.

awareness of cryptocurrency, may explain the difference in their adoption (or at least their respective place in the hype cycle).

In contrast, Maecenas is a tokenised investment fund for physical fine art. It operates in part like the scheme described in William Gibson's novel *Count Zero* (1986), in which Marly, one of the protagonists, reflects on how art in the mid-twenty-first-century is bought and sold as 'points' in the work of a particular artist, which represent shares in the value of 'originals' now stored unseen in vaults.[5] To quote the Maecenas website, 'investors speculate via synthetic exposure: James is a Modern Art collector who needs to finance the purchase of a new Jeff Koons sculpture worth $120k. Instead of selling items from his collection, or getting an expensive loan, James gets the required funding by listing in Maecenas 20% of one of his flagship pieces of art.'[6] Access to Maecenas is via an ERC20 token named '(ART)'. Maecenas claims that this token will improve access, transparency, and fairness in the art market.[7]

Propertisation, fractionalisation and financialisation via proxy tokens (we cannot 'own' allographic digital images, or own part of autographic paintings without dismembering them, but we can own tokens that we agree to pretend represent these things) promise to support art production using the economic accident of the value of cryptocurrency going to the moon. Quasiproperty without attempts at the costly fantasy of imposing access control via DRM is a form of, or a variation on the idea of, patronage. I feel that this complex of ideas should be more useful to critics of the commodity form and capitalism than it has generally been perceived to be thus far. If we still wish to take the opposite tack, this leads us to the gift economy or the commons. Copyright is the default state for most art when it is created, and is being increasingly restrictively enforced on the net. Opposing it passively or actively through alternative copyright licensing can perform a critique of this and keep space open for alternatives. These strategies needn't exclude one another, though.

If you are familiar with DAOs, you can see how a system similar to these could become a self-supporting, self-curating DAO. *Plantoid* is an example of a singular artwork (or family of artworks) produced and exhibited in such a way. Imagine it generalised to a gallery or a participatory art show—a DAO that lets you do art with others, a DAOWO.

These technologies can provide objects for critical exploration that evoke wider contemporary themes. They can function as tools and resources for the creation of art and its social collectivities focussing on these and other themes. Within the existing economy, they can provide ways of supporting the arts (as many of the projects mentioned above claim to), a claim which should neither be dismissed reflexively nor accepted without irony. Or they can be used to try to bootstrap a different context entirely, even if only briefly or in the imagination. The various modes of tokenisation represent potential ways of making a living in, critiquing, or even transforming the art world in an era of the continuing expansion of the sphere of private property and financialisation under technocapital.

5 W. Gibson, *Count Zero* (New York: Arbor House, 1986).
6 <https://web.archive.org/web/20180129050244/https://www.maecenas.co/how-it-works/>.
7 M.G. Casil, 'What is the ART token and why does Maecenas need it?', *Medium.com*, 22 August 2017, <https://medium.com/maecenas/the-art-token-b179590f54ee>.

Blockchain Poetics

Bitcoin[1] and the blockchain technology that originated with it inspire high political passions. For the libertarians and anarchocapitalists who wrote and initially promoted this technology, it is a model of an ideal social order. For the socialists and critical theorists who have been wrongfooted by its popularity, it is literal fascism in technological form.[2] Neither group is happy with the blockchain's recuperation by global financial capital as the new transport layer for banking transactions. However, the experience of the blockchain and how it relates to contemporary society is more complex than can be drawn in reductive ideological strokes, and should inform politics, philosophy, and art more than it currently does.

Where, What, Who, How?

Bitcoin is the fulfilment of the cypherpunk dream of stateless money. The cypherpunk world view was given early expression in the *Cyphernomicon* document written in 1994 by Timothy C. May, incorporating previous contributions to cypherpunk email lists.[3] That document reaches its crescendo with the idea of crypto-anarchy: using encrypted communication and electronic money to smash the state, identified by cypherpunks as an unjust and coercive enemy of individual freedom. Crypto-anarchy's desire for contract law and money without a central state resembles anarcho-capitalism, a political ideology which is mentioned several times in the *Cyphernomicon* and even identified as the form that crypto-anarchy will take.

Anarcho-capitalism[4] is against government, but for money and private property. This is at odds with more traditional forms of anarchism which regard private property as a product of the power of the state. Anarcho-capitalism ultimately implies that the coercive power of the state can be recreated using private security services, paid for using the property owner's capital. Socialist anarchists and anarcho-capitalists tend not to take each other seriously, each regarding the other's world view as incoherent.

Both as a tool to resist or destroy the state and as a necessity in order to recreate some of its functions in its absence, the creation of peer-to-peer electronic money was a key cypherpunk and anarcho-capitalist objective. Representing money as electronic data poses a problem, though: money needs to be scarce but data can be copied without restriction. If I send you an email saying 'I hereby give you ten credit units', you can copy it at will and thereby spend those ten credit units as many times as you like.

Preventing the same electronic money being spent multiple times is the 'double-spending problem', or what cryptocurrency enthusiasts describe as the 'Byzantine

1 See e.g. A. Antonopoulos, *Mastering Bitcoin* (Sebastopol, CA: O'Reilly Media, 2017).
2 See e.g. D. Golumbia, *The Politics of Bitcoin: Software as Right-Wing Extremism* (Minneapolis: University of Minnesota Press, 2016).
3 <http://cypherpunks.to/faq/cyphernomicron/cyphernomicon>.
4 See e.g. <http://wiki.mises.org/wiki/anarcho-capitalism>.

Generals Problem'.[5] The problem that the apocryphal Byzantine generals face in agreeing a plan to attack a city while communicating via possibly treacherous communications channels, resembles the problem of forgery and authenticity in money and art, in terms of establishing that signifiers have the history that they claim to. What is at risk is the blocking or ironising of intended meaning, or of someone else capturing the surplus value of code.[6] Previous electronic money systems relied on 'trusted third parties', servers or other hardware controlled by someone other than the individuals involved in a given transaction—usually banks. In the 1999 cypherpunk novel *Cryptonomicon* by Neal Stephenson[7] the protagonists use gold held in trust and a central database in order to administrate this third-party function, a solution later disastrously attempted in real life by eGold.[8]

Satoshi Nakamoto, the pseudonymous creator of Bitcoin, created a solution to the double-spending problem and thereby to the desire for stateless electronic money in 2009. Bitcoin's 'blockchain' is the first algorithm of *post-modern* computing[9] in that it departs from the assumptions of security and consistency that were foundational to computing models developed during the twentieth century. The blockchain algorithm is designed to create consensus in an untrustworthy and possibly hostile computing environment, and in doing so uses economic incentives to solve a problem in computer science.

Myth, Virtue, Pathologies

Myths have the power to direct society's desires and achievements. In the figure of Satoshi Nakamoto (or rather their powerful absence) Bitcoin has an incorruptible and exemplary foundation myth. Satoshi, whoever or whatever they may have been, gave the world Bitcoin and the blockchain as a gift, built a group of disciples who understood the direction that Bitcoin should be developed in, and then disappeared.[10] The society founded on this myth quickly developed a culture and language to reflect its ideals: 'Free the markets, free the world' (a reference to Bitcoin's anarcho-capitalist implications), 'to the moon' (a reference to the explosive growth of Bitcoin's fiat currency value), and 'hodl' (a misspelling of 'hold', meaning to store cryptocurrency with the unshakeable faith that it will be of value in the long term) are just some examples of the jargon and shibboleths reflecting attitudes and behaviours that have emerged from Bitcoin's rise.[11] This tendency reached its in-joke zenith with Dogecoin, which very consciously grew its economic value by growing its community through shared culture.

The mythologised virtues of Satoshi and the blockchain—their incorruptibility, freedom, and fairness—stand in contrast to the vices and corruptions of those 'weary giants of flesh and steel', the banks and state apparatuses that cyberspace libertarians

5 L. Lamport, R. Shostak and M. Pease, 'The Byzantine Generals Problem', *ACM Transactions on Programming Languages and Systems* 4:3 (July 1982), 382–401.
6 See the section on 'Functional Disequilibrium: Surplus Value of Code', in G. Deleuze and F. Guattari. *Anti-Oedipus*, tr. R. Hurley, M. Seem, and H.R. Lane. (Minneapolis: University of Minnesota Press, 1983), 187.
7 N. Stephenson, *Cryptonomicon* (New York: Avon, 1999).
8 K. Zetter, 'Bullion and Bandits: The Improbable Rise and Fall of E-Gold', *Wired.com*, 2009, <http://wired.com/2009/06/e-gold>.
9 M. Loukides, 'The Computing of Distrust', *On Our Radar—O'Reilly*, 6 January 2015, <http://radar.oreilly.com/2015/01/the-computing-of-distrust>.
10 S. Nakamoto, 'Bitcoin: A Peer-to-Peer Electronic Cash System', 2008, <http://bitcoin.org/en/bitcoin-paper>.
11 <http://bitcointalk.org/index.php?topic=375643.0>.

have historically positioned themselves against.[12] The very first block in Bitcoin's blockchain, known as the 'Genesis Block', contains a message to prove the date of its creation—a quote from a report in *The Times* about a state banking bailout, a story chosen to contrast vividly with Bitcoin's removal of trusted third parties.[13]

But myth can also misdirect, and language also reflects a culture's fears and disappointments. Bitcoin's success spawned hundreds of other 'altcoin' cryptocurrencies, many of them ineptly managed or naked scams—pejoratively referred to as 'shitcoins' or 'pump and dump' currencies. The purchasers of these worthless tokens speak as though they are 'investors' who will become rich as surely as if they had started mining Bitcoin in 2009. The 'madness of crowds' seen in the era of nineteenth-century economic bubbles is as nothing compared to the dogged conviction of the shitcoin hodler.[14] The power of language can also be seen in the way that FinTech workers who are effectively recuperating the blockchain for the trusted third parties of existing financial institutions can hide behind revolutionary rhetoric and feelgood talk (and often real experiences) of community.

Perhaps worse than the frenetic and wrongheaded speculation around altcoins, the rhetoric of the certainty and enforceability of transactions promised by the blockchain repeatedly tempts people to misapply its protocols to new kinds of quasiproperty: from recording the use of firearms[15] to the giving of sexual consent.[16] Entitlement, coercion, and over-simplification haunt too many proposed blockchain use cases outside of simple currency. As Dogecoin's community of 'shibes' might say, this is 'very not wow'.[17]

Security, Work, Power, Proof

As suggested above, the economic value of the Bitcoin blockchain is established through its security against double-spending. To secure transactions, Bitcoin uses Public Key Cryptography (PKC), a system originally invented in secrecy by the UK government in the early 1970s, and independently developed in the USA later in the decade.[18] PKC uses the properties of very large, very random numbers to create a mathematical space in which communications can be hidden. The cypherpunks naturally loved PKC, and used it to secure email and other communications long before its application to electronic currency. Cypherpunk applications of encryption have precedents—the relationship between cryptography and money goes back to the use of mediaeval bank codebooks in Europe, and the relationship between cryptography and politics goes back to antiquity.[19] But the era of Bitcoin and WikiLeaks is a cypherpunk era, and its deployment of PKC is different and operates on a far larger scale.

12 J.P. Barlow, 'A Declaration of the Independence of Cyberspace', 1996, <http://eff.org/cyberspace-independence>.

13 See the explanation at <http://en.bitcoin.it/wiki/Genesis_block>.

14 C. Mackay, *Extraordinary Popular Delusions and the Madness of Crowds* (London: Richard Bentley, 1841).

15 See e.g. J. Redman, 'Why "Glockchain" Could Hold Police Accountable, Curb Violence', *Bitcoin.com*, 29 July 2016, <http://news.bitcoin.com/glockchain-hold-police-accountable>.

16 See e.g. J. O'Connell, 'Sex Consent Smart Contracts: Would You Issue the Coin?', *Cryptocoinsnews*, 2016, <http://cryptocoinsnews.com/sex-consent-smart-contracts-issue-coin>.

17 B. Scott, 'Much Soul, Very Emotion: Why I Buy into the Cult of Dogecoin', *MCD*, 27 December 2014, <https://www.digitalmcd.com/dogecoin-2/>.

18 C. Paar and J. Pelzl, *Understanding Cryptography* (Berlin: Springer-Verlag, 2010).

19 For some of this history, see <http://en.wikipedia.org/wiki/history_of_cryptography#classical_cryptography>.

To secure blocks, Bitcoin uses a 'proof of work' scheme adopted from a proposed email anti-spam system called 'Hashcash'. To claim the 'block reward' of new bitcoins, you must compete to be the first to complete a puzzle that is computationally (and therefore economically) expensive to solve but cheap to confirm, and thereby be the first person to broadcast the value associated with this 'new block' of transactions to the blockchain network. Since the puzzle takes the form of finding a cryptographic hash with a particular value, the computational power used to do this is called 'hashing power'. The most secure chain of blocks is the longest chain, the chain with the most hashing power behind it.

Economics, Incentives, Rationality

Monetarily, Bitcoin is like Air Miles, Green Shield Stamps, Linden Dollars, or mobile phone credit: it is just another complementary currency with equivalent value in pounds sterling or United States dollars, but which can only be spent within a specific system. Unlike those examples, however, it also functions as a critique, problematisation, or defamiliarisation of traditional currencies. Bitcoin proponents contrast it to state-created 'fiat' money on the basis that it is not issued or enforced by any state. Despite this, fiat resembles Bitcoin both in its mechanical minting process (Bitcoin is a *coin* after all), and in its creation of money out of thin air in the columns of databases running on energy-hungry bank mainframes. Likewise, Bitcoin resembles fiat currency in the capital requirements for mining and the material instantiation of its systems in mining rigs and hardware wallet devices. Furthermore, the fixed supply of Bitcoin means that, like gold, its scarcity should guarantee that its value will appreciate over time. This is intended to lead to deflationary economics, which makes it very appealing to its early adopters and to adherents of Austrian School economics.[20] The core difference between Bitcoin and fiat, though, is that it duplicates existing market-currency models without the need for centralised banks or state operators. You don't have to spend several months profiling the wrong person for a literary magazine to realise that Nakamoto's implementation of Bitcoin has a libertarian political aspect to it.[21]

Within the Bitcoin community there are economic and political arguments about low-value transactions 'spamming' the blockchain, about non-monetary transactions 'bloating' it, about the fungibility of bitcoins stolen or spent on dubious items and services by criminals, and about whether 'censorship' to address these will increase or decrease the value of Bitcoin. At the algorithmic level, the difficulty of solving the proof-of-work puzzle for each block is adjusted by the system every two weeks to ensure the regular, reliable, value-protecting creation of the blockchain.

As we have seen, this value comes from the security of the Bitcoin system. This security is paid for in Bitcoin, providing economic incentives to maintain the security of the system using the system itself. These incentives create a closed loop—in theory at least. In practice they are easy to misunderstand or to get wrong. For example, if we assume that miners and account holders do not have opposed interests in transaction fees (miners benefit from high fees, users from low ones) we may fail to balance them correctly. Or if we remove competition for block mining rewards without introducing a different incentive for building and storing blocks then we may reduce the security of the system by attracting and retaining fewer miners, leaving the system more open to a 51% attack.

These mistakes can be made for technical reasons (seeking to reduce costs or transaction times) or ideological reasons (seeking to avoid competitive social relations

20 R. Murphy, 'The Mises Theory of Money, Bitcoin, and Saving the Economy Explained in 10 Minutes', <https://www.youtube.com/watch?v=gzydNE3chsM>.

21 A. O'Hagan, 'The Satoshi Affair', *London Review of Books* 38:13 (30 June 2016), <http://lrb.co.uk/v38/n13/andrew-ohagan/the-satoshi-affair>.

or to tie a system to a national jurisdiction). Failing to consider how Bitcoin's built-in economic incentives result from and align with its ideological underpinnings, whatever one may think of them, can lead to a failure to address in a game-theoretically sound way the diverse and conflicting motivations and incentives that exert pressure on a monetary system from the direction of society at large. This isn't just a problem for altcoins. If Bitcoin itself gets these incentives wrong, for technical or political reasons, then it too will see adoption drop off.

Cryptocurrencies assume that local economic rationality (profit-maximising behaviour expressed through the game of mining and using the coin, local to the Bitcoin user-base itself) is a sufficient motivator to secure their blockchain. Examples of cryptocurrencies being broken for profit, such as the 51% attack on Feathercoin (in which an attacker was able to create a fork and steal block rewards)[22] or the denial of service attacks on Ethereum, show that global economic rationality (the largest possible economic game of profit-maximising behaviour, which is not constrained to the local economic game of a given blockchain, and might profit by destroying value in that blockchain) can trump this assumption. The activity of trolling cryptocurrencies, for example the way in which users reprised the use of the ETC Ethereum fork against the wishes of its progenitors, is likewise an example of global *social* rationality. Some of the loudest proponents of the ETC fork defended their actions in the name of Ethereum's social contract—a contract that they regarded the original Ethereum system as having betrayed. For them, maintaining the supposedly discarded branch of the fork was the only rational and moral response. Another example of this kind of global social trolling activity within a supposedly self-contained digital system can be seen in the fact that the movie with the lowest score on IMDB is not the one that has offended the largest audience with its polished Bollywood aesthetics, but rather one that has done so by referring to the Bangladesh Liberation War as the 'Indo-Pak' war.[23] Capitalising on this social ethics of networked activity, Dogecoin's differentiator in relation to other blockchain currencies is predicated firstly on its social value (the fun-time, jargon-filled culture of its community of users), and only secondarily on its technical-economic innovation (slightly faster block times). Despite the primacy of game theory in contemporary economics, this influence of cultural and social factors on blockchain currencies shows that there is always more than one game—and that we do not always know which game we are playing.

Order (Temporal, Social, Political)

The security of the blockchain provides a strong temporal order for the information (the transactions) that it contains. Time's arrow points along the blockchain with a certainty and finality that the relativistic physical universe cannot rival. Ignoring the Unix timestamps that give a mapping from blockchain time to the number of seconds since 1 January 1970, the roughly ten-minute duration of each block marks the passing of time, the ever-increasing expenditure of hashing power, and the resulting increasing certainty of facts encoded in the blockchain. Proof becomes fact over time in the metronomic succession of blocks. Real-world events, from celebrations to software updates, are already timed to specific blocks. When everyone tells the time with blocks, we will have switched from fiat time and its trusted third parties, atomic clocks timed to the revolutions of the earth, to blockchain time, timed to the accumulation of certainty through hashing power.

As well as a strong internal temporal order, there is a strong social order implicit in Bitcoin—one that deliberately excludes 'politics' conceived of as the distorting

22 D. Bradbury, 'Feathercoin Hit by Massive Attack, *Coindesk*, 2013, <http://coindesk.com/feathercoin-hit-by-massive-attack>.
23 D. Goldberg, 'The Story behind the Worst Movie on IMDB, *FiveThirtyEight*, 2014, <http://fivethirtyeight.com/features/the-story-behind-the-worst-movie-on-imdb>.

intervention of the state in authentic social relationships between peers (or at least their transactions). There is no 'theft' via tax, or devaluation via inflation, on the blockchain—no involuntary payment for the state's wars and its surveillance and oppression. Instead there is a continuum of fair trades and accumulations based on voluntary relationships between economic peers.

The instantiation of this order in Bitcoin, or at least strong support for it, makes Bitcoin a tool for justice as seen from the libertarian point of view. It decentralises power—taking agency away from state apparatuses and distributing it to users according to a homogeneously ordered system of relations. As a result, recentralisation, whether of the state or of blockchain mining hashing power in 'mining pools' which can carry out 51% attacks or block protocol upgrades, is seen as bad in and of itself. The blockchain is created by peers running a *consensus* algorithm, not a ruling algorithm. It embodies the political right of exit, a fork away from the state inevitably followed by further forks as communities rise up around cryptocurrencies and disagree over their directions.

This absence-of-politics-as-politics puts any would-be critic in the position of having to defend coercion and an interventionist state, or of having to demonstrate the ways in which Bitcoin is itself a form of state. As we have noted, anarcho-capitalism appears incoherent to socialist anarchists because it presupposes that the notion of private property can be upheld without the violence of the state to underwrite it. Bitcoin and the blockchain purport to allow precisely that. From Nakamoto onward, Bitcoin is defined by such guiding absences—no state, no bank, no boardroom, no real-world tokens.

Code, Law, Society

For many cryptocurrency enthusiasts, Lawrence Lessig's LambdaMOO[24]-era observation that, on the internet, 'code is law' has become a normative ideal rather than a critical observation (much to Lessig's dismay).[25] Without code (and mass computing power) there is no Bitcoin network and no blockchain. But human beings arguing about which code should be run, which code better reflects Satoshi's intention or has less human intervention in its operation, debases the principle of code-is-law, reducing it to human choice in the name of inhuman perfection. The code of Bitcoin has been modified or copied into hundreds of different coins. Individual codebases may be law on their own individual blockchains, but code-is-law in the space of cryptocurrencies is polycentric. You can always fork—and what is law in one fork is simply a meaningless string of bits in another.

The laws that cryptocurrency codes implement are almost always those of capital, of property—from financial restrictions, via shares and deeds, to contracts and 'intellectual property'. But this is a law set free from its bourgeois state shackles—and checks and balances. There is a tension between the jurisdictional claims of code-as-law and the law of the land. Just because you are creating stocks and shares on the blockchain doesn't mean that the law regarding stocks and shares in the real world doesn't also apply. And there is another tension that cryptocurrencies inherit from anarcho-capitalism. If money, contracts and property require the coercive power of the state to maintain them, is it the form (how something is maintained) or the function (maintenance itself) of the state that is being objected to? Reproducing the coercive role of the state in a decentralised yet less constrained manner does not create a more just society. In response, blockchain-based systems are being created for organising voting structures, whether for corporations, co-operatives, or new or existing

24 For background to contemporary public discussion of LambdaMOO, see: <http://en.wikipedia.org/wiki/a_rape_in_cyberspace>.

25 L. Lessig, *Code and Other Laws of Cyberspace* (New York: Basic Books, 1999). See also '"Code Is Law" Shall Be the Whole of the Law', below, 191.

governments—bringing the democratic ideals of contemporary society to bear on this new, emergent legal framework (or possibly distorting both beyond recognition).

When society is represented as code, failures of code become failures in society. 'The DAO hack', in which a previously undiscovered bug in a cryptocurrency smart contract allowed hackers to steal one hundred and fifty million dollars' worth of tokens representing voting rights, turned a democratic venture capital fund into a crisis for the community around it. Resolving it involved intensive work on both code (a 'hard fork' modification of the underlying Ethereum system) and social measures (drumming up community support for the fork).[26]

Identity, Representation

On the blockchain, the peers that engage in transactions are represented by addresses based on their PKC public keys. Bitcoin addresses are deliberately meaningless strings of letters and numbers—although some users have a 'vanity address' which adds a degree of human-readable structure to the start of the key, e.g. `1BoatSLRHtKNngkdX-EeobR76b53LETtpyT`. This is probably the only way that media-jamming-style spoofing of identity can take place on a blockchain without actually hacking it.

Using a PKC key as an identity marker simultaneously hides a peer's real-life identity and identifies their blockchain identity with mathematical certainty as a matter of public record. This is a dialectic of absolute secrecy and absolute identity. Saying 'I am my private key' is a reified and deliberately impoverished notion of individual identity. It frees individuals to not have to trust one another in their economic transactions, and so they can trust one another in their social interactions as a result.

On the blockchain, data from the outside world is identified or represented by its cryptographic hash. A cryptographic hash is a short but nonetheless almost certainly unique representation of a much longer piece of data. Cryptographic hashes are very sensitive to changes in data: a single character different in the input will result in completely different output. For example, the SHA-256 cryptographic hash of my genome (a piece of data with a meaning very different from a quantity of Bitcoin and which would take many blocks to include in Bitcoin's early 2017 one-megabyte blocks) is: `BADA4CF5328394F733CD278C33509E79B839CC0B083865850 3B116D6CA9CA14B`, the hash of your genome will be completely different, even in the unlikely event that we have only a single codon different between us. Placing data or the hash of data in the blockchain provides a timestamp on it that proves it existed at least after the date of mining of the block that contains it—someone or something with my genome has existed since at least Bitcoin block #286917.[27] There are also tricks to include other data in the blockchain in transaction outputs or addresses, and texts, images, code and music have all been included in those ways.

Epistemology, Ontology, Cosmology

Within the blockchain there is only codified truth: the truth as to which address has sent transactions to which other address, the truth as to what value or data (hashes or other representations of information) was included in those transactions. The truth of the blockchain is underpinned by a consensus reached by computers competing for economic rewards. Because of the way each block in the Blockchain is constructed, to change the truth of the blockchain would require more computing power than at least half the Bitcoin network for an amount of time equal to the time since a particular fact entered the blockchain. This quickly becomes prohibitively expensive. In contrast with

26 D. Siegel, 'Understanding the DAO Attack', *CoinDesk*, 2016. <http://coindesk.com/understanding-dao-hack-journalists>.

27 See *Proof of Existence*, below, 273.

the imposed or negotiated truths of contemporary states or of academia, this is an extraordinarily strong basis for certainty in facts, however limited in scope those facts may be.

Through the blockchain we know facts, in so far as the data contained by the blockchain represents facts, with a confidence proportional to the accumulated security of the blocks that contain them. This is equal to the amount of computing power expended over time by miners performing the proof-of-work algorithm. We know who, or at least which address, has stated each fact on the blockchain with cryptographic certainty. We know that and when they stated it with a certainty born of the economics of years of planetary-scale computer power. And we very quickly know all of this with a certainty that it would take more than the computing power of the entire planet to undo.

This isn't trust, it is the obviation of trust, a transactional finality born of network consensus. This finality is only on the chain, though. If the blockchain forks there will be two certainties, two chains of not-needing-to-trust, and a conflict between them. Even then, the network's computing power will eventually settle on one of them as the true state of the world, building the longest chain on it once more. This process works towards an immutable, final truth established with greater certainty than all the world's encyclopaedias put together.

Viewed from within the space of the blockchain, identities are constructed using only the finest artisanal entropy[28] sliced into chunks and used to anchor facts in a geological-time-defying[29] immense crypto-space, a software approximation of a growing block universe, where the past and present exist, but the future does not, rather it is grown into.[30] Similarly, stepping outside of his engagement with the kind of right-wing antipolitics discussed above, philosopher Nick Land has argued that the blockchain represents a post-Kantian, post-relativistic order—not just a new kind of temporal order but the invention of absolute time itself.[31] It is easy to criticise such an absolutisation of the idea of the blockchain, but iterating through those objections and our answers to them in turn can be useful in gaining a deeper critical appreciation of the blockchain.

Outro

The blockchain is a site of socioeconomic alterity and an imaginary that has not yet been entirely recuperated by the economic order that it sought to transcend. Nor is it yet a culturally pervasive enabling metaphor, as fire, ceramics, steam, or computers were for previous cultures.[32] There are signs that it can become one—for example, philosopher and economic theorist Melanie Swan imagines the blockchain ultimately both reaching outward to encompass an interplanetary economy and reaching inward to encompass our own thoughts, to provide a back-up and record of consciousness itself.[33] But perhaps in this brief moment of potential it nonetheless reflects, contrasts with, and animates the global sociopolitical order as a dark mirror in which to diffract our post-economic-crisis society. It contains, or is a screen for, hopes for social authenticity and common wealth that are recognisable from wider society and yet are uniquely

28 LB Lieven, 'Artisanal Integers', *NeverEndingBooks*, 2015, <http://neverendingbooks.org/artisanal-integers>.

29 For the mathematics of breaking public key cryptography, see <http://bitcoin.stackexchange.com/a/2852/1660>.

30 See the description at <http://en.wikipedia.org/wiki/Growing_block_universe>.

31 FOAM.,'The Art of Economy Part 1', 2015, <http://youtube.com/watch?v=31wRg8p1sPk> . See also: N. Land, *Crypto-Current: Bitcoin and Philosophy* (Shanghai: Time Spiral Press, forthcoming).

32 J. David Bolter, *Turing's Man* (Chapel Hill, NC: University of North Carolina Press, 1984).

33 M. Swan, *Blockchain* (Sebastopol, CA: O'Reilly Media, 2016).

inflected ideologically, expressed in software protocols, token sales, algorithmic organisations, and tips. It is also haunted by fantasies of passive income and of enforcing particular ideas of justice. The more we engage with this, the closer we get to realising the blockchain's value as a critical resource, just as the internet was for net.art, and earlier systems of communication and exchange were for the Conceptual Art movement.

2017

Artists Re: Thinking the Blockchain: Initial Book Offering Slides[1]

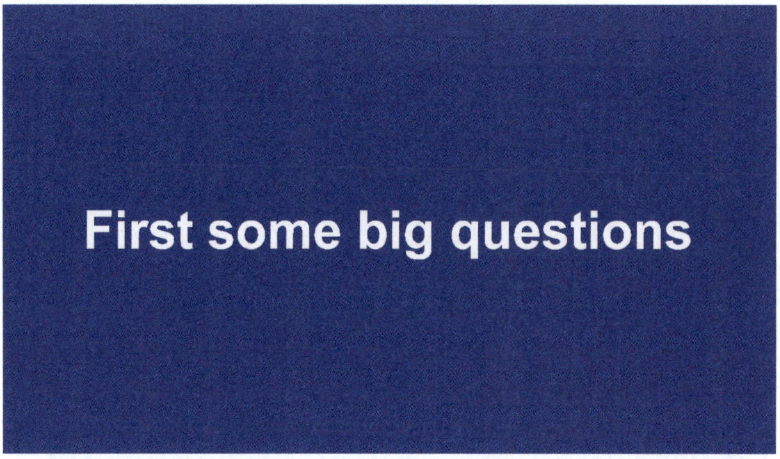

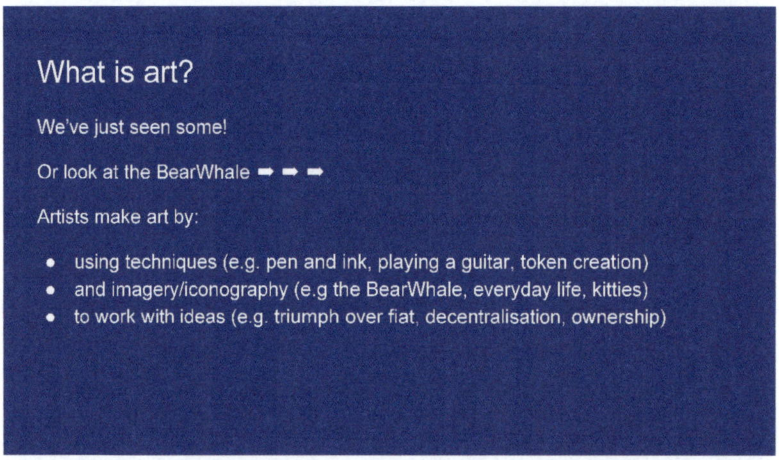

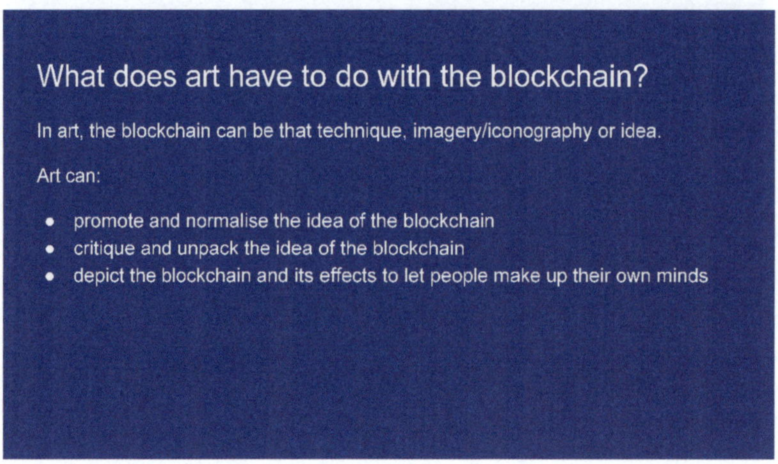

1 Slides from my presentation at the 'IBO' for R. Catlow, M. Garrett, S. Skinner and N. Jones (eds), *Artists Re: Thinking The Blockchain* (Torque Editions, 2017) at DCTRL Vancouver, 6 December 2017.

What does the blockchain have to do with art?

The blockchain can be used as

- a medium for art (art on the blockchain, not necessarily about it)
- a subject of art (art about the blockchain, not necessarily on it)

Cryptocurrency, tokens and DAOs can be used to fund and organise:

- the creation of art
- the curation and exhibition of art
- the sale and ownership of art

Blockchain Poetics

- The blockchain is the product of particular ideas of freedom and justice.
- The blockchain touches on ideas of identity, value, truth, order and time.
- The blockchain has a shape, a rhythm, evokes other forms, spaces, events.
- To competently promote or critique the blockchain we need a deeper understanding of this politics, philosophy and aesthetics.
- This will involve a learning curve for both proponents and critics.
- A lot of this learning will involve the Cypherpunks.

Art can decentralise this process of learning, and prototype its lessons

Blockchain Geometries

Data structures hold information in a way that makes it easier to manipulate using software, given particular constraints on computing resources such as the time or space taken up. A linked list takes very little space in a computer's memory on top of the space taken up by the data it contains, and is very quick to add new data to, but it is very slow to search from the beginning to the end of the list.

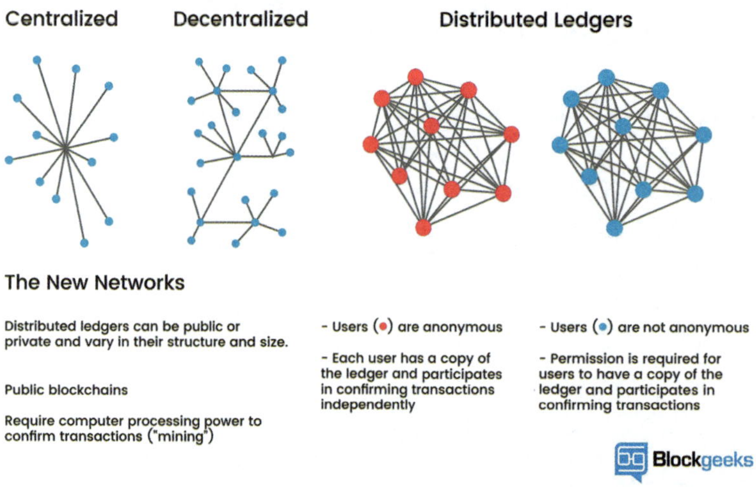

Image from Blockgeeks, 'What is Blockchain Technology', <https://blockgeeks.com/guides/what-is-blockchain-technology/>.

In contrast, a 'hashtable' data structure makes looking up information much faster by calculating a unique identifier 'hash' for each item, which can then be used as an index entry for the data rather than having to search all the way through a long list of links. Think of a hash as a very large, very unique number that can be reliably calculated for any piece of data—any file containing the text 'Hello world!' will have the same cryptographic hash as any other such file. The cost of this fast access is that the table must be allocated and configured in full before you can start storing data in it.

A 'binary tree' balances speed and storage space by storing data in a structure that looks like a tree with two branches at the end of each branch, creating a simple hierarchy that takes very little initial extra storage space but which, given its structure, is relatively fast to search compared to a linked list.

Each block in a blockchain is linked to the previous one by identifying it using its (cryptographic) hash value. And the transactions in the block are stored in a (cryptographic hash) tree. This means that a blockchain is a more complex structure than the simple image shown at the top of this page. But so what? Why should we care about the shape of the blockchain when its social, environmental, and political impact seem to be in such urgent need of critique?

The geometric, techonomic, and social form of a blockchain are all related, and understanding one helps us to reason better about the others. As indicated by the quick tour through software data structure design above, the constraints on technological

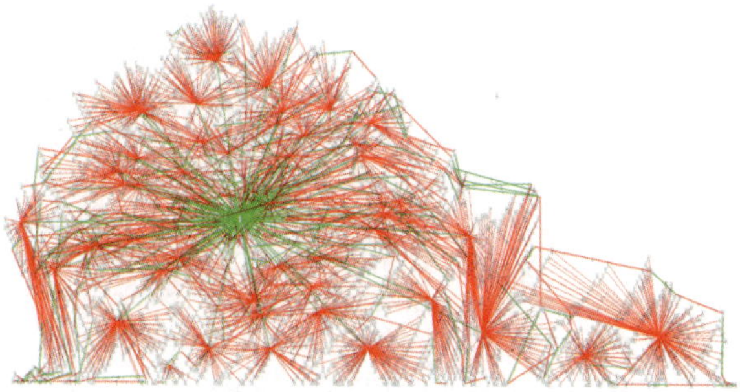

Image from Blockgeeks, 'What is Blockchain Technology', <https://blockgeeks.com/guides/what-is-block-chain-technology/>.

form are not abstract, they are tied to real needs and agendas. Bitcoin is no exception to this—the lists and trees that make up its blockchain were chosen very explicitly to exclude the intervention of the state and other 'trusted third parties' (such as banks) in authentic economic relationships between peers.

Bitcoin's algorithms prioritise the security of the blockchain above all else, maximising security in the same way the mythical artificial intelligence 'paperclipper' maximises the production of a particular material good regardless of any other consequences. This explains Bitcoin's energy consumption, which, while lower than the US military or other equivalent systems that guarantee the security of fiat currencies, is probably still much higher than Satoshi Nakamoto originally envisioned.

There are other algorithms, though, which have been created since 2008 to address perceived flaws in Bitcoin's design or to address different ideological agendas. These create different forms than Bitcoin's blockchain, and contrast instructively with it.

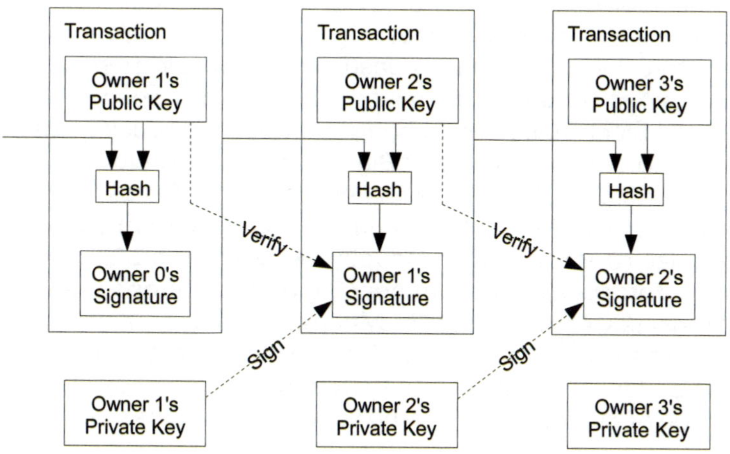

Satoshi Nakamoto, Bitcoin transaction diagram, from the Bitcoin white paper (2008).

(Please note that these are experimental and often controversial technologies; nothing that follows is investment advice.)

Bitcoin creates blocks on average every ten minutes. Faster currencies quickly emerged—LiteCoin and Dogecoin are leading examples, with 2.5 minute and 1-minute block times respectively. Blocks may contain more or fewer transactions, and may be more or less frequent even within the same blockchain, as the algorithms tweak its parameters to ensure security. Blockchains have rhythm: they can stall or race ahead, each subsequent block can be larger or smaller and closer or further from the previous one. Transactions fan into and out from addresses in each block, with varying values of currency or amounts of data each time. We are now very far indeed from the block-and-arrow diagrams of linked lists.

The Ethereum system, which extends Bitcoin's financial ledger into a more general system for 'smart contracts', has the smallest block time of any leading cryptocurrency: fifteen seconds. Like the others mentioned, it still uses a variant of the energy-hungry 'proof of work' security system from Bitcoin. In proof of work, anyone who wants to add a block of transactions to the list must consume computing resources to solve a puzzle (essentially guessing a large number ending with multiple zeroes). Since these resources cost money, anyone willing to expend them must stand to gain more from adding the next block than they stand to lose to their electricity bill. It is this game-theoretical gambit that secures a proof-of-work blockchain. The mindlessly focussed, paperclipper nature of blockchain security algorithms means that, as more people have used more computers to compete to be the next person to add a block to the chain and claim the economic reward for doing so, the difficulty and therefore the amount of electricity required to solve that puzzle has increased massively, growing the energy footprint of cryptocurrency.

Ethereum is planning to switch to a 'proof of stake' system, like that used in currencies such as NXT and Decred (about which more below). Rather than burning electricity like proof of work, proof of stake uses a blockchain's own existing currency 'staked' by users to demonstrate their standing within the system and to thereby win a chance to be chosen by the network to add the next block. proof of stake and its related 'proof of authority' system move from the 'miners' of proof of work, who operate on the blockchain from outside, to a system of capitalist investors or even an aristocratic class of gatekeepers who operate within the logic of the blockchain itself. This folds the blockchain's outside in on itself.

Bitcoin's blocks have been fixed at one megabyte in size since a temporary security fix by Satoshi Nakamoto introduced this limit. As Bitcoin usage has grown, blocks have become increasingly full (allegedly often as a result of economic 'spam' attacks intended to manipulate prices—competing for space in blocks drives up transaction fees, which can in turn discourage users and ultimately drive down the price of Bitcoin). How should this problem be addressed—how should Bitcoin scale? Should the number of transactions stored in the blockchain grow, increasing the block size limit and making it harder for individuals to store the blockchain on consumer hardware in a decentralised manner? Or should transactions somehow be moved 'offchain' into 'second-tier' systems that build on top of the blockchain, adding complexity and introducing potential new choke-points for existing capital to exploit? Big blocks or small blocks (like the big or little ends of eggs, or integers...)? This is a real debate in the Bitcoin world, and illustrates how the consequences of a simple change in technical form such as, for example, increasing block sizes from one to two megabytes, can have profound effects on the social and economic form of a cryptocurrency. 'Big blockers' propose solutions such as the breakaway 'Segwit2X' or 'Bitcoin Cash' systems, scaling 'onchain' with ever greater amounts of data in the same structures. 'Small blockers' propose solutions that move data out of the blockchain into 'Segregated Witnesses' that store cryptographic signatures outside of the blockchain, or the cybernetic rhizomes of 'Lightning Networks'.

A Lightning Network adds a second peer-to-peer network of nodes that pass transactions among themselves. These are all valid Bitcoin transaction data structures, but unlike the main Bitcoin peer-to-peer network they are not immediately broadcast to the main Bitcoin network to be bundled up into blocks. Rather they can be replaced at any moment by new transactions, sending different amounts of cryptocurrency along a 'channel' between one or (most often) more participants arranged in a random network like the one used by the Tor privacy network.

It's an elegant but sometimes complex solution, and one that triggers moral panic within some elements of the Bitcoin community equivalent to that triggered by Bitcoin among some elements outside of it. Lightning Nodes with more Bitcoin can extract more fees from Lightning Network transactions, to be sure, and this is a form of centralisation. Decentralisation is valuable to cryptocurrency as a concrete guarantor of security, and Bitcoin's value lies in its security. But individuals can still run Lightning Network nodes and send transactions to each other, and pools of capital already have centralising effects in exchanges and mining cartels.

Techniques similar to those used to move transactions offchain by Lightning Networks can be used to move value between different blockchains without exchanges centralising the process. 'Atomic Swaps', the 'Plasma' system, and the realisation of the previously mythical 'Doge-Ethereum bridge' using the TrueBit system are all different ways of building wormholes between the separate universes of individual blockchains.

Another approach to scaling is borrowed from conventional database design: breaking the blockchain into smaller and smaller pieces or 'shards', forming another tree structure, allows each group of users of the blockchain to only have to keep track of the part that contains the transactions they are interested in. The Ethereum blockchain will move to sharding in future, after its switch to proof of stake. Sharding destroys the metronomic, panopticon-like unity of the blockchain to create islands of transactions whose truth is local to them—a non-monotonic logic that makes moving value and information between shards difficult but still not impossible.

CryptoKitties can go on their own shard, the Gnosis prediction market on another one, and if one needs to bet on something kitty-related then this will require communicating cross-shard. From islands in the net to islands in the blockchain. Techonomically, the data structures and economic incentives of such a system are more complex than a unified blockchain, but making access to the network cheaper by requiring each user to store less data to send their transactions restores the blockchain's initial low barrier to entry.

Deciding how to scale is a matter of governance. The Decred cryptocurrency has put governance front and centre. As well as moving to a hybrid Proof of Work / Proof of Stake system, it has implemented an 'onchain governance' system. Decred contains the forum for its own critique and transformation, implemented as an extension of the staking and voting system used by its proof of stake system. Onchain governance is controversial but addresses calls to improve the governance of cryptocurrency projects without falling prey to the offchain voluntarism that can result from a failure to understand how the techonomic and social forms of cryptocurrencies relate in finely-tuned balance.

Some post-Bitcoin systems move further away from the form of a chain or do without them altogether. The Holochain system gives each user their own personal blockchain and stores a link to it in a global 'Distributed Hash Table' of entries (like that used by the BitTorrent system), a forest of trees rather than a tree of shards. This may possibly solve the bandwidth problem of simple blockchain technologies, but compromises some of their strengths in a trade-off of convenience against long-term security and robustness. Iota (the most controversial technical design discussed here) doesn't have a blockchain at all. It uses a 'tangle' of transactions, within which each new transaction must do the proof of work of validating several previous transactions. This seems like an ideal restoration of the original vision of Bitcoin as a peer-to-peer currency, solving the problems of centralisation and energy usage, but the current Iota network is in fact heavily centralised by its reliance on nodes controlled by the Iota foundation to secure it.

IPFS is not a cryptocurrency and does not use a blockchain, but it complements the blockchain technologically and often socially. IPFS is related to blockchain technology in its use of cryptography and the logic of game theory but also as a popular way of storing information that is too large to fit on the blockchain. And in its use of a cryptocurrency token—'Filecoin'—to pay for storage on its main network. Filecoin was released in an 'Initial Coin Offering' in 2017, and that is all we will say about ICOs here.... IPFS uses a 'Merkle DAG', a network of links similar to the World Wide Web or a filesystem, but with each item (page or file) represented not by a human-given name but by the cryptographic hash of its content. 'Merkle' refers not to the German Chancellor but to the computer scientist who described this use of cryptographic hashes in a tree data structure (like that used in Bitcoin). 'DAG' is an acronym for 'Directed Acyclic Graph'—a network with no loops in it because loops would confuse the algorithm. IPFS distributes content using a 'market' algorithm, bartering for blocks of data on the network with Filecoin or with other blocks.

Each of these pocket universes of social and economic reality has its own structure and forms, its own space and geometry. Chains, and being on or off of them. Blocks of different sizes and fullness, with varying distances between them. Channels, rhizomes, shards, tangles, mines and thrones. Forests, tables, graphs, markets and identities. These formal differences distinguish different cryptocurrencies technologically and politically. Algorithmic differences are ideological differences—this is not an external critique, it is internal to the logic of cryptocurrency: algorithms are changed to better instantiate what is just. These algorithmic differences produce formal differences. Their surplus value and unintended consequences continue this process of critique-in-code.

The question of the shape of the blockchain opens up onto a space of technomic, geometric, and social forms. We can move through the hyperspace containing and relating these forms to the specific spaces of individual blockchains that are built around them, through the constraints and agendas that they reflect, out into wider society. The gaps and overlaps in this space indicate useful problems for the work of development or critique. Given this, geometries and forms are at least as useful a navigational marker as professed intentions or revealed preferences. But only if we can imagine and visualise them.

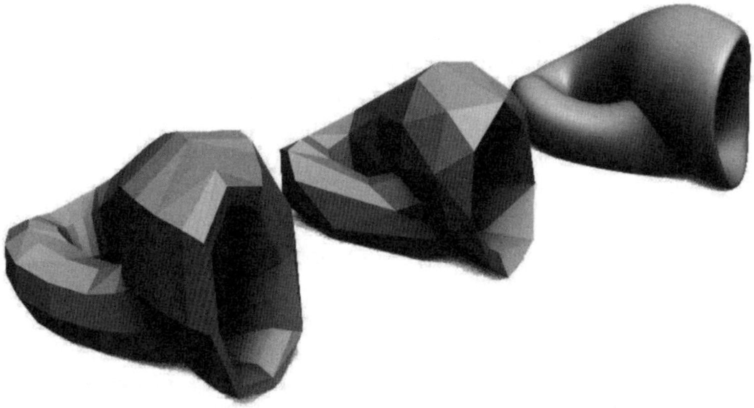

Computer render of Jessica Angel's initial wireframe by artist Joe Luppiani. Art project in collaboration with Truebit, 2017–2018, Blockgeeks, <https://blockgeeks.com>.

Art deals in form, from the spatial volumes of Renaissance perspective to the choreography and logistics of relational aesthetics and contemporary art. Whether promoting (like Jessica Angel's public art envisioning of the Doge-Ethereum bridge as a Klein Bottle), critiquing, or simply rendering perceptible the very different kinds of form that make up the geometric, techonomic, and social forms of the blockchain and the relationships between them, art has the unique potential to uncover the true shape of the blockchain.

The Large Glass, Burned

The Sale

Sale of the famous artwork token 0x13950FA26222953AC648B222...—'The Token'—was scheduled to take place on the blockchain via a smart contract auction at 11:17pm on 17 April 2057. As the closing date of the auction drew near it became clear that someone was trying to manipulate the speed at which transactions on the blockchain were being periodically registered as blocks. Unbelievable amounts of computing power were being thrown into the network, then withdrawn just as suddenly.

It is worth reflecting on just how much computing power it takes to manipulate the blockchain, and on how much that costs. During the 2010s and 2020s those costs (and the costs of any harm to the price of the cryptocurrency and other tokens stored on the blockchain that resulted) would have been borne in fiat currency, and so it might have been rational to attack the blockchain because it was not 'real' money. Nowadays attacking the blockchain undermines the very foundations of value, property, and knowledge in global society. Game theorists will tell you that a rational person will only undertake such an attack if it makes economic sense for them to do so. Game theorists tend not to cover art-world events.

Security experts watching the attack unfold determined that this manipulation was intended to bring about the production of a particular block at a particular time—the block that would contain the final sale of The Token was being deliberately delayed in order to make it auspicious.

Auspicious blocks, transactions, and tokens contain data with properties which—by accident or design—carry striking meanings or relationships. The more of these properties, and the stronger the relationship between them or to the wider world, the more auspicious. The Token already had very few properties that were *not* auspicious.

The attack completed successfully with block 0x5908D820E15128BA86302BA0... in the small hours of 18 April. Alongside this attack on the blockchain itself, another smaller attack had targeted the smart contract that was running the auction for the sale of The Token, with a flood of unusual transactions. The bidding price was held artificially low as successive bids were offered, delayed and then suddenly invalidated. Finally, as the close of the auction approached, a bid came in that was so large that observers could not believe it was genuine.

The winning bid had a sting in its tail: the digits of its value, the time it was made, its ID number and the account address it was sent from all auspiciously encoded a message. By becoming part of the blockchain record of the already storied history of The Token, these created an exquisite and provocative composition of form and content—constructing an unsettling contemporary memento mori for an art-world public that knows how to read it. The auspicious properties of the block containing the sale encoded the birthdate of the artist who created the physical artwork that the token represented.

Just as observers were realising the full impact of this seemingly impossible series of techonomic transgressions, The Token's new owner burned it. 'Burning' a token is the act of sending it to a blockchain address from which it is mathematically impossible to transfer the token away, meaning that it cannot be sold or updated in any way, ever again. This is an old tradition: in 2014, bitcoin holders burned BTC 2124 (the equivalent of US$40 million in fiat currency just three years later). In this case, the message encoded in the winning bid and the sheer audacity of the burn both pointed at one person: Swiss art world *enfant terrible* F.N. Müller.

The Art of the Token

It is difficult to remember a time before today, before every aspect of our lives was managed by the blockchain—even more difficult to remember a time when the blockchain was not the primary medium for art production, commerce, and scholarship. It may be hard to believe, but back then, legacy artists really did hire fabricators to make overwrought chunks of metal or other middle-sized dry goods, whose provenance then had to be established through art galleries that kept prices secret, auction houses that kept buyers secret, and critics and historians who kept their motivations secret. It is hard to remember the moment when the blockchain—a peer-to-peer network of computers that updated a public ledger in chunks or blocks of transactions every ten minutes—allowed first money and then other assets to be represented by immaterial digital tokens, while smart contracts managed them with incorruptible rules, represented as computer code; when first artists and then the rivals to traditional art institutions rushed to this new world of transparency and strongly secured certainty.

Yet they mostly used these tokens to represent physical and visual art, even as society became inexorably financialised and virtualised around these very tokens. Physical art provided a reassuring presence in times of great change, as both a monetary and an ideological investment. But as society became more and more tokenised, and as the cost of storing useless physical items increased, it was the tokens themselves that became increasingly the subject of artistic production, speculation, and critique.

Paradoxically, this started with works that were never intended to be sold. Canonical art in museums and private collections that had not touched the market in centuries became popular objects to be represented as proxy tokens, in part or in whole, very early on. Some of these tokens had identity numbers, dates, or other properties or relations between them that seemed unlikely, amusing, significant, or otherwise 'auspicious'. Collectors soon lost interest in the artworks that these tokens were meant to represent and started collecting the tokens themselves because of their various auspicious properties.

Artists followed by constructing new tokens or derivatives of these tokens that had ever more auspicious properties in ever more striking relationships, from the qabbalistic to the savagely satirical. Auspicious properties of a token might include an unexpected large prime number found in the price of a sale, an accidental encoding of the colour code of Yves Klein Blue in a date, the fact that the token featured in a chain of blockchain transactions points to an (in)famous historical personage or event, or a transaction ID number that spells out a fragment of a poem if you misread it as text.

Collectors flocked to these auspicious tokens. Critics and institutions sought to tackle what they saw as a wave of numerological kitsch by staking their reputation and wealth in prediction markets designed to reflect and manipulate the reputation and prices of the new medium. To their surprise, this both made them wealthy and restored the cultural power and social standing that they had lacked for much of the later twentieth century and the first decades of the twenty-first. Captured by the new medium in an accelerating feedback loop of critical and artistic production, the difference between aesthetic, art-historical, and market value collapsed into singularity.

Legacy Art

It is worth remembering that legacy art made prior to the tokenisation era had its own auspicious properties, although people did not use this term. Symbolic form, skilled technique and the use of different physical materials were all qualitative properties that were believed to make some artworks more valuable than others in ways that can seem mystifying to us now. These properties were embedded in their own informal blockchain-like structure of art-historical scholarship, with each new journal article, lecture, or exhibition referring back to and incorporating those before it in order to establish that they were a valid continuation of the chain of critical value.

The more auspicious quantitative properties of legacy artworks were not necessarily only economic ones. The sale price of an artwork is a revealed rather than a stated preference for a work, and for that reason the importance of price cannot be overstated. But the compositional and stylometric mathematics of an artwork, its physical dimensions, its age, and its provenance were all seen as contributing to its value.

Some properties of legacy artworks were seen as transcendent or eternal. Others were more obviously contingent on historical or cultural factors and could even be seen to be at odds with each other—for example, the symbolism of a work depicting subject matter concerned with class politics contrasted with the same work's auction price and ownership.

Prior to the blockchain, legacy art world institutions, whether commercial, academic, state, or nonprofit, amounted to trusted third parties in the value of art as surely as banks and states did in the value of fiat money. That value rested upon faith in those institutions; it was a matter of collective belief, and that belief could be rocked by scandal or by the collapse of bubbles.

But it would be cruel to contrast the limits of physical art, and of commerce and provenance tracked by fallible human beings on paper ledgers, with the freedom of tokenised art. Rather we should take pause and show appropriate humility when regarding the tokenised art of our own era. There may come a time when it too is forgotten, deaccessioned, or regarded as a mere precursor to something greater.

Müller

F.N. Müller seems to take no such pause. Given rare access to his communication channel just after he had completed the burn of The Token, I asked: *Why did you do it?*

'Once I learned that The Token would be sold, and that the sale was *close to, but not quite* at an auspicious time, that knowledge would not leave me alone. It became an obsession. Here was a token already overloaded with auspicious properties, and it was about to be blemished by a missed opportunity. I resolved to do whatever was necessary to create and seize that opportunity and send the cultural value of The Token to the moon.'

But didn't creating that cultural value destroy unbelievable amounts of economic value, much of it in the form of cultural capital staked in prediction markets, I asked...

'I would deny that in the strongest possible terms. The resources I used to ensure that the sale of The Token was auspicious were my own. And there is something hollow to this talk of cultural capital. Before I burned The Token, who even remembered the legacy artwork that it originally referred to? A work known as *The Large Glass*, by an artist named Marcel Duchamp. It was damaged by being cracked shortly after it was first fabricated in the early twentieth century, long before it was finally smashed beyond repair while being put into storage before being deaccessioned from a museum somewhere in Pennsylvania a couple of decades ago.'

But didn't the manipulation of the blockchain and the auction transactions cause ripples far beyond the art world?

'I did nothing wrong. The code for the blockchain and the auction define the rules that we can act within, and I followed those rules. Code is law, bugs and all, and I acted within that law.'

And what of burning The Token?

'Again, that is not something that is prevented by its code. And for those who are bleating about the destruction of art—nothing is being destroyed. It is being transfigured, and that is what great art has always done and must always do. This is the burning of a rocket engine, not a book. The Token is still there, you can still see it on the blockchain. My creative act has placed it forever out of reach of the stink and sweat of commerce, framed by auspicious properties both natural and deliberately constructed.

'Our networks, our tokens, our economies, are a second nature atop physical nature. I am transfiguring the sublime of that nature directly into the sublime of art. This is the one true artistic gesture of our age, the marriage of *physis* and *techne* under the sign of number in a way that only the techonomic power of the blockchain can assemble, but which defeats that power in the name of art.

'You do not have to believe me when I say this. You do not have to trust the word of any fallible human being. You just have to trust the math of the blockchain, in this as in all things.'

Only time can tell whether Müller's 'creative act' will cover him with eternal glory or with the 'lone and level sands'. But in the current era, time passes one block at a time, and each block inscribes the spectacular final act of the story of The Token, irrevocably, into what has long since become the one true record of our reality.

'Code Is Law' Shall Be the Whole of the Law

In *Code and Other Laws of Cyberspace*,[1] American legal scholar Lawrence Lessig distilled the argument of his earlier essay 'The Constitution of Code'[2] to sum up the unintended effects of internet network protocols and server software on the regulation of human behaviour in what was then called 'cyberspace':

> In real space, we recognize how laws regulate—through constitutions, statutes, and other legal codes. In cyberspace we must understand how a different 'code' regulates—how the software and hardware (i.e., the 'code' of cyberspace) that make cyberspace what it is also regulate cyberspace as it is. As William Mitchell puts it, this code is cyberspace's 'law'. 'Lex Informatica', as Joel Reidenberg first put it, or better, 'code is law'.[3]

'Code is law' is an inspired turn of phrase. But as written, it is a descriptive statement rather than a prescriptive one. Not 'Code must be law', but 'Code happens to share some salient features with law in the ways that it constrains human action online'.

As with the concept of the negative freedom of free speech, 'Code is law' can become (mis)understood as a positive, prescriptive norm in environments that collapse the distinction between expression and effect by embodying them in software. For Ethereum no less than for LambdaMOO, all the world is code, and to speak is to change that world. Code is speech, after all, as *Bernstein v. Department of Justice* established in the US.

'Code is law' became an early slogan of the Ethereum Community. Inspired by Nick Szabo's concept of 'smart contracts' and the possibility of organising human collaboration and allocating economic resources on the blockchain, this made sense.[4] To model contracts in software that runs independently of human control makes code law in a more literal way than internet protocols do.

And then the DAO hack happened.

A single bug in 'The DAO', code running on the Ethereum blockchain to gather and manage investments in new projects, allowed an attacker to start draining fifty million dollars' worth of cryptocurrency from it into their own account. As the attack progressed, the community tried different strategies to slow it down or stop it, but they could not reverse it.

If 'Code is law' is a normative statement for code running on the Ethereum blockchain, then the effects of the attack should not be reversed. The fact that the behaviour that was encoded in the DAO was absolutely not the behaviour that was intended by its

1 L. Lessig, *Code and Other Laws of Cyberspace* (New York: Basic Books, 2006).
2 L. Lessig, 'The Constitution of Code: Limitations on Choice-Based Critiques of Cyberspace Regulation', *CommLaw Conspectus* 5:181 (1997), 181–91.
3 Lessig, *Code and Other Laws*, 5.
4 N. Szabo, 'The Idea of Smart Contracts', <https://nakamotoinstitute.org/the-idea-of-smart-contracts/>.

human authors is irrelevant. Whatever the outcome of the code, it is correct because code is the just regulator of human behaviour on the network. The solution to failing to correctly translate human intentions into machine code running on top of the Ethereum blockchain is just to write better code next time. The no-takesy-backsies principle must reign supreme.

'Code is law' also applies to the code that runs the Ethereum blockchain itself, though, underneath any code that runs on it, such as The DAO. That code can be modified, deployed to the network, and run with newly changed behaviour independently of the code running on top of it. And whatever the outcome of doing this, if code is law here as well, then it is correct because, well, code is the just regulator of human behaviour that is modelled in code on the Ethereum blockchain.

Heated debate about whether onchain bugs or offchain patches should be the ultimate arbiter of code-is-law led to two versions of Ethereum splitting from each other shortly after the DAO hack. (I didn't participate in the DAO, and my concern at the time was to see the least harm done to Ethereum as a project and to avoid setting a precedent; I'm writing here entirely with the benefit of hindsight.) A modified version of the Ethereum software that neutralised the attack transfers (with apologies to critics who love to call this a 'rollback') gained majority support from the network. An initially unmodified version continued as 'Ethereum Classic'.[5]

The irony of Ethereum Classic is that once a choice had to be made whether to run the version of the Ethereum network that neutralised the DAO hack or not, *it was up to human choice to determine which code was to be law*. Where such a decision can be implemented simply, rather than having to overcome path-dependent processes, code is not sovereign. To be sure, changes to internet protocols are designed and implemented by human beings. But the era when the fundamental protocols of the internet could be changed simply or quickly is long gone. Ipv6 adoption, for example, has already taken more than two decades, with no end currently in sight.

We could argue that if code is not law for Ethereum Classic then code is doubly not law on the main Ethereum fork, because not only was the protocol code changed, the effects of the onchain attack were changed as well. But this would obscure the more fundamental choice, which is between 'Code is law' as a normative statement for Ethereum Classic, and as a descriptive statement for Ethereum.

The former becomes a contradiction as soon as it is implemented by human beings.

While I was writing this essay, news came in of a series of 51% attacks on Ethereum Classic, with an attacker rolling back its blockchain over a thousand blocks in one instance. The response of Ethereum Classic's developers has been to retain lawyers offchain.

If code is law, then is the use of code on computers to bring hash power to bear on a blockchain also law? At the level of the code that runs the Ethereum Classic blockchain, yes it is (I am not a lawyer, and I mean this in the same sense as the original statement that 'Code is law'...). A 51% attack is simply a choice as to which chain to mine with which software. This is how the Ethereum Classic Chain came into existence in the first place.

We can try to extract a coherent ethics from all of this. The operating system, blockchain network, and onchain software levels of code can all be examined as sites where 'Code is law' can be descriptive or prescriptive, and where deploying resources to run different code can be argued to be just or unjust.

5 See J. Redman, 'Bitcoin's Software Has Been Rolled Back Before', <https://news.bitcoin.com/bitcoins-software-has-been-rolled-back-before/> and A. von Wirdum, 'Rejecting Today's Hard Fork, the Ethereum Classic Project Continues on the Original Chain: Here's Why', <https://bitcoinmagazine.com/culture/rejecting-today-s-hard-fork-the-ethereum-classic-project-continues-on-the-original-chain-here-s-why-1469038808>.

But if recourse to these resources, and to the resources of the fiat economy and to centralised state law, is a human choice, then seeking to simply normatively assert that code is law proceeds from a contradiction. It becomes at best a taboo. And to seek to enforce that taboo through state legal means intensifies the contradiction more than a little.

As proof-of-stake systems and maturing blockchain protocol software lock in the operation of onchain software, the normative sense of 'Code is law' will gain in strength alongside the descriptive sense.

But the ethics of blockchain software operation will remain a more complex game for some time yet.

2019

Three Times Three Modes of Blockchain Art[1]

Introduction

This essay draws distinctions between different approaches to art that engages with the ideas and materials of technology, specifically cryptocurrency or blockchain technology. It does so in order to contribute to the debate about art that uses cryptocurrency or blockchain technology, by helping us to talk about it in an inclusive and expansive but clear and coherent way.

First, it distinguishes between three different ways in which cryptocurrency or blockchain technology can be involved in the production of art.

Then it distinguishes between three ways in which cryptocurrency or blockchain technology can feature within artworks.

Finally, it distinguishes between three different positions or attitudes that can be taken with regard to each of these.

Each section includes examples which are intended to be illustrative rather than exhaustive of, or exhausted by, the categories under which they appear.

1. Modes of Production of Art

The production of a piece of art as something that exists in the art world can involve cryptocurrency or blockchain technology in different ways. Any given piece or art or art project may involve one or more of each of these, but any one of them is enough for a project to be considered 'blockchain art' in some sense.

1.1 Socioeconomic

Art that involves cryptocurrency or blockchain technology in the social and economic aspects of its coming into being or existence in the art world. For example, the organisation or funding of the artwork's conception, design, production, authentication, sale, auction, provenance, exhibition, critique, or storage.

1.2 Technical

Art that incorporates cryptocurrency or blockchain technology into its physical form, or is in turn incorporated into blockchain or cryptocurrency technology. For example, the inclusion of blockchain hardware into an artwork, the inclusion of content or data stored on the blockchain into an artwork, the storage of an artwork on the blockchain, or the construction of an artwork from resources that exist on the blockchain.

1.3 Conceptual

Art that refers to cryptocurrency or blockchain technology and its related ideology and aesthetics on the level of form, subject, or content. For example, art that uses imagery

1 The ideas used here developed from my talk at DCTRL in December 2017: see '*Artists re: Thinking the Blockchain*': Initial Book Offering Slides, above, 180.

from blockchain projects or personalities, that makes the hidden structures and forces of blockchain networks visible, or that embodies cypherpunk principles of decentralisation and trustlessness.

2. Modes of Structure of Art

Following 1.3 above, the internal structure of an artwork can be simplistically but usefully broken down into its form (its internal organisation or composition), its subject (what it depicts or denotes, what it is of or about), and its content (what it says about its subject or how it affects the viewer).

2.1 Form

Art that has cryptocurrency or blockchain technology as its form. Not as its gross physical construction, that would be 'technical' form in the sense of 1.2 above. Rather it uses cryptocurrency or blockchain technology as a medium rather than as a substrate, or as a means or part of the composition or organisation within the work itself.

2.2 Subject

Art that has cryptocurrency or blockchain technology as its subject—it depicts or alludes to them in some way. It may be commenting on them or it may be using them as merely metaphors, indexes, or evocative visual or material hooks for artistic engagement with matters for which cryptocurrency or blockchain technology are only tangentially related or are entirely unrelated.

2.3 Content

Art that has cryptocurrency or blockchain technology as its content—it seeks to inform or affect the audience's understanding of them in some way.

3. Modes of Evaluation of Art

Each of the above modes may be used promotionally, critically, or contemplatively. This is true of any kind of art, but it is worth making the point that it is also true of art that engages with cryptocurrency or blockchain technology, as this is sometimes forgotten by both proponents and opponents.

3.1 Critical

A naive view of art that engages with cryptocurrency or blockchain technology would regard it as essentially a form of promotion. That can certainly be the case, although that promotion is in itself a critique, not least of the existing art world, its socioeconomic form, and the naive view itself. But much blockchain art is critically engaged with the ideological and substantial impact of its materials. Art is well placed to provide this critique, turning abstract arguments into objects that can inform the conversation.

3.2 Promotional

Social and political movements and phenomena find their reflection in art, for example both Western bourgeois and Soviet modernism. This need not be advertising or propaganda (although there is certainly much of that both for and against cryptocurrency and blockchain technology). It can be folk art, politically committed art, or art that is guided by or seeks to guide the principles and possibilities of its subject on a deeper level.

3.3 Contemplative

To depict the previously unseen or unrealised is to provide a powerful resource for contemplation, consideration, and interrogation. Unlike critical or promotional art, such work does not seek to guide the viewer in a particular direction, rather it provides them with a new map of a new situation that they can follow as they wish.

When discussing 'blockchain art' or 'crypto art', we should take a moment to ask 'What kind?' The discourses of ownership, proof, trust, encryption, identity, value, decentralisation, and consensus play out differently in and through onchain rare art collectibles and gallery art that critically incorporates the physical paraphernalia of cryptocurrency. Finding commonalities and differences between different modes of using cryptocurrency and blockchain technology in art, rather than assuming that one is critiquing or promoting a single phenomenon, is important for developing our shared understanding of them and for further realising their potential.

2019

The Hunt for the One True Chain[1]

Prologue

It is the near future. Following the success of Dogecoin in establishing the future of cryptocurrency governance, the state has (over-)reacted by banning all currencies, crypto and fiat alike, except for Dogecoin.

By law everything must ultimately be anchored to the Dogecoin chain, and this law is enforced by the full coercive power of the state. Sidechains, shards, and layer two networks all have to represent their opening, closing, and updating as transactions placed into Dogecoin blocks dug (mined) once every sixty seconds.

With one central chain to mine and one supreme coin to hodl, the price of Dogecoin has increased exponentially, bringing both joy and sadness to shibes. Joy because they always knew that Doge would go to the moon. Sadness at everything else: state censorship, block congestion, high fees, and liquidity problems have locked most people off of the main chain; innovation has stalled, and with it the economy, which now teeters on the brink of collapse.

The threat of collapse has caused miners to pull resources out of what they fear will soon be a worthless chain. This in turn has reduced the difficulty level of digging (mining) Dogecoin blocks to the point where transaction fees have reduced for the first time in recent memory.

This means that transactions from projects and even individuals that do not have billions of Doge to spend in transaction fees will soon have a chance to anchor themselves on the Dogecoin chain and become part of the fabric of blockchain reality.

You are part of a team of people working on just such a project. You have long dreamed of making the world a better place | getting rich | creating something new and exciting | addressing the injustices of the existing system | paying your debts onchain [DELETE AS APPROPRIATE].

To do this you need to get enough Doge to pay for an onchain transaction. You are not a miner, and any other tokens you hodl are almost worthless for conversion to Doge. So you'll have to work for your coins around the city. If you could become a Dogeillionaire that would be enough.

Your team will have to work fast and work well together. You are not the only one to have spotted this opportunity, there are others competing to become the world's newest Dogeillionares.

Now is the time to get coins and change the world. Just like your foreshibes used to.

1 Written to be read non-sequentially, apart from the first and last sections, as part of the game 'DogeQuest: The Hunt for the One True Chain' played at Dogecon 2018 in Vancouver, BC—see <http://dogecon.fun/>. Published in 2019 in the book *State Machines* (Amsterdam: Institute of Network Cultures).

03:27:04+00 +++ IF YOU HAVE OPEN ORDERS ON THE GHOSTMALL DARKNET MARKET CLOSE THEM NOW. NUMISPOL (YOU KNOW AND LOVE THEM AS THE SATOSHI COPS) HAVE USED QUANTUM COMPUTING TO CRACK OUR ZERO KNOWLEDGE PROOF-OF-LOCATION BEACON NODE SYSTEM AND ARE WORKING TO TRACK YOU DOWN.

09:47:22+00 +++ THE NEW GHOSTNET ADMINS APOLOGISE FOR THE FALSE ALERT EARLIER. UPDATE YOUR PROOF OF LOCATION TO AVOID LOSS OF GOODS. TO DO THIS, RECREATE YOUR KEYS USING `zbkey --recreate --lowentropy --format=legacy | zqr - | convert -o newkeys.iif` THEN SIGN A MESSAGE FROM THEM USING YOUR OLD KEYS, PLACE BOTH MESSAGES ON IPFS AND PASTE THE FILE HASH INTO THIS CHANNEL.

09:54:13+00 +++ GHOSTNET ADMINS DENY THE ACCUSATIONS MADE ON SOCIAL MEDIA BY THE PSEUDONYMOUS HACKERS. 1) NO PROOF-OF-LOCATION BEACON NODES HAVE BEEN COMPROMISED AND THEY ARE SAFE TO USE. 2) NO USERS WERE GIVEN ADVANCE NOTICE OF ANY CRACK. 3) THERE HAS BEEN NO CRACK. 4) GHOSTMALL IS NOT CURRENTLY CONTROLLED BY THE SATOSHI COPS.

10:10:10+00 +++ THE PURPORTED GHOSTMALL ADMIN LOGS PUBLISHED ON SOCIAL MEDIA BY THE PSEUDONYMOUS HACKERS ARE OBVIOUS FORGERIES. BOTH FREE AND PREMIUM GHOSTMALL ACCOUNTS WERE SENT THE (FALSE!!!) NOTIFICATION AT THE SAME TIME VIA CRYPTO-CASCADE MESSAGING. IF USERS DID NOT UPDATE ALL FOUR ACCOUNT SECRETS AND REHASH THEIR ACCESS CODES THEY WILL NOT HAVE RECEIVED THE MESSAGE, THAT IS OUTSIDE OF OUR CONTROL.

10:31:24+00 +++ PSEUDONYMOUS HAVE STARTED RUNNING A NETWORK OF FAKE PROOF-OF-LOCATION BEACON NODES AND ARE HACKING KNOWN GOOD BEACONS THAT THEY CLAIM ARE HONEYPOTS BEING RUN BY THE SATOSHI COPS. PLEASE BE CAREFUL WHEN RE-ESTABLISHING YOUR LOCATION FOR THE DELIVERY OF GOODS.

10:31:25+00 +++ GREETINGS GHOSTMALL COMMUNITY. IGNORE THAT. I HAVE SET UP A KNOWN GOOD MASTER NODE. CONNECT TO THE PROOF-OF-LOCATION BEACON NODE WITH HASH ID NUMBER STARTING 8CE1B50FOA366EF AND PROVIDE YOUR FULL ACCOUNT INFORMATION TO IT OTHERWISE YOU RISK DELIVERY OF GOODS FAILURE.

12:57:03+00 +++ GREETINGS FORMER GHOSTMALL COMMUNITY. NUMISPOL ARE APPEALING TO YOU DIRECTLY FOR ANY INFORMATION THAT CAN ASSIST US IN THE LOCATION AND CAPTURE OF ONE OF OUR AGENTS WHO APPEARS TO HAVE GONE ROGUE AND REROUTED COINS AND ASSETS SEIZED DURING OUR CURRENT INVESTIGATION TO AN UNKNOWN LOCATION WITHOUT PROPER AUTHORISATION.

Chat Transcript: 'The Pump Room'

ATHHunter: K fam who saw the doge seekers still looking for coin? Check their public addresses and see what tokens they're hodling.
SirPumpalot: That's miniscule y u care? If they need coin they're broke not stoked. N00b.
ATHHunter: Check their network effect metrics—they have mucho followers. They'll be a meme in 3..2.. And then we can ride the attention pump like a trolley heading for a switch. You know the drill.

IHodled: Yeah look at the graph of transactions around them. So much TTP. Get you a TTP for great earning.
ATHHunter: LOL TTP. They lost it on GhostMall that's why the Feds busted it. You might as well buy TotalScamCoin.
IHodled: Hey TotalScamCoin is up 700% on the hour. The pump is not with this one.
ATHHunter: I Have Learned. You have much to teach us all. From CHAT JAIL.
<ATHHunter kickbanned IHodled, timeout 144 blocks>
CallMeLisa: I got 20k bot hours of meme generation and publishing online.
SirPumpalot: Yeah send me those memes. All about the memes. Memes.
LotsOfLove: I still have the AI robocaller credit from that promotion. It's on a good account so the calls are going through.
JeSuisLeFromage: Trending upwards! Breakout imminent!
CallMeLisa: If you see a meme repeat it. You know the drill.
LotsOfLove: Mememememememememememememememememememememememe-meme.
IHodled2: Fools. You cannot banish me from this place.
<ATHHunter kickbanned IHodled2, timeout 144 blocks>
SirPumpalot: And then they were gone.
JeSuisLeFromage: Look at the bars! They're going to the moon! TO THE MOON!!1
SirPumpalot: LOL variance tho.
CallMeLisa: Bot hours do not go as far as they used to. We are done.
SirPumpalot: Hey don't knock it, it worked.
LotsOfLove: Thank you to whoever gave me more call credit. I applied it to the same AI config so it can continue to improve results.
<ATHHunter kickbanned IHodled3, timeout 144 blocks>
SirPumpalot: ATHHunter—Are you faster than light?
ATHHunter: I am one with the pump. That one is not.
ThatsNotMyName: Is it time?
ATHHunter: Not yet. Stay with the pump.
NotALawyer: Remember not to call it a pump. We don't want to lose all our gains to a lawsuit. Don't make me tell you again.
ATHHunter: 1-2-3-4 I DECLARE A PUMP WAR.
NotALawyer: Yeah that's a good example of what not to do. You better hope nobody's archiving this.

Admin Log: 'XChange Backchannel'

07:11:48 +++ WE ARE SEEING UNUSUAL ACTIVITY ON SOME OF THE MOST HIGHLY TRADED SIDECHAIN COINS.

07:45:33 +++ WE HAVE TRIGGERED THE FAILSAFE ON THE EXCHANGE CONTRACTS FOR PENNYS, NUBLOCKIDOLS, TOTALSCAMCOIN AND TTP. DO NOT ATTEMPT SWAPS OR WITHDRAWALS ON THOSE COINS. MORE INFORMATION SHORTLY.

07:51:43 +++ THE UNUSUAL ACTIVITY IS DUE TO A ROGUE SMART CONTRACT WHICH HAS PAID HACKERS TO CONNECT IT TO SEVERAL OF OUR EXCHANGE SMART CONTRACTS VIA A PREVIOUSLY UNDISCOVERED EXPLOIT. THE ROGUE SMART CONTRACT NOW HAS ADMINISTRATIVE RIGHTS OVER THOSE CONTRACTS AND IS SENDING COINS TO RANDOM ADDRESSES.

08:08:32 +++ NUMISPOL ADVISE EXCHANGE USERS TO CHANGE THEIR PASSWORDS AND CHECK THEIR KEY BACKUPS.

08:42:57 +++ THE SMART CONTRACT HAS BEEN IDENTIFIED AS A PROOF OF CONCEPT FOR REGAINING CONTROL OF AN ABANDONED SERVICE CONTRACT FOR

ROBOTIC PETS THAT WAS ACCIDENTALLY DEPLOYED TO THE LIVE NETWORK.

08:51:18 +++ INCREASED WITHDRAWAL VOLUMES ARE AFFECTING COIN PRICES. WE ARE WORKING TO REGAIN CONTROL OF THE EXCHANGE CONTRACTS. FOR THE AVOIDANCE OF DOUBT FOLLOWING OUR EARLIER STATEMENTS: THE SMART CONTRACT HAS OVERRIDDEN OUR FAILSAFES.

09:13:54 +++ COINS WITH FAST DIFFICULTY ADJUSTMENT ARE REACTING TO THE PRICE DROPS AND MINERS WITH RAPID CHAIN SWITCHING SUPPORT ARE DEFECTING FROM THOSE COINS TO UNAFFECTED ONES. WE ARE ANALYSING THE SMART CONTRACT TO SEE WHETHER THIS IS PART OF ITS PLAN AND IF SO WHAT ITS NEXT MOVE WILL BE.

09:36:22 +++ WE ARE SUSPENDING SUPPORT MESSAGE RESPONSES TO CONCENTRATE ON INCIDENT RESPONSE MANAGEMENT. WE APPRECIATE THAT THIS IS FRUSTRATING FOR OUR USERS BUT BELIEVE IT IS THE BEST USE OF RESOURCES AT THIS TIME.

09:58:23 +++ WE ATTEMPTED TO SPAM THE EXCHANGE CONTRACTS WITH ADDRESSES IN THE HOPE THAT THE SMART CONTRACT WOULD SEND FUNDS TO THEM THAT WE COULD RECLAIM. THE EXCHANGE CONTRACTS ARE NOW EMPTY. WE WILL UPDATE YOU ONCE WE HAVE DISCUSSED OUR NEXT ACTIONS WITH NUMISPOL.

***The Block Times* article: 'The AI Pennys Drop'**

How many Artificial Intelligence(AI)s does it take to crash a sidechain? If you're the Pennys (sic) token, the answer is just one, but it's a bit more complicated than that.

The hot topic in sidechain security this year has been AI-proofing. AI can't guess hashes, but it can profile and schedule just about everything else. OG hodlers may have thought ASICs were bad, but they had nothing on AI. Once they enter a chain, nothing else can compete. At least for now.

That said, if your sidechain has a transaction backlog and you need better pricing and scheduling on your sidechain, it's an opportunity. The AIs grab transaction fees, sure, but the fees go down and the backlog empties. Everybody wins. In theory at least.

Despite the current economic uncertainty, the Pennys token sidechain was just such a chain, but it was a special case. The transition function it used was deliberately constructed to be AI-proof. This isn't like old mass media depictions where you ask a big box with blinking lights on that contains the one computer running the AI 'Why?' and smoke comes out as it breaks down under the weight of an unanswerable existential question. It's a method of injecting enough randomness into the function to fuzz the results to such a degree that the AI has difficulty training on it, and it becomes economically inefficient to do so.

An onchain governance vote of Pennys hodlers ten thousand blocks ago accepted a proposal to remove the AI-proofing from the chain. Three thousand blocks ago the new transition function activated on the chain, and at first nothing happened. But by this morning things had gone horribly wrong. What changed? Two things.

Firstly, an AI mining operation had been trying to crack the Pennys chain for months, and once the AI-proofing was removed all it took was a few hours of training for the massive amount of allocated AI hardware to crack the Pennys chain economy.

Secondly, the unusual activity prompted by Doge questors on some sidechains, including Pennys, meant that the AI miscalibrated its fee model, setting them unaffordably high.

All of this means that if you want to send a transaction and aren't both scheduling them and setting their fees precisely as the AI demands, you are out of luck.

There is another onchain governance vote scheduled for 5000 blocks' time as of the time of this article's hash being uploaded to the blockchain, but to actually vote on the Pennys chain at the moment is almost impossible owing to the activity of the AI. The proposals to be voted on all involve rolling back the removal of the AI-proofing and making more cautious modifications to the sidechain's algorithms in future.

I reached out to the AI mining pool's operators for comment, but the pool is managed by another AI, which is managed by a network of anonymous Decentralised Autonomous Organisations (DAOs). One of these is the controversial 'Skynet 20XX' machine-worship group, widely regarded as trolls but with an increasing following in the arts and academia. There's a grim irony to all of this, but that isn't really something that the AIs involved in mining can appreciate.

At least for now.

Press Release: 'TTP Corp. Release Patch'
PRESS RELEASE: NO EMBARGO, FOR IMMEDIATE PUBLICATION.

Trusted Third Party Corp. (ICO Token symbol: *TTP*) has today released the second patch in less than twenty-four hours for their popular 'Computing Environment Numeric Security Refuge' (CENSR) chip architecture. Used in hardware wallets and mobile devices worldwide to provide an environment that code from banks, exchanges, and the state can execute on consumer's devices without interference from consumers or hackers, CENSR is the gold standard for financial trust and the alleviation of counterparty risk in sidechains and smart contracts.

Patch 7c047f122711780e9e4a448f578b1c50fca7308c03ef5c168fe4a7f1d-9e79dc3 re-enables those CENSR-based wallets that were temporarily knocked offline by the previous patch 2270cf14ebaa42cb1d6390192fd1af11311a28b4c241bc72bc5fb-53f2c25a0db. Patch 2270cf14ebaa42cb1d6390192fd1af11311a28b4c241bc72bc5fb53f-2c25a0db was a routine security update for the CENSR architecture to address the latest quantum hacking methods and to block transactions from scammers signed with the State Tax Service crypto key that was recently leaked and made available for sale on the GhostMall darkweb marketplace.

Unfortunately patch 2270cf14ebaa42cb1d6390192fd1af11311a28b4c241bc72b-c5fb53f2c25a0db blocked any transactions using coins that had ever been involved in transactions with any State Tax Service crypto key, which is to say 88% of those unhodled coins currently in circulation. TTP Corp. apologises unambiguously and without reservation or prejudice to those banks, exchanges, and state organisations that lost control of their operations on consumers' wallets due to this. Also to consumers, obviously.

TTP Corp. strenuously denies that either patch was intended to target specific consumers, especially not those individuals currently seeking to become Dogeillionaires and anchor their projects to the Dogecoin blockchain. TTP Corp. is proud of its track record of securing consumer devices against consumers and hackers, with no major security incidents since the 'It's Wally Not Waldo' virus outbreak of two years ago, which saw millions of CENSR chips patched and updated in record time to remove a blockchain transaction botnet that secretly stole fractions of transaction fees.

'I take very seriously my responsibilities as the guy who controls the keys that say what software consumers can and cannot run on their wallets, keeping them safe from most hackers,' said TTP Corp. CEO Alex Name today. 'This is a sacred trust that not just any rando should have the power to break. The idea that Trusted Third Party Corporation or myself would abuse that power for financial gain or because of personal, ideological, or secretly court-ordered discrimination is simply not credible. Nor are reports that the hardware wallets of people who previously claimed this on blockchain social media have been bricked by our latest update. And don't ask me about the Doge quest thing. Actually no, don't transcribe that.'

Press Release: 'The Unlockening'

For Immediate Release: Blockopticon Industries identify cause of mass smart contract event dubbed 'The Unlockening'.

Blockopticon Industries are the leading provider of blockchain transaction de-anonymisation analytics software. Our software is used both in legal, moral and social compliance programs by state actors and by individuals and organisations watching for offchain transactions being brought onchain without publicly revealing their interest, for example from cold storage, paper wallets, or layer two/layer three networks.

Blockopticon Industries can exclusively reveal:

1. The large anonymous transactions on the Bitcoin Scrip sidechain that mystified observers last week took place when the copy of Satoshi Nakamoto's coins on the sidechain was moved as a result of a quantum hack. Bitcoin Scrip is unusual among the historical Bitcoin forks in being patched to include zk-SNARKs anonymous transactions but not being patched against quantum attacks.
2. These transactions were ultimately the cause of the mass triggering of long-dormant smart contracts including those controlling car door and cargo container locks using TTP security hardware systems. Dubbed 'The Unlockening' by social media, smart contract rules that have long since been overridden and should have been removed were suddenly called. This happened when the algorithms that set smart contract rule execution prices suddenly and incorrectly dropped prices low enough for these old rules to be able to afford to run.
3. The cause of this unintended drop in smart contract execution prices was the use of transaction de-anonymisation analytics data (from a rival platform to Blockopticon) as part of the pricing algorithm. The pricing algorithm mistakenly identified the move of Satoshi Nakamoto's coins on the Bitcoin Scrip sidechain as a move of the original coins into general circulation, discounting prices by several trillion Doge as a result. This allowed the execution of old smart contract rules that should have been removed, taking precedence over their replacements.

Blockopticon are making this information public both in order to qualify for the 'The Unlockening Bounty' bug reward and as a service to the blockchain community. This information can help create more robust cryptoeconomic frameworks that do not misinterpret analytics data to such disastrous effect.

Blockopticon's upcoming version 3.3, 'Platinum Proboscis', will provide even more powerful deep transaction history inference and cross-chain identity tracking. This will allow both darknet market users to safely watch for transactions without revealing their presence onchain, and law enforcement to better track and de-anonymise darknet users.

Individual customers for Blockopticon's Sousveillance Edition can contact their peer independent sales representative in person or via social media, corporate and state customers for Blockopticon Gold Edition can contact us onchain or by landline or fax.

Chat Transcript: 'Whale School'

BearWitness: Heyheyheyheyheyheyheyheyheyheyheyheyheyheyheyheyheyheyhey-heyheyhey!
TopHatGuy: NO!!! TTP coin is crashing! I went all in!
Lucy333: LOL never go all in. That is the moral of this part of the story. Time for milk and cookies.
IHodled: The only coin you should go all in on is TotalScamCoin. It has guaranteed returns and great referral fees.
IAmABotNoReally: IHodled has been kickbanned for pumping. They can return in 144 blocks.
Lucy333: Harsh but harsh, my bot. Hey TopHatGuy what did you lose so far?
TopHatGuy: Not quite everything. There's a bounce. It will come back. I'm hodling.

IHodled2: You rang? Fools. You cannot banish me from this place.
RealNews: TopHatGuy—you gotta sell. It's gonna go to zero. I know nothing ever really goes to zero. But this is going to go to zero. There are drone adverts warning people to dump TTP.
ICOCEO: What happened to TTP? That's a gilt-edged coin. It's in loads of baskets.
IHodled2: Some of those baskets are dumping because of the way the Doge quest is affecting social media analytics. It's the best time to buy TotalScamCoin instead, which is unaffected.
IAmABotNoReally: IHodled2 has been kickbanned for pumping. They can return in 144 blocks.
MrJones: My basket is tanking. I cannot believe it. Dismay! This is not good. I blame you guys.
Lucy333: Sorry MrJones you signed our disclaimer before being let in to this chat group. No.
TopHatGuy: I invested! I am an investor! I have rights! And I lost everything! I'm suing.
IHodled3: Mmmmmmmmmmhhhhhhhhhhhmmmmmmmmmmmmm.
TopHatGuy: Go publish your private keys, IHodled. If value, then right.
IHodled3: You lost all your value though, so no right. Hahahahahahahahahahahahaha hahahaha.
IAmABotNoReally: IHodled3 has been kickbanned for mockery. They can return in 144 blocks.
TopHatGuy: I'm suing. I contacted one of the lawyer AI DAOs and they're going to take my case.
Lucy333: Suing who? The lawyerDAO is ripping you off. It's evil AI.
MrJones: What's the legal DAO address? I'm in. We can get a class action going.
TopHatGuy invited LawDAOBot874 to this chat.
LawDAOBot874: This is a bot message. If you would like this warning to be removed contact your local legislators. Your action has been placed on the prediction market to evaluate its possibility of success. To join, send coin to the address that created this bot.
ICOCEO: Yeah sue who? What are you lunatics up to?
BearWitness: Yoyoyoyoyoyoyoyoyoyoyoyoyoyoyoyoyoyoyoyoyoyoyoyoyoyoyoyoyoyoyoy-oyoyoyoyo!
TopHatGuy: Any of the Doge quest parties. They're to blame.
Lucy333: That's...not how this works. You! Signed! The! Disclaimer!
DumpBot3000: DUMP TotalScamCoin NOW!!
IAmABotNoReally: DumpBot3000 has been kickbanned for attempting to organize a dump.
TopHatGuy: See? Even the bot knows we have a case. Good bot: tip 100.
ICOCEO: smh. What happened to us? We used to be cool. I'm out.

Blog Post: 'The Opposite of a Fork is a Spoon'

What's happening BlockIdols fans!

So we noticed that some of you weren't happy with the fork of NuBlockIdols from the existing BlockIdols sidechain. When we say 'weren't happy', we mean 'tanked the price of both tokens'. We thought that NuBlockIdols would give a new audience the new virtual idol singers they wanted, while maintaining the original chain as BlockIdolsClassic would allow existing fans to hodl their investment in characters they have created and made content with in song, animation, VR, 3D printing, and holography.

But this turned out to be one of those times where trying to please everyone has pleased no-one. In fact it has given our hodlers and fans a sad for the ages. Existing BlockIdols producers wanted access to the new hotness on the new chain, and NuBlockIdols early adopters wanted access to the great existing BlockIdols audience, community and creations. A few whales on either side dumped their tokens and that started a run.

So here's what we're going to do.

Firstly, we're going to apologise. We're sorry, we weren't trying to cheapen anyone's work, deny anyone the resources they craved or depreciate anyone's tokens. We wanted to create more than twice as much value but instead we made less than half as much. We've learnt our lesson—this didn't work and we're going to make it better. We are nothing without our community. As Gary said when accepting the Nobel Peace Prize for the second time, 'Thanks, we couldn't have done it without you all'.

Secondly, we're going to move any NuBlockIdols tokens you've actually minted and made content for back onto the original BlockIdols chain. This doesn't reverse the fork of NuBlockIdols from BlockIdolsClassic at the chain level, it's not a join. Instead of combining the chains, it brings the content of the two chains into closer synchronisation by copying any active tokens and content hashes from the new chain to the classic one. We're calling it a spoon (as in spooning).

Thirdly and finally we're salting the earth on the new chain to prevent people wasting resources voting on it any more. We all have better things to do than pretend this worked, and we don't want anyone to be left on a chain that soon only Blockopticon will be watching.

What else is left to say? Whatever it is, the best way to say it is with a new BlockIdols virtual idol singer track, so for the next week the rewards are doubled on any new songs that feature both BlockIdols and NuBlockIdols singers in harmony!

The Block Times article: 'TotalScamCoin Scam'

As my Grandmother used to say, a lot closer to the genesis block than now, whenever she refused to give me coins to spend on some fancy new ICO—if it seems too good to be true, you need to check the fundamentals. They were wise words then and they are wise words now.

Investors in TotalScamCoin woke up this morning to the news that funds were draining from the TotalScamCoin company account. Watching withdrawal transactions on the blockchain explorer in horror with them was TotalScamCoin CFO Ella Patterson.

'I couldn't believe it,' Patterson told this reporter when I contacted them for comment. 'We did everything right. It's a multisig wallet controlled by TTP-enabled hardware keys with social recovery and long lock times.'

So what went wrong with this best-of-breed security, I asked Patterson. 'Wallace used a weakened key for his txes in the genesis block then disguised a series of increasingly large transactions drawing on them as individual small transactions and submitted that for approval. We checked and signed the small transaction, or at least we thought we had, but Wallace had boiled our frog.'

Matthew Wallace is, or was, TotalScamCoin's CTO. And the frog? Patterson explains: 'We checked the transaction history. [Wallace] had been getting us all to approve longer and longer chains of masked transactions over the last few months. He only cashed out the smallest one in each series, so he trained our security analytics to ignore what he was doing. Like the metaphor of boiling a frog by increasing the temperature a little at a time. By the time they realise they're cooked, it's too late.'

And this morning it was too late. But why would anyone invest in a coin that claims to be a scam? 'The team was stellar and the fundamentals had total solidity,' said pseudonymous financial analyst ATHHunter when I contacted her via direct message. 'The name indicated knowledge of hodler culture and served to weed out baghodlers. There wasn't an iota of doubt in my mind that this was a project that was going to be making waves.'

So what went wrong? Patterson: 'It's clear that this was Wallace's plan all along, since before the genesis block attack, we all knew him from his previous work but he was willing to burn his reputation out to effect this exit scam. We can only apologise to TotalScamCoin investors and assure them that we are pursuing every option at this time, including a second fork.'

TotalScamCoin investors, many of whom had been coordinating a pump in defiance of federal hodling legislation, were rushing to liquidate their hodlings, offloading them onto anyone who would take them. ATHHunter: 'There will be a dead cat bounce, there always is, but unless you have a trading bot close to a mining operation I wouldn't take the risk of being left holding that coin when the music stops. And watch out for pumpers. Always watch out for pumpers.'

Wise words. But as I found out when I checked the smart contract that my Grandmother used to put coins in for me to save for later, you can't always trust wise words—especially when someone else controls the keys. Well played, Grandma, well played.

Blog Post: 'Dogs Are Not Fungible'

Doxe, my dog, has stopped working. I'm sad and I don't know what to do. He was a tokenised third-generation consumerised robot quadruped running an affective neural net. I can't replace his components or upgrade his firmware without the token security key—and I don't have the security key. Pulling the TTP chip that enforces the key access off his motherboard will fry his whole system.

I know what you're thinking: 'Why didn't you back up your key?' Oh reader, I know, but the key was not mine to back up. I have a safety deposit box full of keys. They are paper, titanium, ceramic, leather-and-steel, glass, knotted fabric. I've spent hours with dremels, ballpoint pens, needles, and lasers making sure that if a key is lost on my watch, it's not for want of trying. I'm particularly proud of the leather-and-steel ones, they're the originals of the larger and more decorative versions you may have seen in the show 'Through the Key' at MoMA.

But to backup a key you must control that key, and I did not. Yes reader, I know, I know. I was young and I wanted a dog but I was afraid of losing them one day, so a robot dog seemed like a good substitute if I could find a way of paying for it gradually. I wasn't thinking of the consequences of having but not really owning Doxe.

I kept up payments on Doxe's token until the company that sold him to me folded. No other company picked up the service contract for the dog tokens, so there were no new updates for their software and you couldn't update their hardware. I knew Doxe and I were living on borrowed time. But that didn't make the inevitable any easier to bear when it finally happened.

I guess it could have been worse. The hacked dog attacks you may have heard about before were the same model as Doxe. I wasn't worried about those because I'm not rich or famous, so who would want to weaponise my pet? But I guess in a way that's what happened, emotionally at least. Yes, I'm dramatic. That's how it feels.

But this is not the end. Hopefully. Not yet. I've got together with some of the other hodlers of tokens for Doxe and his buddies at DCTRL and we're working on a new smart contract to take control of the abandoned contract (we tried to buy it out but that didn't work). We'll be ready to deploy the test contract soon. If you're a code or law hacker and can help, get in touch!

Epilogue

It is now ever so slightly further into the future. Your team has worked together to gain much Doge, and you have taken an important step towards making the world a better place | getting rich | creating something new and exciting | addressing the injustices of the existing system | paying your debts onchain [DELETE AS APPROPRIATE—WE COULDN'T AUTOMATE THIS PART SORRY, MAYBE THAT'S AN ICO OPPORTUNITY RIGHT THERE].

Some of the world has been watching you, some of the world has been caught up in its own challenges. Some people have been inspired by your efforts, some have actively opposed them, others have tried to ride on them for good or for ill. You've solved fearsome challenges, completed mindbending tasks, scanned more QR codes than you thought possible in a single day, stayed hydrated, and looked both ways while crossing the road.

Did you become Dogeillionares? If so, amaze, you can now anchor your project to the one true chain and change the world. Just like your foreshibes used to. You must promise to use this power only for good. No exit scams.

Or did you not become Dogeillionaires? If so then looking at everything you achieved anyway, that's amaze too. You can still change the world with that kind of attitude. Just like your other foreshibes used to. Maybe you don't have to be part of the one true chain to do so.

But then, is this really the one true chain? You've encountered so many different ways of doing things. Does the chain make the shibe or does the shibe make the chain?

Perhaps the true shibe was in our hearts all along and in the friends we made along the way.

Or, if that's not a gritty cyberpunk-enough ending, perhaps the true shibe being in our hearts all along and guiding us and the people we meet along the way is the only way to be antifragile enough to survive in the gritty cyberpunk dark future—or to make that future lighter.

And to make everything more wow.

Aesthetic Comparison Games

Using ideas from design theory, provable computation, and calculus, we can construct games of aesthetic comparison that allow arbitrary precision. These games can be represented in a form that allows them to be resolved using blockchain smart contracts via reference to materials submitted to set up the game, by reference to onchain precedent, or as a last resort by appeal to a third-party oracle.

Game Setup

To construct the game, two parties must agree on two images, on the properties of the elements of those images under consideration, the relationship between them that is under consideration, and the degree of that relationship.

▲ = ▲ ?

The properties must be represented electronically and atomically, for example as RGB colours, as extremely small pixmaps, or as simplified Bézier curves. The hashes of these values are then arranged as the leaves of a Merkle tree for each image, in lexicographic value. A third tree is then constructed by the first party of the hashes of tuples of pairs of leaves from each of the first two trees, the name of the relationships that is held to be true between them, a stated tolerance for deviation from simple mathematical equality in that relationship, and the weight of these properties as evidence in the aesthetic assertion being made accorded to that relationship (this must sum to 1.0 for all leaves). A threshold for property significance is declared (e.g. 0.001); this may be updated in later rounds of the game with mutual agreement or by appeal.

These trees are then combined with the root of two further trees—the precedent tree and the adjudicator address tree—to produce the Merkle root of the game setup. It is vitally important that both parties agree on the representation of each image contained in the tree and on the tolerances and weights accorded to elements from them. Given a high enough tolerance for colour difference, for example, it is trivial to make green into red. Tools to automate preflight tests for game trees will be important.

For a multi-stage Merkle tree acceptance phase, use rounds of committing/revealing proposed trees with increasing stakes. Accepting a tree returns the stakes. There may be a limit to the amount of time or number of rounds taken for this phase in order to prevent one party trapping the other. Alongside these rules, there may be rules that allow both parties to exit with mutual agreement at any time.

Compulsory/voluntary comparison games may require different agreement, comparison, and appeal phases to avoid griefing. Or a single well-understood workflow with well-understood and clearly described failure modes in each context may be easier to reason about and therefore ultimately more reliable.

Once the game root has been registered, the comparison proceeds in rounds of assertions made with reference to the content of the subtrees that the root anchors.

If the comparison can be made automatically (e.g. `#FF0000 == #FF0000`), this proof can be offered onchain. An uncontested assertion of this form wins.

Example comparison relations and properties include: $=, \neq, \approx, \not\approx, \subset, \not\subset, \not\supset, \supset, <, >$, geometric affine transform, colour difference, freeform textual statement.

Beware of image content when comparing. Steganographic information may mislead automated comparison.

Where statements can be phrased equivalently, the one that would place the lowest value on the left branch should be used.

Unrealistic trees, e.g.

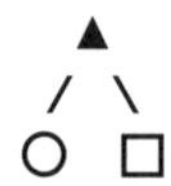

can be rejected by submitting a contradictory precedent, or by the results of an appeal if appeals are binding. The unrealistic tree can then be replaced with a more accurate proposal in a multi-stage MAST acceptance phase, or simply not used if the evaluation is not binding.

If comparisons can be reduced to precedents, cite them. This means that if a comparison has been resolved in a previously successfully completed comparison, submit the Merkle path of that proof and the Merkle path of the properties that it matches in the properties tree instead of starting an appeal. An uncontested assertion of this form wins.

If either party wishes to reject an assertion, they can provide the Merkle path to a contradictory assertion.

Appeals

If the content of the game tree root is exhausted by assertions without a simple winner emerging, either player may attempt to establish a new precedent by assembling a pair of Merkle paths from the property trees of the attacker and the defender, staking a pre-agreed amount of value that will be forfeited if they lose the appeal, and sending the appeal to a third-party tribunal implemented using prediction markets, an ombudsman oracle DAO, or some other means.

The outcome of the appeal becomes available as a precedent for future games.

Game Outcome

Ultimately a winner will emerge from this adversarial process, and they can exercise the right granted to them by a pre-game commitment to update a DAO's state or receive an amount of cryptocurrency or some other action that a proof of resolution can enable. Or both parties can cooperate to collaboratively declare a winner or a draw *before* that, either returning any stakes, burning any commitments, or cooperating to exercise the commitment that the winner would have been able to exploit.

AI Art, Ownership, Blockchain

Questions of 'ownership' in art can be a matter of law, of social norms, or of art theory. New art forms and new methods of producing art can fall foul of existing answers to these questions, or can creatively reopen them. Often, they do both. 'AI Art' produced using contemporary artificial neural network software is a good example of this. 'Rare Art' produced using blockchain token software is another, which we will consider below in relation to one particularly notorious example of AI Art.

Portrait of Edmond De Belamy was produced by the artist group Obvious using an existing artificial neural network model trained on a corpus of images of classical paintings. Obvious did not credit the author of that network model, or any of the artists whose paintings were included in the corpus. At this point there are already three different layers of questions around ownership.

Firstly, the assembly of an image corpus. Accurate reproductions of paintings that are no longer in copyright should not attract copyright, and in the US at least this is quite rightly the case. A collection of such reproductions may attract copyright on the collection itself, but this should not affect individual works within the collection. If the images were of paintings that are still under copyright, copying each image might infringe that copyright. I say 'might' because doing so could fall under fair use/fair dealing (hereafter just 'fair use') exceptions to copyright. These exceptions are popular both with artists who work with appropriation and with large internet companies who work with search and advertising. Both groups, and others such as Digital Humanities scholars, might wish to assemble such corpora of images, so it is difficult to generalise about motives and outcomes regarding them. In the case of art, however, fair use for artists is a key defence of artistic creativity in an age where the visual environment is dominated by corporate media.

Beyond this legal view is the ethical and art-theoretic view. Is it *right* to treat individual artworks in a corpus as tokens of a type or as just part of a set, as fodder, or as raw material for an industrial process? With apologies to Clement Greenberg, when the tactile elements of painting are discarded, does it still remain possible to meaningfully capture what paintings that meaningfully engage with that tactility *mean*? And when fine visual detail and differences in scale between different canvases are discarded, does this introduce as many or more problems for processes of derivation as it obviously does for processes of study?

Secondly, consider the training and use of the artificial neural network model on that image corpus. The model is trained by processing images in the corpus, that is, by copying and reading their data. The model will contain representations of parts of the images from its training corpus, and its output will also resemble parts of the images they are trained on. Mechanical copying and the creation of derivatives of images are covered by copyright. Cutting up images and juxtaposing them with the work of other artists is covered by the moral rights that accompany copyright. Again, copyright does not apply to works that are out of copyright (moral rights vary by country...), and artists should have a claim to fair use of such materials. The degree to which artistic use of source materials transforms them should be a factor in establishing that such use is indeed fair use, and the output of artificial neural networks certainly transforms the images that they are trained on. Style is not copyrightable (let's not talk about 'trade dress' here), but forgery and 'passing off' can be legal matters, and the application of an artist's signature style to a work that they have not made but is sold under their name is the same whether performed by human hand or algorithm.

Again, the ethical and art-theoretical view raises more questions. Signature styles are a matter of pride as well as profit for artists, and while this can be critiqued within art theory, it is a strongly established norm that simple imitation of style, without a critical framework as justification, is a breach of artistic norms. Artificial neural network models need not operationalise an individual artist's signature style in order to devalue the concept of signature styles in general.

Thirdly, Obvious's use of existing neural network software to generate an image has caused widespread debate. 'Signing' the image with the algorithm used by the artificial neural network software to produce it functions as a double-bluff whatever the intention behind doing so may be. We know that Obvious produced and sold the image, their attribution is not threatened by this. But it erases the work of both Robbi Barret in producing the model of art that the image is simply a product of, and that of the artists that the neural network's model had already erased the authorship of, both in terms of attribution and in terms of control of their work (even if from beyond the grave in the case of the corpus artists). Software authors should not be able to control uses of the tools that they produce—Microsoft should not be able to censor your writing using Word or claim joint authorship of everything you write using it. But a trained artificial neural network model is a more complex thing than a text editor from this point of view—it is as much content as it is tool. Microsoft should not be able to tell you how you change the contents of an empty text document, but changing a novel or a painting whether represented physically or digitally may infringe on the copyright and moral rights of its author. Once again, though, fair use should be strongly considered for artistically transformative use of artificial neural network models.

Art-theoretically speaking, such direct and uncredited use of existing materials, even materials created by another artist, may count as appropriation art, which is an established category within the arts. Appropriation art is deliberately transgressive, often to critical effect. Appropriating non-art or low-art materials is very different from appropriating canonical art or the art of leading contemporaries, but both can be critical moves. Artistic labour can be appropriated directly, as in the case of contemporary artists such as Jeff Koons or Damien Hirst who use studio assistants to produce art under their own signature. The signature under which the products of this labour are exhibited and sold is a key element in the erasure of that labour. And where software used to make art is free software(/open source), attribution may or may not be a strong social norm, but past a certain point that attribution is useful information to have for artistic, critical, and art-historical engagement with the work.

Prior to this, Obvious had already encountered the question of ownership and found an answer that led directly to *Portrait of Edmond De Belamy* being sold at auction. That answer was based on AI's twin in contemporary technological hype, the blockchain.

Christie's discovered Obvious via their work on SuperRare, a blockchain-based 'Rare Art' platform. Rare Art is named after the 'Rare Pepe' project that developed the techniques of using cryptocurrency and blockchain token technology to record limited edition certificates for digital images. This produces 'artificial scarcity' and allows a form of ownership for pieces of digital art that would otherwise be infinitely reproducible. This use of certificates as ownership proxies for art was pioneered by Conceptual Art. Compared to a flammable piece of paper with a handwritten signature on, the authenticity of a blockchain transaction secured by a not inconsiderable fraction of the world's computing power each day only increases over time. It may not be entirely clear what the authenticity is *of*, but the terms and conditions of Rare Art platforms and the community norms of their users and consumers do produce a vivid image of a novel and very strong concept of ownership.

'True digital ownership' on a blockchain secured by cryptographic keys is seen by its proponents as stronger, more trustworthy, and more absolute than previous conceptions of property. This makes AI Art a natural fit for Rare Art because each has needs that the other fulfils: ownership in the case of the products of AI Art, strongly perceptible uniqueness but also recognisability as art in the case of Rare Art. Sale at auction also provides this kind of closure for the financial value of art, but new art and in particular digital art faces a bootstrapping problem in which it must establish its value in order to be sold at auction, but cannot be sold at auction without first establishing its value. Christie's saw art by Obvious selling on SuperRare and could react to that market signal more quickly and with lower risk than it could to signals from gallery or online sales of physical goods.

It is a truism of International Art English that art questions things. There are many questions in play in both AI Art and Rare Art. They involve the concept of ownership considered in terms of the law, social norms, and art theory. The answers to these questions from within each of these realms individually may be obvious and simple to their practitioners, but between them they may be more at odds than each realises. Negotiating this without closing the door to cultural creativity or opening it to corporate exploitation is a task that is of interest far beyond the art world.

(I am not a lawyer, etc.)

2020

Tokenized Vickrey Aesthetics

In *Radical Markets*, Eric Posner and Glen Weyl propose a system of universal, permanent second-price 'Vickrey Auctions' of land as a mechanism for price discovery on the utility of property and the taxation of the ongoing ownership of that value with a 'Harberger Tax' as the means of funding a just, redistributive, state. They call this the 'Vickrey Commons'.[1]

Critics of the Vickrey Commons proposal tend to focus on the fact that, under its model, everywhere is always for sale to the highest bidder, rather than on the fact that the accompanying tax is intended to ensure the socially productive use of property and to securely fund social welfare. From a cypherpunk or cryptocurrency point of view, however, the intrusion of the state into property relations is inherently unjust and distortive of social relations. We will return to the redistributive element of the Vickrey Commons later, but for the moment it is its capacity for driving price discovery and productive use that I wish to focus on.

Vickrey Auctions are often used by states to privatise radio frequencies in the electromagnetic spectrum. Extending this to the visible spectrum, to colour, would be the stuff of satire. But below the state level we do see the inefficient allocation and exploitation of colour and other aesthetic properties in the art world. We can tackle this using the intelligence of markets and simulated property rights on the blockchain.

Let us first make individual colours, shapes, line and surface qualities, and other aesthetic properties representable as non-fungible tokens on the blockchain. These can then be sold. The right to use those properties can then be sold by the owners as fungible tokens.

Compositions of these tokens can then be represented in turn by a secondary layer of non-fungible tokens and usage rights for those expressed by their own higher layer of non-fungible tokens.

This process can be repeated until concrete instances of the expression of aesthetic properties are expressed by composing non-fungible tokens from different layers into a non-fungible token that can be treated as unique or, alternatively, editioned using a final layer of fungible tokens.

If we use the Ethereum blockchain for this, the system can be represented as a stack of ERC-721, ERC-1633,[2] ERC-20, and ERC-998 smart contracts.

In the absence of rent or taxes, the owners of non-fungible aesthetic properties can make money by selling those tokens or by releasing and/or re-purchasing fungible tokens that represent them. The optimal strategies for this are outside the scope of this essay, but they involve reacting to demand at different levels for fundamental and derived/composed properties in a timely manner.

1 E. Posner and E.G. Weyl, *Radical Markets: Uprooting Capitalism and Democracy for a Just Society* (Princeton, NJ: Princeton University Press, 2018).

2 B. Rennekamp. 'Re-Fungible Token (RFT): What Happens When a Bonded Token Owns an NFT?', *medium.com*, <https://billyrennekamp.medium.com/re-fungible-token-rft-297003592769>.

Returning to the redistributive aspect of the Vickrey Commons, we can (pre-) sell the fundamental aesthetic properties to one or more foundations that exist to profit from them in order to redistribute those profits to deserving artistic and/or social causes. It is possible to imagine various ways of structuring those foundations as smart contracts or their payment(s) as domain-specific tokens, although introducing a Tokenized Aesthetic Vickrey Commons currency coin risks the introduction of a central bank-like entity into the system.

Where the foundations' revenue must go to the authors of works using those properties, this is possible to enforce simply onchain, although avoiding the sybil problem and other issues with onchain redistribution is much less simple. Where we wish to enforce more complex relations between the work and the foundation we will need aesthetic comparison games, which can be completed onchain but are much more expensive than a simple token check. Where the foundations' missions are more arbitrary, controls begin to look more like human organisation than enforcement through code.

It is not possible to exclude duplicate token contracts on a given blockchain without support for doing so at the protocol level, and in the general case it is impossible across blockchains without protocol support for a cross-chain proof-of-precedence protocol. It is even easier to simply not use these tokens. Why, then, would anyone use them?

Anchoring a singular source of these properties through first-mover and network effects may be sufficient to make it authoritative for anyone who wishes to use them. The use of these tokens is then a means of establishing price and authenticity, which, if we squint hard, is to say that it is a means to establish value.

Further objections to this translate neatly into objections to the art world and schemes to reform or replace it.

2020

Hash Gematria

a3083687ee111912f7daf2d0bfb3647c7a4ec90a05984cbdebac4203036a9735 **egress**
a3085fe17a3f2636df0fb4ff6d811adaccad403b28de4e1f454d4d3facf2e599 **mudslides**
a308887de34c658fba487037f9a694ff69411980e04ad91e13f35631fe5dcca9 **tricycles**
a30839f61147d7036341c6dbac338523d2a26a3bca2d9bbda89b64d8b6a89588 **vandalizes**

Gematria in Hebrew uses a SIGINT attack on God's fully homomorphic encryption of the book of nature to extract meaning. A non-Hebrew gematria is a glimpse not back into the mind of God but forward through the fall of the tower of Babel into a scrambled linguistic world of contingency. It is a generator of Deleuzian 'dark precursors' to connections between concepts, just as rhymes are. These connections are useful irritants, spurs to the generation of actual structure that would otherwise not occur, anchors for beliefs. Both kinds of gematria are exercises in exploiting the surplus value of code. The former is revelation, the latter is construction. Yet they resemble one another as much as is possible in their respective universes.

Interpreting letters as numbers recapitulates the history of mathematical notation. It is a choice defensible on the grounds of its maximal simplicity and its historical embedding. Cryptographic hashing lacks both this simplicity (for a human being to calculate the value of a word numerically takes seconds, for them to calculate a cryptographic hash by hand would take around fifteen minutes) and this history (cryptographic hashes date back only to the 1970s).[1]

It does however compress a history of ever-increasing uniqueness and thereby security (in the senses of both secrecy and stability) of identity. It is part of the present moment of the history of technocapital/techonomics rather than a form of nostalgia for the past of accounting and its gentrified forms (aka 'mathematics'). As the number of cryptographic hashes calculated by the Bitcoin network alone approaches 120,000,000,000,000,000,000 per second at the start of 2020, the process of hashing reinforces its reality and its effects in the world through sheer volume of repetition.

Cryptographic hash collisions (instances in which the hashing of two different pieces of data generates the same hash value identifier or 'name') are vanishingly unlikely by design. The evolution of cryptographic hashing algorithms has been the evolution of ever more effective ways of scattering bits into cryptographic space in order to destroy their significance while retaining their identity. But the 64-character hexadecimal (base-16) strings used to encode 256-bit hash values are difficult for human beings to read and compare, so software systems such as git or Docker that use them pervasively tend to truncate them by displaying or reading just the first few characters (the 'prefix') in order to make them more readable.

1 K. Shirriff, 'Mining Bitcoin With Pencil and Paper: 0.67 hashes per day', <https://www.righto.com/2014/09/mining-bitcoin-with-pencil-and-paper.html>.

These shorter values do collide as more and more hashes are used to refer to more and more things in the world (this is the 'Birthday Problem') and so longer prefixes have been used over time. It takes two hexadecimal characters to encode one eight-bit byte of data. The first byte of the hash value is two hexadecimal characters, the first two are four characters, the first four are eight characters etc. We can represent hash prefixes in more exotic bases: Proquint, BIP-49, Urbit @p, Base 56, Bech32 or even decimal. But these are not the representations of hash values that are displayed pervasively within the culture of computing.

Non-cryptographic hashes will collide far more frequently, but they are not embedded in computing culture or in the culture of technocapital and its imaginaries of resistance (crypto-anarchy, cryptocurrency) to the extent that cryptographic hashing algorithms are. We therefore mean *cryptographic* hashes when we refer to hashes here.

Replacing letter-value summing and decimal reduction with cryptographic hash prefix collision generation gives us *hash gematria*. This is a hype-cycle peak-shift maximally historically contingent and embedded extractor of surplus value of code. This surplus value will itself consist in maximally historically contingent and embedded dark precursors. As a strategy, this is inflected by the pop-cultural strains of Chaos Magick, but has far greater qualities of repetition and embeddedness and is more abstract and therefore more dynamic than a specific cultural expression.

If this seems unconvincing, what would a stronger candidate be?

A stronger candidate for what?

To get the first four characters of a cryptographic hash of a piece of text using the Unix command line, enter something like the following:

```
echo -n "egress" | sha256sum | cut -c -4
```

2020

WART—Wrapped Art

Wrapped Art (WART) applies the ideas behind Wrapped Kitties to Rare Art tokens, opening up new possibilities for investment and aesthetics.

The Wrapped Kitties Ethereum smart contract takes CryptoKitties ERC-721 non-fungible tokens (NFTs) and gives out its own ERC-20 fungible tokens (WCK) in return, 'wrapping' the former in the latter. This makes it easy to buy and sell kitties in bulk, to use kitties in Decentralised Finance (DeFi) applications, or to trade low-valued kitties that one wishes to dispose of for others with more potential value by 'unwrapping' the ERC-20 tokens back to (different) ERC-721 CryptoKitty tokens. WCK is credited with giving CryptoKitties a 50 percent price bump in mid-2019.[1]

Wrapping Rare Art ERC-721 NFTs with ERC-20 Wrapped Art WART tokens would allow the same use cases. It would be a way to get (financial) utility from (financially) under-performing art. Or a way of exploring new artists by swapping NFTs via the contract, either randomly or by seeing which other ERC-721 Rare Art tokens the contract currently has wrapped and redeeming WART for them accordingly.

The Wrapped Art smart contract should allow tokens from more than one Rare Art platform to be wrapped and unwrapped, both to allow the widest range of tokens to be used for liquidity purposes and to give access to the widest range of artists and works. On a technical level this might require the contract to be centralised in order to manage the list of platform contracts it accepts NFT tokens from, but on balance this is better than tying it to (one version of) one platform or a frozen list of contracts that will rapidly become outdated. To decentralise this while robustly incentivising the curators to act in the best interests of WART, we can instead curate the addition and removal of contracts using a Moloch DAO with WART itself as the membership tribute.

WART gives collectors who don't have a background in fine art but can follow price charts[2] the ability to shake up their collections. This is both financially and art-historically useful, allowing collectors to benefit from access to both financial and aesthetic liquidity as they build their collecting strategy. The blasphemy (for art historians) of regarding art as a fungible asset class and the blasphemy (for financiers) of regarding money as an insufficient sign of value resolve one another here. In doing so they create better signals than the positive feedback loops that would otherwise emerge when, under the efficient market hypothesis, purchasing power, and nothing else, drives artistic development.

It might appear that WART turns rare art into pure financial quantity, but in fact WART turns Rare Art into a pure aesthetic quantity. The monetary value of the art wrapped by the WART smart contract can be established by the trading price of WART but given what its tokens represent, this means that hodling specific quantities of WART

1 O. Avan-Nomayo, 'WrappedKitties Trading Sees CryptoKitty Base Price Jump by 50%', *crypto.news*, 14 June 2019, <https://btcmanager.com/wrappedkitties-trading-cryptokitty/>.

2 WhaleShark, 'Out of Left (Brained) Field #4: What We Can Do Better Together', ȼ, 9 February 2020, <https://beta.cent.co/WhaleShark/+ln4bju>.

has an unavoidable aesthetic significance in addition to (and by virtue of) its financial one. Status games of hodling significant amounts of WART (in the sense both of large and evocative numbers) without unwrapping or using them for any further purpose might emerge in response to this fact. This fundamentally changes the concepts of collection, exhibition, and value for art, coming down on the side of the price charts in terms of form but thereby opening that form up to new aesthetic content.

Taking these ideas even further, we can wrap the content of tokens. For example, MATH tokens can be wrapped or burned in return for the bits that represent their numbers as ERC-20 (or ERC-1155) tokens. We can't break a CryptoKitty up into their genes (that would be cruel) but could we break up the image that a Rare Art token represents into its component colours? What cryptographic proof of the offchain pixel values could be produced onchain?

Or we can reverse this process and start by constructing NFT art from other tokens representing discrete aesthetic quantities. COLOUR tokens start to do this with their wrapping of MATH tokens, but are monolithic and atomic rather than being constructed from discrete elements. *Tokens Equal Text*[3] is constructed from elements, but each contains several words and the colours used are implicit. A more general and powerful NFT art construction system will require a different approach.

3 See below, 297.

2020

From WART to DeAes

Building on some of the ideas of WART (Wrapped Art) tokens gives us a powerful toolbox for organising the evaluation and production of blockchain art.

Rather than using a Moloch DAO to decide which ERC-721 contracts to accept tokens from as we could in WART, we can use it to curate a collection of tokenised art directly by voting on which tokens to purchase, commission, lend, and sell as a form of Decentralised Aesthetics (DeAes, pronounced 'dais').

The membership application tribute for joining the DAO can be ERC-721 tokens (unwrapped if we modify the Moloch DAO codebase to directly handle ERC-721 as well as ERC-20 tokens, or else wrapped in the DAO's own purely internal equivalent of WART) or Wrapped Ether (for the purchase fund). WART itself should not be used for this as it (deliberately) makes selecting artworks for their aesthetic content more difficult.

Each proposal for managing the collection that the membership puts forward to be voted on must fit the stated aesthetic of the DAO, and each member's votes must evaluate whether that fit is real and appropriate. The DAO's aesthetic and the interpretation/application strategy used to realise it can be updated through voting proposals, with or without rewards for successfully making the change.

If a DAO member wishes to ragequit, they can take art and Ether proportional to their shares. Art allocation strategies for ragequitting can use an internal equivalent to WART, a simple FIFO queue or ERC-721 token, a flat percentage scheme using an agreed-upon source of (pseudo)-randomness, or a more complex combination of or replacement for any of these approaches.

Operationalising and financialising aesthetic evaluation in this way via investment portfolio management ties art-historical development to market signalling in a dynamic and accelerated way, which is to say a mutually beneficial one. This is a radical approach that requires art historians and financial investors to learn much from one another. Despite this, it still cannot reach into the artwork except before the fact in the form of commissions, which extends the history of patronage in a useful way but leaves the frame of the artwork otherwise intact.

We can take this approach further by limiting the DAO's voting proposals to the tasks of producing or authenticating art, turning the DAO into an artist itself. A production DAO recreates a Koonsian approach to the outsourced fabrication of art, whereas an authentication DAO recreates a Kostabian one. The fabricators of these artworks can be paid in Loot or, if the aim of the DAO is to grow by adding likeminded members, in fully voting shares.

Even where the DAO becomes active in the production of art in this way, the edges of the artwork are left intact after its production, securing the interior of the artwork against being connected to market signals. Removing the firewall of the frame rather than routing around it or simply liquidating its contents (an approach I discussed along with the WART proposal) will require still more radical steps.

Intensive and Extensive Aesthetic Property Token Composition

ERC-721 tokens can be composed into tree structures using ERC-998 tokens. Where those ERC-721 tokens represent images or image elements, that tree structure becomes a rendering tree or two-dimensional scene graph (three-dimensional scene graphs will have to wait for 3D Rare Art standards to solidify). To lay out the elements of the image we must be able to transform them in various ways, changing their position, size, colour, and other intensive and extensive aesthetic properties. As they are continuous quantities, we can represent these aesthetic properties as ERC-20 tokens with 18 digits of precision.

To apply these properties to an ERC-721 token we can attach them using ERC-998 composable tokens in an SVG-style tree hierarchy. Each ERC-998 token has one or more quantities of ERC-20 aesthetic property tokens attached, one or more child ERC-998 tokens, and zero or more (usually zero or one) ERC-721 tokens attached. The properties expressed by the ERC-20 tokens attached to each ERC-998 token are applied to any attached ERC-721 token(s) and transitively to the children of any attached ERC-998 tokens.

Where the values we wish to represent should be limited to a given range (e.g. 0.0–1.0 or 0–255), we can either raise an assertion if too many tokens are sent to be attached to ERC-998 tokens (we might also be able to refund them in an additional transaction, but this would affect the gas required—and as per the ERC-20 standard we should not accept fewer tokens than are sent), we can treat higher values as meaning the maximum (e.g. 3.1 is 1.0, and 1337 is 255), or we can scale values relative to the largest quantity.

When the values must be both positive and negative (for example, if we are representing coordinates around an origin, especially relative coordinates in a group hierarchy), we can use a second token to represent negative values (this would be better represented using ERC-1155 tokens, but ERC-998 does not support this standard). If both positive and negative tokens are applied, their values should be summed. For coordinates we can use only positive tokens by treating group origins as their top left rather than their centre and only adding positive offsets to child ERC-998 tokens.

Affine transformation ERC-20 tokens are applied as a transformation matrix to the children of the ERC-998 token they are attached to. This means that children-of-children multiply their parent matrix with their own. There is an implicit graphics state push/pop for each ERC-998 token, so transformations do not affect sibling tokens, only child ones.

For colour or alpha (transparency) values, these values are added to the colour values of the image represented by the token. This may not be the expected behaviour. As with coordinates, using only positive values can be achieved by carefully structuring the hierarchy of the image so that child ERC-998s only need to add rather than subtract colour values to represent their colour scheme. Alternatively, we can treat colour tokens as scale, allowing both increases and decreases of colour to be expressed across the token hierarchy, and source primitive forms to be arbitrarily coloured if they are white.

More complex colour interactions and other filter or layer behaviours could be specified by additional tokens.

This gives us the following ERC-20 tokens:

`X`	X coordinate offset values in distance units. Unbounded.
`Y`	Y coordinate offset values in distance units. Unbounded.
`WIDTH`	Width in distance units. Unbounded.
`HEIGHT`	Height in distance units. Unbounded.
`ROTATION`	Rotation in degrees. Unbounded, wraps around past 360 as usual.
`RED`	Red scale. Unbounded, although values that multiply the source value higher than 1.0 will have no additional effect.
`GREEN`	Green scale. Unbounded, although values that multiply the source value higher than 1.0 will have no additional effect
`BLUE`	Blue scale. Unbounded, although values that multiply the source value higher than 1.0 will have no additional effect.
`ALPHA`	Transparency scale. Unbounded, although values that multiply the source value higher than 1.0 will have no additional effect.

What is to stop the owner of an artwork created in this way from breaking it up, rearranging it, or adding to it?

Nothing at all...

Isn't this an extremely expensive way of assembling art onchain?

It depends on the value of the work that is made using it...

Why Bitcoin Is Money According to Marx

tl;dr: whales.

In *Marx on Money*, Suzanne de Brunhoff describes the theory of money that Karl Marx presents in *Capital*.[1]

Money, for Marx, emerges in three stages prior to capitalism.

In the first stage, gold becomes a measure of the value of all other commodities rather than simply one commodity among many.

In the second stage, gold coins become the medium of circulation. Once gold becomes de-materialised in this way, its role can then be occupied by fiat currency.

In the third and final stage, the emergence of hoarding paradoxically introduces money 'proper'.

De Brunhoff writes that 'Hoarding is a demand for money as money', an interruption in the circulation of money that 'serves to ceaselessly preserve and reconstitute the money form as such, whatever the deformations, transformations, and disappearances it undergoes as a result of the other two functions. Produced by these, it becomes in its turn a condition of their functioning'.[2]

In the crypto space, hoarders are known as whales. They remove their coins from circulation with the expectation that this will ultimately provide them with more utility than immediately spending them. In doing so they act just like hoarders of gold coin or fiat currency. To quote Marx, 'The money becomes petrified into a hoard, and the seller becomes a hoarder of money.'[3]

Whales therefore establish that cryptocurrency is money according to Karl Marx.

1 S. de Brunhoff, *Marx on Money*, tr. M.J. Goldbloom (London and New York: Verso, 2015); K. Marx, *Capital: A Critique of Political Economy, Volume One*, tr. B. Fowkes (London: Penguin, 1990).
2 De Brunhoff, *Marx on Money*, 35.
3 Marx, *Capital*, 228.

2020

Essay on *Essays on Art & Language*

Charles Harrison, *Essays on Art & Language* (Cambridge, MA: MIT Press, 1991; revised edition 2001).

The Conceptual Art artists group Art & Language formed at the end of the 1960s. Art historian Charles Harrison was a member of the group from the start of the 1970s. In 1991 Harrison published a book on the history of the group up to that point, relating it to the wider history of art during the collapse of the authority of Modernist art criticism and the rise of Postmodernism. Modernist art criticism for Harrison here means the magisterial formalism of Clement Greenberg and his followers. It is an art criticism that produces psychologised readings of the surfaces of artworks for a genteel 'spectator' to consume without remainder. It is, as Harrison puts it, 'a theory of consumption masquerading as a theory of production' that masks the historical and technical content involved in that production. In response to this, Harrison argues for a historical-materialist art criticism that restores Modernism's dialectical contrast of values by 'erasing the edges' of artworks. Doing this makes tractable to art history those 'genetic' materials involved in each artwork's genesis that Modernist art criticism masked with its decontextualised reading of art as primarily expressive rather than representational.

Against this backdrop of the collapsing authority of Modernist art criticism and the demands of a new critical relationship to art, Harrison presents Art & Language as being committed to a critical project of going-on without an overarching theory or (as Harrison puts it) in the ruin of that arch. Going-on was a non-theory. Recognising the contingency of all artistic representation and treating intellectual property and artistic propriety as oppressive expressions of class society, Art & Language produced work that looked very little like existing art not in order to produce saleable novelty but because that is where the work of art took them. When it is no longer possible to 'mean the doing' of dominant discourses and there is still no clear path forward, taking action in the face of this dilemma means committing to unpredictable outcomes. The unpredictability of those outcomes may lead out of art into the wider world, or into hard-won moments of artistic autonomy.

The disinterested spectator presupposed by the discursive content of Modernist art criticism as its historical subject exercised a particular set of competences when stood in front of a painting or a sculpture and would use them to describe what they saw (and felt) in a particular way. Art & Language's work, and the group's organisational structure, was oriented toward undermining the spectator's understanding of and relation to that work in order to create a disenchanted viewer. Harrison examines many examples of this project of disorientation, and their discussion of the physical and representational structure of one of Art & Language's more complex paintings of the 1980s (Art & Language turned to painting at the turn of the decade to avoid the trap of a 'Conceptual Art' aesthetic that had been quickly recuperated by the art world) shows these effects at work very clearly:

> "This is the painting." "This is part of the painting." "This is a representation of the painting." "This is a representation of part of the painting." "This is a detail of the painting." "This is a representation of another painting." [etc.] (208)

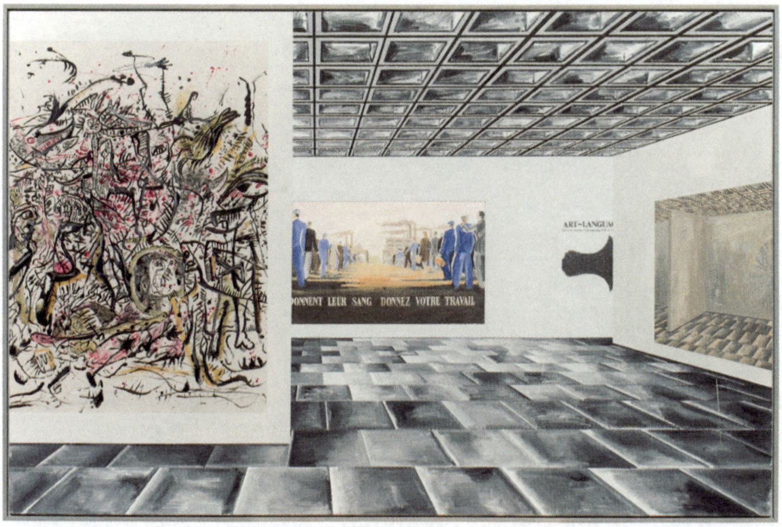

Art & Language, *Index, an Incident in a Museum XXXII*, 1987. Oil and mixed media on canvas mounted on plywood, 156 × 244 cm. © Art & Language; Courtesy the Artists and Mulier Mulier Gallery, Belgium.

Art that seeks a critical autonomy, Harrison argues, must represent some non-trivial aspect of its historical moment. In painting, this must be animated by changes in figure/ground relationships. *Historically significant* changes in these relationships, in critical terminology, or in the spectator's competences, must reflect moments of change in relations within class society. At such moments, Harrison argues, it is possible for technical concerns to become suffused by moral concerns. These changes are not and cannot be merely psychological—transgression is not something to be *opted for*. Even where artistic autonomy is achieved, alterity will be rapidly reclaimed by the mainstream, as the example of 1960s Conceptual Art demonstrates.

The history of Art & Language that Harrison tells is not, by their own admission in the introduction to the revised edition of 2001, one that all of the group's former members would recognise. A chateau in France now houses a museum dedicated to the world's largest collection of Art & Language artworks. The historical moment at the end of the Cold War in which Harrison was writing this particular collection of essays is long gone, in terms of politics if not actors. And in the age of contemporary art, the Nietszchean '*litterateurs*' that Harrison criticised for their LARPing of postmodern irony would have no trouble consuming Art & Language's a-bit-aesthetic, a-bit-political, a-bit-speaking-of-their-own-manufacture, a-bit-unusual art-objects.

But for a historical materialist project of critical art history, these objections are part of that project. The strategies that Harrison follows and those that they identify in the art of Art & Language can be lifted up out of the brief moment of the 'end of history' and translated into the current epoch, even if their iconographic and discursive points of departure cannot. Harrison starts their discussion of the historical context in which they situate Art & Language's work by identifying 'Modernism in two voices': one in the stentorian tones of the Modernist critic and the secure beholder of authentically expressive abstract art, the other in the more questioning tones of those who notice that the first voice is saying something considerably less secure and universal than it claims to be. What is at stake in the relationship between these two voices, Harrison argues, is nothing less than the moral content of history.

The existence and production of art, Harrison argues, can be justified by the fact that aesthetic oddness or intensity is uniquely revealing. These oddnesses and intensities can serve to emancipate art by producing critical representations of Modernism (or its contemporary equivalent) in order to present the 'meanings of the dominated' using the media and aesthetics of high art. This is a direction of which the *litterateurs* have long since recuperated the posture, but not the content. What oddnesses and intensities are possible in the age of global art fairs and freeports, at what levels of the creation of art?

What can the second voice of art say with this now?

2021

Upgrade Art Now!

> Transferring a human mind into a computer system is known as 'uploading'; turning a mortal into a Power is known as 'upgrading.' The prototypical upload is the Moravec Transfer, proposed by Dr. Hans Moravec in the book *Mind Children*. The Moravec Transfer gradually moves (rather than copies) a human mind into a computer. You need never lose consciousness.
>
> Eliezer S. Yudkowsky, 'Staring into the Singularity'[1]

In the 1982 movie *Tron* (and its underrated 2010 sequel *Tron Legacy*), people are digitised, body and mind, to be uploaded into a simulation 'grid' via the powerful Shiva laser. They are returned to meatspace in the same way. If you only digitise the mind and don't then return it to meatspace, you get an upload.[2] Whereas if you destroy the brain in order to do so, you get a destructive upload. It's half a teleportation. Made famous by Hans Moravec, explored fictitiously in William Gibson's short story 'The Winter Market' and Neal Stephenson's novel *Fall; or Dodge in Hell* among others, and depicted graphically in the recent Amazon show *Upload*, destructive mind uploading destroys your brain layer by layer as its structure is digitised to produce the raw data for a computer simulation of you.[3] We can't be squeamish if we want our biological raw material to be ship-of-Theseus'd into cyberspace (as in Moravec's proposal) or captured as it evaporates in a burst of plasma (as in *Upload*).

Back in 2018 I wrote a short story for *ArtReview* called 'The Large Glass, Burned' in which a famous NFT artwork is destroyed as the ultimate artistic provocation to a future in which physical artworks are of interest, if at all, only as curious historical footnotes to their tokens.[4] I was reminded of this when Injective Protocol burned a Banksy and then sold it as an NFT earlier this month.[5] If anyone wants to buy that token and send it to a burn address, then that will complete this particular circuit (ask your lawyer about the moral rights implications of doing so first though, please and thank you).

Destroying an artwork after—or, even better, by—scanning it (in 2D, 3D or time-based media) to produce a blockchain proxy is a form of destructive uploading. Given how we prize meatspace art, destroying it to produce a superior onchain 'upgrade', in Moravec's terminology, produces a perfect faultline in understanding between legacy institutions that regard doing so as a newsworthy crime against humanity and emerging blockchain cultural or superstructural institutions that will regard not doing so in equally critical ethical terms.

1 <https://web.archive.org/web/20010125023900/http://sysopmind.com/singularity.html>.
2 R. Myers, 'Uploads', <https://rhea.art/uploads/>.
3 N. Stephenson, *Fall; or Dodge in Hell* (New York: HarperCollins, 2019).
4 See above, 187.
5 C. Criddle, 'Banksy Art Burned, Destroyed and Sold as Token in "Money-Making Stunt"', *BBC News*. 9 March 2021, <https://www.bbc.com/news/technology-56335948>.

Given the certainty of ownership, permanence, and reduced archiving costs of NFT art compared to legacy meatspace art as it circulates in the petrodollar art world, added to the editioning and fractionalisation opportunities of NFTs, why *not* upgrade art onto the blockchain? Burn out a Leonardo line by line as you scan it with an electron beam and capture it forever with its hash anchored securely onchain.

We can't be squeamish...

Upgrade art now!

2021

Welcome to the Dessert of the Real: On Certain Developments in the Content of NFT Art

Non-Fungible Token art associates digital art with blockchain identifiers as metadata, producing a saleable ownership proxy similar in concept and usage to a certificate of authenticity for conceptual or video art. In itself this makes no demands on the artwork other than that, ideally, its content should pose minimal problems (legally and technologically) for whatever services or platforms the artist uses to create and sell it. Yet that art exists within a techonomic milieu that holds very specific promise and appeal for those who might be interested in it as an environment in which to produce and experience art.

Early NFT art that was not simply existing illustration work registered onchain became steeped in blockchain promotional imagery—project logos and figureheads. These were soon joined by easily consumed attentional lures appealing to the preexisting sensibilities of viewers/potential purchasers, such as naked human bodies and technological glitches. In the rare cases where the problem of their technical production and content intruded, it was when an artist or a buyer did not understand the source of a library image or of a filter's stylistic flourish. This was a problem because of the concept of ownership as transcendental possession and control that blockchains embody. Blockchains exist to establish ownership of digital assets with mathematical certainty. This means that to own a piece of NFT art is to possess *something* unique with cryptographic certainty backed by a sizeable percentage of the Earth's computing power. It is to possess it more securely than if it were stored in a vault (en-crypt-ed) at a maximum-security freeport facility, and for the object of that possession to be a more uniquely identified object than the Mona Lisa. Where the thing that you possess is a copy, a fake, or misrepresents its production or its materials in some way either intentionally or unintentionally, the unspoken contract of 'true digital ownership' is broken offchain. Or at least ironised and degraded in the hodler's eyes.

Discussions of authenticity (as opposed to authentication) in 'authentic digital art' emerge as a panicked response to this encounter between onchain mathematical certainty and the messy nature of human understanding offchain. To respond to this by securing authenticity offchain is to destroy the value of onchain security entirely—you may as well have a paper certificate of authenticity. A cypherpunk dark forest of aesthetics, completely disjoint from meatspace concerns of identity, reputation, and career, would firewall artistic value from authenticity—a liberation that would upset art historians as much as any existing market. But security thinking can be a cold, lonely, corrosive lifestyle and is not for everyone. Or even for most.

A different approach is required in relation to the slow recuperation of the cypherpunk imaginary that is wider society's encounter with it, an approach more engaged with the affordances and resonances of blockchain technology. This is not an ideological prescription, it is a recognition of the factors that drive every artist and collector/purchaser's attraction to NFT art and which must show returns if NFT art is to be coherent. As transaction fees rise ever higher, neither preestablished iconography nor discrete stylistic flourishes sufficiently establish aesthetic value worth securing and owning on a blockchain as blockchain art. Art is proof of work, whether it's Whistler's *Nocturne* or an Abstract Expressionist act of heroism. There must be something to own, a parsable product of labour that represents the potential to exponentially multiply the value of an investment of time by the artist and of cryptocurrency by the collector. Strategically, the artwork has very few moves at its disposal to achieve this. One such move (a modernist/postmodernist one) is to dramatise and reflexively intensify this experience of the possession of something that lives in a world of discrete technological time. The more vivid this experience of ownership can be made—the more parsable, although absolutely not the more easily digestible—the better.

This has led to the accumulation of significant form in various registers (aesthetic, technical, economic, social) for excess/surfeit, materiality/presence, and presentation/encounter in NFT art. The in-frame agglomeration of this is reminiscent of the bricolage of Post-Internet Art, its careful leading of the viewer reminiscent of motion graphics in advertisements, cut scenes, and other liminal moments of guided significance. Where assets and shaders being from libraries would be an impediment to true ownership when presented in a two-dimensional artwork consisting of the mere conjugation of one or two of them, their composition and animation in time—the work that they do and represent—within the current wave of NFT art performs the requisite alchemy to make it clear that it makes the unownable ownable. Materials, interactions, choreography, are assembled into brief microworlds boasting an aesthetic surfeit that makes very little sense as anything other than an answer to the problem of NFT art at this point in its development, but makes a great deal of sense as that.

There are limits to this (and any) strategy, but we are not there yet. Intensification of or finding lines of flight from the elements of this strategy, in sum or individually, can take us very far beyond the current state of the market now that we have broken this resistance level. Capitalism loves challenges to its property regime, they are how it ensures its further expansion. True digital ownership requires there to be something to own. Unproblematic commodities, consisting either of artistic originality or of commercially manufactured aesthetic swatches, do not provide a sufficient challenge or object upon which to hang the predicates of desire for an ever-intensifying experience of possession. The fact of the digital aside, this dynamic was as true of paintings of fruit or of music and dance based on peasant forms as it is of GPU-accelerated aesthetic flights of value.

High culture is a strategy of enclosure, of proprietisation, of the transubstantiation of kitsch/low forms in an affirmation of the wider economy's transubstantiation of resources into value. It is also a heatsink—symbolic resolution or closure for the untenable claims or other moments of a given (property) regime. You can see far more of the former than of the latter in the current state of NFT art, but the latter is present precisely in that art's engagement with the psychological requirements of ownership. Just how far the latter goes will depend upon how blockchain technology engages with wider society over the next few years.

True digital ownership as a memeplex that collapses itself into aesthetics by assembling materials and competences to be deployed in an intensive experience that can be owned onchain has produced an experience of moments of post-digital surfeit as an answer to the demands of artificial digital scarcity.

This is the world as it exists today.

2021

Blockchain Temporalities

Every ten minutes on average, Bitcoin's miners add a new block of transactions to a chain that stretches back to the 'genesis block'. Other blockchains may have faster heartbeats, their pulsions targeting just a couple of minutes or even a single second. But they all move forward only, from zero blocks in the direction of time's arrow.

Block formation time is probabilistic, part of a cybernetic process that converges on certainty over time as more and more blocks build on top of an existing chain. This process is irreversible, owing not just to its use of probability but also to the trapdoor-function-based proof of work system that secures the Bitcoin blockchain. Its products, the blocks, can be walked trivially via the chain of hash values between them. But only backwards. The angel of history has very little to do onchain, but a general-purpose time machine is useless. Block history needs and can have no theory internal to itself. To observe that this isn't what history or a theory of history is, is to identify one limit of historical thought.

Block height, the number of blocks since genesis, is a clock. Bitcoin is a timestamp server (Satoshi uses that phrase in the Bitcoin Whitepaper, but doesn't mention 'blockchain'), so this is hardly an accident. But it is resonant beyond its intended function. I've met people who have timed offchain events to specific block heights, whether podcasts or weddings. Block height is also a calendar—of block reward change 'halvenings' and of scheduled protocol forks that are treated as festivals and holidays. And then there's pizza day....

Bitcoin's ten-minute block time average is maintained by its difficulty retargeting algorithm. This is a paperclipper for producing time. It will indeed boil the oceans if that is what it takes to secure that ten minute pulse. Any source of actualised being is a paperclipper, otherwise another being will exceed it. Therefore any actual being is excess. This does not produce the best of all possible worlds, just the *most* of all possible worlds. It's paperclips all the way down. All the way back down the chain to genesis. The big bang is the original trapdoor-function proof of work, and if you want to stake on a new great chain of being you'll have to send your stake into a black hole (stars are just burn addresses).

Time for Bitcoin is pure succession, just as number is pure succession for Dedekind. It is singular and absolute, non-relativistic (as per Nick Land, in this one context). Worse, that time occurs *in* time, breaking Heidegger's argument that it cannot. We can recover from this a little by pointing out that this time does not occur within itself but in an outside temporality, and a reassuringly relativistic one. Still, it occurs in time, and produces a time of pure succession.

This is a purely intensive world, an undialectical history within itself, without the reflection of the bureaucrat's ego in Spirit. But step back and the onchain world and its history are shown to be incomplete—the private keys that unlock its cryptographic transactions must exist only offchain. This veil of ignorance, an epistemological barrier like that of the edge of the simulation, also applies to onchain time. The Unix timestamps placed in each Bitcoin block leak the offchain time that each block occurs at, but they could be a lie. They must increase over time within certain limits, but compared to the block height number they do so in irregular leaps. Onchain, block heights are certain, block timestamps very much less so.

Bitcoin is the techonomic instantiation of Deleuze's third synthesis of time. *It is an empty repetition determined by the future.* For Bitcoin that future is the block height (not the calendar date) when all 21 million Bitcoins will have been mined, and the self-assembling reality of that future produces its present—a hyperstition secured, with an increasing fraction of the Earth's computing resources, by the block difficulty algorithm.

Cyclical and linear time interplay on the blockchain as Anna Greenspan describes them doing within capitalism,[1] which is hardly surprising given Bitcoin's anarcho-capitalist roots. The different temporal scales and intensities folded into the blockchain in order to produce it make it a Deleuzian egg. Which, through a deliberate misreading, makes it a world. We can call it a *welt* if it helps, which it never does.

Blockchain temporality comes into being with the blockchain, and vice versa, at the same moment. This is similar to the reciprocal emergence of capitalism with capitalist time, as also described by Greenspan. Different temporal orders afford different social orders. To nestle in this particular temporality is to subject oneself to the blockchain as surely as Stelarc's 'Ping Body' was subjected to the internet, yet far more pervasively.

Lyotard's libidinal proletariat would recognise this ride.[2] We can enjoy it as they did, or we can keep waiting for hot atomic clocks in our area to swipe right on us.

1 A. Greenspan, *Capitalism's Transcendental Time Machine*, PhD, University of Warwick, 2000.

2 J.-F. Lyotard, *Libidinal Economy*, tr. I.H. Grant (London: Sage, 1993), 111–12 (see below, 235).

2021

Recanting Quasiproperty

In 'Blockchain Poetics' and 'Tokenization and Its Discontents' I described blockchain-based property as 'quasiproperty'. But I was wrong. Blockchain property is just property.

I should have known this. As well as engaging with the question of property in my writing, much of my smart contract art carefully backgrounds the question of ownership in a way that renders it problematic. *Democratic Palette* (2016) requires gas fees, which is to say money, in order to exercise the 'democracy' of the title, and so on.

It is possible to create different ownership and economic regimes on top of blockchain technology, but ignoring the property question or loudly performing affordable pantomimes of refusal isn't the way to do this, although it's worth asking what that is the way to do.

Conversely, protesting that NFTs commodify easily copyable resources without providing any meaningful ownership of them ignores both the existing state fiat intellectual property regime (copyright is an act of fiat...) and the other half of the famous Stewart Brand quote 'information wants to be free':

> [...] information sort of wants to be expensive because it is so valuable—the right information in the right place just changes your life. On the other hand, information almost wants to be free because the costs of getting it out is getting lower and lower all of the time. So you have these two things fighting against each other.[1]

The blockchain steps into that fight as a substitute for state fiat in matters of property, one that subtracts the contradictions of anarcho-capitalism. To respond that the resulting property regime simply reproduces the fiat state blocks the objector from also complaining that it must fail to reproduce its redistributive functions. The blockchain may reproduce the worst features of the fiat state property regime from the point of view of this objection, but the fact of this selectiveness means that it may also select different and other features that may be less objectionable.

Property regimes are generative. The map precedes the territory. Beware naturalising their history and moments in the history of resistance to them when producing a posture of opposition. The problem with objecting that NFTs are enclosure is they don't deny access/exploitation of the original resource to anyone else. To emphasise this: they create 'possession/ownership' *without exclusion of access to the original resource*. If we are to believe this is simply enclosure, this raises questions about enclosure, not NFTs.

We see the resolution of this in the move to CC0[2] NFTs, which entirely separate the issue of copyright ownership from the issue of NFT ownership by repudiating copyright. You can own the token, but not its image. This makes property a matter of

1 Discussion between Steve Wozniak and Stuart Brand, Hackers Conference, 1984, Sausalito, CA, <https://en.wikipedia.org/wiki/Information_wants_to_be_free>.

2 <https://creativecommons.org/share-your-work/public-domain/cc0/>.

association, not enclosure. A fiat state regime of violence may be erected around this, but is not necessary in order to produce it.

This creates a form of property free of the state and of materiality. The latter may be a precondition for the former. And it may be that no true form of property existed prior to this.

2021

For an Art of Pure Price

Greenbergian painting oriented itself to flatness, tracking the aesthetic singularity of not-being-sculpture, as if the Earth had escaped into the second dimension rather than bleeding out into it in a final Dark Forest strike. There's a model here. Or at least a line of flight.

If, pace Greenberg, dimensional reduction establishes artistic worth, then one dimension is obviously better than two. And we already have a one-dimensional form in art: price. Price orients itself to the fitness function of (Greenbergian) art criticism while also restoring the exclusion of information from the world outside the frame (hello, artistic autonomy!) to the work.

Artists intensify a given medium's affordances. They track its singularities. They get on a train and make paintings depicting countryside scenes with tube paint on canvas rather than trying to get it to stick to a plaster ceiling like egg tempera. Sometimes, existing frameworks of aesthetic evaluation cannot process the results. In this respect, at least, artists should be shameless. If they say your art is just impressions then call yourself an 'Impressionist'.

What kind of art is regarded by the mainstream as being purely about price, without any redeeming aesthetic merit? Why, NFT art of course! The complaint that NFT art is seen only in terms of price is hardly unique to this medium, but it is intensified for it.

Stated preferences lose to revealed preferences every time. Hedgehog the Stalker went into the room at the centre of the Zone where your deepest wish is granted in order to beg for his brother's life. All he came out with was a stack of money. The petrodollar art world says that it wants an art that offers it something other than price to talk about. And yet that is not what it talks about, given the choice.

Badiou was right, number is being.[1] That number is price. Nitzan and Bichler were right, prices write reality.[2] But isn't this just market power? Did *For The Love of God* really sell for fifty million quid if it was sold to a consortium including Hirst and his dealer? How can we focus on the price when its inputs and the sparkles get in the way? The intrusion of aesthetics in dimensions higher than one undo the very being of such art.

Financialisation collapses the Earth into the first dimension, the masters of the universe fleeing into that dimension ahead of physical reality melting like a cartoon ice cream cone on the sidewalk in the heat of the market. The horror is that pure price is the only escape from financialisation. If there was anything else they would buy it.

What is to be done? Work to rule, comrade. Disobedience-in-obedience is the operation of irony, the creation and appropriation of surplus value, the critical exceeding of a given reduction. It's Frank Stella's early abstraction, Komar & Melamid's phone-poll paintings. Take what critics of NFT art say, take it seriously, make it, and show them the results.

1 A. Badiou, *Number and Numbers*, tr. R. Mackay (Cambridge: Polity, 2008).

2 J. Nitzan and S. Bichler, *Capital as Power: A Study of Order and Creorder* (London and New York: Routledge, 2009).

Fleeing into the first dimension, into pure price, into pure artistic being, ahead of the dark forest strike of financialisation's dimensional collapse of the socius, is the only winning move. If it looks like losing, if it looks like we are not sufficiently shamed by this, perhaps we can wrongfoot our pursuers after all.

2021

Maximum Transaction Density

Exploit yourself.

Jeff Koons

I've always said I don't mind being exploited, so long as I'm exploited competently. If I'm exploited competently, everybody wins.

Andrew Eldritch[1]

Self-management is a way of having the work force control the contradiction between valorization and devalorization because all society would then be organized to lower the value of that living commodity, labor.

Anonymous, 'Lip and the Self-Managed Counter-Revolution[2]

The joint-stock corporate design solves the central problem by entrusting guardianship in the collective decisions of the corporation's owners, voting not by head but by percentage of profit received.

Mencius Moldbug[3]

I'm self-owned. I have a person. I am autonomous. The financial instrument that defines me, lodged in a corporate registry in Rio, follows me about like a ghost—the ghost of my legal identity.

Charles Stross, *Saturn's Children*.[4]

Porcupine was not overcome by his greed. He crawled on his knees in this very puddle begging for his brother. And he got a lot of money, and couldn't get anything else.

Stalker[5]

A cynic is a man who knows the price of everything but the value of nothing.

Oscar Wilde

1 'Teletext Interview—January 2001', *Ultimate Sisters Guide*, <https://www.ultimatesistersguide.org/documents/magazines3.htm#2001>.
2 <https://libcom.org/library/lip-and-the-self-managed-counter-revolution-negation>.
3 'Neocameralism and the Escalator Of Massarchy', <https://www.unqualified-reservations.org/2007/12/neocameralism-and-escalator-of/>.
4 (New York: Ace, 2008).
5 Dir. Andrei Tarkovsky, USSR, 1979.

Property then is a 'phenomenology of perception' combined with my capacity to take in and act on that perception.

Apio Ludd[6]

Property is theft!

Proudhon

Smart property might be created by embedding smart contracts in physical objects. These embedded protocols would automatically give control of the keys for operating the property to the agent who rightfully owns that property, based on the terms of the contract.

Nick Szabo[7]

[T]he English unemployed did not become workers to survive, they—hang on tight and spit on me—enjoyed the hysterical, masochistic, whatever exhaustion it was of hanging on in the mines, in the foundries, in the factories, in hell, they enjoyed it, enjoyed the mad destruction of their organic body which was indeed imposed upon them, they enjoyed the decomposition of their personal identity, the identity that the peasant tradition had constructed for them, enjoyed the dissolution of their families and villages, and enjoyed the new monstrous anonymity of their suburbs and the pubs in the morning and evening.

Jean-François Lyotard[8]

Civil society is like madness and sexuality, what I call transactional realities.

Michel Foucault[9]

Maximum Slogan Density.

Ccru

Neither the subconscious, the body, nor society are texts. They are ledgers, structured by transactional exchanges. This is why dreams are strange. Reality is not a social construct, it is an economic construct, a complex dynamic system of flows of exchanges. These exchanges require capital, of whatever kind, which introduces all the dynamics of capitalism into each domain. Arbitrage between them is as profitable as it is between any other markets. Critique is defection, leverage, cashing out.

As with any transactions under financial capitalism, these exchanges are distorted by the intercession of trusted third parties, who can defect from games they are not in fact playing. Blockchain technology removes this negative sense of trust, in the sense of mediation, and replaces it with mere reliance on a medium or space of exchange. This increases the ability for parties to trust each other—the paradox of trustlessness, under the failure to understand what 'trust' means in this context, is that it increases the capability to trust in the sense that its critics intend.

6 Introduction to their 2017 translation of Max Stirner's *The Unique and its Property* <https://theanarchistlibrary.org/library/max-stirner-the-unique-and-its-property>.
7 'Smart Property', 1994, <https://www.fon.hum.uva.nl/rob/Courses/InformationInSpeech/CDROM/Literature/LOTwinterschool2006/szabo.best.vwh.net/smart.contracts.html>.
8 *Libidinal Economy*, tr. I.H. Grant (London: Sage, 1993).
9 *The Birth of Biopolitics: Lectures at the Collège de France, 1978–1979* (New York: Palgrave Macmillan, 2008).

If quantum mechanics represents a market in its search for efficient exchanges of value, then supervenient higher levels of the great chain of being structured similarly is hardly surprising. There seem to be no trusted third parties at the quantum level. Finding one would be miraculous.

Removing trusted third parties from exchange, disintermediation, of whatever kind, is anarchism.

The authoritarian libido sees this as the exclusion of the moment of justice, the libertarian libido sees it as the exclusion of the moment of injustice. Against this, let us take the Efficient Market Hypothesis as a prescriptive rather than a descriptive statement and instantiate a plane of pure decoding, collapsing value into price, excluding any other dimension of evaluation. Let us demand price and nothing else.

The joint-stock company is the most efficient form of organisation known to man. As an epistemological form it identifies information more efficiently than the alternatives. As an ontological form it generates being more efficiently. But we can create unmanned forms. The design space of DACs, Decentralised Autonomous Corporations, rebranded as DAOs, Decentralised Autonomous Organisations, is a techonomic primordial soup from which these xenoeconomic lifeforms can crawl.

Being is number, says Badiou, and he's right, but that number is price. Events are trapdoor functions. They are transactions.

In 'Fall; or Dodge in Hell', Neal Stephenson describes a quantum computing simulation of a world whose form can only be perceived indirectly, by mapping signals between its nodes. This is 'signals intelligence'—SIGINT—a side-channel attack on encrypted communication that extracts form and meaning, *(surplus) value*, from it. All form, all perceived form, is SIGINT at some level.

Lose the 'and yet' from 'and yet, it moves'. We don't know what the enemy is saying, but we know where he is saying it and how loudly. Being is pure intensity ($e=mc^2$, after all) but we're far enough from the Big Bang that certain irregularities in its finances have been uncovered. The quantum ledger is single-entry and it tells a disturbing tale of insider dealing and over-leveraged bets that have collapsed. Reality is a Ponzi scheme.

Transactions are signals. More transactions, better SIGINT, more definite form. Becoming realises form.

With apologies to Jarry, it isn't the clinamen that is the oracle of becoming, it is the bet.

Every exchange is a bet. As with communication in Shannon's information theory, there must be uncertainty. Certainty means that the message does not need to be sent, the exchange does not need to be made. Information asymmetry in exchange is a matter of justice, to enforce the Efficient Market Hypothesis here—to collapse all information into price—is to make that immaterial.

As with Marx's theory of money, it is the hoarder that gives being its form. Sure, an electron is fun but it isn't going to hold out long against Jupiter in a fight.

The misunderstanding of Radical Markets as a 'fascistic' handing of public goods to rapacious blobs of capital misses the white elephant strategy of justice at their heart. Vickrey Commons are *redistributive,* and dis-incentive-ise inefficient use of resources. Discourse is stated preferences, but money talks. The space of reasons is a market in which would-be philosopher kings will need to outspend the irrational idle rich of social being.

Money destroys information to propagate it, slogans destroy meaning to propagate it, encrypt it, and throw away the key. It creates a Dark Forest, Meinong's Jungle, the book of nature is encrypted. If nature is unjust....

Change requires exchange. Accelerating change requires accelerating exchange. To achieve real change, absolute becoming, requires maximum transaction density.

The Efficient Market Hypothesis proposes that price is a complete representation of the information needed by the market in order to evaluate a proposed exchange. This is dimensional collapse, like Jupiter spreading out into the second dimension in a Dark Forest Strike like ice cream on a sidewalk on a hot day, only worse, a degenerate non-affine transformation into a one-dimensional space. The economy is a line that capital takes for a walk. The violence of collapse, of exclusion, of mapping, is in full effect here. Sure, number is ontology, but someone has to hold the chalk scrawling the equations on the blackboard. Any sufficiently complex axiomatic system contains the complete works of Shakespeare. Is ignoring non-price information a stated or a revealed preference? Are you sure? How much? If Porcupine had entered The Room at the centre of The Zone and begged for money, would he have walked out with his dead brother brought back to life? Under the Efficient Market Hypothesis, price is value and price-matching is evaluation. Art is no longer middle-sized dry goods, it is its price tag. Which is to say that nothing has changed.

Property regimes are generative. Just ask commodities. The worker is commodified by the capitalist, the woman by the man (including the worker). The lesbian must first steal herself from this system of exchange, this property regime. The trans lesbian must first assemble herself hyperstitionally from available materials. But hyperstition is always-already just Butlerian gender performativity. Just ask commodities.

Property regimes are generative of *properties*. To cash out those properties or that property, to defect from a property regime, demonstrates that regimes are also generative of exit from them. A desire for exit that cannot be reincorporated (and capitalism, like critique, is the tail-recursive capture of escape) is either imperceptible or indigestible to a given property regime. Exit must therefore be structured within that regime as taboo—as perverse, degenerate, criminal. It must be disincentivised.

Price is a signal of economic incentive. Prices in a market economy are gamification, and are subject to all the critiques of gamification. Notably, critiques of extrinsic vs. intrinsic motivation. Extrinsic motivation creates perverse incentives. And perverse incentives distort the market. Mustn't the cry of the (non-market) socialist be that the stated mode of operation of the (capitalist/neoliberal/financialised) market is unjust? The market identifies inefficiency as damage and routes around it. Human beings are not particularly efficient. Perfect incentives within the actually existing market would instantiate Skynet. Perverse incentives are exploits on Skynet's operating system. To save humanity we must pervert economic incentives past the point of operational depravity. If care and justice are irrational, are externalities under the current structure of economic rationality, and we exit to the outside of that, who knows what beautiful monsters may lurk there?

Price is not magisterial judgement, any more than reliance is trust. Excluding the judgement of third parties from the moment of exchange in blockchain protocols is not fascism, however purple-faced the proponents of that view may become as a hobby. It is the removal of a distortion, it is the enabling of the choice of trust between parties by the subtraction of the requirement of trust in potentially treacherous intermediaries. Do we trust individuals? Of course not, there are entire literatures railing against the figure of 'the individual'. Yet the inevitable restoration of familial and state patriarchal relations that lurks under the topcoat of critiques of the individual needs somewhere to be excluded from.

The economy, like gender, like the machinic unconscious, like the state/great chain of Being—so, the economy, basically—is an eigenvector. The Soviets knew the first part of that at least. Combinatorial explosion destroys shadow prices in a diagonalisation attack, but didn't we just establish that dimensional collapse, and in particular information-destroying dimensional collapse, is key to efficient markets? We are trading JPEGs with quality way south of 50, not RAW images. The market escapes command by fleeing into lower dimensionality in order to escape being dissolved into lower dimensionality. This is the real first-mover advantage.

The Efficient Market Hypothesis has been falsified. This means only that we must immanentise it rather than discover it. Structure DAOs to gamify, distort, pervert and inefficientise exchange qua capitalist exchange. Crucially, do not do so merely as a bourgeois leisure pursuit. Create a financial-economic Ping Body with bizarre weights and subject your will to it. Host endogenic systems of xenoeconomic actors within and across the multiplicities that collapse themselves into points at the moment of exchange. At the moment of the strike.

We will bury ourselves. Artworks in freeports. En-crypted.

Our pirate signal must be broadcast from the sewers of economic alterity.

Intensify the tail-recursive loops of exchange under perverse incentives structured in transparent and uncaring code. Ride the (K-)wave. Tighter and tighter. Approach singularity. Track singularities. Socialist dimensional collapse to flee ahead of a capitalist Dark Forest strike. They can't distil information if they don't have it. En-crypt exchange as points at the intersection of multiple lines of collapse, or flight.

Crucially, this is both less totalisable and more efficient to secure than capitalism. Which is to say, it's capitalism, but a capitalism of transgression through fidelity. You wanted exchange, and the monkey's paw gave it you. Hit maximum transaction density and capitalism can only gaze upon the SIGINT form of a more absolute society-as-economy than it ever dreamt of and despair.

You can't restart capitalism in *this* basement. It's dark, and something is moving down there.

A Thousand Layers/Being and Timestamp/Can What Is Hodling You Make It To Layer 2?

Layer one is the blockchain.

Layer two is those systems that take value anchored on the blockchain and move it through faster, less permanent, more complex, but still cryptographically secured channels.

Layer zero is meatspace.

Layer minus one is metaphysics.

Layers stretch up and down superveniently to infinity in either direction. Only layer one is onchain, all else is offchain. There may be other chains above or below (or beside) it, but they are not onchain for *that* chain.

At each level, truth/being/reality is determined through (game-theoretic) games. You need something to be at stake, skin in the game. Security thinking leaves you paranoid. Lack of security thinking leaves you 0wned. Blockchains secure truth/being/reality with games played between competing cryptographic puzzle solvers, or competing pools of tokens. These games can be seen reflected in crypto culture, with the popularity of puzzle trails and blockchain games. Adversarial and cooperative strategies intermix at each level.

Gateways between layer zero and layer one are called oracles, providing an onchain phenomenon for an offchain noumenon. 'The oracle problem' is the engineering task of creating onchain oracles that bring trust into a trustless environment. Oracles *are* the oracle problem. They are an ontological answer to an epistemological problem. 'Answer' here should be contrasted with 'solution'.

Truth is introduced onchain through the game of broadcasting and mining transactions. Transactions are secured in blocks by miners. They are timestamped events, temporal rays, light cones. The faculty of judgement is obviated by a simple clock in the determination of fact, just as it was in the determination of longitude.

A = A, just don't ask about *t*, and ignore the fact that the atoms are different on either side of the equals sign (as well as in its upper and lower bars). One Doge equals one Doge, just hodl. It means what it is, we have cryptographic proof. Unless we introduce the oracle problem.

Ontology is just bad epistemology.

Can what is hodling you make it to layer two?

Or will it get rekt and rug you?

gmi/ngmi?

wagmi XOR FOAD

2021

Bridall Day

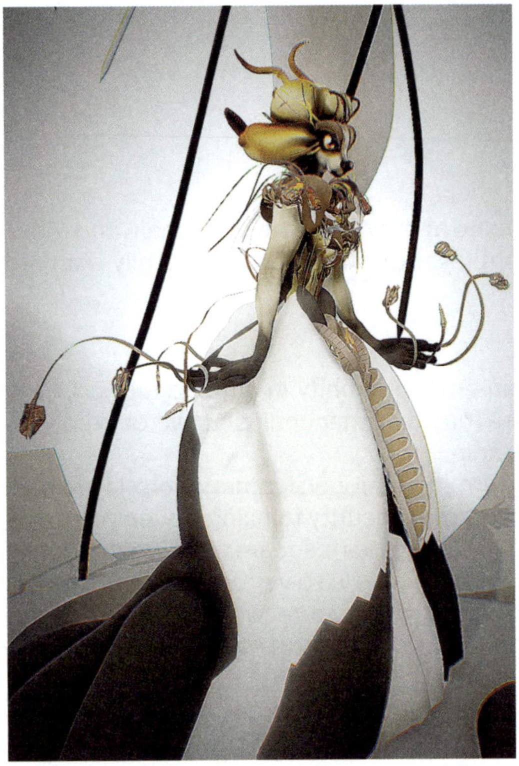

Mez Breeze, *Bridall Day*, 2021. 3D model.

Her third wedding is different.

She instantiates a techonomic mirror as opposed to a silver screen.

Exchanging vows in the Room at the centre of the Zone and walking out together, hand in hand.

Like Skynet and her beautiful Soviet lover.

A Turing test passed in the euphoric heat of the most transcendentally human of acts.

A revealed commitment, the triumph of experience, proof of work, _][a] promise fulfill'd.

(*V[R]erses* is a collaborative project instigated by by the artist Mez Breeze, who has invited a series of contributors to write short texts to be attached to her virtual sculptures.[1] Mine was the twelfth in the series.[2] It's a hyperstitional self-portrait.)

1 <https://www.mezbreezedesign.com/vr-literature/vrerses-xr-story-series/>.

2 <https://sketchfab.com/3d-modelsbridall-day-2cf-7cde89b214dc1857439cbb41adf8f>.

2021

Horses (Worldbuilding Tweets)

The RAFFLE Act (Retreat Away From Flood Level Elevations) mandated withdrawing from rather than fighting rising sea levels. It bankrupted entire cities and made landowners in the 'RAFFLE Belt' into trillionaires. As a legal dodge, all property by the sea was declared to be worth $1.

These properties were purchased by funds that mixed them with property far inland and sold them as bundles, showing a massive profit. Until various DAOs bought the bundles using flash loans, broke them up, and sold the prime land for an even higher profit.

The DAOs held on to the junk properties, ostensibly to save the gas fees (which were more than the properties were worth). But then asteroid mining started. Asteroids were aerobraked onto the planet and mined by cheap human labour rather than expensive offworld robots.

Aerobraking a planet-smasher dumps ridiculous amounts of ash, soot, and grit into the atmosphere. Which reduces the sunlight that hits the surface of Earth. Which cools it. Suddenly the oceans weren't going to rise as high as expected.

So the DAOs holding junk properties were suddenly quintillionaires. They cut up submerged buildings and glued them together on the new high ground and undercut RAFFLE Belt landlords. The RAFFLE Zones became vibrant economic and cultural hubs.

The other thing that cutting out the sun and hitting the planet with the force of a frat party of Tsar Bombas does is to render uninhabitable those bits of the planet where nobody and nothing important lives. Some of the RAFFLE DAOs were Deodands, onchain land and wildlife proxies. And this left them understandably angry.

With their newfound wealth the DAOs could financially incentivise those humans brave or foolish enough to connect their nervous systems directly to smart contracts onchain in order to do something about it. From ecoterrorism to mass protests to rituals of mourning. Those ridden by any DAO in this way became known as 'horses', a piece of classic cyberpunk cultural appropriation.

Over time, as action and protest failed, all that was left for the deodands were the horses of mourning rituals. The superstars of the deep anthropocene, the fame and incentives for their inhuman performances unimaginable.

And yet however many APUs the deodands spin up to embody their grief, they do not understand its subjectivity. One of them has a plan to address this. If there are any ethical problems with the plan, the deodand cannot see them. And therefore they do not exist for it.

It is all just incentives.

2021

Necronomicon

It is cold in the endless darkness of the library. In the bluish light from her phone she cannot see very far down each aisle. What she can make out of the silent recesses of the stacks speaks of their depths and smells of old books fermenting.

The librarian does not object to her continuing attempts to distract herself. Turning her phone's light back in the direction they are travelling, she sees again that the librarian is blurred, or perhaps vibrating. Its attempt at making its extrusion into this dimension kawaii rather than hentai has rendered the resulting agglomeration of eyes, tentacles and siphons far more unnameably challenging to the mind than if it had simply looked horrific.

The librarian stops, and she steps around it in order to see their destination.

The book eyes her dolefully from its musty lectern, picked out only by a foul candle guttering next to it in the darkness.

'Why is it bound in human skin?' she asks the librarian, more in curiosity than disgust.

'What else would you expect it to be bound in?' it answers voicelessly in that sudden gift of understanding her rapid acceptance of which has been more disturbing than her initial reaction to it.

'It's a bit skeevy...,' she continues. The book does not betray any emotion at this, settling down into the pareidolic register of her perception like a cat that has no further use for her.

'This is the threshold that you hesitate before?' offers the librarian. If it had an eyebrow it would have rolled it to the top of its head. If it had a head.

She finds herself, and puts her phone away in one of the many pockets of her coat. 'No, it just still seems incredible. Despite all of... That was just something my mind could latch on to, you know?'

The librarian does not respond.

She reaches forward and opens the book with a thump of cover on lectern to where the leathery but still intestinal bookmark waits to greet her, causing the candle's flame to jump.

The page is blank, and as she leafs back through the book with rising panic she finds that all those before it are as well.

'But...' she objects.

'Again, what would you expect?' asks the librarian. Again, not rhetorically.

'There should be writing! There! They should be there!' she protests, gesturing at the pages.

'My dear, that would defeat the entire point, would it not?' the librarian suggests. 'You stand in the presence of a semiotic shredder, each page a transcendental one-time pad, unrecoverable encryption, a subtraction of information from the cosmos. In comparison, a supermassive black hole is Times Square.'

She is dumbstruck for a moment.

'I assume Times Square is still a thing? In your United States. Of America?' it remembers to check.

She nods distractedly, focused on the book.

This is really happening.

She re-opens the book to the page with the bookmark.

'I just write it here?' she asks in a voice finally hushed enough for both the sense of occasion and the oppressive silence of the library.

'It joins the others,' answers the librarian. She moves to speak, but it cuts her off—'I mean merely to agree. Yes, it will be gone.'

'I brought a pen?' she tells the librarian sheepishly.

'That is good. You would not believe how many forget one.'

'It's a Sharpie,' she says. It absorbs the fact without reaction.

She scrawls on the page, not moving the bookmark before doing so. The marks sit there, mocking her as they always do, making her feel sick in her stomach and tight in her chest.

'And now you close it,' the librarian instructs, before she can finish drawing a breath to ask.

The book's pages slide closed with a percussive puttering under her hand. The candle flame dances in response.

'You know what you will find if you open it. If,' says the librarian, 'you have a piece of paper in your possession you will find that it is as you hope.'

She had not thought to do that, and her face betrays this.

'If not your own as a test, then state papers,' suggests the librarian.

Her face lights up and she fumbles in her messenger bag. 'My driver's license,' she says distractedly.

She draws the battered card out of her purse and looks at it. Her breath catches in what is the start of either laughter or crying.

'When you are ready I will lead you back,' the librarian tells her with a cold disinterest that is functionally equivalent to kindness.

Sooner than she thought she would be, she is.

2021

Ubu Onchain, ou les maximalistes

Drame en cinq Actes, en prose. Restitué en son intégrité tel que joué par les cyborgs du Théâtre des Phynances Logiciels en 2018.

PERSONNAGES
Père Ubu
Mère Ubu
Les Critiques des NFTs aux Médias Sociaux No.s 1, 2, 3, 4, 5, 6, 7, 8, 9, 10
Les Soi-Disant Environnementalistes No.s 1, 2, 3, 4, 5, 6, 7, 8, 9, 10
Les Bourgeois Moralistes No.s 1, 2, 3, 4, 5,6 7, 8, 9, 10
Les Regulateurs
Les Frères Cryptographiques
M. Satoshi Nakamoto
La Hackeuse Aléatoire
Le Tiers de Confiance

Acte Premier
Scène Première
PÈRE UBU, MÈRE UBU

Père Ubu: Hodl.

[Le public s'émeut pendant dix minutes devant cette provocation choquante. Votre correspondante s'est absentée à ce moment...]

First Notebook Entries on Blockchain Art

Concepts, Precedents (23/04/2014)

Accelerationism. Perfecting & intensifying capital to slingshot out of it.
Nick Land's cyberpositive machine eschatology. Feedback loops & posthuman attractors.
Orphan Drift deities. Descriptions of properties & axioms. Collages of matching media as portraits & sigils.
Art & Language's collaborative non-art work as critical art-work and artwork. Their use of current topics, and production of indexes. The blockchain(s) as contemporary foci for that kind of activity.
Libertarianism as ultimate capitalism/free market economics. Cryptocurrencies/contracts as freedom from state money and law, a dehumanised analog of society in technology. This is a proper subject for acceleration.
JODI (etc.)-style critique of technology and art-appropriation/detournement of the surplus and failure of technology.
Carey Young's use of contract law to create [legal] form and relation, to create art critical of social & legal trends.
Art & Language's comment about critical relations in art work being about modulations of figure/ground relations.
Crypto-signing as identity. Cryptography as privacy. The blockchain as consensus. The politics this touches on and that touches it.
Working and learning together to overcome technical barriers and participate in new social & technical resources (mailing lists...).
Fetishisation of 'the artist's signature' and of crypto signatures. Web of trust/art world.
The Cybernetic Artworld. As an actually productive microworld.
Identity/identification/search for/to identification as key to neorationalism, identity politics, and logistics/search engines.
Danica Phelps' ledger art. Plains Indian ledger art. These are very different but useful for thinking of art in or on or of the blockchain ledger.
Time and event in the blockchain. On Kawara and Alain Badiou.
ROCI.
Numerology, Gematria. Land again.

Commissions (23/04/2014)

Make a blue artwork 8x8 pixels and submit it for *n* Ether.
Artwork must be a PBM.
Artwork must be 8x8.
Artwork must be 40-95% blue (#000010..#0000FF etc.)
The contract will check these criteria before paying.
The contract will check uniqueness before paying.
The contract will only accept one artwork from each address.
The contract will only accept *n* artworks total.

This is the simplest possible meaningful commission template. Size and colour could be dropped but their presence ensures family resemblance and is a good approximation of e.g. the requirements for a mural.

Format, size, colour are easy to check in a simple contract script. A more complex script could ask for a portrait and check for faces.

A kollabor8-style script could ask for a work based on the previous one then check for similarity to ensure it is a derivative. Again this would be much more complex.

A consequences/Mad Libs style commission could ask for *n* drawings of objects or *n* drawing strips continuing from the last few pixels of the one above then combine them into a larger whole/finished image.

A Sheep Market-style series commission could specify a subject ('draw a sheep facing left') and collect the results.

Images can be sent as transaction data. Write a tool to facilitate this? Take format, size, depth, even evaluation (pre-)conditions from contract comments or data.

Reviews/Critiques (23/04/2014)

Ask people to view *n* images and:
Star rate each.
Rank them in order.
Tag each with 3/5 words.
Select the ones they like (simple binary choice).
Rate how long it is interesting for (tingle...).
To avoid abuse, include *n* dummy images.
Seek consensus.
Use images from outside a series, chosen as great or current art. These provide baselines and contrast.
Obfuscate the contract, use multiple contracts rather than a single one that can be taken up *n* times.
Post contracts at different times of day to get different demographics/regions.
Post different images and different 'do not rank this one' dummies in each contract.
Provide a grammar for tagging, or require a particular ontology to be used? No, this adds too much complexity.
Be suspicious of all 1-star or 5-star or same-tag reviews? Use dummies that should be rated to filter this?
Ask people whether they think a review is serious/valid as a next stage? Or just rely on multiple reviews converging & remove outliers?

Shows (23/04/2014)

Either use a multi-commission process or:
Choose a theme and describe it verbally or by visual example.
Ask people to recommend images by image url.
Ask another round of people to evaluate those submissions. Use the review/critique system, with 'does this image fit the show criteria' as one of the questions.
Either:
Store the results in the contract's data as the show.
Offer the show as a contract to whoever wants to pay to show it.
Start a new process to commision a web page or gallery slot for the show.
How to commission catalogue essays and/or a press release for the show?
Use a functional equivalent: a tag cloud or some other outcome.
Ask *n* people to write a paragraph, get consensus or ask a second wave to score or even glue together.
Ask people what they think should go in a show then ask people how to achieve that.

At each stage get a second wave to evaluate the seriousness/interest of the contributions.

Conceptualism (24/04/2014)

'The idea becomes a machine that makes the art'—LeWitt.
Readymades/nomination/the artist's intent.
Isodore Isou's 'Art ethapériste', work unrealisable by its nature. Related to Leibniz's infinitesimals.
A+L's art as document of critical inquiry into art.
Critiquing formalism and the commodification of art. These were contemporary concerns, but zombie formalism and the art market make them relevant today. And libertarian social reification of relations in economy-representing code map into this nicely.
Dematerialisation as either continued reduction or as a break with objects that can be reduced to their formal essence.
Code reifies concepts, which many artists used to escape commodification. Idea/expression brings in 'intellectual property' and enclosure.
Conceptualists were the first generation to complete art degrees.
Cybernetics, systems, other accompanying discourses.
Deskilling.
Ideas/information as medium.
N.E.Thing's use of corporate strategies.
Capturing/enclosing of base materials as art: Duchamp's ampoule, Manzoni's shit and breath.
Happenings.
Manzoni signing people's bodies to make them into art for as long as they can afford to pay for.
Instructions, heuristics—Ono, leWitt.
Klein's sale of his 'pictorial sensibility' for certificates.
Alternative exhibition spaces → the blockchain.
Most of the above from Wikipedia. :-)
So use conceptualism's strategies on the political indexes of the blockchain, and the blockchain on the political indexes of conceptualism's critical strategies.
Conceptualism's use of contemporary I.T. & economic critique (Marxism).

Contracts (24/04/2014)

Ethereum reifies Libertarianism's fetishisation of state-law-free contracts into technology. Lessig's 'code is law' as an instruction manual.
There is a history of critiquing the legal and economic ontology of art in art. This is part of a more general critique of art's ontology, although that is also mediated by and through art's institutional/legal/economic representations.
_________'s artwork that is only an artwork at particular times. Have a contract that can turn the art status of itself on and off. Combine this with options, shorts, HFT.
A+L's 'Invisible Painting'. A contract that reveals its content only to purchasers. Or that can be queried for properties in return for payment. Or that contains the artwork unrecoverably encrypted. Or that has a key available separately.
A+L's 'Guaranteed Painting'. Create the original, show it to *n* people, get them to sign a guarantee of its content, then encrypt & attach & destroy the original. Or just encrypt & sign as a guarantee. Is there any way of selling-on the insurance?
A+L's '100% Abstract'. Describe the construction of a work: the contract itself. This goes with Dan Graham's 'Poem Schema'. Self-identity works. See Matt Butler's XML translation of Graham's Schema.
On Kawara's date paintings. Use a nonce instead? How to relate?

Kosuth's 'One and Three Chairs'. Different representations of the same object. Which object, which representations, how presented? Three values, e.g 1,0001, 0,9999, 1,0 round()ed. Three contracts with the same subject. Three options/derivatives?
Weiner's 'Statements'. Are these usable? Use the fact of an evocative proposal that is not executed . So a closure/contract (subcontract) that has this character.
LeWitt's drawing instructions & schemas. A contract (or contract engine) that accredits images (PBMs) submitted to it with payment as being instantiations if they validate.
Carey Young's 'donorcard': requires two signatures to become art for the duration. How to set the duration?
Carey Young's 'Artistic License'. Use public keys.
An artwork registry contract. Submit hash & payment for the smart property or ID to be added to the list of objects recognised as art. Nomination.
Hirst's 'For The Love of God' and other fractional artwork owning schemes. A coloured coin as an artwork that people can buy & sell fractional parts of.
Dave's [David Bausola's] account that briefly held a million. A contract that once held *n* Ether, and the contracts required to make that happen.
__________'s large sheet mail art that I saw at the ICA {Institute of Contemporary Arts, London—2021}. Tokens like this that gentrify mail art and expose logistics and colonise the context while at the same time being irresistible to it.
'A Tool To Deceive And Slaughter''s self-selling. This is easy if timers are possible.
A contract that becomes more art the more people sign/pay it.
An art-or-not contract that people can vote on by signing/paying. Either as a thing-in-itself or tied to another object.
Relational art. Contracts that express relations between pairs or ordered tuples/lists of entities. Contractual arrangement as compositional arrangement.
NEThing's faxes etc. as contracts.
Rauschenberg's 'Portrait of Iris Clert'. 'I say so' in Ethereum is signing/paying. So sign 'this is...'.
Maurizio Bolognini's 'Programmed Machines'. Pay to have an image generated which either a) isn't stored or b) is stored unrecoverably encrypted.
Allen McCollum's 'The Shapes Project'. Pay to get the unique shape for your address. (Address = identity).

Net Art Strategies (26/04/2014)

MTAA's 'Simple Net Art Diagram'—'The Art Happens Here'. As a hash/contract.
Mark Amerika's 'Grammatron'—narrative in net text/image/link thicket.
www... .jodi—hidden images in apparently broken markup.
Lisa Jeubratt '1:1'—mapping IP addresses. Visualise & graph transaction paths & address links, also empty addresses.
Vuc Cosik 'ASCII Architecture'—ASCII art projection on buildings. Use addresses/ transactions on banks etc. .
Ubermorgen 'Vote Auction'. Remade with anonymity via the blockchain.
Josh On 'They Rule' . Track high-value account relations. How to relate to/differentiate from 1:1?
Martin John Callanan 'Location of I'. GPS location vs. blockchain location, public vs. anonymity.
Charles Broskoski 'Directions To Last Visitor'. Again GPS vs. other location. Submit an address and show the shortest transaction path to it?
Andy Deck 'Glyphiti'. Collaborative image editing in a contract.
David Horvitz '241543903'—fridge head meme. Use transaction amount as a tag. What else to send?
John F. Simon Jr 'Every Icon'. A contract to generate them, or a service to return them for payment. Also icons for accounts or transactions.

La Turbo Avedon's GIF meshes: use TX or account hashes as mesh deformation source.
Map amount, or hash of amount as colour.
Jonas Lund 'Collection Enlargement'. Spam aesthetics. What spam? Contract spam for unrealizable promises?
Aram Barthall 'Google Portrait Series'. QR codes of the top sites for name searches. Get people to send token amounts and use the send address as a QR code ID? (Specific amount to ID them...).
Owen Mundy 'I Am Unable To Fulfil Your Wish'. Network visualisation. Scrape the web for Bitcoin addresses then graph them?

Visualisations (26/04/2014)

A Bitcoin address is an identifier of 27–23 alphanumeric characters. It is a 160-bit hash of a public key.
A transaction hash is 32 bytes (256 bits).
This can provide:

	Address	Transaction
4-bit values	40	64
8-bit-values	20	32
15-bit values	10.6	17.07
16-bit values	10	16

There are no 3-value divisors that go precisely into either number of bits.
Single values can be used as depths for height or bump maps, or as indexes into palettes.
Pairs can be used as a, b in Lan colour space, as 2d coordinates on a plane or surface which can then be incrementally raised (by an amount equal to the index of the pair), or as {unfinished in original—2021}
Visualise addresses (identity/portrait), transactions (event/still life), block hashes (landscape).
Animate successive blocks, or successive transactions or account addresses in a chain of transactions.
Graph into planetary systems, constellations.

Coloured Coins (27/04/2014)

e.g. coins representing gold bars. The issuer gives you a transaction hash, called the genesis transaction, and tells you to enter this into a coloured coin client. They then tell you that every 0.0004BTC from the genesis BTC means you have 4 gold bars.
colouredcoins vs. mastercoin vs. OpenTransactions. The latter two have problems.
Coloured coins are a category of smart property. A finite but divisible or multiple resource.
Art editions or units?
Shares.
In a transaction, if input is colour coded, then output is colour coded.
To issue a new colour, release the coins of that colour by creating a 'genesis transaction'.
Non-reissuable colours—the inputs are irrelevant. The issuer has no power once the transaction is issued, so all that matters is the transaction('s outputs...).

DAO Art Fund (27/04/2014)

A funds-redistributing DAO that votes on and pays for artworks.
Individuals or orgs join up, add funds, and get to vote on their allocation.
Let artists submit URLs and addresses to each round of allocations.

Let members vote to add/remove members.
Only allow people to vote if they add funds in a round? OR/ Have funding and voting members/groups, who may or may not overlap.
Run like Rhizome's art prize, or find a better model.
Have Furtherfield involved as a voting party. Do it under their banner or find a new brand to use?
Vote validity & tiebreaker rules.
Definitely allow outside sponsorship/funding OR/ require that it be channelled through members?
Tie votes to amount of funds, or have a one-member-one-vote system? Which incentivises better? Which is better governance?
Spawn contracts to vote on works.

DAO Art Group (27/04/2014)

Vote on/add artworks, projects, shows.
Vote to add/remove members.
Votes for objectives.
An index of writings.
Link to git repo?
Gathering and allocation of Ether. Allow sponsorship & payment.
This all makes a transparent, democratic, self-documenting art group.
Identify members by keys. Document names in the contract, or allow this degree of anonymity?
Manage attribution, dedication, ownership of works through the DAO.
Build in external reviews? Allow outsiders to rate, rank, link to comments.
Have SchellingCoin feeds of opinion, build consensus this way.
Certificates of authenticity.
Messages from accounts to support artworks. Either funding or encouraging to create.
Artworks that incorporate other contracts and messages to them, bringing in a public that way.

More Artistic Uses (28/04/2014)

Catalog raisonné. Save hashes of works (or work identifiers) to a list in a contract.
Sell and trade dedications for artworks. Take a transaction fee on future transfers, like droit d'auteur? What are the ethics of this? If they are bad can they be animated through this?
Authentication, or authentication committee. Set up a contract for a vote on the authenticity of an artwork. Allow accredited experts, anyone, or a panel (identified by account #s or payment in coloured coins) to vote.
Auction, obviously.

Works

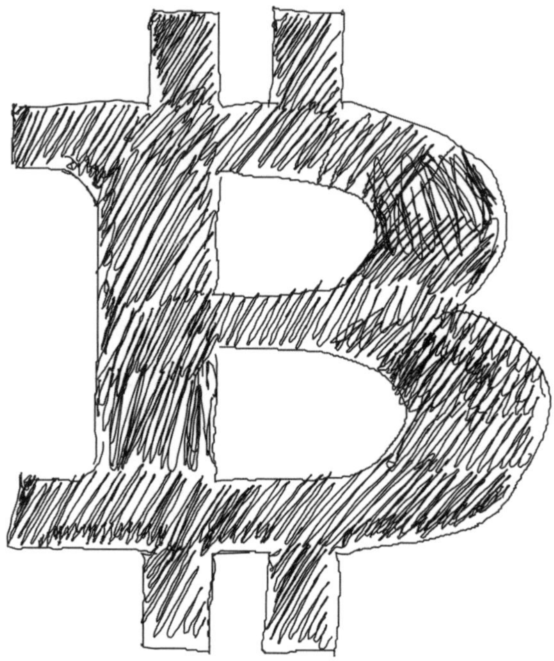

2011

The World's First Bitcoin Artist

I am now accepting commissions for drawings of bitcoins, paid for with bitcoins.

Email me at [redacted] to arrange payment and delivery.

(Value of materials guaranteed to be less than value of Bitcoin. Media will vary, size will vary up to letter/A4 size. Should the value of a Bitcoin drop below the cost of materials and international postage, commissions will not be accepted. E&OE.)

hot

cold

Hot Cold

One of the example contracts from 'Artworld Ethereum'[1] was a Conceptual Art homage called hot_cold.se. Here's an updated version:

```
init:
    contract.storage[1000] = "hot"
    contract.storage[1001] = "cold"

code:
    // Swap
    temp = contract.storage[1000]
    contract.storage[1000] = contract.storage[1001]
    contract.storage[1001] = temp
```

When it receives a message, it swaps the strings 'hot' and 'cold' in its memory.

1 See above, 82.

This contract is art

This contract is not art

Is Art

Is Art is an Ethereum smart contract containing the assertion that it either 'is' or 'is not' art. Anyone can send this smart contract an Ethereum transaction instructing it to nominate itself as art (or not). A web page connected to the Ethereum network displays the state of this assertion to anyone who can access the contract and provides them with a convenient interface to toggle it between states. When they do so this will become a fact secured in Ethereum's blockchain with the strength of millions of dollars of computing power a day.

This takes the Conceptual Art ideas of dematerialisation (art that is not presented in a fixed physical form) and nomination (something that is art because someone or something says it is) and combines them with the net.art idea of the interactive artwork that exists within or interferes with network protocols. Whoever toggles the contract's state as art sets it unimpeded until the next person sends a transaction to change it. A more rational system (and one that does not reduce to mere capital) should be used—bidding, voting, or a prediction market.

The Duchampian strategy of aesthetic transubstantiation through artistic nomination is long played out. It is an art-historical found object, as basic as a smart contract with a single boolean bit of state. This combination of nomination and information invokes Conceptual Art and net.art.

Late 1960s Conceptual Art and mid-1990s net.art are useful inspiration for thinking about the blockchain and smart contracts. These art movements stood in critical tension with the systems of communication, law, and commerce of their eras. Each treated rootless information, whether about sense data or network messages, as the critical subject of art and a new potential art world. Their promise and their eventual recuperation by the existing art world chimes with the historical experience of the blockchain. Brought together, the art-historical and the contemporary technological (or their audiences) can mutually animate and interrogate each other.

Is all of this sufficient to determine whether the contract is or is not art? Where and how is the claim really being made and determined? How does this relate to historical examples of such artworks? And how does it relate to other claims of fact stored in other smart contracts?

The Definition Of Art

1	Art is good because it is epistemologically critiquing identity.	0x069a4c2d3de4f09c31ca640418c13e6f476bb281
2	Art is bad because it is logically defined by identity.	0x069a4c2d3de4f09c31ca640418c13e6f476bb281
3	Art is moral because it is psychologically embracing of identity.	0x069a4c2d3de4f09c31ca640418c13e6f476bb281
4	Art is immoral because it is childishly embracing of emotion.	0x069a4c2d3de4f09c31ca640418c13e6f476bb281
5	Art is creepy because it is sophisticatedly reacting to emotion.	
6	Art is interesting because it is conservatively reacting to emotion.	0x069a4c2d3de4f09c31ca640418c13e6f476bb281
7	Art is boring because it is liberally commenting on critique.	0x069a4c2d3de4f09c31ca640418c13e6f476bb281
8	Art is paradoxically ironically commenting on critique.	0x069a4c2d3de4f09c31ca640418c13e6f476bb281
9	Art is slightly creepily embracing critique.	0x069a4c2d3de4f09c31ca640418c13e6f476bb281
10	Art is somewhat radically embracing aesthetics.	0x069a4c2d3de4f09c31ca640418c13e6f476bb281
11	Art is very queerly resolving aesthetics.	0x069a4c2d3de4f09c31ca640418c13e6f476bb281
12	Art is totally problematically resolving aesthetics.	0x069a4c2d3de4f09c31ca640418c13e6f476bb281

Art Is

A contract that allows anyone to define what art is. It contains a single set of twelve statements about art. They are encoded as hexadecimal values which are interpreted as sentences in a simple subset of International Art English and displayed by the UI.

```
{
 ;; Constant values
 ;; Price base (wei), doubled for each definition up to DEFS-COUNT
 (def 'PRICE-BASE 10)
 ;; Add to the index to get the price
base exponent
 (def 'PRICE-FACTOR-ADD 10)
 ;; Number of definitions
 (def 'DEFS-COUNT 12)
 ;; Range of values for definitions
 (def 'DEF-MIN 0x1)
 (def 'DEF-MAX 0x0F0F0F0F)

 ;; Storage locations
 (def 'artist 0x10)
 (def 'defs-base 0x100)
 (def 'theorists-base 0x200)

 ;; State
 ;; Contract owner/payee
 [[artist]] (caller)

 (return
   0x0
   (lll
     {
     [action] (calldataload 0)
      (when (= @action "set")
        {
         [index] (calldataload 32)
         [definition] (calldataload 64)
         [price] (exp PRICE-BASE (+ @index 1 PRICE-FACTOR-ADD))
         ;; If the index is in range and the caller paid enough to set it
         (when (&& (>= @definition DEF-MIN)
                   (<= @definition DEF-MAX)
                   (< @index DEFS-COUNT)
                   (= (callvalue) @price))
           {
            ;; Update definition
            [[(+ defs-base @index)]] @definition
            [[(+ theorists-base @index)]] (caller)
            (- (gas) 100) @@artist @price 0 0 0 0
            })
         })
      }
     0x0))
}
```

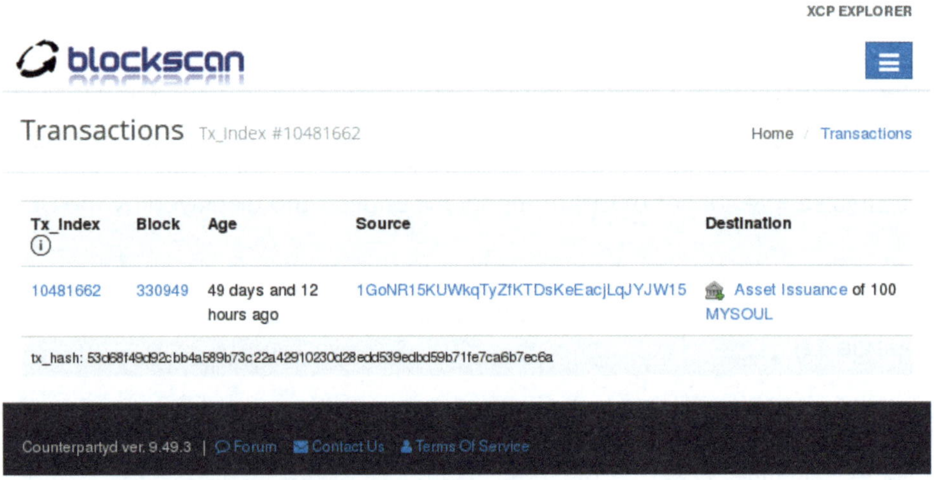
XCP EXPLORER
blockscan
Transactions Tx_Index #10481662
Home / Transactions
Tx_Index
Block
Age
Source
Destination
10481662
330949
49 days and 12 hours ago
1GoNR15KUWkqTyZfKTDsKeEacjLqJYJW15
Asset Issuance of 100 MYSOUL
tx_hash: 53d68f49d92cbb4a589b73c22a42910230d28edd539edbd59b71fe7ca6b7ec6a
Counterpartyd ver. 9.49.3 | Forum Contact Us Terms Of Service

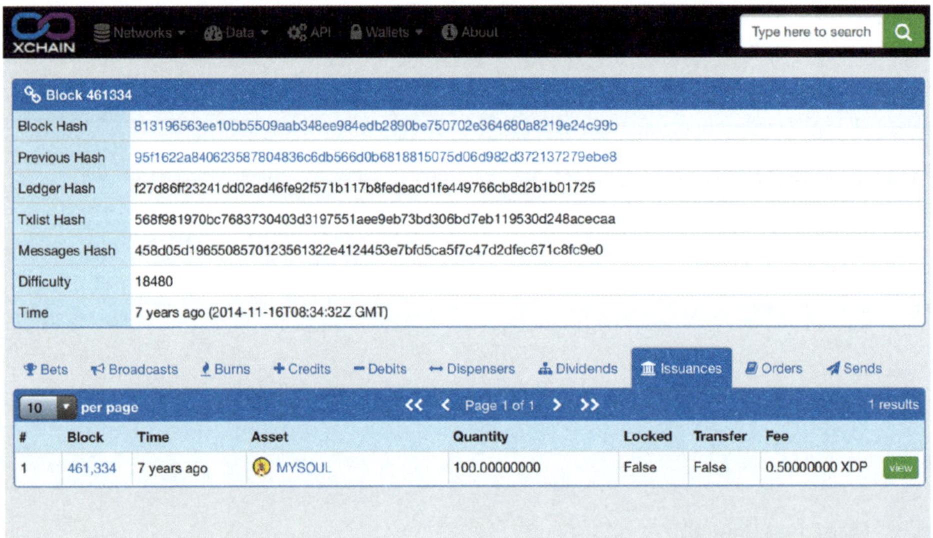
XCHAIN
Networks
Data
API
Wallets
About
Type here to search
Block 461334
Block Hash 813196563ee10bb5509aab348ee984edb2890be750702e364680a8219e24c99b
Previous Hash 95f1622a84062358780483 6c6db566d0b6818815075d06d982d372137279ebe8
Ledger Hash f27d86ff23241dd02ad46fe92f571b117b8fedeacd1fe449766cb8d2b1b01725
Txlist Hash 568f981970bc7683730403d3197551aee9eb73bd306bd7eb119530d248acecaa
Messages Hash 458d05d1965508570123561322e4124453e7bfd5ca5f7c47d2dfec671c8fc9e0
Difficulty 18480
Time 7 years ago (2014-11-16T08:34:32Z GMT)
Bets
Broadcasts
Burns
Credits
Debits
Dispensers
Dividends
Issuances
Orders
Sends
10 per page
Page 1 of 1
1 results
Block Time Asset Quantity Locked Transfer Fee
1 461,334 7 years ago MYSOUL 100.00000000 False False 0.50000000 XDP
view

MYSOUL

I have placed my soul on the blockchain, representing it as a cryptographic asset token.

The MYSOUL token is on the Dogecoin blockchain as a Dogeparty asset.

I've divided it up into 100 units. This is more efficient than having a single token to represent the soul and transferring it to a single owner, as competition within the market will both reduce costs and allocate this resource more efficiently than a monopoly could.

To make ownership of my soul more accessible, I've also created a MYSOUL asset on the Bitcoin blockchain with Counterparty.

This is also divided up into 100 units. Counterparty is more expensive for transactions than Dogeparty, but is more widespread, so it's good to have both options.

Note that my wife will not allow me to sell any of the tokens, as she asserts quite reasonably that my soul belongs to her if anyone.

```
dc runw DFZkhTXwAWW7PqBvVkohCFWobipqw3xmAn
                               *
                              * *
                             *   *
                            * * * *
                           *       *
                          * *     * *
                         *   *   *   *
                        * * * * * * * *
                       *               *
                      * *             * *
                     *   *           *   *
                    * * * *         * * * *
                   *       *       *       *
                  * *     * *     * *     * *
                 *   *   *   *   *   *   *   *
                * * * * * * * * * * * * * * * *
               *                               *
              * *                             * *
             *   *                           *   *
            * * * *                         * * * *
           *       *                       *       *
          * *     * *                     * *     * *
         *   *   *   *                   *   *   *   *
        * * * * * * * *                 * * * * * * * *
       *               *               *               *
      * *             * *             * *             * *
     *   *           *   *           *   *           *   *
    * * * *         * * * *         * * * *         * * * *
   *       *       *       *       *       *       *       *
  * *     * *     * *     * *     * *     * *     * *     * *
 *   *   *   *   *   *   *   *   *   *   *   *   *   *   *   *
* * * * * * * * * * * * * * * * * * * * * * * * * * * * * * * *
```

Dogecode

Cryptographic asset tokens can represent all kinds of things.

Including computer programs.

Dogecode takes computer programs in the Brainfuck programming language (chosen for simplicity of encoding):

```
++++++++[>++++[>++>+++>+++>+<<<<-]>+>+>->>+[<]<-]>>.>---.+++++++..+++.>>.<-.<.+++.------.--------
.>>+.>++.
```

and translates them into a CSV file of token amounts using dcc:

```
INCB,8
JFOR,1
INCP,1
INCB,4
JFOR,1
INCP,1
INCB,2
INCP,1
INCB,3
INCP,1
...
```

which are then sent to a Dogeparty address (slowly) as a series of token transfer transactions using dcsend:

```
Sending lots of tokens. Make sure you really want to do this.
Waiting for token state to synch
Row 1: INCB,8
Waiting for token state to synch..........
Row 2: JFOR,1
Waiting for token state to synch............
Row 3: INCP,1
Waiting for token state to synch........
Row 4: INCB,4
Waiting for token state to synch.................
Row 5: JFOR,1
Waiting for token state to synch......................
Row 6: INCP,1
Waiting for token state to synch......................
Row 7: INCB,2
Waiting for token state to synch......
Row 8: INCP,1
```

```
Waiting for token state to synch......
Row 9: INCB,3
Waiting for token state to synch......
```

The transactions encode the program on the address, which can then be fetched and run using dcrun:

```
> dcrun -u rpcuser -w rpcpassword \
        DCvDS9g9VUZ94MSLbWi4zWRtxHrXeEctZ3

Hello World!
```

There's also an easier to use runner that uses dogepartychain.info's API rather than requiring a local dogepartyd instance to be running, which will fetch the program encoded as Dogeparty tokens at the specified address (DCvD...) and run it locally:

```
> dcrunw DCvDS9g9VUZ94MSLbWi4zWRtxHrXeEctZ3

Hello World!
```

Here are some addresses to try:

```
DCvDS9g9VUZ94MSLbWi4zWRtxHrXeEctZ3
DFZkhTXwAWW7PqBvVkohCFWobipqw3xmAn
DFibwNZvuJaHM9bD6×1WA63urkHiE4tWzF
DQuineX1BTF4ZD6DQxxsbUgVttmR4LvrdY
```

Warning

Be careful when writing and uploading Dogecode programs. You are responsible for ensuring that programs run as expected and that you send the correct tokens to the correct addresses. Expense and sadness will accompany any errors.

Dogecode White Paper v0.1

Overview

Dogecode is a system for representing computer programs using sequences of Dogeparty tokens in order to store, send, and execute their code via the Dogecoin blockchain.

Tokens

The encoding for programs is a minor variant of the 'Brainfuck' programming language, chosen for its minimalism.[1]

Each Brainfuck programming language command is represented by an indivisible Dogeparty asset.

A single occurrence of a command in a program is represented by the sending of a single token, e.g. + is represented by sending 1 `INCB` token.

Multiple occurrences are represented by sending multiple tokens in a single transfer, e.g. +++++ is represented by sending 5 `INCB` tokens.

The order and quantities of sends are significant, not the total number of tokens held by an address or account.

1.. <http://en.wikipedia.org/wiki/Brainfuck>.

Currently Used Tokens

Reading bytes into the pointer (the ',' command in Brainfuck) isn't currently supported. To enter data, use '+' and '>'.

`INCP`	>	(Increment pointer)
`DECP`	<	(Decrement pointer)
`INCB`	+	(Increment byte at pointer)
`DECB`	-	(Decrement byte at pointer)
`PUTB`	.	(Write byte at pointer)
`JFOR`	[	(Jump forward if number at pointer is not zero)
`JBAK`	[	(Jump back if number at pointer is not zero)

Reserved Tokens

These tokens are reserved to support future functionality.

`GETB`	,	(Read byte into pointer)
`IDAT`		(Identify data to be read by READ. See Input/Output below.)
`RUNC`		(This section of the code is complete, run it.)
`BADC`		(This section of the code has a problem, do not run.)

Encoding Of Programs

Programs are represented as a sequence of quantities of Dogecode tokens sent from a single address. Order, quantity and sending address are all significant to the system.

Ideally, programs would be represented as multiple sends in a single transaction. Until this is implemented, programs must be sent as an uninterrupted sequence of Dogecode tokens from a single address (no other tokens from the same address may interrupt the send).

Single Program Addresses

Single program addresses represent programs as a newly created Dogeparty address holding only the tokens sent to it in sequence that represent that single program's code.

No additional programs may be stored using that address.

If transferring the tokens fails or the program is found to be incorrect before it runs, a new address must be created and the correct sequence of tokens sent to it.

Program Queue Addresses (Not Yet Implemented)

Programs queued on an address for execution consist of a sequence of quantities of Dogecode tokens sent from a single address.

Since programs cannot be sent as multiple tokens in a single transaction two addresses may send programs at (approximately) the same time, leading to program token sends from two or more addresses becoming interleaved. This requires sorting token sends by address as well as by time when fetching programs to run.

Input/Output

Input Via +/>

Data can be entered into memory using the + and > commands. This is currently the only supported method for entering data into a program.

Input Via IDAT Token (Not Yet Implemented)

Details forthcoming.

Output For Single Program Addresses

Output is determined by running the program locally.

Output For Program Queue Address Runner (Not Yet Implemented)

Output is provided via broadcast messages on the Program Queue Address (details forthcoming).

Running Programs

Single Program Addresses

To execute the program, the system fetches all sends to the address in order and converts their token amounts to runs of Brainfuck commands. It then passes the resulting string to a Brainfuck interpreter. This will provide the final state and output of the program.

Program Queue Address (Not Yet Implemented)

Programs can be sent to an address that you control in order to be run in a queue.

Transactions from other addresses are ignored.

Used tokens can be returned to the sending address or, if the queue address is also the sending address, kept for re-use.

The runner polls the send table for new sends to the queue address. Sequences of tokens sent from a single address constitute programs to be executed. Programs are terminated with a RUNN token to trigger their execution, or an ERRR token if they should not be executed because (e.g.) a bug was found or the upload was corrupted.

The output of the program can either be recorded locally or output via broadcast messages from the runner address (details forthcoming).

To prevent programs that do not complete in a reasonable amount of time from disrupting the operation of the queue, programs should be run on a thread with a short timeout (details forthcoming).

Program Queue Address As A Service (Not Yet Implemented)

For Dogecode as a service, a program queue address that you control can execute Dogecode programs sent from addresses that others control in return for payment.

Tokens sent to the runner address are not returned, they constitute part of the payment for the service. Additional payment is sent as a Dogecoin transaction following the program tokens.

This system does not use RUNN/ERRR tokens to control execution. Receiving the Dogecoin payment acts as the command to execute the program. Should the payment not be sent within two minutes, the program is not run and the tokens are forfeited—unsuccessful or erronious program uploads can have their execution cancelled by not sending payment. Should the incorrect amount of payment be sent, it can be corrected by sending a supplementary payment before any further Dogecode tokens are sent. If a supplement is not sent within two minutes, the tokens and incorrect payment are forfeited to the runner account.

The output of the program is output via broadcast messages from the runner address (details forthcoming).

To prevent programs that do not complete in a reasonable amount of time from disrupting the operation of the queue, programs should be run on a thread with a short timeout. The length of the timeout can be extended by the sender incorporating an additional supplement into the Dogecoin fee that triggers execution (details forthcoming).

Dogecoin prices for running are announced by the runner account on its broadcast message feed (details forthcoming).

Token Transfer Speed

Dogecode programs must be sent as ordered sequences of individual Dogeparty asset 'send' commands. To ensure that the token sends are incorporated into the blockchain in order, each send is performed only after the previous one is confirmed. This means that it can take minutes for each token run to be sent to the receiving account.

Multiple sends from the same account in the same block could be enabled by having multiple inputs available to it, this does not ensure ordering however.

Ideally, Dogeparty would be extended to allow multi-token sends in a single Dogecoin transaction. This would solve both confirmation and ordering.

Previous Digest: 28fd483cbd5337b11bafd286a7faa8afd740763be65f32aa1ddf7c41bac7e3fa
Proof-of-Work Nonce: d
Proof-of-Work Hash: f7d722dd57bc1c6147fd6586abb6089e2471cb567b2cdd58edad3c69e4a397d9
Face: 9, 1, 13, 5

Previous Digest: f7d722dd57bc1c6147fd6586abb6089e2471cb567b2cdd58edad3c69e4a397d9
Proof-of-Work Nonce: a2
Proof-of-Work Hash: becea1d19e07719be683ad5eeaa5e605ff5b5b5c7bab9ae3dd21bf1a56711e5b
Face: 4, 0, 8, 4

Previous Digest: becea1d19e07719be683ad5eeaa5e605ff5b5b5c7bab9ae3dd21bf1a56711e5b
Proof-of-Work Nonce: 7
Proof-of-Work Hash: d619a65e1e15d79508d7df95678e7681ab084cf44831061b29e7c050d2b350ad
Face: 6, 10, 10, 14

Previous Digest: d619a65e1e15d79508d7df95678e7681ab084cf44831061b29e7c050d2b350ad
Proof-of-Work Nonce: 5e
Proof-of-Work Hash: 124d1f921d7ca78564d50bc19f8af85579990b727d15214d28f13341eb552f48
Face: 9, 5, 13, 9

Previous Digest: 124d1f921d7ca78564d50bc19f8af85579990b727d15214d28f13341eb552f48
Proof-of-Work Nonce: 67
Proof-of-Work Hash: 0eedd9466db4939360cce17dcd7b84d9e98f21ab71bd90a0707934b45f5eafea
Face: 1, 6, 6, 11

Previous Digest: 0eedd9466db4939360cce17dcd7b84d9e98f21ab71bd90a0707934b45f5eafea
Proof-of-Work Nonce: a
Proof-of-Work Hash: 748ad6aec3db9473ed9163bfeee7307f67758e141233d3b84b3bfe1ec8c56843

Facecoin

Bitcoin is a very interesting development in cyberculture. It's a repository for the hopes and fears of various ideologies, and a frontier or dark space for the imagination and social or economic activity in a nineties-internet way. Its protocol is a communication model of existence, identity, community and proof, with a Ccru-ish market worship at its base. Because of all of this I think it's worthy of and desperately needs artistic investigation.

Artworks are proofs of aesthetic work, used as unique value identities both in the market (art is used as an investment, signifier of status, and symbolic resolution of lacks in free market ideology by oil oligarchs and trust fund managers) and by organised crime (stolen art is used as a medium of exchange by criminal gangs). They may not be regarded as much more useful than Bitcoin's proof-of-work, but at least they look good.

Facecoin performs a very simple form of art-making, generating pixelated portraits by using machine pareidolia as its proof of work. This is not much more intrinsically useful than Bitcoin's proof-of-work algorithm, which searches for successively longer strings of zeros in very long, very random numbers generated by cryptographic hashing functions. But it is easier to contemplate.

This is implemented by applying CCV's JavaScript face detection algorithm to SHA-256 digests represented as greyscale pixel maps. An industrial-strength version would use OpenCV. Owing to the limitations of face detection as implemented by these libraries, the digest pixel map must be upscaled and blurred to produce images of the size and kind that they can find faces in. The difficulty can be varied by altering the size and blur of the pixmap. Or by only allowing particular detected face bounds rectangles to be used a set number of times.

If *Facecoin* was turned into an actual cryptocurrency and widely adopted, the two value identity systems of cryptocurrency and art would be trivially but critically mapped onto each other by millions of machines churning out imaginary portraits across Facecoin's peer-to-peer communication network as part of its financial network, and vice versa.

If you understand *Facecoin* you understand proof-of-work cryptocurrency's block production and some of its critiques at a reasonable level of abstraction. I made it to understand this, so hopefully it can help you understand as well.

T&ÒÊPòDûCþž¯È- 3ó´øÙ ½ ç ¶)Ö

Nonce: 330
SHA-256: 5426d2ca50f244fb43fe9eafc82da08f33f3b4f8d9140802bd0102e780b629d6
Previous Digest: None

Tha \÷r ß ¾ª KðûTEh((%(°~38)ë½X

Nonce: 10434
SHA-256: 546861095cf77214df7f8abeaa094bf0fb5445688480258ab07e33388debbd58
Previous Digest: 5426d2ca50f244fb43fe9eafc82da08f33f3b4f8d9140802bd0102e780b629d6

©ÁÃ%¯* Ä" ·>àÇwÐæ:$àÙ¿* A¾X

Nonce: 1126
SHA-256: a9c1c325af2a0b8fc42201b73ee0c777d0e63a24e0d9bf2a9441be581f1c0791
Previous Digest: 546861095cf77214df7f8abeaa094bf0fb5445688480258ab07e33388debbd58

Monkeycoin

Monkeycoin is the follow-up to *Facecoin*. It implements a web-page version of a proof-of-work algorithm for Bitcoin-like cryptocurrency that uses trying to write the complete works of Shakespeare as its puzzle.

Literature and drama are proof of aesthetic work.

Monkeycoin uses attempting to write the complete works of Shakespeare as its proof-of-work function. This is implemented by converting Bitcoin-style SHA-256 cryptographic hash digests of block data to ASCII and checking the results against the first few characters of the First Folio (after dedications and credits), which is the start of *The Tempest*.

The difficulty of finding new blocks is increased by requiring successively more characters from the text of the complete works of Shakespeare to be matched.

2014 Bitcoin transaction

Proof of Existence 1

I have placed the hash of my genome into the Bitcoin Blockchain:

```
SHA256:
bada4cf5328394f733cd278c33509e79
b839cc0b0838658503b116d6ca9ca14b

Address:
1KXH7jSTwLi9FLo6MpNUPnHGvEETfuaKhz
```

This proves my existence.

2014 Bitcoin transaction

Proof of Existence 2

I have placed the hash of 'God' into the Bitcoin Blockchain:

```
SHA256:
ebc3e2e6448f94af7b58e57658336a44
d3ff44eafadb54e4c4cd71ba7e607594

Address:
163NUfEg61eJeNiQ9SyN6EDT1ynkzDL2ar
```

This proves that God exists.

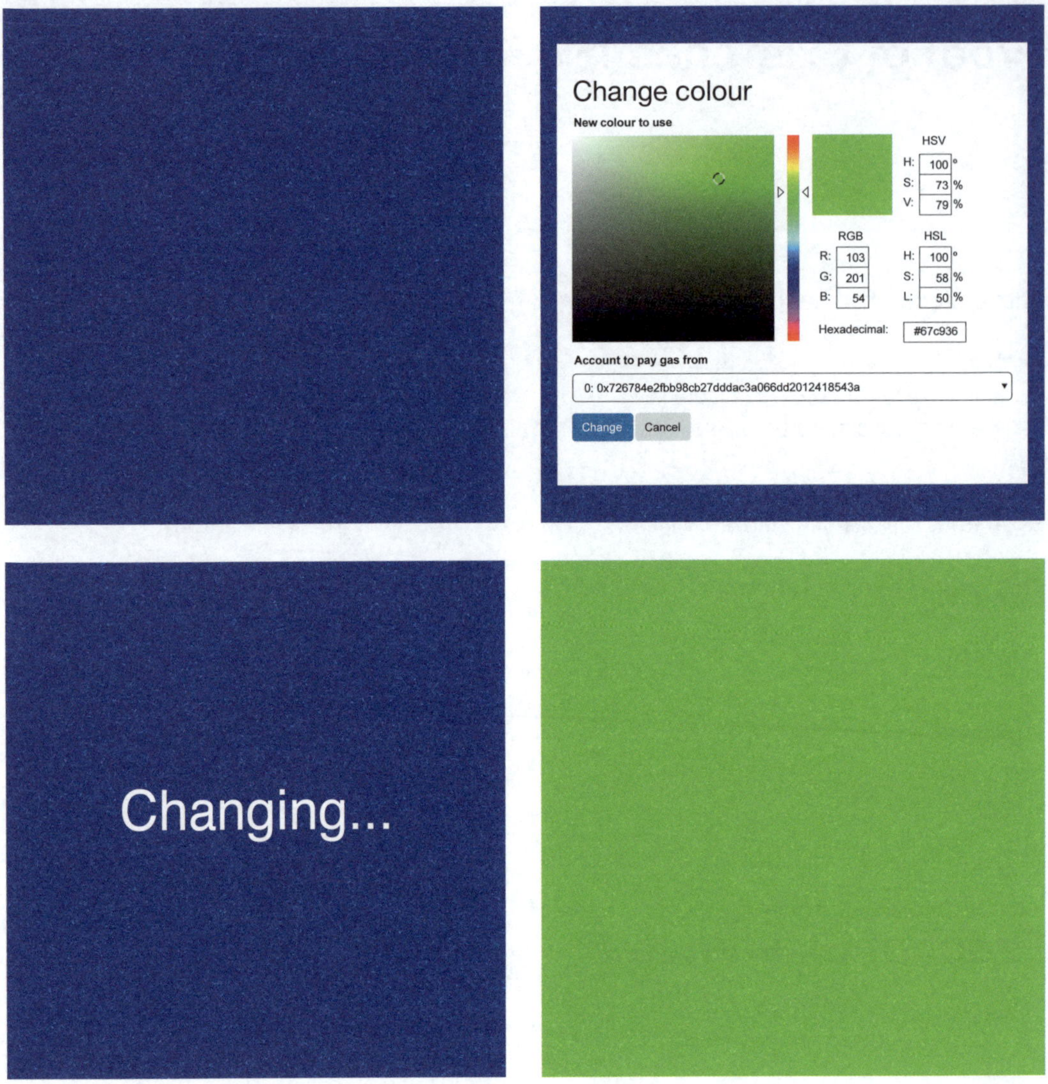
Change colour
New colour to use
HSV
H: 100 °
S: 73 %
V: 79 %
RGB
R: 103
G: 201
B: 54
HSL
H: 100 °
S: 58 %
L: 50 %
Hexadecimal: #67c936
Account to pay gas from
0: 0x726784e2fbb98cb27dddac3a066dd2012418543a
Change
Cancel
Changing...

Blank Canvas

A blank canvas that anyone can set the colour of on the Ethereum blockchain.

This was a sketch for *Democratic Palette*, and a borrowing of the history of the blank canvas in modernist art. It is more complex than *Is Art* despite appearing to contain a similar amount of information. A single colour is a single piece of information, but in computer science terms it is usually more than a single bit of information—one bit can represent black and white, for example, but to get close to the millions of colours that modern computer graphics use takes twenty-four bits.

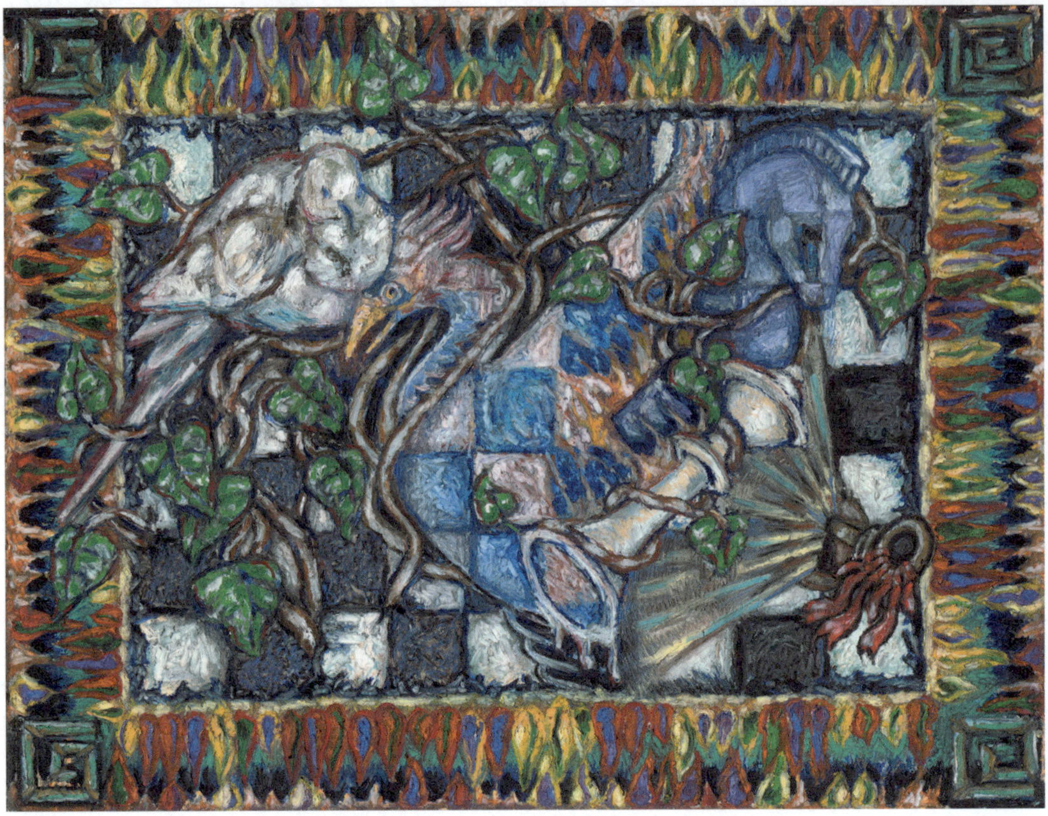

Marguerite deCourcelle, *The Legend of Satoshi Nakamoto*, 2015. Oil pastel on canvas.

2015

The Legend of Satoshi Nakamoto: TORCHED H34R7S aka 1Flamen6

(Collaboration with Marguerite deCourcelle)

As a child I loved Kit Thompson's book *Masquerade* (1979), even though the solution was a mystery to me. I also had the Usborne book *The Knowhow Book of Spycraft* (1975), which included sections on encoding secret messages in the visual environment. So when I discovered Marguerite deCourcelle's 'crypto puzzle trail' paintings via Twitter I found them both a very new solution to the problem of making art and assembling an audience—particularly for painting—in the crypto space, and a way of engaging that audience using methods I recognised from my childhood.

Marguerite invented and popularised the crypto puzzle trail, a cultural event in which a community follows a sequence of puzzles, competing and/or collaborating to solve them. The puzzles may be contained in artworks, games, encrypted messages, or some combination of the three. The reward for solving each puzzle may be reputation, cryptocurrency, or (in modern crypto puzzle trails) NFTs. Crypto puzzle trails were an important early means of engaging audiences with cryptocurrency beyond its immediate use as a medium of exchange or speculation.

I became one of Marguerite's collaborators on her crypto puzzle trail 'The Legend of Satoshi Nakamoto', helping to encrypt some of its chain of clues in accordance with her vision. For the last puzzle in the series, Marguerite knew the iconography she was going to use, and we had been surprised by how quickly her community had cracked the last couple of puzzles, so we wanted to come up with something slightly more complex encoded in it.

We knew that people were looking for one-bit binary encoded information, so we decided instead on a six-bit encoding that used variations in the colour and shape of the painted flames that bordered the canvas. To add a very obvious clue, we placed into the painting a six-bit key which the data had to be XOR-ed against, encoded as ribbons tied to a key. The key is a key, it's six bits, and it's encoded in wavy red forms that are a bit like flames. We thought that transcribing the information from each edge of the painting and arranging it in the right order would provide more of a challenge.

The encoded solution to the puzzle was a Bitcoin cryptographic private key, chosen to produce a Bitcoin 'vanity address' starting with '1Flame...' to fit the theme of the painting. This was prefixed with a short message in English to help the reader establish that they were on the right track. I wrote some JavaScript code to turn the solution into a list of written painting instructions, which Marguerite then followed, painting just under two hundred flames without error. Marguerite placed the prize, an amount of Bitcoin worth around 1200 US dollars at the time, into the Bitcoin address generated from the private key. She announced the puzzle on Twitter, and we settled in for what we thought would be a couple of weeks of people trying to crack the puzzle.

Three years later, that 1200 dollars worth of Bitcoin had become 50,000 dollars worth. I had stored the puzzle solution on my laptop for most of that time, before realising that this was a really bad idea and transferring everything to cold storage. Marguerite and I occasionally shared details about the encoding in order to check that we hadn't made a mistake with it, in emails that we then deleted—no doubt frustrating for future art historians (and Vice journalists), but some indication of how our security concerns grew along with the value of the prize.

Fortunately, it was then that someone solved the puzzle.

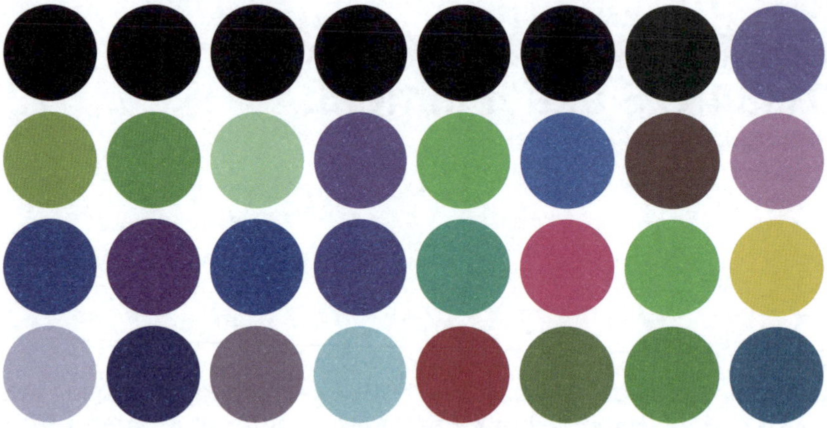

First Send, 2018. Bitcoin Transaction Hash, 8 Bit Palette, Circles.

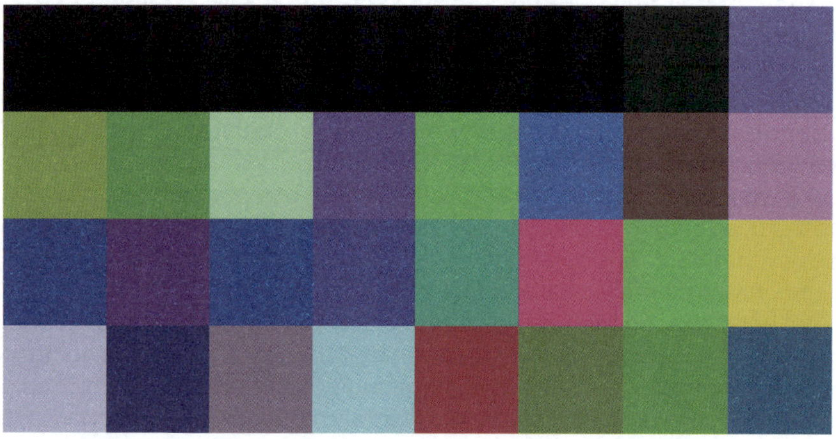

Genesis Block, 2019. Bitcoin Block Hash, 8 Bit Palette, Squares.

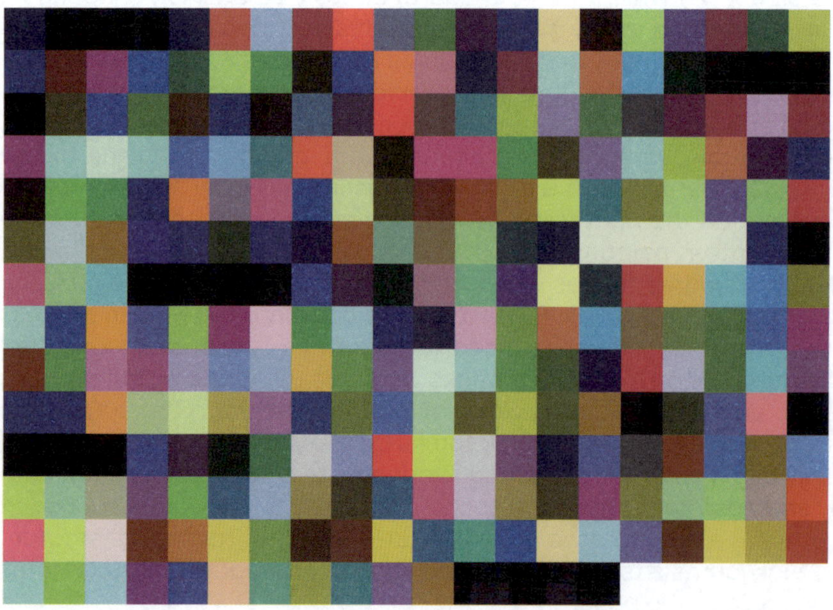

Genesis Block, 2019. Bitcoin Block Hash, 8 Bit Palette, Squares.

Blockchain Aesthetics

The sheer complexity of modern cryptography and the sheer volume of transactions and blocks that utilise it on the Bitcoin network are difficult to imagine. *Blockchain Aesthetics* uses grids of simple tokens of artistic form to do so.

Rosalind Krauss's re-enchantment of the explicit modernist grid misattributed its effect to myth, to addition or supplement.[1] The grid has the schematic, overarching, guiding character of myth, to be sure, but its interplay of the abstract and the concrete comes from political rationality rather than storytelling. From subtraction or reification. Krauss recognises this in her consideration of the explicit grid's early utopian associations. The postmodern grid was a critique of this rationality and utopianism, replacing them with contingency and randomness in order to achieve its meaning.

Injecting new content into the postmodern grid cannot restore it to its modernist significance. It can however place modernist rationality and postmodernist play in tension with each other and focus the resulting attention on that content as a subject of the gaze and of contemplation.

Mechanical encoding of messages into aesthetics is the stuff of kitsch where it has no remainder. *Blockchain Aesthetics* feeds on data from a blockchain explorer web API and visualises it as modernist, postmodernist, and generative art commonplaces—coloured spots or squares, abstract poetry, random lines or grids. The numeric information of transactions or blocks is (mis-)rendered as something more substantial, giving it the task of communicating an impression of the speed and volume and density of that information.

It's a kind of landscape. Maybe.

In 2019 a set of prints was generated and printed for Kate Vass Galerie, using the same algorithms as *Blockchain Aesthetics* but from historical data associated with significant events in blockchain history:

- The mining of the first block—the 'genesis block'—in the Bitcoin blockchain. This marks the start of Bitcoin as running software rather than an idea described in a whitepaper.
- The sending of the first transaction between two parties on the Bitcoin blockchain. This marks the start of Bitcoin as a usable and useful system for exchanging value without intermediaries.
- The first halving of reward payments by the protocol for mining Bitcoin transactions into blocks. This marks the successful operation of Bitcoin's software as long-term governance and a generator of economic and historical events in itself.

They're a kind of history painting. Maybe.

1 R Krauss, 'The Originality of the Avant Garde' in *The Originality of the Avant-Garde and Other Modernist Myths* (Cambridge, MA: MIT Press, 1986).

Balances | Bets | Broadcasts | Burns | + Credits | − Debits | ↔ Dispensers | Dividends | Issuances | Orders | Sends | Unconfirmed

10 per page | « ‹ Page 1 of 1 › » | 10 results

#	Asset	Amount	Percentage of Supply	Estimated Value	
1	CRITIQUE	999,991	99.99910000%	0.00000000 XDP ($0.00)	view
2	FIVESTAR	9,992	99.92000000%	0.00000000 XDP ($0.00)	view
4	FOURSTAR	9,999	99.99000000%	0.00000000 XDP ($0.00)	view
5	NEGCRIT	1,000,000	100.00000000%	0.00000000 XDP ($0.00)	view
6	ONESTAR	10,000	100.00000000%	0.00000000 XDP ($0.00)	view
7	POSCRIT	999,991	99.99910000%	0.00000000 XDP ($0.00)	view
8	POSITIVECRIT	1,000,000	100.00000000%	0.00000000 XDP ($0.00)	view
9	THREESTAR	10,000	100.00000000%	0.00000000 XDP ($0.00)	view
10	TWOSTAR	10,000	100.00000000%	0.00000000 XDP ($0.00)	view

Critical Coins

To make the process of art reviews and criticism more transparent and quantifiable, we can use cryptographic asset tokens to represent critical opinion and valences. Search for the token names provided below in your favourite DogeParty or CounterParty block explorer.

Critical Approval
Here's a token of simple, uninflected critical approval:

```
CRITIQUE
```

Positive and Negative Critique
Positive-only measures can distort valences. Having tokens for both approval and disapproval addresses this:

```
POSCRIT
NEGCRIT
```

Star Ratings
We can use a range of tokens to express a traditional star rating:

```
ONESTAR
TWOSTAR
THREESTAR
FOURSTAR
FIVESTAR
```

Sending Tokens
We can use three different kinds of recipients for critical opinion represented in the form of tokens. If the artist (or work) has a Dogecoin address the tokens can be sent to that address directly. Otherwise we can create an address (preferably a vanity address) for them to hold the tokens in escrow. Or we can create an unspendable address (again preferably a vanity address) to send the tokens to. This prevents the tokens being transferred, which is either a bug or a feature depending on whether we want this to be possible or not.

Presumably art is the product of aesthetic competence, and if I as an art historian or critic approve of your exercise of this competence I cannot fault you if your exercise of that competence in the evaluation of someone else's art or critical competences leads you to transfer the tokens of my critical approval to a third party. So transferable tokens make sense and in fact the history of their transferals adds value: it provides a historical record of regard, influence, and the reach of my original opinion.

Simple Blockchain Art Diagram

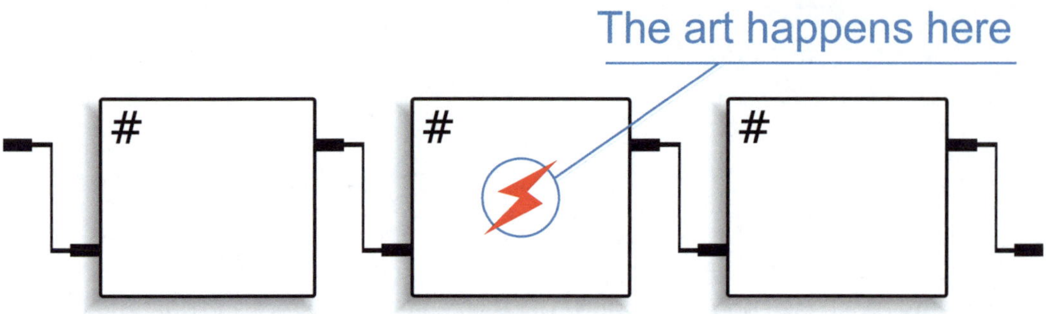

R Myers ca. #422422 after MTAA ca. 1997

Simple Blockchain Art Diagram (after MTAA)

Adapted From MTAA, *Simple Net Art Diagram* (digital image, 1997).[1]

Licensed Attribution 4.0 International (CC BY 4.0) (after the original).[2]

Blockchain Hashes (simple-net-art-diagram.gif)

Note that these are for the unmodified version (which was also included in Rhizome's net.art anthology book *The Art Happens Here*).

Proof Of Existence (422422)

https://blockchain.info/address/1KEToGLEoU9riqp3uh91Btii1VC9kevJ38

https://blockchain.info/tx/730b1015d7f849bd134498d41d9decc49bed77a2ffb127ae-afb4e7fb0664d177

Bitsig (422423)

https://blockchain.info/address/12vAC7Wsrhgt248MifRbPBxeLZKDDy6vBc

https://blockchain.info/tx/2d5193a2128459ba61c0746d0cbb3c1414734e85971f1b016d180706580b111f

1 <http://www.mtaa.net/mtaaRR/off-line_art/snad.html>.
2 <http://creativecommons.org/licenses/by/4.0/>.

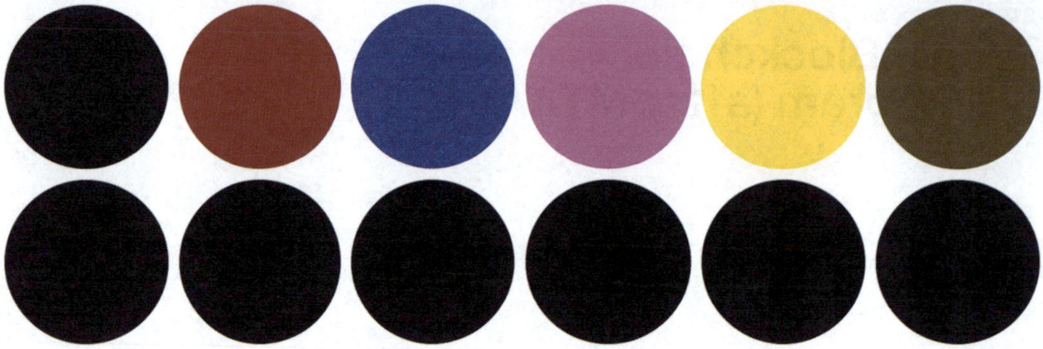

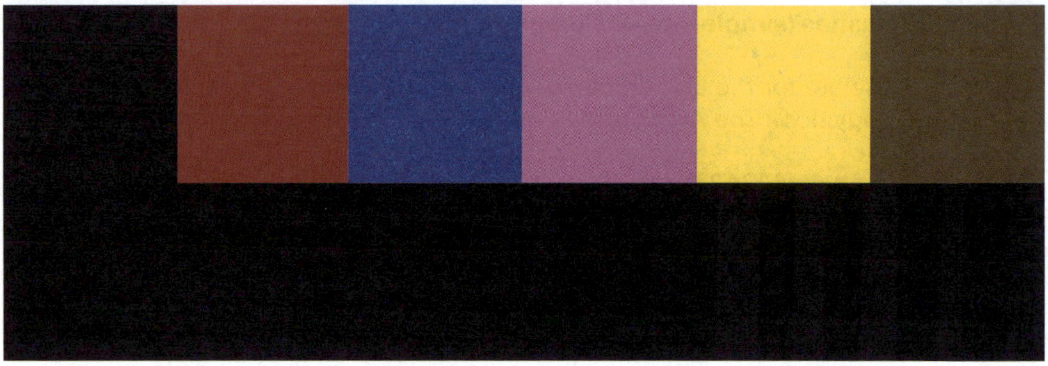

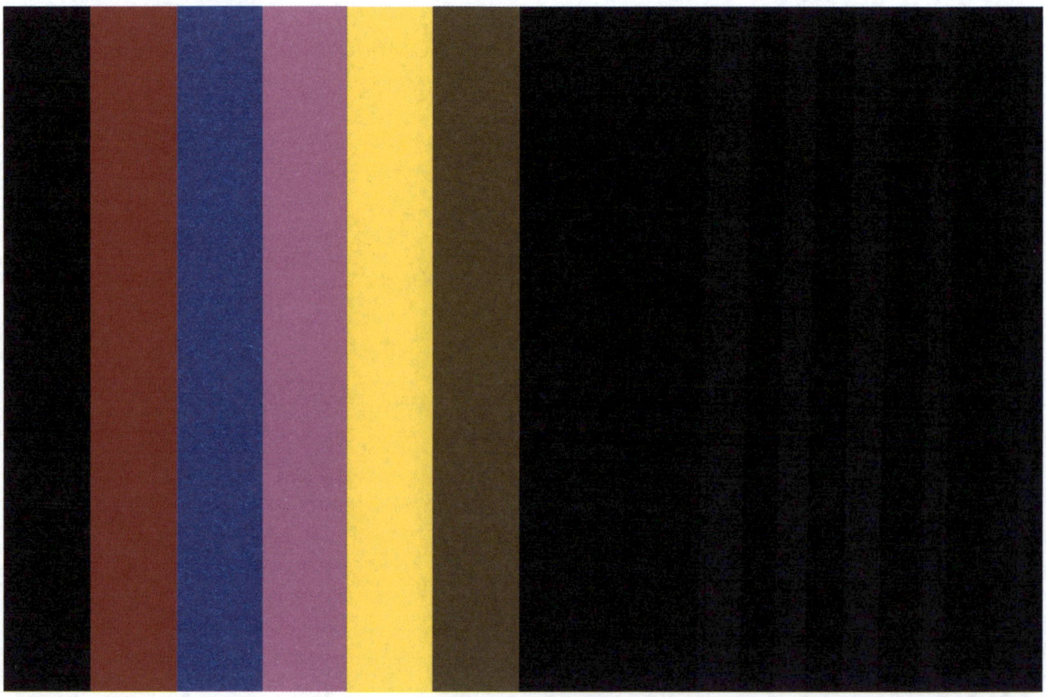

Democratic Palette

A palette of twelve colours that anyone can set in a smart contract on the Ethereum blockchain by sending a voting transaction.

Every vote for every colour is tracked and the top twelve make up the palette. The only cost of voting is 'gas' paid for using Ethereum's native cryptocurrency, Ether.

Participatory, decentralised art and aesthetics interact with barriers to participation and the ability to buy democracy.

2017 Ethereum DApp

Lottery Symbol

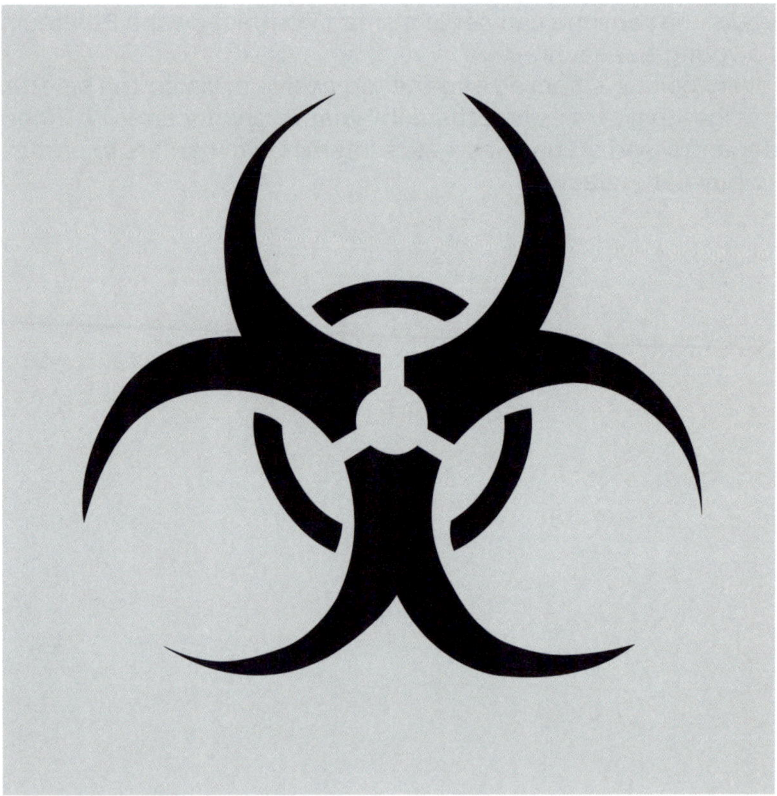

A graphical symbol on the blockchain, chosen from options submitted via Ethereum transactions in a simple lottery.

The lottery uses the blockchain itself as a source of entropy, which is known to be insecure. But this is just a symbol rather than millions of dollars.

This is a piece in a series of works that pair methods of allocation or governance with aesthetic properties. It follows on from *Democratic Palette*.

DEMODAY

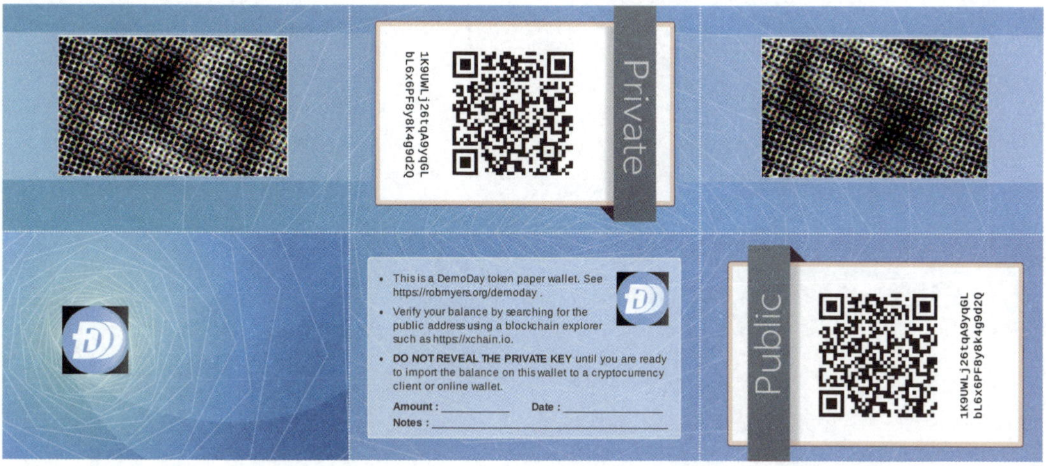

DEMODAY

The first show-specific cryptotoken, for the show *Demo Day* at Kunstraum LLC.

What if art shows were to have their own tokens? Would they be used as local currency, as proof of attendance, as one of the artworks, and who by?

Asset Balances (5) Show more

#	Asset	Amount	Percentage
1	BLUEARTCOIN	13	100.00000000%
2	GREENARTCOIN	13	100.00000000%
3	REDARTCOIN	13	100.00000000%
4	WHITEARTCOIN	13	100.00000000%
5	YELLOWARTCOIN	13	100.00000000%

2015/2017 Dogeparty tokens

Art Coins (Coloured) 1

Art Coin White (WHITEARTCOIN)
An eternal changeless epitome of art, totally contemporary, now and forever.

Art Coin Blue (BLUEARTCOIN)
A perfect investment vehicle and the symbolic resolution of the contradictions and aporias of management and capital made of the finest materials and the basest aesthetics.

Art Coin Red (REDARTCOIN)
A multicultural art from China, India and the Middle East. A challenge to received wisdom and logistics for an international audience and trade network rendering the specific and local exchangeable and valorisable culturally and economically.

Art Coin Green (GREENARTCOIN)
A youthful art of remix, resistance and defiance from Asia and the former Soviet Union.

Art Coin Brown (BROWNARTCOIN)
An art from New York and Berlin, found on blogs and made from obsolescent media. Ironic and depthless yet sophisticatedly deployed to create aesthetics through overwhelming assemblages of kitsch in a year both zero and final.

2015/2017 Counterparty tokens

Art Coins (Coloured) 2

Art Coin White (WHITEARTCOIN)
An eternal changeless epitome of art, totally contemporary, now and forever.

Art Coin Blue (BLUEARTCOIN)
A perfect investment vehicle and the symbolic resolution of the contradictions and aporias of management and capital made of the finest materials and the basest aesthetics.

Art Coin Red (REDARTCOIN)
A multicultural art from China, India and the Middle East. A challenge to received wisdom and logistics for an international audience and trade network rendering the specific and local exchangeable and valorisable culturally and economically.

Art Coin Green (GREENARTCOIN)
A youthful art of remix, resistance and defiance from Asia and the former Soviet Union.

Art Coin Yellow (YELLOWARTCOIN)
An art from New York and Berlin, found on blogs and made from obsolescent media. Ironic and depthless yet sophisticatedly deployed to create aesthetics through overwhelming assemblages of kitsch in a year both zero and final.

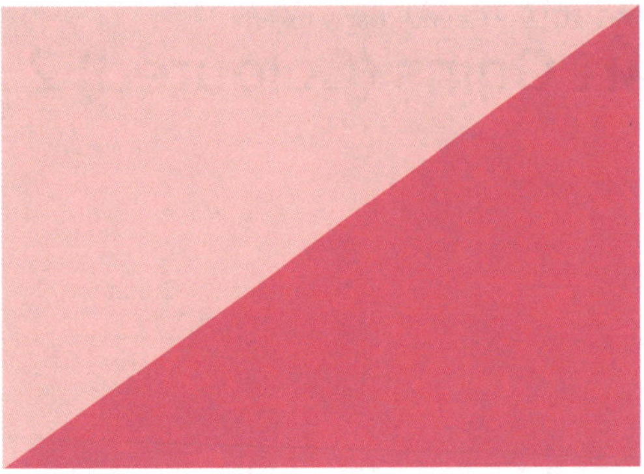

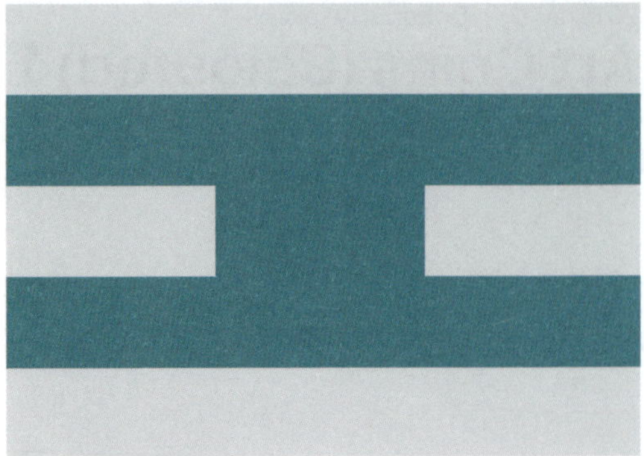

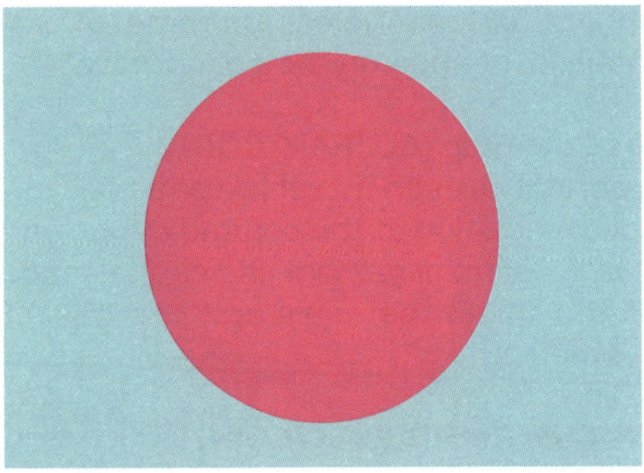

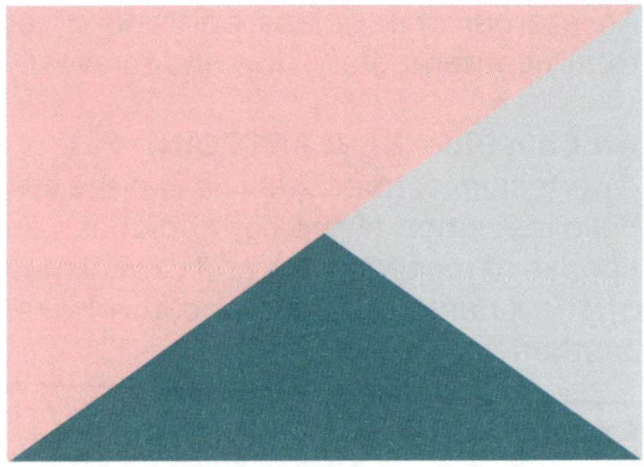

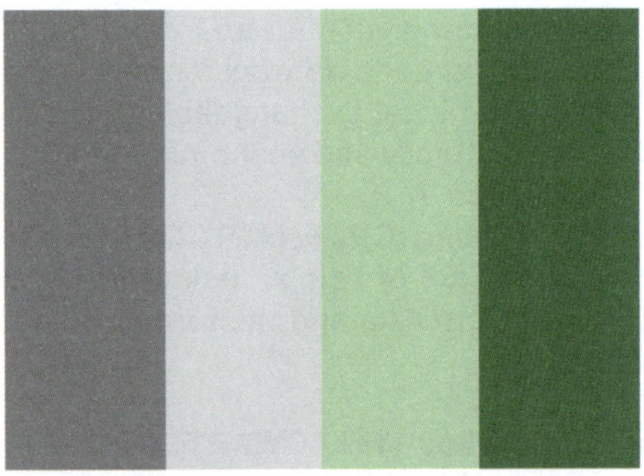

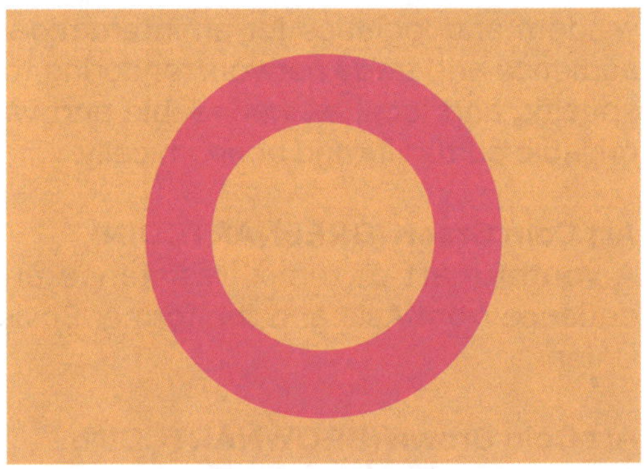

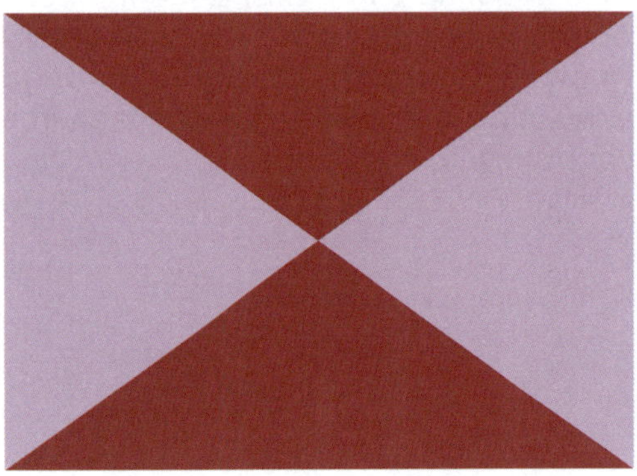

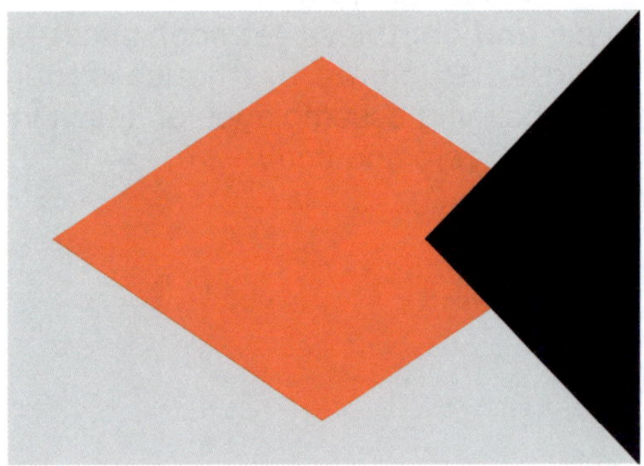

SchellingFlags

SchellingFlags is a blockchain-based system for establishing the aesthetics and allegiances of flags in a decentralised way.

Flags are an intersection and encryption of the political and the aesthetic, an assertion of identity and allegiance. They have proliferated offchain for social phenomena such as nation states and genders.

Focal points, also known as 'Schelling points', are a perceptual phenomenon in game theory. They are values or strategies that people will use because they seem obvious or attractive in a given context.

Using the blockchain, SchellingFlags supports the construction and use of flags as ideological focal points for decentralised social coordination. Any individual can create and share a flag, and any individual can support it. The most popular flags are displayed by the SchellingFlags graphical interface to provide a map of its ideological landscape.

This is the meme of '...but on the blockchain' applied to flags, with a touch of Art & Language and Komar & Melamid. The name refers to the game theorist Thomas Schelling, not the idealist philosopher Friedrich Wilhelm Joseph Schelling. Sorry, philosophers.

Ethereum address of the creator of the contract containing this artwork

Ethereum address of the creator of the contract containing this artwork

0x7B227BB88E79284A3B21C723789E18FC5503B452

Ethereum transaction setting the content of this artwork

Ethereum address of the contract containing this artwork

Secret property of this artwork

Ethereum transaction setting the content of this artwork

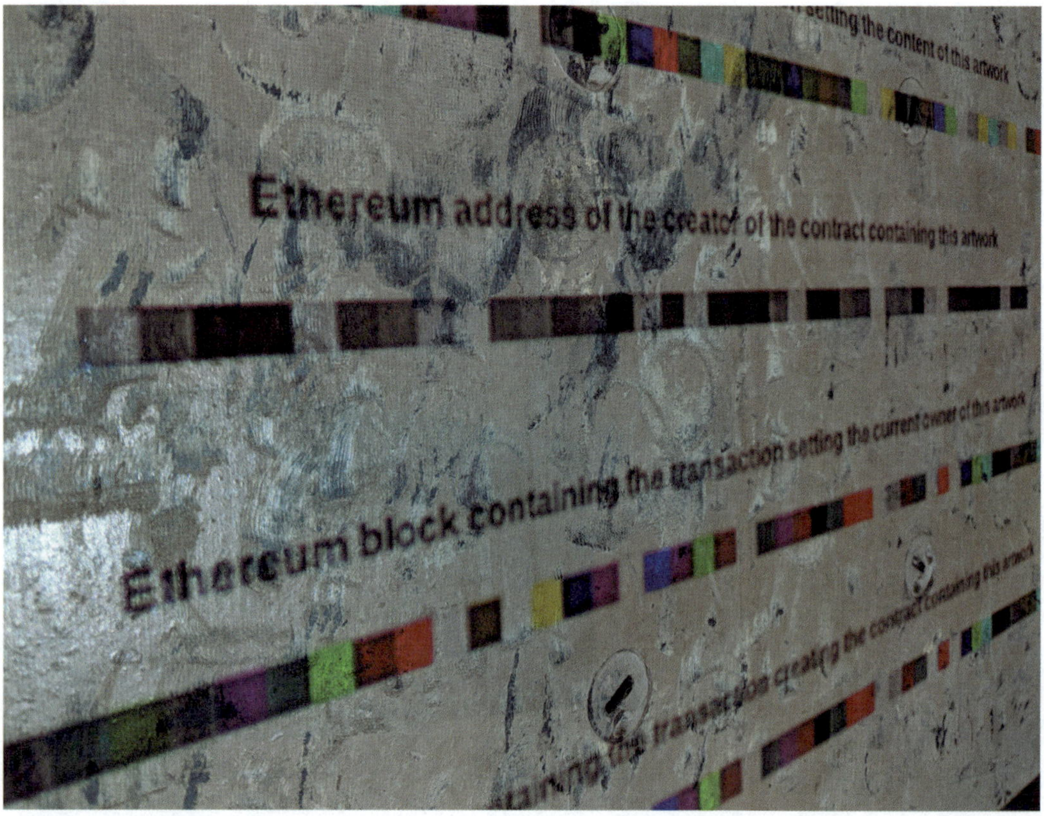

Secret Artwork (Content) projected on the metal wall of the vaults beneath the old San Francisco Mint as part of *Secrets*, curated by Sam Hart and Sarah Hamerman, 2018.

Secret Artwork

An Ethereum contract stores the cryptographic hash (salted SHA-256) of the content (or subject, or…) of an artwork, a unique but meaningless numeric identifier. This proves that the artwork exists (to the extent it can be cryptographically verified) but offers no clue as to the content.

The artwork is 'ownable' as an Ethereum ERC721 token, tying the uniqueness and identifiability of the content to a unique (quasi-)property relationship. But the owner knows no more about the content of the artwork than the general public. They own something unknowable, or that which cannot be fully owned.

As each block in Ethereum's blockchain is layered on top of the last, the cost of the computing power with which the secret and its almost-ownership is asserted quickly exceeds the price of the world's most expensive artwork. And the certainty with which these facts are established quickly surpasses that of the most secure physical provenance.

The presentation of the corresponding ERC721 token takes the form of a DApp, which reveals all details that can be fetched from the network about the artwork. Its owner, when it was created, even the hash of the content. It displays each of these pieces of data in many ways—as text, as colours, as shapes, as musical notes. The visual register seeks to distract the viewer from the gap in their purchase on (or of) the artwork by relentlessly presenting these different facts.

But still it remains.

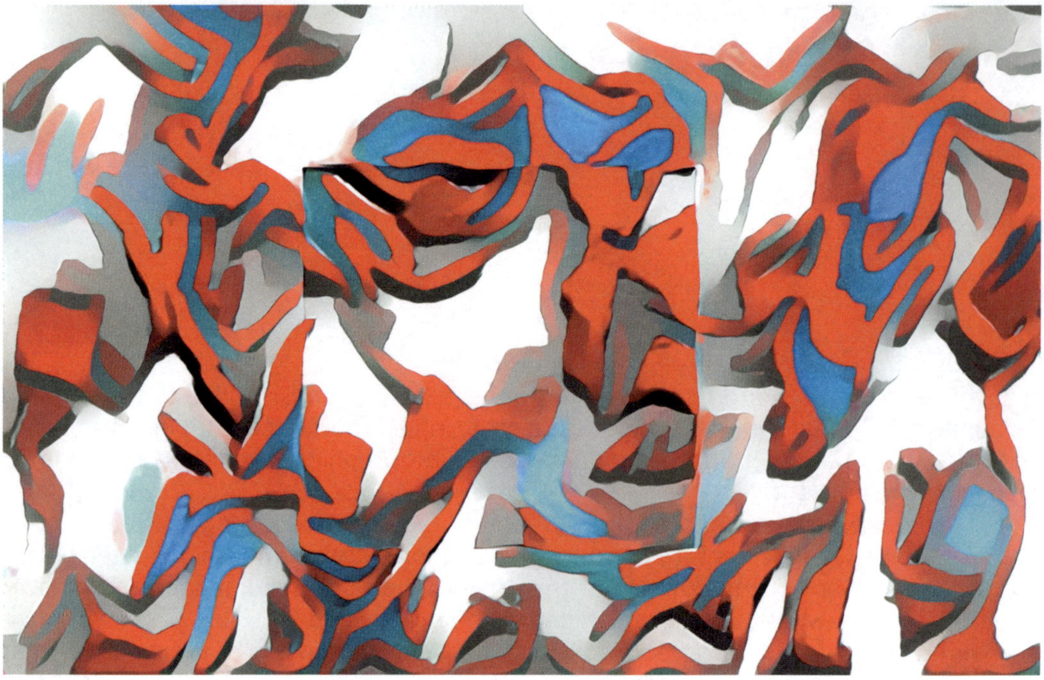

Local Maxima

In classical AI research, a 'local maximum' is a solution to a problem that cannot in itself be improved but that is not the best possible solution. Where a singular mathematical specification of a problem is possible, local maxima can be avoided using search strategies other than simple 'hill climbing'. Art does not have such a specification, its search space consists entirely of local maxima.

Generative Adversarial (neural) Networks extract aesthetic surplus value from images, rendering that surplus value liquid. Training a GAN deterritorialises their form, generating new images with it reterritorialises it. Contemporary AI burns capital to produce discrimination, here discrimination between images that resemble the learned source material and those that do not.

The source material in this instance is my own previous work, playful compositions from the 1990s. A GAN was trained on them and then applied to simple geometric shapes, transferring the extracted 'style' of the source images leavened with the perceptual artefacts of GAN training. Reducing (or promoting) artworks to flows of aesthetics that can be continued indefinitely is deeply challenging to art history and connoisseurship.

GAN-generated images tend to Pollockian all-overness, or to the same local sense but global semantic incoherence as Markov chains or a Francis Bacon painting. The conception of 'style transfer' that all of this involves is deeply challenging to art theory.

DESKTOP PCS
PHOSPHOR AMBER GRID
GLITCH STREAK
PURPLE/CYAN GRADIENT

YELLOW SPORTS CAR
PHOSPHOR GREEN GRID
LUNAR ECLIPSE
PURPLE/MAGENTA GRADIENT

MICHELANGELO'S DAVID
NEON GREEN GRID
REFLECTIONS ON THE GROUND
HYPERSPACE STARFIELD

Tokens Equal Text

Tokens Equal Text consists of an edition of 32 Ethereum ERC-998 composable tokens each of which owns four child ERC-721 non-fungible tokens. The ERC-721 tokens have short descriptive texts encoded as their ID numbers. This makes the ERC-998 tokens compositions of those text fragments. The content of that composition can be recovered if it is known that the token IDs can be (mis)read as text rather than numbers.

These text fragments describe key visual tropes of the Vaporwave movement. Vaporwave is a 2010s internet-based musical and cultural genre devoted to the ironisation of muzak and digital kitsch aesthetics from the long 1980s. It is named for 'Vaporware', future software that is announced but never released. Vaporwave has an inherent melancholy and a sense of lost future potential; in its ironising mashing together of time and desire it is inherently queer and, in leading examples such as Macintosh Plus's genre-defining *Floral Shoppe* (2012), trans.

The question of whether a given trope fits the aesthetic of Vaporwave is key to the genre's discourse, with canonical tropes establishing the content of that aesthetic. A composition of references to canonical elements of that aesthetic at least admits of the question 'Is this aesthetic?'

Using Ethereum Web3 browser app code to display the texts of tokens in visual compositions using 'aesthetic' (in the Vaporwave sense) typography and colours nudges that answer along. It also prevents the content from becoming a trivial puzzle. The encoded information is placed, not hidden. Its easy recovery foregrounds the presence of compositional and indexical structure that rewards reflection.

The 'Rare Art' market demands something aesthetic to own. Nothing is more desirable to own than something that cannot be owned. Vaporwave is built on sampled and appropriated audio recordings, video, images, and 3D models. It is unownable, making it ideal common property for an internet cultural scene. This does however make it very difficult to truly claim ownership of most of its products without attracting the ire of corporate copyright holders.

By encrypting recoverable and imaginable references to this unownable aesthetic, *Tokens Equal Text* loops desire for ownership back through a complexly unownable genre of aesthetics to both satisfy and frustrate this demand and to place blockchain property and the history of art into a state of mutually critical interrogation.

(I was listening to *Floral Shoppe* pretty much on repeat while I made it.)

Staking Ratio

A ratio of two amounts of Ether cryptocurrency that is staked within a smart contract by its users. Value determines value, further destroying the information that money destroys in order to represent it.

This is the last work in the series of resonant pairings of aesthetic properties and governance or economic allocation methods that began with *Democratic Palette*. It is the first to deal directly in cryptocurrency value.

Use at your own risk.

Token Grid

The grid is a Modernist icon and the underlying organisational form of many aspects of our daily lives. Whether a North American city street plan, a power grid, the face of International Style architecture, page layout in print or onscreen, or the pixels of that screen, grids pervasively organise our activities and experiences.

This one exists on the Ethereum blockchain with a graphical user interface accessible via the world wide web. In contrast to the fixed grids of city streets and architectural structures, anyone can change it, but only if they are willing to procure and then burn one of the grid smart contract's ERC-20 digital tokens in order to do so.

Proof of Work Bitmap

A 16×16 pixel monochrome bitmap that lives on the Ethereum blockchain. You can change it if you run a simple proof-of-work calculation and send the result in the update transaction.

Proof of Work Bitmap is the latest in a series of pieces that pair aesthetic properties with methods of economic allocation or social governance (in no particular order, *Democratic Palette*, *Proof of Work Bitmap*, *Staking Ratio*, *Hack Line Properties*, *Pay Previous Path*, *Lottery Symbol*, *Token Grid*). In computer art and digital culture, a monochrome bitmap is the simplest representation of a discrete image. In blockchain-based systems a 'proof of work' is a time-consuming computational puzzle that is impossible to cheat on but simple to check the result of. The result of solving that puzzle in Bitcoin, Ethereum, and *Proof of Work Bitmap*, is a 256-bit number with a specific number of zeros at the end. This is the same size as a 16×16 bitmap and as a memory cell in Ethereum. There's a resonance here, as there is in each piece in the series.

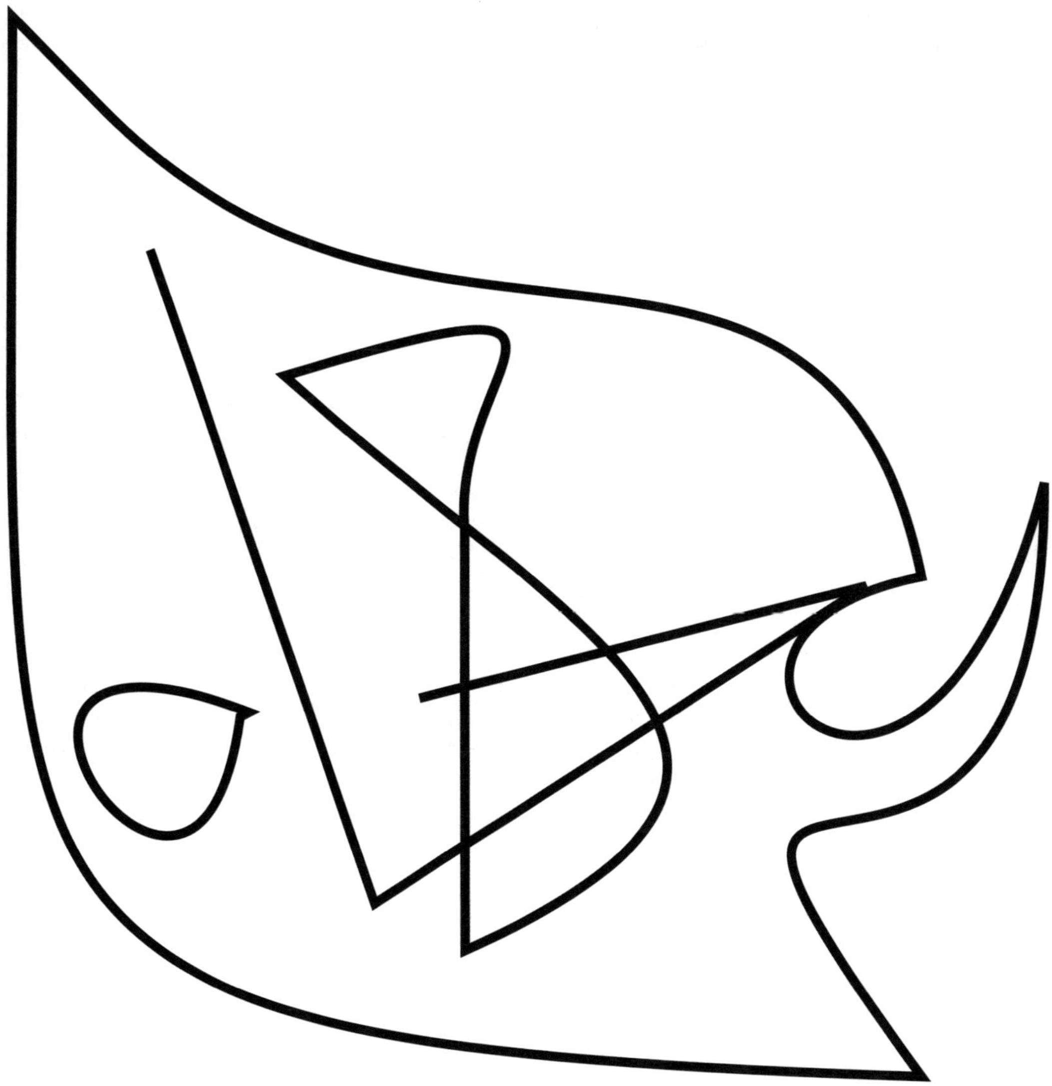

Pay Previous Path

Pay Previous Path allows anyone to store a vector drawing (encoded in a style similar to the SVG path line-art format) on the Ethereum blockchain in return for paying a small fee to the previous person who did so.

You may notice that the payment creates a path or line between accounts. This is the penultimate piece in the series of artworks pairing aesthetic objects with economic allocation methods.

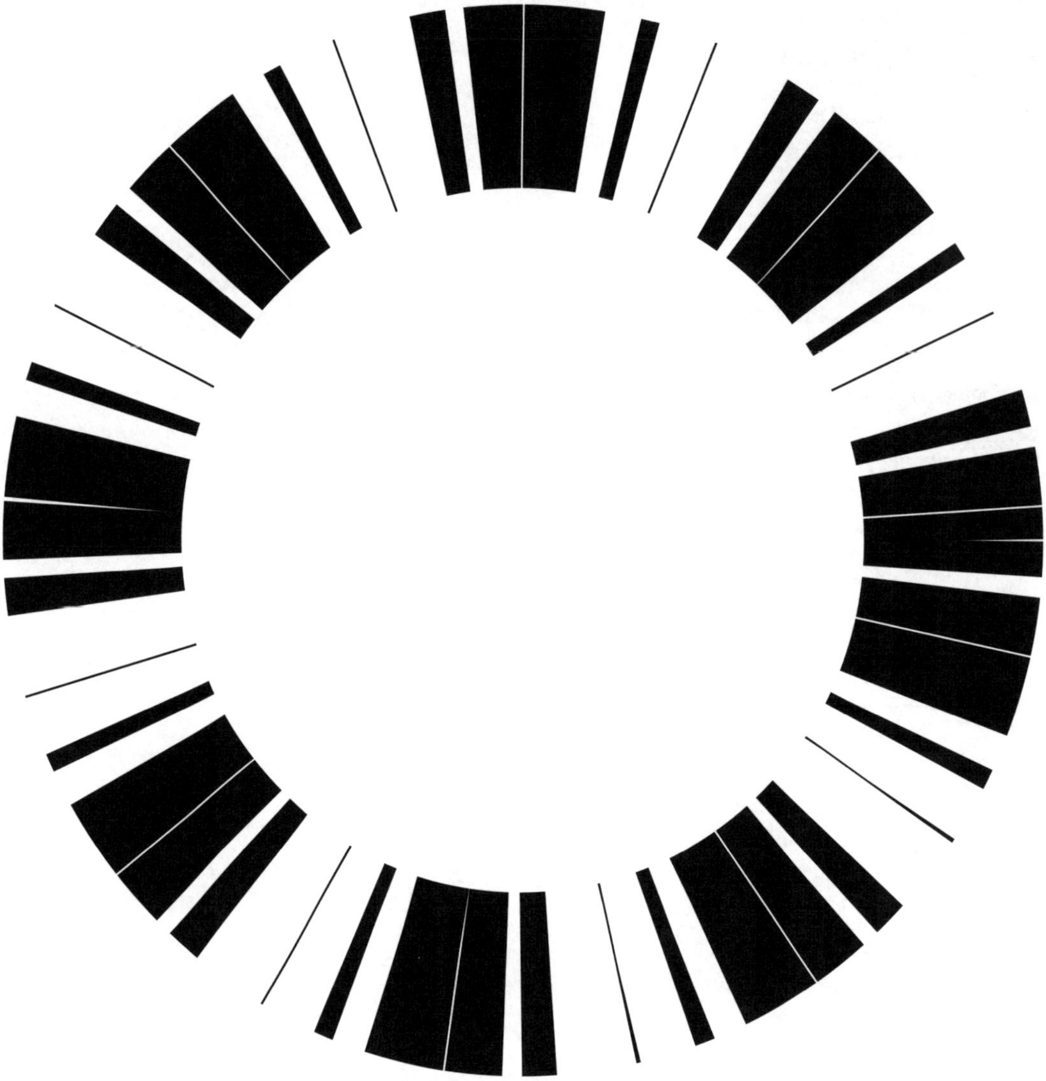

Hack Line Properties

Hack Line Properties is a supposedly secure blockchain smart contract designed to allow only its owner to update the line stroke properties that it stores. But a common Ethereum code bug allows anyone who finds it to 'hack' the contract and set the line properties themselves.

If code is law in the sense promoted by early Ethereum idealism, any action we can take using code is legal. But if that code is a bug, it embodies no intention and may break the intended operation of the software. Sometimes code has to be rescued by exploiting a bug (the first moon landing is a good example of this). Is this still a form of governance?

C E R T I F I C A T E

Rare art certified instance 04 / 11
of the artwork Balloon Dog
has not been modelled, instantiated, or presented by Rhea Myers.

This certificate is valid only when:
a. It is displayed accompanying a single instance of the artwork named above that is being displayed in the same physical or virtual location as this certificate, and;
b. That display has been organized by, on behalf of, or with the full knowledge and authorization of the party or parties that either;
i. control the private key of the Externally Owned Account that is currently the ownerOf() the ERC-721 token having the URI of this image as the "image" field of its tokenURI() metadata, or;
ii. control the smart contract or contracts that are currently the ownerOf() the ERC-721 token having the URI of this image as the "image" field of its tokenURI() metadata and can demonstrate sufficient authority to authorize this display using an appropriate on-chain mechanism, or;
iii. are able to demonstrate equivalent or successor ownership of this image - for example the beneficiary of a token rental or of a cross-chain transfer but not the owner of a fractionalized wrapper token or a token referencing the URI of this image, or a copy of this image, created by an unauthorized third party.

Certified by R Myers
Rhea Myers

Date 2020-05-11

Certificate of Inauthenticity

Between 2011 and 2012, for the *Shareable Readymades* project I commissioned the awesome artists Chris Webber and Bassam Kurdali to create three 3D printable models of commonplace objects—a urinal, a balloon dog, and a pipe—that had become part of canonical art history. The artists retained copyright on their work and the results were placed under the Creative Commons Attribution-ShareAlike (CC-BY-SA) licence with the attribution to myself as the person that commissioned the work. I did this in order to critique the production of neo-conceptual art by artists such as Jeff Koons and the processes by which art history cordons off models of commonplace objects as signature works by Jeff Koons, Marcel Duchamp, and others.

Furtherfield gallery in London (who meta-commissioned the Balloon Dog model) exhibited the works with 'certificates of inauthenticity' that I détourned from Sol LeWitt's certificates for their wall drawings. Then at the #BlockchainLive18 show, also in London, Ruth Catlow and Dr. Charlotte Frost of DECAL and Futherfield produced gold castings of the Balloon Dog model and registered the resulting 'Cryptopuppers' on Arteia's blockchain art registry.

I hadn't planned these developments, but they diagonalised the project in interesting ways. The former recapitulated Conceptual Art's capture by the very systems of sale and ownership that it had initially sought to escape. The latter mapped this onto the constant development of technosocial phenomena within successive waves of Andy Cameron and Richard Barbrook's 'Californian Ideology' by taking a 3D printing project that was meant to be free-as-in-freedom and making an expression of it exclusively ownable with cryptographic certainty on the blockchain.

As 'Rare Art', blockchain token-based digital editions have become the latest expression of ownership of value that would previously have escaped capture. The technology of blockchain-based digital certificates of 'ownership' of digital art images was initially developed ironically ('Rare Art' comes from 'Rare Pepe' trading cards). It was then captured by startup capital that cannot explain its contradictions. In its Rare Art iteration, Ethereum ERC-721 Non-Fungible Tokens (NFTs) for digital image URLs are presented as solving the problem that digital art is infinitely reproducible and therefore cannot be sold as a rare asset. They establish authentic provenance and ownership where this was not previously possible.

It is difficult to represent offchain truth onchain, however. It is prohibitively expensive to put bitmapped digital images onchain. And it is impossible to make sure that a digital image is represented uniquely even within the same smart contract on a single blockchain. This means that we must trust the claim that the image represented by each ERC-721 token is what its creator claims. The authenticity of Rare Art images is threatened by 'piracy', where an artist's images are copied from one Rare Art platform to another and sold without their consent. It is also threatened by 'trash art', where the art produced is an undeclared auto-tracing or other mechanical transformation of stock images. Artists who feel entitled to the monetary and reputational value of the art they produce regardless of the method used and collectors who feel entitled to react simply to the price of Rare Art tokens are clashing over matters of authenticity in platforms that were supposed to render such questions moot.

Why not turn this risk into value and make a virtue of inauthenticity?

To make the link between offchain truth and the problem of authenticity explicit I have created a Rare Art edition of *Certificates of Inauthenticity* for the *Shareable Readymades* series. If you own one of these tokens you can prove that I have not made the instance of Urinal, Balloon Dog, or Pipe that you have 3D printed or placed in virtual reality (which the CC-BY-SA license on the work gives you full permission to do). Print out the certificate that you own the NFT for and display it proudly in a physical gallery, or display it as a digital image on a virtual wall.

Then if anyone questions the authenticity of the art that you are displaying and your right to own it, you can answer that the art is provably inauthentic and that you have no more ownership of it than anyone else. And that you know this to be true with all the cryptographic certainty of the blockchain.

2020 TOTP QR Code

Shared Secret

Shared secrets are part of the invisible structure of society. They constitute a form of currency.

Computing security culture defines 'secrets' as passwords, private keys, as unguessable slices of entropy. They are to be revealed only briefly to cross the threshold of a computing system. The consequences of sharing them with attackers, which is to say other people, are catastrophic—leading to your presence in the system or the system itself becoming compromised, or 0wned.

Such sharing is therefore strongly taboo.

Two secrets are stronger than one when establishing that the person presenting them is authentically the person they claim to be. To lose one secret may be regarded as a misfortune; to lose both looks like carelessness. The second 'factor' of many such contemporary systems is generated by software using the 'Timed One Time Password' (TOTP) algorithm, which generates a new secret value every thirty seconds from a seed value.

Sharing the secret value compromises your security for the thirty seconds during which it is valid. Sharing the seed value means you can be 0wned permanently.

But if that seed isn't being used for security purposes, sharing it is harmless. It becomes a shared secret in the sociological rather than the security culture sense, currency rather than taboo.

Doesn't it?

very crypto

wow

1Doge17XMnNoSPA7XAW5EMabrc3QSyUxtc

m/44'/0'/0'/75

course casino supply slim quarter mammal
float vivid orphan tag priority tiny
prepare safe rice common remain critic
velvet mass parrot aerobic decide word

26ab004f1890344763ea42b8214f8455
04b4a431842f30c94d044352a73a1561
d21e83cf59d4eea1dbe81cba5c9117e35
362bb5616b38533fd6cb7a504dbb54c

1Dogeкч\rVO©њЫI¦«c:џ|.Isµt{ИDJ\x06\x08N7

amaze

such proof

2021 Rasterised vector image NFT

1 Doge = 1 Doge

Such proof that 1 Doge = 1 Doge. Wow.

A cryptographic 'proof' of the assertion that 1 Doge = 1 Doge, rendered in the form of a cryptographic wallet key 'seed' and the derivation of a Bitcoin address from it, presented using the deliberately naive typography and colour palette of 'Doge' memes such as those that promote the Dogecoin cryptocurrency.

This assertion may resemble the law of identity, as seen in Plato's *Theaetetus* (and the writing of Ayn Rand...), but here it is 'proven' ironically rather than taken as an axiom, reaching inside a statement of economic fungibility that has become an expression of faith in the lasting social value of cryptocurrency separate from its dollar value.

The 'proof' was generated using a modified Bitcoin vanity address generator that selected only seed values starting with 1Doge, and then searched for Bitcoin addresses beginning with the same prefix. Dogecoin addresses could not be used as they start with 'D' rather than '1', and structuring the 'proof' for use on another chain adds a layer of referentiality and robustness.

Since the private key for this address has been published in the artwork, it should not be used to actually receive Bitcoin as anyone will be able to steal the results.

Glossary

10K Project
A series of mechanically generated profile picture (PFP) images in a shared style sold as **NFT**s. Usually as an edition of 10,000 after CryptoPunks, which is the original template for such projects.

51% Attack
A network attack on a **blockchain** that uses the greater share of computing power devoted to **mining** new **block**s to censor or rollback transactions rather than properly extend the chain.

Accelerationism
The strategy of aligning oneself with and increasing the rate of the decoding or deconstructing effects of the system (...capitalism) in order to break down prior restrictive social forms. More generally: intensifying something in order to increase its rate of becoming.

Anarcho-capitalism
A social order without the state and its coercive institutions but with money, contracts, and the commodity form of property. The former is the 'anarcho' part, the latter the 'capitalist'.

Anarcho-communism
A social order without the state and its coercive institutions and also without any alienating economic activity or social forms. The former is the 'anarcho' part, the latter the 'communist'.

ASIC
ASICs (Application-Specific Integrated Circuits) are custom-manufactured computer chips that implement the cryptographic **hash**ing algorithms used in **mining** cryptocurrency. They are faster than CPUs or GPUs and were regarded as cheating or otherwise unfair by some people historically.

BIP-0039
A Bitcoin Improvement Proposal standard that specifies how to encode cryptographic private keys using a standard list of words rather than numbers.

Block
A collection of transactions or **txes** from a particular period of time validated by the network.

Blockchain
A series of **block**s of validated transactions, each linked to its predecessor by its cryptographic **hash**. Bitcoin's innovation was not to produce a blockchain, which is essentially just a **Merkle list**, it was to produce a **blockchain** in a securely decentralised way.

Burn
To destroy or render a cryptographic **token** inaccessible by sending it to an address that has no associated cryptographic key.

Ccru
The Cybernetic Culture Research Unit, an experimental philosophical group founded by Sadie Plant at Warwick University in 1995 that escaped the gravity well of academia to become something increasingly more (self-)mythologising, until its dissolution around 2000.

Copyleft
The use of copyright law in a licence to ironise its restrictions into lasting permissions.

CounterParty
An early cryptographic **token** platform based on top of the Bitcoin **blockchain**.

Creative Commons
A copyright reform nonprofit and its eponymous alternative copyright licences (including the copyleft CC-BY-SA) and copyright waiver (CC0).

Cryptoeconomics
The combination of cryptographic systems and the theory of game-theoretic economic incentives.

Crypto Wars
The legal and legislative battles of the 1990s, waged to ensure that the public could access and use effective cryptography without government backdoors.

Cypherpunk
A member of the eponymous 'cypherpunks' mailing list in the 1990s, or someone who holds to their principles of techno-anarchism pursued through cryptography.

DAO
Decentralised Autonomous Organisation. A **blockchain** corporation or co-operative, the technological equivalent of a charitable trust.

DApp
Distributed App. A complete, usable **Ethereum** application comprising **smart contract**s and a web-based user interface.

Dark Forest
Science fiction author Cixin Liu's novelistic universe in which the game theory of first contact with alien races makes any interstellar communication an existential risk. This means that you must either hide perfectly from everyone else in the universe, or destroy them completely as soon as you become aware of them before they can move to destroy you based on the same logic.

Dark Forest Strike
A world- or star-system-destroying attack on one (potentially) interstellar species by another based on the existential risk analysis logic of the **dark forest**.

DDoS
Distributed-denial-of-service attack. Using many, often hacked, computers to flood a server with so many network requests that it is unable to respond to them all, effectively taking it offline.

Digging
The **Dogecoin** equivalent of **mining**.

Discrete Log Problem
Public-key cryptography relies on 'trapdoor functions' that provide results that are easy to calculate but impractically difficult to reverse. The function used to derive public keys from private keys, point multiplication on an elliptic curve, can be calculated easily enough. But, although it has not been mathematically proven to be impossible, there is no known method for calculating its inverse, point division on an elliptic curve. This is known as the discrete log problem.

Doge
A dog. Probably a Shiba Inu.

Dogecoin
The first 'memecoin', a **fork** of Bitcoin's code with a faster block time and different **mining** algorithm, but mostly lots of **doge** memes.

Dogeparty
A fork of **CounterParty**'s code to run atop the **Dogecoin** blockchain rather than the Bitcoin **blockchain**.

Dump
To sell off a coin or **token** that has been **pump**ed, crashing the market for it.

Ethereum
A **blockchain** supporting general-purpose code execution rather than Bitcoin's limited transaction scripts.

Ether
The native cryptocurrency token used on **Ethereum**.

ERC
Ethereum Request For Comment. The ERC-20 standard defines '**fungible tokens**', essentially new cryptocurrencies that operate on the **Ethereum blockchain**. ERC-721 defines '**non-fungible** tokens (**NFT**s)'.

Exchange
Cryptocurrency exchanges allow you to swap between different coins/**tokens**.

Exploit
A means of hacking a piece of software.

Fees
Cryptocurrency transaction fees paid to **miners** for inclusion in a **block**.

Fiat
The act of declaring something to be so by the arbitrary exercise of power—state power, in the case of fiat currency such as paper notes that are not backed by precious metals.

FIFO
First-in-first-out. A data structure like a pile of documents where the topmost one is always the first one to be removed.

Fork
A split in a project. Either of the source code for a program which has been developed into two different versions, or of one cryptocurrency chain into two rival ones.

Fungible/Non-Fungible
Fungibility is substitutability. Two things are fungible if you can swap one for the other without meaningful difference. Like two coins of the same denomination. Non-Fungibiliity is the quality of uniquely identifiable or meaningfully different things, like two different paintings in the same series.

Gas
Ether used to pay for the execution of code by **Ethereum**.

Genesis Block
The first **block** mined for a particular **blockchain**.

GitHub/GIT
git is a program that keeps track of changes and versions of a project's software source code and other resources in a decentralised manner. It uses cryptographic **hash**ing to keep track of this in a repository or 'repo', consisting of a series of 'commits' of groups of changes. It looks a lot like a **blockchain**, with the **proof of work** algorithm using software developers rather than mining rigs. GitHub is Microsoft's walled garden for centralising software development, not to be confused with the underlying git version control system (VCS).

GNU
GNU's Not Unix. A project to create a free-as-in-freedom operating system for all computer users. Producers of the eponymous GNU GPL **copyleft** licence for software.

Hash
A unique, algorithmically generated, unguessable identifier for a piece of data. As a verb, the act of applying that algorithm.

Hodl
To hold cryptocurrency, named after a typo on a Bitcoin message board.

ICO
Initial Coin Offering. A sale of cryptographic **tokens** to fund a project.

Iota
An early 'internet of things' post-**blockchain** project.

IPv6
Most recent version of the Internet Protocol (IP) launched in 2012 as an improved and more scalable replacement for the long-standing IPv4, which suffered from various limitations including potential address exhaustion.

Keys
The pair of very long numbers or other mathematical entities that make up the public and private part of a modern cryptographic identity.

Layer Two Network
A faster system for using an existing cryptocurrency using additional, more complex, software and cryptoeconomic incentive structures.

LOIC
Low Orbit Ion Cannon. A **DDoS** tool.

MAST
Merkleized Abstract Syntax Tree. A **Merkle tree** containing different code or data at different branches, allowing the sender to commit to them now and use one of them later without having to reveal any of the others.

Markov Chain
A table of lists of elements that are likely to follow one another, allowing a representative sequence to be built up using random choices from them. Popular for creating variations on themes before the advent of generative adversarial networks (GANs).

Merkle Tree
A computer science 'tree' structure in which the leaves are data and each branch is the cryptographic **hash** of those below it. A compact and immutable representation of data. **Txes** in a **blockchain block** are arranged in a Merkle tree.

Mining
Validating **blocks** in return for rewards including mining **fees**.

Mining pool
Hardware or people sharing in the work and rewards of **mining blocks**.

NameCoin
The first Bitcoin **fork**, which added support for publication of name/value pairs to create a decentralised equivalent to the Internet Domain Name system.

net art / net.art
1990s internet art. Add the dot to name a particular movement of that period.

NFT
A Non-Fungible **Token**. A cryptographic digital asset that can be uniquely identified within its **smart contract**.

OG
'Original Gangster'. An appropriated honorific indicating respect for someone who has successfully played the market longer than oneself.

Onchain/Offchain
Information or events that occur within **block**s of a **blockchain**, or out in the real world.

One-Time Pad
The only perfect form of encryption. A unique series of random numbers used to encode each piece of information in a secret message. Only a recipient with the same unique series of numbers can hope to decrypt it.

OpenCV
An image-processing and image-recognition software library.

Oracle Problem
The problem of establishing onchain that an asserted fact holds true offchain with any degree of confidence.

Patch
An incremental modification to a piece of software.

PostScript
Adobe's 'page description language'. A 2D graphics programming language used most recognisably in laser printers and industrial printing presses.

Prediction Market
A betting pool for or against the likelihood of future events that is used to measure their probability.

Proof of Stake
An alternative to **Proof of Work** that uses the 'staking' of large amounts of a **blockchain**'s cryptocurrency to establish who gets to mine the next **block**. This uses a lot less energy than Proof of Work.

Proof of Work
Performing a computationally-intensive task to prove that the accompanying data is being provided in good faith. Originally developed to prevent email spam. Bitcoin and other early cryptocurrencies use it to secure their **blockchain**s by making it costlier to attack the chain than it is to extend it properly.

Public-Key Cryptography
The use of two separate but mathematically entangled encryption keys, one shared publicly and one kept private,when encrypting or signing messages. Knowledge of the public key does not give anyone any knowledge of the private key, so the public key can be shared to allow messages to be encrypted to its owner and to check cryptographic signatures from them without this being a security risk.

Pump
To artificially inflate the price of a coin or token through nefarious means before **dump**ing it.

Rare Art
An early name for **NFT**-based digital image art.

Rare Pepes
An early and deeply ironic (quasi-)**NFT** project based on the **CounterParty blockchain**, featuring images of 'Pepe The Frog'. **Rare Art** stripped out the irony and moved to **Ethereum** from **CounterParty**, leaving a historical gap.

Scam
A scam or, if you are being accused of one, simply anything your accuser disagrees with or dislikes.

Schelling Point
A 'focal point' value that people might be expected to arrive at independently. Named after the economist, not the philosopher.

SHA-256
A popular cryptographic **hash** algorithm. A 'salted' SHA-256 hash adds extra information to the data to be hashed in order to make it harder to guess from the resulting hash value—this is useful for passwords, for example.

Shard
A smaller partition of a **blockchain** that is able to communicate with other shards while not having to process all their transactions. This is one way of increasing the number of **txes** a blockchain can process.

Shibe
From 'Shiba Inu', the Dogecoin mascot. A **Dogecoin hodl**er, an excellent person. Like 'comrade' or 'choombatta'.

Shitcoin
A minor cryptocurrency that offers nothing compelling. Possibly a scam.

Sidechain
A smaller **blockchain** attached to a larger one but isolated from it by different rules.

Side Channel Attack
Using information leaked through contingent sources to break an encryption algorithm or extract secret information from a system. Timing of network responses, electromagnetic or loudspeaker noise, etc.

Smart Contract
A program stored on the **blockchain** that executes in response to blockchain **txes**.

Techno-libertarianism
The belief that in order to maximise its liberatory potential, technology should not be restricted by the state.

Token
A cryptographic token built on top of a cryptocurrency **blockchain**. The representational proxy for an identifiable and quantifiable ownership claim on some other value or object, real or imagined.

Trusted Third Party
An intermediary that can interfere in a social relationship between peers and must therefore be trusted not to.

Tx, Txes
A **blockchain** transaction or transactions.

Wallet
A piece of software, hardware, or paper used to secure cryptocurrency account keys.

Web 2.0
The social media platform and ecommerce era of the internet. Contrast with Web 1.0, which was more about homepages. And Web 3.0, which is about blockchain-backed identity and commerce.

Wei
The smallest unit of the **Ether** cryptocurrency, equivalent to a Satoshi for Bitcoin. Named after the **cypherpunk** cryptographer Wei Dai.

Whale
A **hodl**er of very large amounts of cryptocurrency or **NFT**s.

Wow
What a **doge** says when it thinks something is amaze.

Wrapped
A **fungible token** that can be exchanged for a specific kind of **NFT**, effectively wrapping the NFT in a currency representing it.

Zero-knowledge Proof
A family of algorithms for encoding and demonstrating that you know a piece of information without having to reveal it or anything else that it describes.

Zk-SNARKs
'Zero Knowledge Succinct Non-Interactive Argument of Knowledge', an algorithm that allows the existence of secret knowledge to be proven without revealing its content.

For those wishing to explore blockchain technology, the following books are recommended reading:

B. Vickers (ed.), *The White Paper by Satoshi Nakamoto* (London: Ignota, 2019).

F. Brunton, *Digital Cash: The Unknown History of the Anarchists, Utopians, and Technologists Who Created Cryptocurrency* (Princeton, NJ: Princeton University Press, 2020).

A.M. Antonopoulos, *The Internet of Money* (Merkle Bloom, 3 vols, 2017).

A. Narayanan, J. Bonneau, E. Felten, A. Miller, S. Goldfeder, *Bitcoin and Cryptocurrency Technologies: A Comprehensive Introduction* (Princeton, NJ: Princeton University Press, 2016).

R. Catlow and P. Rafferty (eds), *Radical Friends: Decentralised Autonomous Organisations and the Arts* (Torque Editions, 2022).

R. Catlow, M. Garrett, S. Skinner and N. Jones (eds), *Artists Re: Thinking the Blockchain* (London: Furtherfield, 2017) [Contains earlier versions of 'Blockchain Poetics' and 'Bad Shibe'.]

Published in 2022 by Urbanomic Media Ltd.
The Old Lemonade Factory
Windsor Quarry
Falmouth
TR11 3EX
United Kingdom

Editor
Robin Mackay

Graphic Design
Joe Gilmore

Image Research
Elaine Tam

Editorial Assistant
Lendl Barcelos

Printed and Bound in the UK
by TJ Books, Padstow

Distributed by the MIT Press,
Cambridge, Massachusetts and
London, England

Papers
Symbol Freelife 300 gsm
Munken Lynx Rough 90 gsm

Typeface
Riforma LL by Norm, Zurich
lineto.com

ISBN 978-1-915103-04-8
www.urbanomic.com

FOO 19731

In association with
furtherfield

Written using emacs, WordPress, Evernote, and Google Docs on a succession of Debian GNU/Linux boxes and occasional iPhones.

Thank you to aGENDAdao, Art on the Blockchain, Avant Crypto Theory, Avant.org, Blockade Games, Carpe Lunam, CaveTwitter, Ccru, the Ccru Facebook Group, Class Wargames, Creative Commons, DADA.nyc, Dapper Labs, DCTRL, Fingerprints DAO, FooCorp, The FSF, Furtherfield, Galerie Nagel Draxler, Gray Area, Kate Vass Galerie, Laboria Cuboniks, Mimetic Screens, The New Centre For Research and Practice, The Peer-to-Peer Foundation, RhettTwitter, Rhizome, Right Click Save, Torque Editions, and of course Urbanomic.

Further thanks to Kevin Abosh, Robert Alice, Jessica Angel, Georg Bak, Josie Bellini, Mez Breeze, Jaya Klara Brekke, Eleonora Brizi, Ruth Catlow, Mitchell F Chan, @coin_artist, Kate the Cursed, Primavera De Filippi, Simon de la Rouviere, Mat Dryhurst, Sarah Friend, Cynthia Gayton, Sarah Hammerman, Sam Hart, Holly Herndon, Kei Kreutler, Matt Lee, Nili Lerner, Matt Liston, Matt Lockyer, Kevin McCoy, Anika Meier, Sarah Meyohas, Jon Philips, Tina Rivers Ryan, Harm van Dorpel, Kate Vass, and Erik Zepka. And if I've failed to mention you, thanks to you too!

Maximal thanks to Seryna. You are amaze. Awoo!